A Playful Production Process

A Playful Production Process

For Game Designers (and Everyone)

Richard Lemarchand

Foreword by Amy Hennig

The MIT Press
Cambridge, Massachusetts
London, England

This book was set in Stone Serif and Stone Sans by Westchester Publishing Services. Printed and bound in the United States of America.

Uncredited illustrations by Richard Lemarchand.

Library of Congress Cataloging-in-Publication Data

Names: Lemarchand, Richard, author.
Title: A playful production process : for game designers (and everyone) /
   Richard Lemarchand ; foreword by Amy Hennig
Description: Cambridge, Massachusetts : The MIT Press, [2021] | Includes
   bibliographical references and index.
Identifiers: LCCN 2020052141 | ISBN 9780262045513 (hardcover)
Subjects: LCSH: Video games—Design. | Interactive multimedia.
Classification: LCC GV1469.3 .L46 2021 | DDC 794.8—dc23
LC record available at https://lccn.loc.gov/2020052141

10 9 8 7 6 5 4 3 2

To Nova

Contents

Foreword

I'm fortunate to count Richard among my oldest colleagues and dearest friends.

We first met in 1995 when I joined the design department at Crystal Dynamics, and I'll confess I instantly had a professional crush on him. Between his boundless creative energy and good humor and his Oxford degree in physics and philosophy, there was something simultaneously silly and serious about him that I immediately adored. I knew I wanted to work with him but had no idea that our first encounter would lead to a creative collaboration encompassing fifteen years and seven games, and a friendship that would span twenty-five years.

We were both fledgling game developers at that point, still finding our feet with less than five years' experience under our belts. The industry was young too, and game design as a discipline was still largely uncharted territory (forgive the pun). We made plenty of mistakes along the way, but as Rich says, we learned to be "fearless about failing." Project by project, with me in the creative director role and Rich as lead designer, we adopted and developed many of the philosophies, practices, and methods outlined in this book. We learned how to be game designers and interactive storytellers together.

Richard's playful "what if" mindset helped me to untether from the sometimes overwhelming scope of directorial responsibility, and his grounded, practical, organized, responsible nature kept me anchored when there were a thousand tasks to keep track of and hard decisions to be made. As it turns out, this dichotomy precisely defines the qualities that a good designer—particularly in a leadership role—needs to develop.

Twenty years of hands-on, in-the-trenches game development, coupled with a decade of teaching experience, make Richard uniquely qualified and equipped to write this book. Inside these chapters, you'll find a treasure trove of useful techniques and practical advice on the whole arc of game development, from blank-page ideation to the final product.

Even more important, I think, are the "soft skills" of collaboration and communication that Rich describes, cultivated by experience:

Curiosity—the inquisitive urge to dive into research and the ability to blend inspirations from disparate sources (music, art, literature, comics, movies, history) into your game design.

Flexibility—the understanding that game development is controlled chaos, a sustained act of mutual faith from beginning to end that requires us to be adaptable, collaborative, holistic thinkers.

Generosity—the awareness that we do our best work when the design flows around everyone's contributions, that our craft is improvisational by nature, and that we "plus" ideas when we "yes, and" each other. Even if the final result is a little jangly, it's better for having everyone's fingerprints on it.

Humility—the strength to know that a light hand on the reins is best, and that leadership is not about taking control but giving up control to empower others. The mantle of authority cannot be artificially bestowed; it must be earned from the team every day.

Respect—the recognition that any collaborative endeavor is a crucible of healthy conflict and productive debate, which requires a climate of candor and trust.

This is the ethos that Rich has developed and honed over his career and the qualities he demonstrates every day with his colleagues, students, and friends.

I know that readers will enjoy spending time with Richard in the chapters of this book as much as I've enjoyed knowing him over the years and will gain as much as I did working alongside him. Rich's wisdom and character—his enthusiasm, thoughtfulness, kindness, and his patience as a leader and a teacher—shine through the words on every page.

Amy Hennig
President, New Media Division
Skydance Media

Introduction

We must collect our thoughts, for the unexpected is always upon us.
—Charles Baxter, *The Feast of Love*

Making games is hard. The problems we face, both creative and technical, often seem impossible to solve. Everything in game development takes much longer than you think it's going to. Then just when you've got a handle on your game, something new comes along to derail your plans. If you let it, game development will mess you up and burn you out.

Creative people usually start learning how to make things when they're kids, often by trial and error, using the undiluted powers of a child's imagination and curiosity. As we get older, we probably get taught some artistic technique—how to shade a drawing, how to blow into a clarinet, or how to hold a chisel while we're turning wood on a lathe. But it's likely that no one ever teaches us about the metastructure of the creative process: how to manage our time and plan our projects.

In our teenage years, many of us adopt the natural way of trying to make our work excellent: we just put more time into it. We stay up late the night before an assignment is due. Maybe we stay up all night. We show up for class bedraggled and exhausted, hopefully with a completed assignment but too tired to answer questions about it with a clear mind. By the time we become adults, these partially successful but pretty dysfunctional ways of working have become deeply ingrained habits, and if we're not careful, we bring them to everything we do. If we become game developers, we bring them to game development. For a long time, I thought that the path to an excellent game inevitably meant lots of late nights, lots of coffee, and putting everything in your life—apart from work—on hold for the last few months of a project.

The good news is that none of that is true. You can unlearn those bad habits. Over the course of my career, I learned how to ensure that I made great-quality work without running out of time—and without having to stay up all night.

My name is Richard Lemarchand, and I'm a game designer. I worked in the mainstream of the videogame industry for over twenty years and got my start at MicroProse in the UK, where I became a junior member of the group that founded the company's console game division. I moved to California in the mid-1990s to work at Crystal Dynamics, where I was involved in creating the game series *Gex*, *Pandemonium!*, and *Soul Reaver*. I remain passionately grateful for everything my mentors, teammates, and friends at MicroProse and Crystal taught me. Between 2004 and 2012, I was a game designer at Naughty Dog in Santa Monica. I helped to finish *Jak 3*, before becoming lead game designer on *Jak X: Combat Racing*. I then led or co-led the design of all three PlayStation 3 games in the *Uncharted* series. *Uncharted 2: Among Thieves* became a huge success for Naughty Dog, winning ten AIAS Interactive Achievement Awards, five Game Developers Choice Awards, four BAFTAs, and more than two hundred Game of the Year awards. The work that we did together at Naughty Dog is a testament to the wisdom, courage, and playfulness of those teams.

In 2005, I began giving talks and mentoring games students at the University of Southern California. These experiences, along with the arrival of the indie games scene, prompted me to think about how I could spend more time looking at games through the lenses of art and culture, research and criticism, impact and education. I was offered a position at the USC School of Cinematic Arts, and I left Naughty Dog to join USC in 2012. I have been teaching and making games among the talented faculty, staff, and students of USC Games ever since.

This book is rooted in the things I learned throughout my industry career and is based on an intermediate design and development class that I teach almost every semester. My class is designed to help students who are no longer beginners in their game design practice but who are not yet experts. It's a class in both game design and game production, two things I see as inexorably intertwined. Game design is the process of coming up with ideas for a game and then making them work in gameplay; you can think of game production as "project management," ensuring that things run smoothly as the game gets built. Design and production are two sides of the same coin—they have different faces, but you can't have one without the other. Why not try to bring these two disciplines closer together? After all, they share the same goal: to make an excellent game.

When I joined the game industry, all of our practices and processes were still in their infancy. We did our best to structure our work but made a lot of mistakes. As time passed, we learned in stages, first figuring out the importance of preproduction and its differences from full production, then realizing the importance of postproduction. Finally, we recognized that we were missing out on the very first step: we had something to learn from the ideation processes used in games academia and in other mature design disciplines. These four project phases—**ideation**, **preproduction**, **full production**, and **postproduction**—are going to give us the roadside markers we need to chart a course on a journey from first glimmerings to finished game. You can see them in figure 0.1.

Imagination and design are closely connected. The dreams we dream at night and by day can lead to the greatest accomplishments in art and literature, science and technology, industry and entertainment. But until we make decisions and act upon them, we are not designing, only speculating. Furthermore, game design and interaction design

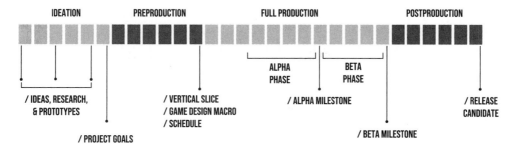

Figure 0.1

The four phases, milestones, and deliverables of the playful production process. Image credit: Gabriela Purri R. Gomes, Mattie Rosen, and Richard Lemarchand.

are fundamentally different from other processes of media design and creation in some important regards. The things we make are interactive and dynamically systemic, and that introduces a vast number of unknowns, variables, challenges, and problems into the creative process. How can we stay in control of the design process, ensuring that we make the right decisions at the right time? This book will show you how.

The game industry has always been plagued by the problem of "crunch," uncontrolled overwork that harms individuals, communities, organizations, and games. This book will help you address or avoid this problem. To be clear: I like hard work, and I believe that creating excellence usually involves some extra effort at some point. But there's a difference between hard work and crunch. Hard work is sustainable if you do it in a controlled way, giving yourself time to recharge between times of extra effort. Crunch is not sustainable. It burns people out, makes them miss important events in the lives of their family and friends, and, for a huge proportion of the game developers affected by it, causes them to leave the game industry, taking with them all their hard-won wisdom and experience.

When challenged to organize or improve their creative methods, some people use the essentially chaotic nature of creativity as an excuse to avoid taking control of their process. It's true: a lot of creativity is chaotic. But that chaos, while it must be respected, can also be harnessed and organized with the right tools to create good working habits and the best possible outcomes for our projects. Most of us will struggle with our bad habits and blockages for the whole of our creative lives; that's perfectly normal. If you are content with the status quo, close this book now. If you want to unlock more of your own game-making ability, then keep reading. True learning almost always comes with a struggle, so get ready for a few growing pains. Use this book in a way that makes sense for you, to get rid of whatever old habits aren't serving you well anymore and to pick up new habits that will help you become the kind of creative person you want to be.

This book will help you acquire new skills around game design, production, and implementation, skills that will help you conceptualize and create your future projects with greater efficiency, more creativity. and less pain. It will help you find new ways to make great games and interactive media while preserving your physical and psychological well-being and that of your teammates. I hope it will also be useful to people from related disciplines: interaction designers, experience designers, contemporary artists, and immersive designers for theme parks, VR, and theater. All these practitioners struggle with the same challenges that game designers do—devising entirely original and innovative participatory experiences, using design patterns and tools that they themselves are inventing. Indeed, the skills and techniques in this book could be applied to any complex design process in almost any field.

Design and production are aspects of the creative process where objective facts, analysis, and rationality meet the subjective judgments of experience, art, and audience. When we're striving to make something great, it's valuable to acknowledge the importance of the creative vision, values, and goals driving a project. At the same time, we need to reconcile creative people's aspirations toward excellence and innovation with the practical constraints of time and money.

We also need "soft skills" of collaboration and communication. It's not enough to be good at designing and making games if your teammates and collaborators feel bad about the project, each other, or you. This is probably the most challenging part of any collaborative creative practice, and this book will give you some practical advice about how to communicate and collaborate well.

I've written this book from the point of view of someone with my particular creative background, working in storytelling character-action videogame design. But I've tried to use language that acknowledges the incredible diversity of genres and styles that we see in game design, interactive media design, and all their adjacent art forms. In doing so, I hope to draw together the art and practice of design and production in a way that is useful to everyone, from every discipline and on every team. It's my goal to help you meet even higher standards of excellence in your work than you have reached before and to do so without burning out. If I do my job well, you will achieve more with less wasted effort, working smarter, not harder.

Using this book, you will design and create games using the **playcentric** process used in the USC Games program and described by Tracy Fullerton in her book *Game Design Workshop: A Playcentric Approach to Creating Innovative Games*.[1] You will design iteratively in a cycle of decision-making, implementation, playtesting, and design revision. You will learn what it means to envision and refine a set of **project goals** over the course of a project.

You will learn a design and production methodology based on the **"Method"** used at studios like Naughty Dog and Insomniac, which also incorporates attitudes and elements from **agile development**. You'll capture your ideas using **blue sky thinking** and **research**. You'll meet milestones where you deliver a **vertical slice**, a **game design macro**, and a **schedule**. You will learn how and when to **scope** your project in a way that reliably results in a high level of quality. You'll take your project through **alpha**

---

1. Fullerton, *Game Design Workshop*, 4th ed., 12.

and beta phases, and create deliverables related to each. Ultimately, you'll learn what it takes to finish a game—or any kind of interactive project.

Throughout the book, you will find references to three concepts that I believe lie at the heart of healthy game development practice: respect, trust, and consent. **Respect** has awareness of and regard for the thoughts, feelings, wishes, and rights of others, valuing their lived experience, their agency, and their autonomy. It's important that we respect our colleagues, and it's important that we respect the people who play our games. **Trust** follows naturally when we learn that others respect us. It's trust between teammates and professional peers that makes the difficult work we do together possible, when we can count on each other to share in our work in a way that helps and supports everyone in our endeavor. Trust is also important in the relationship between game developers and their audiences. **Consent** is crucial at every stage of our journey. We must ensure that the people who interact with us do so willingly, that someone consents to work on our team for a certain amount of time, and our players consent to see what our game has to show them. Respect, trust, and consent are the foundations of community, and communities are what make and play games.

I anticipate that the first time you use this book, things won't go perfectly, and that's okay. We are all prone to overlooking important things, slipping back into old habits, and just falling afoul of bad luck. What's important is to try some new processes, tools, and structures, to explore new ways of working, to create positive and lasting change in your creativity and your life. The methods I describe here are a collection of best practices from the past few decades of game design. I'm sure that the coming years will bring us even better techniques. Maybe you will be a part of that evolution.

If you've spent some time in the game industry, you might find that what I have to say in this book presents a slightly idealized view of the game development process. I'm fine with that. Game development, like life, is messy. I've been through the cycle of having my ideals crash into the realities of the world. But time and again, I discovered communities of people who were able to live up to ideals that others said were unrealistic. In doing so, they were able to create wonderful new things previously thought impossible. Idealism is valuable: it's part of how we make the world better. Where idealism meets experience, wisdom is born.

Phase One: Ideation—Making Ideas

1 How to Begin

Throughout my time in the game industry, I had a feeling that there is a special phase right at the start of a project, before preproduction, where we begin to figure out what kind of game we're going to make. When I joined the USC Games program, I learned the name of this phase from Professor Tracy Fullerton: it's called ideation, and it's a long-standing part of the design process in fields like graphic design and industrial design.

In her book *Game Design Workshop: A Playcentric Approach to Creating Innovative Games*, Tracy suggests that we begin our design process by deciding on the "player experience goals." She says:

> Player experience goals are just what they sound like: goals that the game designer sets for the type of experience that players will have during the game. These are not features of the game but rather descriptions of the interesting and unique situations in which you hope players will find themselves.[1]

During the ideation phase, we are going to figure out what experience goals to set, along with some other things about our game. Taken together, we'll call these our project goals.

Some of the projects I've worked on have been sequels, where we already knew roughly what kind of game we were going to make. But what about when we're starting from scratch? How do we overcome the famous "blank sheet of paper" problem, where we're paralyzed by overwhelming choice, and because we *could* do anything, we can't decide to do anything?

The right way to tackle the blank-sheet-of-paper problem is to stop thinking about the big picture. Remove the idea of the finished project from your mind—it's too big to grapple with yet—and start with one of these three types of ideation activity:

- Blue sky thinking (coming up with ideas)
- Research (digging for ideas in books and on the Internet)
- Prototyping (building simple things to play with and evaluate)

---

1. Fullerton, *Game Design Workshop*, 4th ed., 12.

We'll look at these activities in detail in the next few chapters. As soon as you start to tackle one small part of the project, you will find yourself making rapid progress with the big picture.

In the ideation phase, we will define the one, two, or three things that will make our game unique and distinctive. When we have some creative direction to guide us in the next part of the process, we'll be ready to set project goals to mark the end of the ideation phase. The project goals will be specific so we have direction, but they'll also be open-ended to give us room to maneuver as we move forward. We'll look at this closely in chapter 7, "Project Goals."

We're also going to spend some time in chapter 6 looking at "Communication as a Game Design Skill." Communication is the cornerstone of creating an environment of respect, trust, and consent on our teams and helps us to become better collaborators and creative leaders.

You'll notice references to other chapters throughout this book, including chapters later in the book that you haven't read yet. Don't worry—you don't need to jump ahead to be able to understand the part you're currently reading. The book is structured to introduce things in a good order. These connections are intended to help you if you are interested in a particular subject or if you're trying to understand how different parts of the process fit together.

You can stop a blank sheet of paper from being blank by scribbling a mark on it. Then you can turn that scribble into an excellent drawing. Let's get started.

2 Blue Sky Thinking

"Blue sky thinking" refers to activities we can use to come up with ideas, seemingly from nowhere and without limits. Blue sky thinking can involve spontaneous and improvisational thought or speech—writing down or saying the first thing that comes into your head—or it can be more structured and methodical. In either case, it's about getting away from the known and the familiar and into a realm of new and innovative ideas.

In this chapter, I'll quickly tell you about my favorite blue sky thinking activities: brainstorming, mind maps, and automatism. These activities can help us make a mark on the blank sheet of paper, to give us a starting point for the design of our game.

Brainstorming

Brainstorming is an activity for groups or individuals where we come up with ideas spontaneously and write them down. It's good for generating long lists of ideas very quickly and can also help members of a team get to know and understand one another.

Brainstorming works best when we closely follow a short list of rules. You'll find various versions of these rules online, but here is my favorite set:

- **Set a time limit**. Rookie brainstormers often overlook this crucial rule. Brainstorms work best when they're short. Twenty minutes forces everyone to work fast, and thirty minutes is a good maximum. If you get on a roll, go longer. Time pressure in a brainstorm pays off in multiple ways, including helping you focus on the next most important rule . . .

- **Focus on quantity over quality**. You're not trying to come up with the *right* idea or the *best* idea during a brainstorm. You're just trying to capture *all* the ideas. You'll pick the best ones later. Encourage everyone to say the first thing that comes into their mind. If your team likes competition, set a goal to come up with more ideas than you've ever come up with before. However, this could descend into chaos if you don't . . .

- **Appoint a facilitator**. Put one member of the group in charge. They will be tasked with moving things along, contributing ideas to get the brainstorm started, and making sure that . . .

- **Only one person speaks at a time**. This keeps the session energetic without becoming chaotic and gives the team members a chance to demonstrate respect for each other, developing trust. The facilitator should also make sure that . . .

- **Everyone gets a chance to speak**. Good ideas can come from everyone on the team, but some people might be reluctant to speak up. A good facilitator will notice when someone wants to contribute but is having trouble jumping into the conversation and will make and hold space for their voice. The facilitator or someone else on the team should also be tasked to . . .

- **Write everything down**. Capture all the ideas. Writing the ideas on a whiteboard where everyone can see them is good, but a shared online document or writing in a notebook is fine too. Every last idea is worthy of being recorded, no matter how obvious or weird it seems.

- **Welcome unusual ideas—the weirder the better**. This rule complements "focus on quantity over quality." In a brainstorm, we're trying to get away from the familiar and into fresh territory. An idea that seems unworkably strange could later prove to be a source of brilliant originality and innovation. The facilitator should regularly remind everyone about this rule, to help break down the social resistance that we all have to saying things that seem silly or odd.

- **Say "yes, and"—combine and improve ideas**. This is a great way to keep things moving along—especially when your mind goes blank. Use the "yes, and" technique from improv comedy and theater, by taking one of the earlier ideas and adding to it or modifying it.

- **Don't discuss the ideas during the brainstorm**. This rule is often *very* hard for analytical people like game designers to follow. We all want to start dissecting ideas as soon as we hear them, to see if they're any good. *Don't do this during the brainstorm.* The time for discussion comes later. For now, remember the time limit and focus on generating as many new ideas as possible.

Evaluating Brainstorm Results

After the brainstorm, set some time aside to sort through the ideas you captured and begin to evaluate them with lively discussion and debate. I know from my own experience that people often brainstorm and then never look at the results again. Instead, they get stuck on whatever ideas randomly lodged in their memory. Turning a brainstorm into a strong project idea is just like panning for gold—it takes time and attention.

Talk over the ideas with your teammates and review each one using whatever criteria are appropriate for you and your team. You might be particularly keen to find new styles of gameplay or new subjects for the narrative design of your game. You might have a particular impact goal in mind for your project or have a set of technical considerations that you want to embrace. Continue to look for new and interesting combinations of seemingly unconnected ideas.

Some people find it useful to assign priorities to their ideas. Copy the ideas into a spreadsheet, with a single idea on each row. In a column next to the ideas, assign a priority of high, medium, or low to each idea. Set the priorities in whatever way is appropriate for your team; at the very beginning of ideation, it might just be your level of excitement about each idea.

You could continue this process by making additional columns for how interesting, exciting, or practical each idea is—or any other evaluation you come up with. You can have different columns for different team members, to show who likes which ideas. This can be valuable for discovering shared interests and building consensus among teammates. As a central idea for your game starts to emerge, you can prioritize ideas based on how well they seem to fit with the emerging direction.

Prioritizing our ideas helps us begin to make design decisions and, in doing so, to set a creative direction. We want to keep exploring widely during the ideation phase, but we also want to begin steering our thoughts in a particular direction. Doing something as simple as prioritizing our ideas begins the process of decision-making in a way that isn't threatening, because we're not ruling anything out yet. It's rather like setting the sails of a ship to catch the wind from a certain direction. It will make sure that, even though we could end up anywhere on the wide horizon, we won't be sailing around in circles.

If everyone on the team is excited about the same ideas, that's great. If different people are excited about different things and can't come to an agreement, then someone in a leadership position can help to decide a direction. Tracy Fullerton holds that an important aspect of game team leadership is finding ways to connect ideas to one another, to achieve a synthesis that the whole team is excited about.[1]

There is some debate in creative circles about the value of brainstorming, and sometimes it's overemphasized as the one and only source of good ideas. I personally think a short brainstorm makes for a good starting point. Brainstorms get a lot of ideas on the table quickly and are valuable for developing the team's understanding of their collective interests and passions.

Mind Mapping

Mind mapping is a more structured version of brainstorming and works well when you've arrived at a core concept that you want to explore in greater depth. The technique is very simple: write down the core idea in the middle of a whiteboard, screen, or sheet of paper, and begin to brainstorm, following all the same rules described above. Each new idea should be connected to the core idea or to another idea that has already been written down in the mind map. You can see an example of a mind map that is partway through creation in figure 2.1.

---

1. Private communication, May 25, 2020.

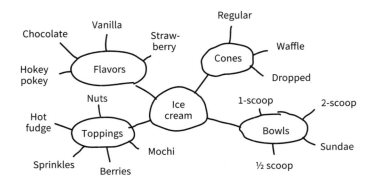

Figure 2.1
A work-in-progress mind map centered on the concept of "ice cream."

Draw lines between the ideas, clearly showing the relationships among them. You'll soon have a radiating pattern showing clusters of ideas with a built-in hierarchy of "parent and child." Sometimes a "child" idea will take over as the center of a new major cluster—that's okay! Let your mind map get messy and follow where it leads you. Mind mapping's spatial structure will help draw your attention to possibilities that you're overlooking. You can find many great digital tools to help with mind mapping if you search the Internet.

Automatism

In the early twentieth century, a group of artists known as the Surrealists became fascinated by the new idea of the unconscious mind, wanting to explore it in pursuit of knowledge, freedom from restrictive social convention, and new types of art. They developed techniques for doing so, many of which they described as games. If you're interested in this type of creative exploration, I strongly recommend *A Book of Surrealist Games* by Alastair Brotchie and Mel Gooding.[2]

One technique the Surrealists liked was called automatism (from the word *automatic*, meaning "done spontaneously"). To use automatism, simply sit down with a piece of paper and a pencil, or at a computer, and set a timer for anywhere between four minutes and an hour. Start your timer and then *keep writing* (or drawing, if you prefer) until your timer runs out. Don't pause or hesitate; force yourself to transcribe whatever comes into your mind. Follow your stream of consciousness. If you do this honestly, it will be easy. Don't review or analyze what you're writing down or drawing.

A lot of what you set down will be nonsense or banal. That's okay. Some of what you write or draw will be very personal and might surprise or even shock you. It's important that everyone should have the right to keep the results of an automatism exercise

2. Brotchie and Gooding, *A Book of Surrealist Games*.

private. Some of what you put down will be interesting, unusual, moving, or otherwise powerful. That's the gold you've been in search of. You can use it as a starting point for a brainstorm or a mind map.

Other Blue Sky Thinking Techniques

That's just a small selection of blue sky thinking activities. There are many others, like "cut up," which Tracy Fullerton describes in chapter 6 of *Game Design Workshop*.[3] You might also use journaling, storyboarding, Wikipedia:Random, or your favorite divination technique.[4] Keep a notebook throughout your project; it will hold your ideas, plans, sketches, and diagrams, but it's also a place to doodle and free associate. If you search online for "ideation techniques," you'll find many more prompts for blue sky thinking.

Designers, Spreadsheets, and the Power of the List

Game designers end up making a lot of lists in the course of their work. Lists of raw ideas, lists of game mechanics and levels, lists of features and content, to-do lists and task lists. Some people take to this more easily than others, but being a good list-maker is a learnable skill and a great way to get ahead as a game designer.

Most of the design documents we used during my time at Naughty Dog were spreadsheets. The first time I saw a spreadsheet, I felt quite frightened! It looked like something from an accountant's fever dream, and I couldn't understand what to do with it. Today, I love spreadsheets—they are one of the most powerful tools in the game designer's toolkit and the best way to organize information quickly and easily.

Spreadsheets give you easy access to the vertical and horizontal dimensions of your page using a grid of boxes (called cells). Yes, game designers spend a lot of time making lists, but in fact we more often make tables with rows and columns of cross-referenced information. As soon as you have listed out the names of the characters in your game, for example, you'll need to keep track of what animations they use, how fast they can move, and so on. Tables are what spreadsheets are good at. Formulas that add up columns of numbers are a snap to learn. Conditional formatting that color-codes the information in the cells lets you see what's important, quickly and intuitively. Watch an online video about how to use spreadsheets, and soon you'll love spreadsheets too.

The phrase "the power of the list" is popular among people interested in project management. Lists have power because knowledge is power. Lists that we look at regularly help us keep all our ideas present in our minds. Having access to an up-to-date list of something relating to your game (like a list of all the different characters, or all

---

3. Fullerton, *Game Design Workshop*, 4th ed., 179.
4. "Wikipedia:Random," Wikipedia, https://en.wikipedia.org/wiki/Wikipedia:Random.

the collectable objects in the game) is to have the power to make that part of the game excellent and to do it in an efficient way. Power must be shared in a healthy team, so always put your lists in a public place and tell your teammates where they are. Be the person who keeps lists current—it demonstrates that you're a responsible designer. It's much more efficient to maintain a list day to day throughout a project than to have to update it when the information it contains is suddenly needed.

Lists help us avoid making mistakes. Checklists are used by everyone from airline employees to surgeons to prevent life-threatening accidents and errors and to empower junior staff to speak up when they notice something going wrong.[5] Becoming a better list-keeper is a simple and effective way to make better games.

People sometimes think of creativity as a mystical process practiced only by innately brilliant auteurs. I believe in the existence of *eureka!* moments, those flashes of inspiration where we suddenly seize upon something new and great. But I also believe in the truth of Thomas Edison's admonition that genius is "one percent inspiration and ninety-nine percent perspiration." That's why we have to brainstorm quickly and in quantity, to work through ninety-nine so-so ideas and find the one perfect idea we're looking for.

Creativity is everywhere in our lives and in even the most mundane of our actions, and it's accessible to everyone who cares to create. Creativity needs passion to push it through to the completion of the creative act, so take note of what you get excited about.

Finally, if you want to innovate in game design, don't rule out ideas because they don't fit onto the game mechanics that you're already familiar with. Instead, consider taking an idea that is simple and complicated at the same time ("musical taste," "jealousy," "New Year's resolution") and exploring it using the ideation strategies that we'll discuss in the next three chapters: research and prototyping.

---

5. Don Sadler, "How to Avoid Surgical Errors," OR Today, June 1, 2016, https://ortoday.com/how-to-avoid-surgical-errors/.

3 Research

Research is one of my favorite parts of the ideation phase, and it was important in the creation of every *Uncharted* game. We wanted to root our stories in historical and geographic fact, because we knew that "grounding" them in this way would help our audience suspend their disbelief. We wanted to pass what *Uncharted* director Amy Hennig calls the "Google test"—if you searched online for some historical event or place in the game, you'd find a trail of facts leading you onward to the real world. We thought this might pique people's curiosity, maybe even making our games subtly educational.

I think that almost every game can benefit from some research to give it foundations in the real world. The creators of fantasy and science fiction worlds have to work particularly hard to make their creations seem grounded and believable, and the details needed to do that will come from reality.

Research on the Internet

Before the Internet era, we'd have to go to a library or buy a lot of books to research a game. Now that we have Wikipedia, Google, and the 366 million registered Internet domain names, we have an incredible wealth of information just a few clicks away.

I love to explore Wikipedia, Reddit, and Google Images, both for credible knowledge and information and for things that seem spurious, mistaken, or ridiculous. Be sure to double-check your sources if you want real facts. You can use research to dive more deeply into a subject that you've discovered through brainstorming and to help give your mind maps more branches.

Image Research

As well as text-based research, I'm a big fan of image searching. I like to save images into a local folder on my hard drive and then use them to spur conversation among the team. Images usually convey information much more quickly than text and will give different people different ideas, which is useful when you're trying to explore widely.

Once you've collected a good crop of images, you can assemble them into a mood board, a single page or screen of pictures arranged around a certain idea or theme. Putting two seemingly unconnected pictures next to each other can cause entirely new ideas and feelings to emerge, as in the famous Kuleshov effect.[1] Creative industries like moviemaking, marketing, and videogame design use mood boards to convey a concept quickly and effectively and to open up discussion about future direction. It's almost never too early to start building your own mood board or image montage, using Microsoft Paint, Adobe Illustrator, or an online service like Pinterest.

Don't Neglect the Library

Research on the Internet is great, but, ironically, the seemingly wide-open Internet can easily keep you inside the invisible walls of your preconceptions. So make sure you head to a local library as part of your research process. A skilled librarian and a physical collection of books can lead you toward ideas, facts, and artworks that you wouldn't otherwise discover.

Field Trips

Some of the best research happens outside your studio, home, or office. Pixar is famous for their research trips to unusual, far-flung places—the unearthly world of Paradise Falls in their 2009 film *Up* was created with help from a visit to the tepui mesas of Canaima National Park in Venezuela.

But you don't have to have a big budget to do great field trip research for your game. Chances are there is somewhere local you can go to find inspiration and knowledge that informs your design and grounds your game in reality.

Take note of the processes and systems that you see in the world around you. What aspects of daily life could become interesting parts of your game's mechanics, environments, and storytelling? People-watching is a great part of any research field trip. Take your notebook with you and write everything down. Without invading anyone's privacy, take photos. Ask for permission where necessary. Introduce yourself to parts of the world that you see every day but have never looked at in detail. Get lost in your own town and look at the familiar with fresh eyes.

Interviews

Conducting interviews can be an excellent way to find ideas and ignite your creativity. Later in this book we'll look at the importance of placing people at the center of your design process, using playtesting and other techniques. This is what Tracy Fullerton calls playcentric game design, and it is part of a humanist tradition in design that reaches back into history.[2] Humanism in design can be seen in the nineteenth century

---

1. "Kuleshov Effect," Wikipedia, https://en.wikipedia.org/wiki/Kuleshov_effect.
2. Fullerton, *Game Design Workshop*, 4th ed., 16.

Arts and Crafts movement, in the work of twentieth-century architects like Friedens-reich Hundertwasser and the team of Arakawa and Madeline Gins, and in the innovations made in human-centered design at the Silicon Valley creative agency IDEO, to name but a few.

You can start talking to people about your game's design before you even have an idea for your game. Many great design projects start with interviewing people about their lives, their thoughts, and their feelings. Choose someone you'd like to design a game for, and ask them questions about their daily activities, their leisure time, their interests, even their hopes, needs, and fears. Write down their responses or make an audio or video recording of the interview. You'll get back a wealth of surprising, interesting ideas—one of which might spark the genesis of your next game project.

Shadowing

Sometimes it's hard to get good information about people just by talking to them—we all have biases that skew what we think and say, and people often overlook details that could be interesting to us as designers.

Shadowing gives us a way to dig deeper into people's lives, interests, and preferences. It is a research technique that has its roots in management studies in the 1950s and was developed as part of the human-centered design practice of design and consulting firm IDEO. Shadowing involves accompanying someone, with their permission, as they go through their day. We observe the person we're shadowing and take notes, make audio and video recordings, and gather data such as how much time they spend in locations and activities. By seeing people going about their lives, observing them discreetly and without interference, we can gain a deeper understanding of their behavior, opinions, and motivations.

Shadowing can also help us see how individuals, friends, and families use their game-playing leisure time—how they relate to and interact with each other when they're playing, whether they're playing together or if one person is playing and others are watching. New ideas for cooperative and competitive games might emerge in this way. Shadowing is useful in the design of "health games" designed to create positive outcomes in the health of their players and in the design of "serious games," "applied games," and educational games. It could also be helpful in the wildly innovative work of experimental game designers and art game makers.

Research Notes

Make sure to keep a record of your findings in the form of research notes. Doing research on the Internet, it's easy to go into a click-trance and emerge with nothing to show for it but your browser history. Take the time to copy-paste text, images, and links into a research notes document, giving yourself and your team something you can refer back to throughout the course of your project and whenever you're stuck and need some inspiration. An idea that didn't seem relevant early on might prove to be useful or even transformational later.

Research should be a rich part of your ideation phase, and you can discover many more blue sky thinking and research techniques in the IDEO Method Cards deck. This useful, inspirational, and highly innovative tool from design agency IDEO has fifty-one techniques to "keep people at the center of your work!"[3] Situation Lab's award-winning "imagination game," *The Thing from the Future*, designed by my USC Games colleague, the late Jeff Watson, and Carnegie Mellon University design professor Stuart Candy, is another great card deck tool, created for designers and others looking to have playful and thoughtful conversations about the future.[4] Mary Flanagan and Helen Nissenbaum's *Grow-a-Game* cards help designers be more intentional about the ways in which they integrate human values into their game-based systems.[5]

For some of us, research is so enjoyable that it can easily eat up all our ideation time. Set limits on the time you spend researching, so that you don't spend too long down the rabbit holes you'll discover. Try to find a good balance between free-form exploration and more structured investigations of particular topics. Keep referring back to the concept you were originally researching and try to stay on track.

Not all your time has to be goal-directed; there is great beauty and value in untrammeled thought. Just be wary of swimming in circles. Explore outward, upward, inward, or downward, but check in regularly to see if you're making good use of your time. If you do your research well, you'll create wonderful new experiences that are grounded in our shared realities. The world is a great teacher. Let it tell you something about your game.

3. IDEO Product Development, *IDEO Method Cards*.

4. Jeff Watson and Stuart Candy, *The Thing from The Future*, 2017, Situation Lab, http://situationlab .org/project/the-thing-from-the-future/.

5. Mary Flanagan and Helen Nissenbaum, "Grow-A-Game: Overview." Values at Play, https:// www.valuesatplay.org/grow-a-game-overview.

4 Game Prototyping: An Overview

Brainstorming and research are good, but the lifeblood of ideation is not really thinking; it's *making.*

A little thinking goes a long way, but nothing can replace the discoveries made and the design lessons learned by creating things that people can play with. So the most important activity to get busy with during ideation is prototyping.

I can't stress this enough: you should start with a small amount of blue sky thinking, perhaps a single brainstorm, and maybe do a little research, just twenty minutes or so. After that, you should immediately start building your first prototype. If you're doing ideation right, this prototype will be the first of many. As Autodesk Fellow and technology pioneer Tom Wujec points out in his TED Talk "Build a Tower, Build a Team," "design is a contact sport."[1] Until we start to build, we can't discover the hidden assumptions that could harm or help our project.

I've noticed that when people sit down to do some prototyping for a game, they often start trying to build a complete game straightaway. Things rarely go well for people who do this. They pour energy into work that is based on preconceptions, work that doesn't really help to guide their design, and they start to get burned out before they've even really begun.

So before I start giving you strategies to prototype your game, I want to emphasize something very clearly:

Your prototypes are not demos of your game.

I will guide you toward making a demo (short for "demonstration") of your game later in our process when we talk about the creation of a vertical slice. Making a demo *will* become an important part of designing your game.

But for now:

Each prototype you make explores one or more ideas for your game.

A true prototype tests a very small number of things—maybe just one thing. If you can discover just one player activity that is interesting, fun, emotional, or otherwise compelling, then your prototype has served its purpose, and will act as a foundation for future

---

1. Tom Wujec, *Build a Tower, Build a Team*, 2010, https://www.youtube.com/watch?v=H0 _yKBitO8M.

design work. (More on player activities in a moment.) If you don't discover anything good, you can start over again with a new prototype.

During ideation, you should aim to make as many different prototypes as you possibly can. If you're fast and focused, each prototype might only take you two or three hours to make, playtest, and iterate upon. It's okay if you're slower, but keep your prototypes simple and to the point.

Game Mechanics, Verbs, and Player Activities

Game mechanics are the rules and processes in a game that make up its functioning and interactivity. They govern what the player can do and how the game starts, unfolds, and eventually ends. Game mechanics make possible what game designers often call the verbs of a game—the "doing words." For example, your player-character might move, act, speak, or buy.

Some game verbs are more "atomic"—pressing a button to make a character jump is a basic verb atom in certain types of games. Other game verbs might be more "molecular" and are made up of groups of these verb atoms. For example, *explore* is a game verb that might be made up of the atomic verbs *walk*, *jump*, *climb*, *crawl*, and *move the game camera*. Of course, just like an atom is made up of subatomic particles, atomic game verbs can be broken down further. *Climb* might be made up of the subatomic game verbs *reach left*, *reach right*, *drop down*, *dyno jump*, and so on.

Player activity is a term we use to describe how the player uses a particular verb. A player activity might be running around looking for the exit in a first-person game using the WASD keys, the mouse, and the Shift key. It might be trying to get three of the same items in a row in the grid of a match-three game by tapping on a touchscreen; or it might be navigating through a story for the second time, trying to find a different ending by clicking on the links in a Twine game. Player activities are the result of the combination of your game's mechanics, verbs, and narrative, along with the player's perceptions, thoughts, actions, and intent.

Like many game designers, I tend to use these terms interchangeably, but I think that talking about mechanics and verbs as player activities when we're prototyping reminds us to keep the player's actions and experiences in the foreground of the discussion. Player activities are often sequenced into loops, and we'll look more at the "core loop" of a game in chapter 10. When we get into a deeper analysis of a game, we might talk about patterns of player activity, where we see different groups of players using the same mechanics and verbs to express widely different styles of play. The most famous identification of patterns of player activity is Richard Bartle's famous player types of killer, achiever, socializer, and explorer.[2]

---

2. "Bartle Taxonomy of Player Types," Wikipedia, https://en.wikipedia.org/wiki/Bartle_taxonomy_of_player_types.

For each prototype you make, ask yourself:

✓ What player activity am I prototyping here?

✓ What game verbs am I investigating?

✓ What kind of experience does this player activity produce?

✓ What tone or mood does the player activity have?

✓ What interesting gameplay and story things can I do with this player activity right now?

✓ How much could I do with this player activity if I had the time to devise different situations and scenarios in which to use it?

✓ **What question am I trying to answer with this prototype?**

This last point is very important. The designer Chaim Gingold, who is known for his work on *Spore* and *Earth Primer*, has a lot of excellent advice to give about making prototypes. He wrote an essay called "Catastrophic Prototyping and Other Stories" for Tracy Fullerton's book *Game Design Workshop*, and you can also find it online. Chaim advises us to design each prototype to answer a question we're asking: "For example, you might be thinking about mouse-based control schemes for a school of fish. Your question is: how do I control these fish with a mouse?" Chaim points out other benefits of prototyping, like using prototypes to persuade teammates that an idea will work. He also gives advice about working quickly and economically, not trying to do too much at once, and using our time well. Chaim's essay is excellent—go read it now.[3]

Three Kinds of Prototyping

Depending on your background, you might have strong preconceptions about prototyping. I want to shake them up by offering you three different kinds: playful prototyping, physical prototyping, and digital prototyping.

Playful Prototyping

A prototype is a way of bringing an idea to life, and this is what a toddler does when they pick up a toy animal and jiggle it around, making a growling sound. The ideation process is all about putting some wind in the sails of your design, and in my experience, there is no better way to start than by picking up a toy or other object and saying, "Let's imagine . . ."

For example, I might use an action figure and some boxes to figure out how a game character should scramble up a pile of collapsing rocks. I might use two toy cars to show how a racing game mechanic works, or I might use a spoon and a fork to play-act the body language of two nonplayer characters during an argument.

---

3. Chaim Gingold, "Catastrophic Prototyping and Other Stories," January 20, 2011, http://www.levitylab.com/blog/2011/01/catastrophic-prototyping-and-other-stories/.

As toddlers get older, they start to play make-believe, taking on roles and acting out scenarios. This can be a part of playful prototyping too. At Naughty Dog and Crystal Dynamics, my colleagues and I would often use playacting as a way to bring clarity to our design ideas and to problem-solve.

In countless design meetings, I have stood up and begun to act out an activity that might be performed by a character in our game: peering through a keyhole, crawling through a narrow space, pulling on a chain. In doing so, I'm illustrating ideas and encouraging discussion. Tracy Fullerton told me that Walt Disney was famous for acting out the postures and actions of his characters—such as the witch with the poison apple—while his colleagues drew furiously to capture his expressions and gestures.

As soon as we can see (and partly imagine) something in motion before us, we begin to make discoveries about our design ideas. Is the keyhole too low? Is the crawl space too narrow? Is the chain too heavy to lift? I won't say more about playful prototyping here; it's so wide-open that you can invent your own techniques. This probably shouldn't be the only prototyping strategy that you use, but it might turn out to be one of your favorites.

Physical Prototyping

One of the greatest innovations of the playcentric game design process that Tracy Fullerton describes in her book *Game Design Workshop* is the use of physical prototypes. Physical prototyping involves the creation of board games, card games, and other kinds of nondigital play activity like a sport or a playground game. This can, of course, lead to the design of great board games, card games, and sports, but it is also a powerful way of designing a digital game. For example, BumbleBear Games' superb real-time strategy platform videogame *Killer Queen* was initially prototyped as a physical team game.[4]

Tracy told me that she started using physical prototyping to help designers break away from the solved problems of existing genres of play and explore innovative new game design spaces. It turned out to be such a powerful technique that physical prototyping is now a bedrock of the way that game design is taught in the USC Games program.

How to Make a Physical Prototype

It's easy to make a physical prototype, and you can use a wide range of materials in building one. The most commonly used elements are paper—copier paper will work fine—and pens, pencils, or crayons. You don't have to be able to draw well; stick figures are fine. For construction, you'll need tape or glue and scissors. Index cards are useful and versatile; the rigidity of the cardstock makes them equally useful as playing cards or as construction material for game pieces and environmental elements. Some plastic, wood, or glass counters are good for representing game pieces or resource tokens. Sticky notes are often used.

---

4. "'Killer Queen' Game at IndieCade 2012," https://www.youtube.com/watch?v=9y3OI3KCdYk.

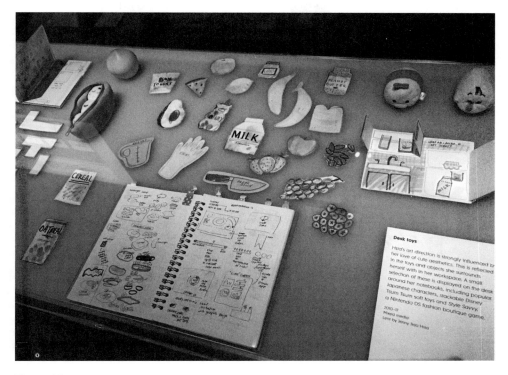

Figure 4.1
Jenny Jiao Hsia's physical prototypes for *Consume Me*, "Videogames" Exhibition at the Victoria and Albert Museum, London.

Think about a player activity that you want to investigate. It might be picking up a piece of fruit with a fork, trudging through a sandstorm, or sorting magic beads by their color. What are the underlying systems that you want to represent? How can you abstract them into the conventions and representations that work in board games and card games? In this way, you can use physical prototyping techniques to begin to investigate the verbs and game mechanics that will make up your game.

You can also start to physically prototype more complex patterns of player activity. If you want to make a game where a character explores a system of caves, you could make a simple board game with a track to move along, full of cave-ins, switchbacks, and underwater sections. If you want to make a game about the world of international finance, you could mark up index cards as stocks, bonds, and cash, and begin to design a system of legitimate trades and shady activity.

Invention is the order of the day in physical prototyping. You might be an experienced board game designer who can easily find parallels in the player activities, verbs, and mechanics of physical games and digital games. If, like me, you have less experience as a board game designer, your process might be looser. Your physical prototypes might even feel more like playful prototypes. As Tracy Fullerton reminded me, "It's important to remember that prototyping is always about answering questions, so if you don't have a question that will be answered by a physical prototype, then use another format!"

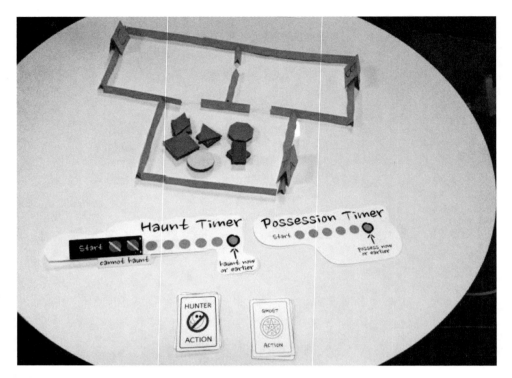

Figure 4.2
A physical prototype of a digital game, *Daunting Dollhouse*, by Chao Chen, Christoph Rosenthal, George Li, and Julian Ceipek created in a USC Games IMGD MFA class. Photo credit: George Li.

Playtesting a Physical Prototype

Once you've built your physical prototype, it's time for the most important activity in this book, and one that we'll come back to over and over again. It's time to playtest.

Playtesting is the foundation of a healthy game design practice. I'll describe my approach to playtesting in great detail later in this book, but for now, I want you to get other people to play your physical prototype as often and as early as you can. Don't worry too much about the presentation of your prototype: as long as people can read your writing, understand the symbols you've used, and handle the playing pieces, you're ready to start.

Write out the rules of the game so that your players can learn it without talking to you. Doing this and then conducting "rules tests" is an important part of every game designer's early education. It develops our understanding of the complexity of systems, the challenges we face in communicating game design ideas, and how every aspect of a game is open to interpretation. You might use the "Wizard of Oz" method from the academic discipline of human-computer interaction, where you (the designer) stand in for the computer that could be running the game in the background, giving information and taking actions on behalf of the game.

As you watch your playtesters, carefully write down your observations. What do they understand about what they can and can't do in the game? What do they then try to do? What do they fail to understand? What do your playtesters get excited about, and what makes them frustrated? What makes them laugh or feel sad? What other emotions do they show? What kind of activities do your playtesters seem to want to do over and over, and what are they reluctant to try?

Iterating on Your Physical Prototype   One great thing about physical prototyping is that it's quick. You can make fundamental changes to your design with a few strokes of your pen or snips of your scissors. You're less likely to hold on to an aspect of your design that isn't working just because you invested time in creating it and have become emotionally attached. This is crucial, because what you must do after nearly every playtest is iterate on your design. Add, remove, and alter things, all the while looking to improve your design. What constitutes an improvement? You are free to decide, but you must acknowledge the results of the playtest.

I sometimes encounter people who think that playtesting is bad because it "dumbs down" a game's design. Thinking like this could not be more wrong. *There is no greater reality in the world of game design than an unmediated encounter between a player and a game.* The player can never be "playing it wrong" and is rarely "just not getting it." (These are excuses that people sometimes make when their designs aren't working.) The player's actions and experiences are authentic expressions of the quality of a game's design, and the best representation of their work that any game designer can have. As I once heard the game designer and educator John Sharp put it: "Game design is like stand-up comedy: the designer and the comedian immediately know whether something has worked or not."

However, game designers should never blindly follow or reactively respond to what players do in a playtest or seem to want in a game. Skillful designers learn to interpret the results of a playtest in the context of their creative goals, and you are at liberty to determine the future course of your game's design, in the light of the results of a playtest, based on your goals.

Game designers are often advised to "follow the fun" in a playtest, and that's great advice, if it's fun that you're after. I love fun in games, I love thinking about what makes a game fun, and I think that almost every human being finds having fun to be central to their happiness and well-being. But not everyone has fun in the same way, and games don't have to be fun in a traditional sense; maybe they don't have to be fun at all. Some of my favorite games, like Liz Ryerson's *Problem Attic*, deliberately refuse to provide the traditional type of pleasurable fun that we get from other games.[5]

It's important in a playtest to be clear about your creative goals, so that you can iterate in the right direction. This will become increasingly important later in our process. While you're prototyping, it's a good consideration but not crucial. For now, it's okay if you spin in circles or get lost a little bit, as long as you're making and learning.

---

5. Liz Ryerson, *Problem Attic*, 2013, https://lizryerson.itch.io/problem-attic.

That's why the physical fact of game pieces on a table in front of you is so good: it gets the ideas you're exploring out into the world, where they can be seen more clearly. You can pick out the good ones more easily and build upon them or revise them.

Physical Prototyping throughout Development   Physical prototypes are good for getting a game design started during the ideation phase, by helping you make sometimes unexpected discoveries about the core game mechanics, narrative, and aesthetics you want to use. But physical prototyping is valuable throughout preproduction and full production too, whenever an open design question can be investigated quickly, easily, cheaply, or thoroughly using physical prototyping techniques.

Strategy games, where the player manipulates systems of resources, lend themselves very easily to physical prototyping at every stage of development. The levels and scenarios of action games and narrative experiences can be mocked-up easily and quickly with physical prototypes, allowing us to answer detailed questions about the player's flow through space, line of sight, and resource availability. This makes physical prototypes useful long after you've got a working digital version of your game. You can use physical prototyping whenever you're working on the "micro design" of a game (more about this in chapter 18).

It's my belief that almost every type of game can benefit from the inventive use of physical prototyping. You'll have to decide for yourself how much physical prototyping is useful for your project, and when it's useful.

Digital Prototyping   If your goal is to make a digital game, then digital prototyping provides a supercharged next step in the ideation process and will lead you directly toward designing and building your game.

Stated in a general way, digital prototyping is the process of using software to make game prototypes that run on a computer. Maybe your digital prototype runs on a personal computer, a phone, a tablet, or a game console, probably with a screen and audio output. It might use a keyboard, mouse, or game controller for an interface, or some other kind of input: voice recognition, gaze-tracking, or a special alt-controller. Or it might run on some other kind of computing platform, like a smartwatch or even a medical implant. Maybe the software you use to build the prototype is easy to use, with a drag-and-drop interface, or maybe it's more complex and requires some knowledge of programming.

In all these cases, we will use the same guidelines that we used for making playful prototypes and physical prototypes: we'll focus on just one player activity at first, trying to find something that works and that we want to keep.

To make a digital prototype, you need some preexisting ability with digital game development. Maybe not a lot, but some. Providing you with that ability is outside the scope of this book, but I can give you some pointers on how to start learning digital game development, and I'll do so in chapter 5.

Every Game Developer Is a Game Designer

To close out this chapter, I'd like to get some terminology straight with you. You might have noticed me switch from talking about *game design*, a term I've used throughout most of this chapter, to mentioning *game development*. Are they the same thing? They're very similar, but I think it's worth distinguishing between the terms.

A game's design is the abstract pattern of elements that make up the game in a way that will produce a good experience for the player. Game designers are concerned with the process of conceptualizing and planning a game, although that planning is tied up with the building of the game in a way that makes it hard to disentangle the planning from the building, as we'll see throughout this book.

When we talk about *developing* a digital game, we mean the process of using software tools, writing code, making art and audio assets, creating animations and visual effects, and tying everything together into something that a player can open and play. So a game developer could be an artist, animator, software engineer, audio designer, composer, game designer, writer, user experience designer, producer, quality assurance professional, or could belong to some other discipline. Most game developers will have some primary role on a team, like environment artist or gameplay programmer. Some people have the job title of game designer, and their role is usually to generate and gather design ideas, and to lock down designs for the game—maybe level design and systems designs.

I believe that every game developer—whether they are an artist, sound designer, animator, or programmer—is also a game designer, because the moment-to-moment decisions they make as they carry out their work have a fundamental impact on the design of the game. "The devil's in the details," or "God lives in the details," perhaps depending on how much trouble the details are giving you. As designers Ray and Charles Eames once said: "The details are not the details. They make the product."[6]

It's particularly important for people with "game designer" in their job title to remember that, in fact, every developer on the team is also a game designer. Everyone on the team contributes to the design of the game, and the best game designers realize this, gathering design ideas from all across the team, as well as coming up with ideas themselves. The game designer's responsibility is to synthesize the best ideas into a coherent whole.

Now that we have a solid understanding of game prototyping, we'll move on to the next chapter and a detailed discussion of the process of building a digital game prototype.

---

6. Daniel Ostroff, "The Details Are Not the Details," Eames Office, September 8, 2014, https://www.eamesoffice.com/blog/the-details-are-not-the-details/.

5 Making a Digital Game Prototype

In this chapter, we'll talk about the process of making a digital prototype, starting with choosing a game engine and perhaps a hardware platform for our game. We'll discuss how we can go about building, playtesting, and iterating on the design of a digital game prototype, and the creative opportunities offered by sound. We'll look at the question of whether to follow where a digital prototype is leading us or to guide our direction in some other way, and we'll look at the deliverables that result from a digital prototyping process.

Choosing and Using a Game Engine

The digital prototyping process starts when we decide what game engine we are going to use to prototype (and maybe later develop) our game. A game engine is a piece of software used to build games. Some are easy to use, and some are more challenging to learn. Most are made by companies, and some by groups of volunteer developers. Many are free to use, and some require payment.

The game engines that are currently the most widely used in both the game industry and game academia are Unity and the Unreal Engine. Both are available as free versions you can download, both come with useful and constantly improving tutorials, and both offer a vast number of features, giving you immense game-making potential. Other game engines are easy to discover with some research on the Internet. Wikipedia's "List of Game Engines" article is a good place to start.[1] If you haven't done much programming, consider using Twine, Bitsy, or Emotica. Remember that every game engine is worthy of respect, and good game design is always about creativity and constraints. Some of my favorite games of the last ten years have been made in easy-to-use game engines.

If the game engine you would like to use is not yet available to you, just find a game engine that you can use today and start building immediately. As game designers, we should always be ready to prototype using whatever means are at hand. Remember that

---

1. "List of Game Engines," Wikipedia, https://en.wikipedia.org/wiki/List_of_game_engines.

what you know how to do right now is enough to allow you to explore and express your game design ideas.

Once you've chosen an engine, your next step is learning how to use it. If you are able to learn how to use software by reading web pages and books, watching videos, and posting on forums, then your path ahead is clear. All you need to do is to set aside the time to learn, and you'll quickly make progress.

If you find it hard to learn in isolation, you can take a class or go to a workshop, find an indie game developer meet-up group in your area, or find a friend who will teach you. Create an environment where you can regularly meet in person with other people who have more skill than you and are willing to share or trade expertise, and your knowledge and skills will soon start to grow exponentially. If you want more help and inspiration, I recommend Anna Anthropy's excellent book, *Rise of the Videogame Zinesters*.[2]

Choosing an Operating System and a Hardware Platform

You have another choice to make around this time: what hardware platform and operating system will your prototype run on? You can choose to make games for PC or Mac using Windows, macOS, or Linux. You might make games for a phone or a tablet using Android or iOS or for a game console that uses a proprietary operating system. Some game engines make it easy to export your game to multiple operating systems and hardware platforms.

You could develop games for virtual reality, augmented reality, or mixed reality. You could make a game to be played on a health tracker or a watch or with some earbuds. In his book *Play Anything*, Ian Bogost argues that the world is full of playgrounds, ready for us to have fun with if we can recognize them.[3] I encourage you to regard every game engine and hardware platform that you approach as a playground, rich with potential for interest, emotion, challenge, and reflection.

Depending on your game and team, it might be important to choose your hardware platform as early as possible. As game designer and producer Alan Dang pointed out to me: if you're thinking about using a platform that brings a lot of constraints—such as specialized input or output methods—the greater your need will be to hurry up and choose.

Build Your Prototype as a Toy, Not a Game

As I mentioned in the previous chapter, people sometimes make a mistake when they start prototyping: for their first digital prototype, they try and build a complete game.

---

2. Anthropy, *Rise of the Videogame Zinesters*.
3. Bogost, *Play Anything*.

They make a player-character and some enemies. They'll add a score counter and a way to earn points. They'll devise a set of rules and a narrative frame, and set up a beginning, middle, and end of the game.

I understand this impulse to start to plan a game in detail from the very beginning. But doing so puts the cart before the horse. I know from my experience as a game designer that the correct path is to take one step at a time, and for me, when I'm digital prototyping, that often means starting by building a toy.

A toy is an object that elicits play. It could be a store-bought toy like a doll or a ball, or it could, in the imaginative hands of a child, be a found object like a bucket or a bicycle tire. The important thing about the toy, for our present discussion, is that it's a system that either has some *mechanical, interactive* element, some *narrative* element, or both.

For example, a ball will bounce when thrown at the floor, and we can try to catch it after the bounce—we could easily imagine it as a cartoon character that says "ouch" on every bounce. A doll can be posed, will stand and fall, and has a certain narrative character that comes from its visual design: it might look like a nineteenth-century doctor or a thirtieth-century space pilot. A bucket can be used as a basket or worn like a helmet. An empty bicycle tire can be rolled down a hill or thrown like a frisbee.

These interactions with a toy sound like the player activities we discussed in the last chapter, don't they? You might not be used to thinking about the things we do when we play with a toy as the fundamental building blocks of the digital games you play, but they have potential as the atomic verbs of gameplay. Posing a doll or throwing a ball is philosophically no different from the running, fighting, and collecting that we do in a commercial videogame.

So begin your digital prototyping by building toys—small, simple, playful systems. What you're looking for are the most fundamental verbs and player activities that you will use in your game. At the same time, be on the lookout for verbs and activities that dovetail nicely with the narrative ideas you have in mind. For example, "to fly" is a verb that goes well with stories about pilots, astronauts, and birds.

Perhaps you'll start with something tried and true, like a character that can run and jump, a piece of land with a cursor that can place buildings, or a grid with objects that can slide around and that will disappear when three are lined up. You could add your own spin to these familiar player activities, or you might strike out in a new game design direction, making a plant that throws out seeds when it's flicked, a hoop that makes soap bubbles when it's waved, or a musical instrument that makes strange sounds when you shake it.

Try to keep your prototypes focused on exploring whether the player activities (a) can create a feeling and appear interesting, (b) are easy for players to understand and use, and (c) could be useful in the kind of game you want to make. Adjust these priorities as you see fit, but always stay clear about what you're trying to figure out with each prototype.

The Importance of Sound for Digital Game Prototypes

Some people have a tendency to neglect sound design when they're prototyping. That's another big mistake. As game designers, we usually only have three sensory modalities with which to communicate with our players: sight, hearing, and touch.[4] While not everyone can implement the touch-based "haptic" design of a vibrating game controller or mobile device, most of us can implement sound in our digital prototypes, and we should make sure that we do so, for a number of reasons.

In *Game Feel: A Game Designer's Guide to Virtual Sensation*, Steve Swink discusses the vital role that sound plays in shaping our experience of a virtual space as having physical properties. He says, "A sound effect can completely change the perception of an object in a game," and gives an example of an animation of two circles moving toward and then away from each other.[5] Without any sound, the circles look like they just pass each other by. With the addition of a "boing!" sound effect at just the right moment, they suddenly look like rubber balls bouncing off each other.

Sound design can tell you whether a character is wearing sneakers or metal boots. It can tell you whether your arrow bounced off stone or ice, and it will certainly make your interface selections feel satisfying or annoying. Steve Swink goes on to describe the way that nuances of sound design can convey information not just about objects or an event but about the space that the event takes place in: "If that massive hammer hits the ground and the sound echoes and reverberates, the sense conveyed to the player is that this impact happened inside a giant warehouse or other massive, empty, interior space. If the impact is muffled, it will sound more like striking the ground outside."[6]

That's not all that sound can do. In his excellent article "Designing a Movie for Sound," Academy Award–winning sound designer Randy Thom lists thirteen different "talents" that sound contributes to film and, by extension, to games and their digital prototypes:

Music, dialogue, and sound effects can each do any of the following jobs, and many more:

- suggest a mood, evoke a feeling
- set a pace
- indicate a geographical locale
- indicate a historical period
- clarify the plot

---

4. Game designers working in location-based entertainment can also use olfactory (smell) design to enhance their players' experiences. But there are many more sensory modalities than the five senses of sight, hearing, taste, smell, and touch. Proprioception, our sense of where our body is in relationship to itself, is an important consideration for virtual reality designers, and humans have around twenty other senses that game designers might use in their designs. We'll come back to the senses in chapter 7. For further information, refer to "Sense," Wikipedia, https://en.wikipedia.org/wiki/Sense.
5. Swink, *Game Feel*, 159.
6. Swink, *Game Feel*, 160.

- define a character
- connect otherwise unconnected ideas, characters, places, images, or moments
- heighten realism or diminish it
- heighten ambiguity or diminish it
- draw attention to a detail, or away from it
- indicate changes in time
- smooth otherwise abrupt changes between shots or scenes
- emphasize a transition for dramatic effect
- describe an acoustic space
- startle or soothe
- exaggerate action or mediate it[7]

Steve Swink also points out in *Game Feel* that, interestingly, sound isn't bound by realism in the way that images usually are. Students of filmic sound design learn early on that many of the iconic sound effects that we know aren't tightly tied to reality but are adopted by poetic resonance and by convention. When you think of the crisp "crump" sound that you've heard whenever someone walks on snow in a movie, you're actually thinking of the sound of someone crushing a leather pouch of cornstarch, a convention established long ago by an innovative and unknown movie Foley sound designer. As Steve Swink says:

> The record scratch for the King of All Cosmos speaks in *Katamari Damacy* or the orchestral hit when a special move is completed in *Tony Hawk 3* prove that mapping an unexpected sound effect to a particular event can have delightful results. These have nothing to do with the reality of the things they are attempting to portray, but they feel satisfying. As in a cartoon, it's not necessary to limit your thinking about how to apply a sound effect to the emulation of reality. You can convey an impression of physicality with a noise much different from the apparent reality of the object.[8]

So, this is one reason why we should make sound design a part of our digital prototyping process: it opens up a huge vista of possible experience for our game that reaches beyond the auditory and into our perception of space, mass, friction, momentum, and other physical properties.

Another important reason to include sound in a digital prototype relates to emotion. Once, early in my time at Crystal Dynamics, I heard someone say that "the eye is connected to the brain, but the ear is connected to the heart." I forget who said it, but I have never forgotten their words. They were making the point that in films and games, while picture and sound both convey logical *and* emotional information, the picture tends to be less emotionally charged on its own, while sound design plays a huge role in shaping emotional experience. For an example of this, take a look at Christopher Rule's minute-long film, *Scary Mary*, a recut trailer for Disney's 1964 film *Mary Poppins*

---

7. Randy Thom, "Designing a Movie for Sound," FilmSound.org, 1999, http://filmsound.org /articles/designing_for_sound.htm.
8. Swink, *Game Feel*, 161.

with new sound design that recasts the children's story as a terrifying thriller.[9] In *Scary Mary* you'll hear the important role that both sound design and music can play in conveying information and creating emotion.

Mark Cerny recently told me that he has a strong focus on the importance of 3D audio technology in games, and the enhanced locality and presence it brings. 3D audio technologies mimic the way that sound waves interact with an environment; *locality* relates to being able to perceive the positions of noise-making objects in space, while *presence* is the psychological impression of actually being in a certain environment. As Mark says, the "locality actually affects the design (you know exactly where the enemy you can't see is) and the presence is connected to your emotional relationship with the game."

In his 2014 GDC Microtalk, composer Austin Wintory suggested that instead of bringing in a composer late in a project, as many game developers regrettably do, it would be excellent to bring them in at the very beginning of the creative process.[10] New creative opportunities open up when we bring a composer into a game project early in its life cycle, as the composer's expertise can intertwine with that of the game designer. It's very easy to drop music and sound into most digital prototypes, and you'll learn an enormous amount by doing so.

Playtesting and Iterating on a Digital Prototype

As soon as you have a prototype in which a player can do something, you must playtest it. I try not to spend more than a single hour building gameplay before I run the game, grab a passerby, and ask them to play for a few minutes. Game designers are pretty good at evaluating what's working in their games. We think of something that seems like it might be fun or interesting, we build it in our game engine, and we try it out. Maybe it's good, and we like it. Maybe we think it's boring and stupid, or otherwise doesn't work. In both cases, we should playtest what we built.

Our own ability to understand what's good and bad about something we've built is radically limited by the fact that *we built it*. We've been thinking about it for a long time, and we understand how it works in intimate detail. Maybe our prototype is only fun to us because we understand it so well. Someone else might get bored or stuck straightaway. On the other hand, maybe we think our prototype is boring because we understand it so well. If we give it to someone who doesn't know it at all, we might discover that they find it interesting, pleasurable, and fun.

We'll take an in-depth look at getting the most out of playtests in chapter 12, but for now, when you're playtesting:

- Don't explain too much. Don't explain *anything* if you can get away with it.

- Don't help your playtester at all or otherwise interfere with what they do.

---

9. Christopher Rule, "THE ORIGINAL Scary 'Mary Poppins' Recut Trailer," 2006, https://www.youtube.com/watch?v=2T5_0AGdFic.

10. Austin Wintory, *GDC Microtalks 2014: One Hour, Ten Speakers, a Panoply of Game Thinking!*, https://www.gdcvault.com/play/1020391/GDC-Microtalks-2014-One-Hour, 31:45.

- Watch your playtesters play. Notice what they do and listen to what they say.
- Take lots of notes about what you see and hear while they're playing.
- When you're talking to your playtester after they've played, resist the urge to explain anything. Instead, ask questions that draw them out about the experience they've just had.

After every playtest, including the very short playtests that you do when you're building a prototype, it's time to evaluate the results of the test and then iterate on your design.

- What should be amplified because it was successful?
- What needs fixing because it might eventually work?
- What should be removed because it isn't working and probably won't ever work?

There can be some tough calls to make here. The more you grow as a game designer, the better your judgment will become about the potential of your prototypes. Once you've decided what to keep, change, and chuck, do another round of work on your prototype, and then test it again. This iterative cycle of plan-make-playtest-evaluate-repeat is one that will remain with you throughout most of your game's development.

In a professional environment, it's good to run "friends and family" playtests every week or as often as you can manage. In a classroom setting, run weekly "musical chairs" playtest sessions with very short rounds, to get as much feedback as possible about every game or prototype.

How Many Digital Prototypes Should We Make?

The answer to this is simple: you should make as many *different* digital prototypes as you can in the time that you have allocated for ideation. This is especially true for designers who want to innovate and discover new types of games and new styles of play. For someone with digital game-making experience, it might only take a few hours to create a strong player activity prototype—and maybe as little as twenty minutes. If you stay focused on very simple prototypes, you might be able to make a huge number of them in a single day.

Sometimes you'll strike gold straightaway, with your very first digital prototype. You'll find a player activity that works so well that you just know you want to follow where it leads. Sometimes it will take a while to make a prototype that you and your playtesters like, and that's okay. It's important not to get discouraged and to keep making new things. The seam of gold that you're looking for will eventually appear, either with a bolt from the blue or just because you and your playtesters like one of your prototypes better than the others.

When to Follow Where a Prototype Leads

Whenever you've made a digital prototype you like, you'll have a choice to make. Should you use your remaining ideation time to continue to iterate on the successful prototype? Or should you explore some wildly different directions? It might be safer to iterate on a successful prototype, but I like to err on the side of more exploration, especially early in the ideation phase. The uncertainty around this kind of decision is part of what makes creativity both scary and exciting. It's up to you to find the right balance for your working style.

I've often seen people discard prototypes that are working very well, and they usually do it out of ego. They don't like what they made because it doesn't match their expectation of what they thought their game would be like. Maybe they judge it as not cool or innovative enough, even though it has the potential to be both with a little more work. They junk it even though their playtesters were having a wonderful time, wanted to play more, or were moved by what they played.

Guard against this. Yes, ego is essential for creative people: it's a source of creative vision. But it can easily derail or block our process, if it's unwisely motivated. During ideation we have to reconcile our vision with our openness to new ideas. This takes effort, but the only way to develop this essential creative muscle is to work it.

Ideation Deliverable: Prototype Builds

A deliverable is a thing provided by a project's developers to its stakeholders (the people running and/or financing the project) as part of a development process. Our prototypes are the first of several deliverables that we'll make throughout our playful production process.

The best way to deliver a prototype as a deliverable is by creating an executable file. This executable allows us to play the prototype when the file is run, and making the executable is known among software developers as making a "build." Making a build is an important part of the overall development process. The details vary from engine to engine, and the game engine that you're working in will offer documentation about making one (though not every engine can or needs to make builds).

It's better to deliver builds instead of project folders for a number of reasons, whether you're sending your work to a game publisher, project manager, professional peer, or professor. A build is easier and more convenient to deal with—in a couple of clicks, you can be playing the game. A build is also usually much smaller than a project folder in terms of file size.

While I never throw away the project folders for my old prototypes, I keep an archive of prototype builds alongside them. When I want to look at an old prototype later for inspiration or research, it's easier to find and run a build than to load up a project file (as long as the old build still runs).

Build Notes

For every build that we create, we should make some build notes. These will be useful for anyone we send the build to and for ourselves if we go back to look at the build later. On professional projects, the notes for a build can run to many pages and might describe in detail all the work that was done to create the build. For prototypes, it should be enough to provide the following.

A **description of the inputs** is valuable to anyone trying to play it, especially if the prototype doesn't teach its controls through gameplay.

Keeping a **list of attributions** for any found and third-party assets that you're using is a good habit to get into. You're probably not going to publish your prototypes, and some limited use of copyrighted materials is permitted for personal work and in academia, but there's no knowing which of your prototypes might turn into a successful commercial work, when the presence of copyrighted assets would be a problem. Remember, found assets can only be used commercially if they have an appropriate license like Creative Commons or Open, or if they're subject to fair use. It's no fun to have to hunt through your project folder seeking out the license statuses of the things you found on the Internet. If you keep a list of the found assets as you go along, you'll save yourself valuable time later on.

Additional instructions can be useful—for example, to tell the player if the prototype is open-ended or has some goal that can be reached.

It's important to keep a list of the **credits** for your game, starting from the very beginning of the project. People who do even a small amount of work on a project should be credited, except under special and carefully negotiated circumstances. The game industry has had a big problem with the unfair erasure of people's contributions to games, and every responsible game designer should work to counteract this problem. The International Game Developers Association has produced a useful Crediting Standards Guide that you can use in your crediting process.[11]

Masterpiece Syndrome

You might have heard of masterpiece syndrome, where creative people get so excited about their next project that they become overwhelmed by the responsibility. Masterpiece syndrome often kicks in when a project is bigger and potentially better than any you've worked on before, whether it's your first professionally made game or a university thesis project.

Masterpiece syndrome is similar to the blank-sheet-of-paper problem we discussed in chapter 1. People become paralyzed by the seemingly infinite options for what to make and how to make it. You want this game to be the best thing you've ever made, an instant classic, a modern masterpiece (for you, at least). But the pressure is so intense that it can be incapacitating, especially if you start to compare the things you're making to all of the masterpieces made by the game designers you love.

---

11. IGDA Credit Standards Committee, "Crediting Standards Guide Ver 9.2 [EN/JP] [2014]," IGDA .org, August 15, 2014, https://igda.org/resources-archive/crediting-standards-guide-ver-9-2-en-jp -2014/.

In an attempt to inoculate people against masterpiece syndrome, I give them this quote about "the gap," from Ira Glass of *This American Life* fame:

> Nobody tells this to people who are beginners; I wish someone told me. All of us who do creative work, we get into it because we have good taste. But there is this gap. For the first couple years you make stuff, it's just not that good. It's trying to be good, it has potential, but it's not. But your taste, the thing that got you into the game, is still killer. And your taste is why your work disappoints you.
>
> A lot of people never get past this phase, they quit. Most people I know who do interesting, creative work went through years of this. We know our work doesn't have this special thing that we want it to have. We all go through this. And if you are just starting out or you are still in this phase, you gotta know it's normal and the most important thing you can do is do a lot of work.
>
> Put yourself on a deadline so that every week you will finish one story. It is only by going through a volume of work that you will close that gap, and your work will be as good as your ambitions. And I took longer to figure out how to do this than anyone I've ever met. It's gonna take a while. It's normal to take a while. You've just gotta fight your way through.[12]

The right way to deal with masterpiece syndrome is to think less, act more, and embrace failure. Being fearless about failing is a central part of my game design philosophy. If one of your prototypes doesn't work—that's fine. Just move on to building the next thing. If you make a lot of prototypes, then on the day that you run out of ideation phase time, one of them will stand out as the best, and you can keep working on it—or a variation of it—in the next project phase.

The Emotional Side of Prototype Playtests

Prototype playtests usually have a wonderful, festival atmosphere, and in my classes it's great to see lots of playful, experimental, innovative software showing up. However, prototype playtests can also have some anxiety attached to them. People are bringing in work that they've made under time pressure, and might be sitting on some masterpiece syndrome. If you're doing it right, playtesting can be pretty painful. It's agonizing when a playtester gets stuck and you can't help them, and the feelings that you have when someone doesn't like your game can be difficult to deal with.

I try to look out for anyone who isn't feeling good about the prototype playtesting process (or the prototyping process overall) and offer them some support. I point out the things that I like about their work, as well as offering some constructive critique, and they will often start to relax and see the value in what they've made.

I always encourage designers to seek out this kind of support whenever they need it. If design *is* a contact sport as Tom Wujec says, then it's rather rough-and-tumble, and we owe it to ourselves and each other to be kind, compassionate, supportive, and respectful as we go through the complex, emotionally charged process that is game

---

12. Ira Glass and Daniel Sacks, *THE GAP by Ira Glass*, 2014, https://vimeo.com/85040589.

design and development. It can be hard to ask for help, but tolerating the discomfort that comes with doing so is an essential skill for collaborators and leaders alike.

✄   ❀   ✄

The best general advice that I can give you about prototyping is just to throw yourself into it with urgent, joyful abandon. Don't think too hard—just make, make, *make!* Enjoy everything you do, and don't get stressed out about the quality of your output. Don't be afraid to abandon the idea that inspired a prototype and let the prototype lead you in a new direction. Notice what is appearing in front of you in the world and pursue it. Like a mountain range emerging from the mist, the chain of your prototypes will help your creative vision come into better view.

As Mark Cerny recently told me: "For *God of War*, it's about making each moment *epic*. For *Control*, it's about the bureaucratic sureality of narrative, environment and game mechanics."[13] Prototyping will help you define your creative direction, which will find expression in what I see as the most important deliverable outcome of the ideation phase: our game's project goals.

---

13. Private communication, May 31, 2020.

6 Communication as a Game Design Skill

Game designers are communicators. The games that we make communicate ideas and feelings to our audience of players. Games are highly conceptual, built of logic, number, space, and language. These are conveyed in image, sound, touch, and the other modalities of our senses. Games convey meaning in many complex and sophisticated ways, and this is part of what makes game design such a fascinating artistic practice.

Of course, as well as communicating with our players, the people who make games have to communicate with each other. And if the process of communicating with our players is complex and sophisticated, it stands to reason that the way developers communicate with each other will be too, creating both problems and opportunities.

Communication, Collaboration, Leadership, and Conflict

Like most game developers, I place a strong focus on communication, collaboration, leadership, and conflict as core aspects of game development. These "soft skills," relating to the way that team members work with one another, are as much a part of the creation of an excellent videogame as strong game design, ingenious programming, or beautiful art and audio.

Communication is important because making a game involves much discussion of abstract concepts related to our game's design and of concrete facts related to its implementation. Unfortunately, most of us aren't nearly as good at communicating as we'd like to be. The simplest of communications—about street directions or a homework assignment—can be confusing and frustrating. I've seen that frustration amplified ten thousand–fold as someone tries in vain to describe a complicated game design idea to a teammate, each person muddying the conversation with their own preconceptions and biases.

To make things even more complicated, communication, like all of our cognition, is profoundly affected by emotion. Emotion affects our ability to say things and to hear them. Have you ever put off telling somebody something difficult because you could tell that they weren't in the right mood to hear it? Or have you found a conversation becoming difficult because you got defensive about something that was said? Happily, we can improve our ability to communicate, by learning practical skills like the ones I'll introduce you to later in this chapter.

Collaboration is important for most game developers, because few of us make games entirely on our own. Most of us work in teams, from triple-A developers to indies and students. Even the people we think of as game-making auteurs, working in isolation to bring their unique vision into being, collaborate with other people: those who make the software tools and write the shared code libraries that we all use, and those who give design feedback and advice.

Working with others can be fun, enriching, illuminating, and energizing. We can accomplish things working together that we couldn't possibly achieve on our own. It can also be difficult, frustrating, agonizing, and even scary. Fortunately, the ability to collaborate well is also something that can be learned.

Collaboration is built into the heart of the USC Games program as a very important aspect of game-making. Film editor, director, and sound designer Walter Murch—a USC School of Cinematic Arts alumnus—famously emphasized the importance of collaboration when he said, "Half the job is doing the job, and the other half is finding ways to get along with people and tuning yourself in to the delicacy of the situation."[1]

I have two interpretations of Murch's "delicacy of the situation." I think that he is referring to subtleties in the relationships between the individuals doing a job together, and he's also talking about the complex balance of elements in the creative work they're making. Taken together, this is "the situation": the community of people collaborating to make a creative work and the work itself. The two things are deeply interconnected. If teammates don't get along—if they're always miscommunicating or fighting against each other—then the creative work they're making probably won't hit the right notes.

Good collaboration isn't just about getting along easily, though. In my experience, it's best when people are willing to challenge each other respectfully, to make sure that we're reaching the best design decisions possible. But there's a difference between productive disagreement and destructive argument, and we must learn to tell them apart.

Leadership is a key game development skill, whether we're a game director in charge of the design and development of an entire project or the most junior person on a team. Leadership isn't just about leading; it's about working with leaders. Everyone on the team, right up to the game director, must be able to recognize when to lead and when to follow. This is particularly important for the discipline leads on a team (the lead artist, lead programmer, and so on), who must figure out when to make a decision on their own and when to check in with the game director.

Good game development leadership is about knowing when more work needs to be done on something and when it's time to move on to something else. It's about making timely decisions so that other people can move ahead with their work. It's sometimes about refusing to make a decision yet, because we're still figuring out the design, and then working with others so that they can still move forward. Game team leadership is about recognizing the emotional state of a development team,

1. Walter Murch interview in Wohl, *Editing Techniques with Final Cut Pro*, 524.

as individuals and in groups, and bringing positivity and balance where it's needed. It's also about helping team members who have come into conflict resolve their differences.

It can take a long time to develop genuine leadership ability, but you'll find that the ability to lead is closely connected to good communication, collaboration, and conflict management skill.

To get a sense of the wide-ranging skills of a game director, I recommend Brian Allgeier's excellent *Directing Video Games: 101 Tips for Creative Leaders*. The "Organizational Improvements" and "Team Culture" sections of Clinton Keith and Grant Shonkwiler's *Creative Agility Tools: 100+ Tools for Creative Innovation and Teamwork* contain a lot of wisdom for people seeking to improve their game development leadership skills. *Creativity, Inc.: Overcoming the Unseen Forces That Stand in the Way of True Inspiration*, by Ed Catmull and Amy Wallace, offers great advice about creative leadership, alongside practical examples and a real understanding of how creative teams work.

Conflict between the members of a game development team is an important aspect of every one of these subjects we've been discussing. Of course, it's easy to see conflict as a problem, but in fact conflict is essential and necessary to every collaborative creative process. We just have to learn to handle it well, working through disagreements respectfully and productively. We also have to learn not to avoid or ignore conflicts when they happen, which can lead to even bigger blow-ups down the line. I recommend *The Big Book of Conflict Resolution Games* by Mary Scannell as an excellent exploration of these subjects.

Communication, collaboration, leadership, and conflict can be difficult to discuss, since the things we can say about them often seem so obvious as to be banal. As subjects, they're also quite loaded with social taboo, so that discussing them in a straightforward way might mark you as a weirdo, hypercritical, or a snitch. But we need to make sure that we're communicating and collaborating well if we're going to build a team that values respect, trust, and consent.

Luckily, there are lots of good techniques for helping us with what is essentially *talking about talking*, and many of them feel like games. We'll look at some of them in the course of this book.

The Most Basic Communication Skills

Sometime while I was at Crystal Dynamics, I was introduced to the basic skills that underlie all effective communication: clarity, brevity, and active listening. These three simple ideas resonated with me very strongly. I've used them throughout my career, and every game developer can benefit from keeping them in mind. Let's take a look at these, one at a time.

Be Clear

Clarity is the essence of good communication. If a message is not clear, it cannot be understood.

Game designers often have to work extra hard to be clear. The ideas we're proposing and the work we're doing are often complicated and abstract. We have to choose our words carefully and should try to be specific and exact. For example, it's important to distinguish between the player and the player-character.

Our quest for clarity is complicated by the fact that the names for concepts that game designers use are not always widely agreed upon. What you call graybox I might call blockmesh. That's why I try to avoid using jargon until I'm sure that the person I'm talking to understands a particular term.

Catchy new nicknames for game design concepts are invented all the time and then fade into history: clutch, mobs, tanking, nerfing—these are all useful shortcut terms that we can use on a team when we've agreed that we know what they mean. But resist using jargon just to show off your game design chops. It's usually counterproductive, and it keeps people with useful ideas out of the conversation if they happen not to have heard a term before.

Of course, if a piece of communication isn't clear, the surefire way of bringing clarity is for the person who didn't understand to say so. Early in my career, I was given one of the best pieces of game development advice that I ever received: I was told that if I didn't understand something, I should not worry about seeming ignorant; I should just ask for an explanation. Right up to the present day, I've found that if I say when I don't understand something, it makes the conversation better, sometimes for everyone in the room. The person I'm asking can usually just restate what they mean quickly and easily, and I often notice others benefiting from a moment's additional explanation.

I don't usually feel perceived as lesser when I do this—if anything, having the confidence to ask for clarification makes a person seem more capable. And asking means that I never have that awful feeling anymore, that I would sometimes get at the very start of my career, of drifting further and further away from the deep meaning of a conversation because I'd missed some important idea near the start. So, help bring clarity by asking questions.

Keep in mind that the freedom to ask questions is often attached to social privilege, in belonging to an identity that is in the majority. We need to create just and equitable working environments, where everyone feels able to speak up. Team leaders and senior team members have a role to play here in setting a tone in meetings so that we do not interrupt and speak over each other, by speaking up to support colleagues' ideas or questions, and by doing one-on-one check-ins with people whose ideas may be getting overlooked. Creating team cultures where everyone has a voice takes effort, but it's important for us to realize that there are tangible steps we can take to do so.

Be Brief

"Brevity is the soul of wit" runs the old proverb. Whether "wit" means intelligence or humor, if a message is delivered quickly, it's more effective. A meaning lands more impactfully, or a joke rings out more sharply. To communicate with someone, we have to hold their attention, and everyone's attention is limited. So get to the point and say what you have to say as quickly as you can, while still being clear.

There's a tension to hold here—sometimes brevity and clarity are in competition with each other. You'll have to decide whether you're being brief enough while also being clear enough. And boiling down a complex concept to a simple encapsulation takes effort. As the seventeenth-century mathematician Blaise Pascal said, "I would have written a shorter letter, but I did not have the time."

To strike a good balance, consider saying a little less than you might be inclined to say, and ask if you're being clear. The person you're talking to can then guide the conversation with follow-up questions, instead of patiently listening while you tell them something they already know.

Someone once told me that when you're going into a game design conversation with a long list of issues to get on the table, it shows good leadership and collaborative skill to pick the three biggest issues, and talk only about those (for now, at least). That way, you don't overwhelm people, and the most important things get the attention they deserve. We can always come back to the other issues later, once these big things have been taken care of.

Game designers can often find it challenging to be brief: our work is fascinating and rewards deep discussion. But I've seen in my professional life how much valuable game development time can be eaten up by discursive note-giving and long-winded presentations. Pause and consider whether you could be more concise.

Listen Actively

Listening is the most undervalued communication skill. Listening actively means paying attention to what someone is saying. This might seem obvious, but even people who are good listeners get distracted by their own thoughts. If you have a lapse in your attention like this, apologize and ask the person you're speaking with to repeat what you missed.

There's another meaning of active listening: it's when you show someone that you're following what they're saying by looking at them, nodding occasionally, and saying "mm-hmm" or "uh-huh" as they speak. Many of us do this naturally as we listen in conversation; I think it's like the "handshaking protocol" that computers use to establish and maintain communication over the Internet. It says, "Yes, I'm still receiving you—keep going." The same kind of language can be used to signal when a subject is outliving its welcome. "Uh-huh, yep, I got it" says that it's time to move on to the next topic.

Overt displays of attention like this don't come naturally to everyone. If you don't like doing it, don't worry. There's another way to confirm for someone that they've been understood. I was taught this technique partway into my game design career, and I find it enormously effective for eliminating misunderstandings and saving time. The technique is called either mirroring or reflecting, and it is very simple. At the end of a complex statement or question that you've listened to, you say, "Let me mirror that back to you to see if I've understood you correctly," and then you summarize what you think you heard the other person say. What will most likely happen is that the other person will say, "That's almost it, but . . ." and then fill in some small detail that you hadn't quite got.

This might seem ridiculously simple, but it works like magic. When discussing the complexities of game design, it's very easy for misconceptions to creep into our understanding of what we're doing. Mirroring reliably exposes potential misunderstandings with almost uncanny effectiveness. Most every time I use this technique, I discover some small but important detail that I'd overlooked or misunderstood. Often those misunderstandings wouldn't have amounted to much apart from lost time. Sometimes they could have led to dire consequences. Make mirroring a part of your communication toolkit.

You get bonus points for active listening by stopping everything else that you're doing and focusing your whole attention on the person you're listening to. In our multitasking lives and with our phones almost always in our hands, it's becoming quite rare for people to do this. But the divided attention of multitasking often comes at a price of work that is inefficient and error-prone, and communication that is ineffective or uninfluential.

If you're reading social media while talking to someone on the phone, you might miss something important that they say. If you keep coding while a teammate is telling you something important about the game's design, they might walk away from your desk thinking that you didn't hear them or that you don't care. The best active listening lets others clearly know that you value what they're saying, which has a strong emotional benefit and builds respect and trust.

Clarity, brevity, active listening. When things go wrong in your communication— when things get confused or emotional in a way that is creating problems—come back to those three friends and they will steer you right.

Sandwiching

I am well known for my use of and love for the communication technique known as sandwiching, to the point where I sometimes get teased about it. I don't care— sandwiching is a powerful technique to use when giving someone constructively critical feedback about their creative work or their performance on the job, and it has served me well in both industry and academia.

When giving someone feedback, start with a compliment, telling them something you like. This is the first slice of bread in the sandwich. This can't just be empty praise: you have to be authentic, so choose something that you *actually* like. If you can't find anything you like at first, look again. I believe there is something to admire in every act of creativity—it might be that the person put in some effort, or that they really aced some small detail, even though there are major problems to discuss.

This first compliment plays a few roles. First, it's a clear and easy way to show respect. Respect is the basis for trust, and trust is what we want to nurture if we're going to be able to give and receive the constructive criticism we need to make our work great.

Second, it's actually useful for creative people to hear what *is* working for others in their game or in their performance. Without praise for the things we're getting right, it can be hard to know for sure what is of value in our work.

And third, a compliment may play some role in creating good emotion around the current act of communication. If we're feeling good about the work and about the person critiquing it, we may be more able to hear what they're saying when they give us their constructive critique.

I will often mention several things that I like when I'm giving feedback, because I know that the more clearly I signal to someone that I like their work and respect their abilities, the more deeply I can dive with my constructive criticism.

The filling in the sandwich is constructive criticism, and just as the filling is the most nutritious and flavorful part of a sandwich, your constructive criticism is the most important information that you have to convey. Throughout this book we'll be discussing game design as an iterative art form, and the constructive criticism that we receive about our work is an important part of the iterative loop. We build something, we give it to someone to play, they give us their constructive criticism (in one way or another, in this case, verbally), which we then evaluate. In light of the feedback we've received, we make changes to what we built, and we playtest again.

So, the constructive criticism you give talks about what you *didn't* like about what you just played (or about someone's performance), but it does so in a way that is useful. It doesn't tear down; it builds up. In order to do this well we have to choose the words of our constructive criticism carefully.

In chapter 12 we'll look more deeply at giving and receiving good feedback. But to get you started, I have three very simple principles for giving constructive criticism: *be direct*, *be specific*, and *criticize the work, not the person*.

When giving constructive criticism, *be direct*. Don't try and mix the bread of your compliments in with the sandwich filling of your constructive criticism. Don't beat around the bush or try and disguise your criticism as a compliment. Don't hint at your criticism or frame it passive-aggressively. Have the courage to come right out and say what you think isn't good, what you don't like, or what you think could use more work. Don't be unkind or aggressive: speak calmly, and in a friendly, collegial way. You're taking the time to use sandwiching, so you've earned the right to be direct with your constructive criticism.

By *be specific*, I mean that it isn't enough to say, "This isn't good" or "I don't like this." You should say *why* you think it isn't good, or why you don't like it. Instead of saying, "This jump mechanic isn't good," say, "This jump mechanic isn't good because there's a noticeable pause between pressing the button and the player-character leaving the ground—it feels sticky and unresponsive."

The third principle—*criticize the work, not the person*—was something that I picked up from Naughty Dog studio president Evan Wells. Evan makes it a simple rule to always criticize what we can see of the game on screen, hear through the speakers, and feel through the controller, making sure never to criticize the person who made the work we are looking at.

If you follow this rule of criticizing the work, not the person, you lower the chance that someone will get discouraged or angry, and you keep everyone's focus on improving the quality of the game. This might seem obvious, but it's surprisingly easy to stray from saying, "This game mechanic isn't good" to saying, "The way that *you* made this game mechanic isn't good." By staying focused on the work, and what could be improved about it, we can always devise an actionable plan for making it better, without alienating the person doing the work.

So that's the first slice of compliment bread and the filling of constructive criticism— what about the second slice of bread? When we're sandwiching, it's usual to conclude the feedback session with another compliment. I usually try and find something I hadn't already mentioned, but it can be enough just to remind them what you liked. Sometimes there's something more to say that's complimentary in light of the constructive criticism. ("I think that, given that there's more work to do on the jump controls, the part that I liked—the animations and sound effects—will feel even better once these problems are solved.")

The second slice of bread is often thinner than the first—the concluding positive comments are usually given more quickly, especially if the constructive criticism was received well by the game maker. If someone shows signs of having a difficult-to-deal-with emotional reaction to my constructive criticism, I'll take rather more time to give some additional compliments at the end and will open up into a conversation, giving the game maker a chance to respond to my comments or explain their work. I'll take the time to hear them out, and maybe in our conversation we can get to a place where the game maker feels good about their work and has an actionable plan for making it better.

Some people call this technique "the compliment sandwich," and some call it "the poop sandwich." That might mean they think that constructive criticism is poop, but it's more likely that they had a run-in with someone who didn't use authentic compliments and instead used sandwiching as an excuse to be unkind. You can use sandwiching as an opportunity to change the minds of skeptics and to show them that this technique actually works.

Sandwiching isn't the be-all and end-all of good feedback; it's only a starter kit. It works best when you don't yet have a strong bond of respect and trust with someone, maybe when you don't know them very well or don't get along with them easily.

Building respect and trust between team members is a key aspect of a strong game design practice. Respect comes from valuing each other's experience, ability, values, and intentions, and having a shared understanding that the respect is mutual. Trust arises when you know you can rely on someone else to act in everyone's best interests, to make good decisions, and to be a good collaborator, being generous to the team while also acting in pursuit of their own values.

The more your relationship with someone develops and strengthens, the less need there is for sandwiching. The bread in your sandwiches will get thinner and thinner over time, until it disappears completely, and you can give someone your constructive criticism directly and have it land well with them. You'll soon create a team culture rich with strong values around collaboration, which will in turn allow your team to make truly excellent games.

Respect, Trust, and Consent

The strongest teams are those where the team members respect each other, have strong bonds of trust between them, and make sure that everyone is consenting to the ways we're involved in the work we're doing. We show each other respect by using our communication skills, listening attentively to what each of us has to say, and giving full consideration to each of our worldviews. Showing respect doesn't cost us anything apart from our time and attention, as long as we hold an attitude that everyone's experiences and beliefs have value. When we show each other respect, we're showing that we value each other, including our work, time, and skill.

When we work together in an atmosphere of respect, doing the difficult work of game development together, then trust follows naturally. If I have helped you in the past and shown you that I respect you and am willing to prioritize your effort and well-being as well as my own, then you will come to trust me. In the future, we will be able to do difficult work together more quickly, efficiently, and with less stress. Trust between team members makes everything run more smoothly in the extremely complex work that we're doing together.

Consent is important everywhere in our lives, including on our game development teams. We have to be sure that everyone on our team clearly understands what we're asking them to do, and has agreed to do it, without coercion. This is applicable especially around questions of overtime and compensation—whether we're working for the numbers of hours that we expected to work when we joined a team, and whether we're being paid properly for our time. It is also relevant around ethical matters pertaining to our work: whether we agree with the values in the games that we're making.

If we build and maintain an environment of respect, trust, and consent, then we are setting ourselves up to flourish as game developers. To create this environment, we need to communicate and collaborate well. Communication truly is a game design skill.

7   Project Goals

We've made three types of deliverables so far in the ideation phase: lists of ideas, research notes, and prototypes. There's a final deliverable for us to create before we're done with ideation, which all these other deliverables lead us toward: a set of project goals.

If we establish some clear goals for our project at the end of ideation and commit ourselves to them, then we give ourselves a creative direction to propel us into the next phase of the project and to help us throughout its whole course. For me, project goals come in two types: experience goals and design goals.

Experience Goals

The idea of an experience goal was first introduced into the game design literature in 2008 with the second edition of Tracy Fullerton's *Game Design Workshop*.[1] As Tracy told me, "I added [the concept of experience goals] because I was trying to clarify the process we were using in [the USC Game Innovation Lab], which was so different from the way that people were speaking about game design process in general—as feature- or pillar-driven."

An experience goal is the kind of experience you want your players to have, often described in terms of an *emotional* experience. While there are many reasons to play a game, the emotions that games give us are usually why we spend time with them: the satisfaction of winning and the frustration of losing, the tense anxiety of a stealth game, the nuanced melancholy of an arthouse game, or the joyful laughter of a party game.

Your project goals don't have to describe how you'll create the experience through the design of your game—although, as we'll see later, your prototypes should have given you a decent idea of how you'll do it. By focusing on the experience that we want the player to have, we can begin to free ourselves from our preconceptions about what playing a game is or isn't like. We can move away from traditional, limited ideas

---

1. Fullerton, *Game Design Workshop*, 2nd ed., 10.

about fun, and explore the wide, deep expressive power of game design. It's my belief that establishing an experience goal for our game at the end of ideation is the key to innovating in game design and to understanding games as an art form.

Tracy Fullerton, the MDA Framework, and Naughty Dog

As I mentioned, I get this focus on experience goals from the work of Tracy Fullerton. In *Game Design Workshop*, in a sidebar essay about working on *Cloud* with game designers Jenova Chen and Kellee Santiago and a team of students in the USC Game Innovation Lab, Tracy says:

> When we began working on *Cloud*, we had only an innovation design goal: to somehow evoke the feeling of relaxation and joy that you get when you lie back in the grass on a clear sunny day and look up at the clouds wandering across the sky. . . . At some time or another, we've (all) dreamed of flying up in the clouds and moving them, shaping them into funny creatures or smiley faces or lollipops, or whatever comes to mind. It seemed like entirely new territory for a game. It seemed risky and interesting. So we decided to give it a try.[2]

Tracy calls it an innovation goal here: she had not yet coined the term *experience goal* when she wrote this essay. We can see now that the *Cloud* team was setting an experience goal. They didn't initially know how they were going to create this relaxing, joyous experience. They didn't even know if they could create it. But by setting an intention and beginning to explore toward it, they made their first bold move toward a new frontier for game design.

That move would set in place a design philosophy that changed the game industry forever. The core of the *Cloud* team would go on to found thatgamecompany, and to create the award-winning games *Flow*, *Flower*, and the 2012 Game of the Year, *Journey*. Tracy has used similar experience goal–setting techniques throughout her own award-winning practice, from *The Night Journey*, the game that she codesigned with the renowned artist Bill Viola, to her widely acclaimed *Walden: a game*, a playful and systematic take on the work and world of Henry David Thoreau. Tracy has continued to push the envelope of what games can do, innovating in her process as well as her art.

The famous MDA framework—mechanics, dynamics, and aesthetics—also places a focus on player experience. The framework was proposed by Robin Hunicke, Marc LeBlanc, and Robert Zubek in their groundbreaking 2004 paper "MDA: A Formal Approach to Game Design and Game Research" and seeks to help us both design and analyze games.

The aesthetics in MDA are the experiences produced as the player plays in the dynamic system determined by the rules of the game. One of the goals of the MDA authors was to help us understand the often-nebulous idea of "fun" in a deeper way, and to expand our thinking about the kinds of experiences that games could give us.

---

2. Fullerton, *Game Design Workshop*, 4th ed., 252.

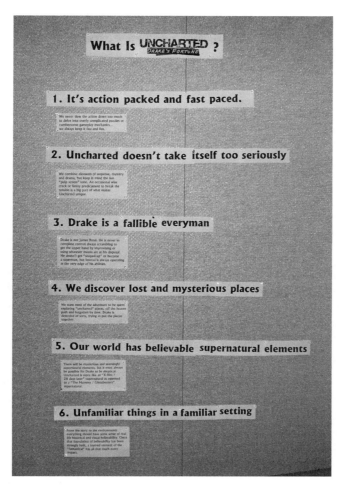

Figure 7.1
What is *Uncharted*? (Naughty Dog, circa 2006). A transcription of this text is available in appendix B. Image credit: *UNCHARTED: Drake's Fortune*™ © 2007 Sony Interactive Entertainment LLC. *UNCHARTED: Drake's Fortune* is a trademark of Sony Interactive Entertainment LLC. Created and developed by Naughty Dog LLC.

Setting experience goals (figure 7.1) was how our team at Naughty Dog developed the world of *Uncharted*. Working with senior concept artist Shaddy Safadi and the team, *Uncharted: Drake's Fortune* game director Amy Hennig defined the type of experiences that we wanted to create in a concise set of rules, which we displayed in a public area in the studio. These rules helped us stay on track throughout the development of the entire series. I see them as experience goals, defining a space of possibility in a way that helped us design the *Uncharted* games.

Types of Experience

Most everyone knows what it means to have an experience, but when challenged to say what experience is, many of us struggle. The nature of firsthand experience (what psychologists would call subjective experience) is tied up with the nature of consciousness, and philosophers throughout history have been baffled, amazed, and inspired by this topic.

To have an experience is to have a sense of a self, with something happening to that self. Experience might be physical, mental, emotional, spiritual, religious, social, subjective, or virtual and simulated. Intellect and consciousness produce different categories of mental experience, like thought, perception, memory, emotion, will, and imagination.[3]

All these types of experience could form the basis of excellent and interesting games, when used as experience goals. Some of them seem particularly useful for game designers.

Thought, Memory, Imagination, and Willpower

Thinking of something, knowing something, and remembering have associated experiences, of what it's like to do each thing. The same with imagination, which gives us the ability to make plans, and will, in the sense of "willpower," the faculty that allows us to make decisions and to take action. Games trade heavily in these types of experience. I know that if I touch those spikes, the hedgehog will drop all his rings, and I think that I will try to bounce off three mushroom people in a row this time.

Thought, memory, imagination, and will are fundamental parts of our experiences of games and—if we wanted—we could set an experience goal for our game that involved our players thinking something, remembering something, or imagining something. This might be particularly important for the creators of educational games. Willpower is, of course, at the very center of game design, since the decisions and actions of our players drive most (though arguably not all) types of game design. Game designers talk about this in terms of agency and autonomy.

Perception

Our perceptions are the experiences that we have as a result of the operation of our senses. Most schoolkids know the five traditional senses of sight, hearing, taste, smell, and touch, but the sense of proprioception, the kinesthetic sense of where your body is in relation to itself, is an important one for game designers. Our vestibular sense of balance and acceleration is also important for designers, especially for games that get us moving around.

Thermoception and nociception—temperature and pain, respectively—haven't often been used by game designers, though experience designers for theme parks and virtual reality often use hot and cold air to reinforce the experience they're shaping. The famous *Painstation* interactive art piece created by Tilman Reiff and Volker Morawe in 2001, which the brave can play at the Computerspielemuseum (Computer Games Museum) in Berlin, uses pain as a negative reinforcement for losing in a *Pong*-like game.

---

3. "Experience," Wikipedia, https://en.wikipedia.org/wiki/Experience.

Our bodies have a large number of other internal senses, which tell us whether we're hungry or thirsty, blushing, suffocating, and whether our stomachs, bladders, and bowels are full. All these senses are fair game for designers seeking to make innovative types of experience.

Emotion

The emotional feelings that games give us are what draw us into a game and keep us playing. For many years, game designers often didn't think beyond the two emotions that dominated the first five thousand years of the history of games: the joy of victory, and the frustration of defeat. We shouldn't underestimate the power of these emotions, though. As Jesper Juul points out in *The Art of Failure: An Essay on the Pain of Playing Video Games*, the failure that we experience in games is not without its own kind of pleasure. Other emotions are often present alongside joy and frustration: the delight of play, the curiosity that drives exploration, and the satisfaction of completion.

Today, game designers are interested in the wide range of emotion that games might provoke in their audience of players. Perhaps as a result, out of all the different types of experience, emotional experiences are often by far the most useful to us as experience goals for our games. In most every art form that I can think of, our experiences of thought, memory, imagination, will, and perception weave together in a complex braid that results in the powerful, nuanced emotion that great art brings out of us.

Therefore, it seems very important that game designers be "emotionally literate," able to discuss a wide range of possible emotions with clarity and accuracy. For many of us, that's harder than it sounds. Many cultures down the years have made it taboo to speak extensively about emotion. Men in particular have often been made the subject of that taboo.

To help people expand their emotional literacy, I remind them of the characters of Joy, Sadness, Fear, Anger, and Disgust, five of the characters in Pixar's 2015 film, *Inside Out*. These characters were based on the work of Dr. Paul Ekman, a UC San Francisco psychologist who pioneered the study of emotions in their relation to facial expressions. Ekman's research identified seven primary emotions that people from cultures throughout the world show in their faces: the five that the *Inside Out* characters are named for, and also surprise and contempt.

This palette of seven emotions could be a strong starting point in helping us set an emotional experience goal for a game. It's probable that a story-driven game will invoke all seven emotions at different times, but we can give our whole game an overall direction by choosing to focus on just a few of these, or maybe on just one.

For a wider view of emotion, look to the work of Dr. Robert Plutchik, a psychologist at the Albert Einstein College of Medicine, who proposed a psychoevolutionary classification for emotional responses. Alongside most of Ekman's primary emotions, Plutchik added anticipation and trust, and showed different levels of emotional intensity in each group. His work is often illustrated with the "wheel of emotions" shown in figure 7.2.

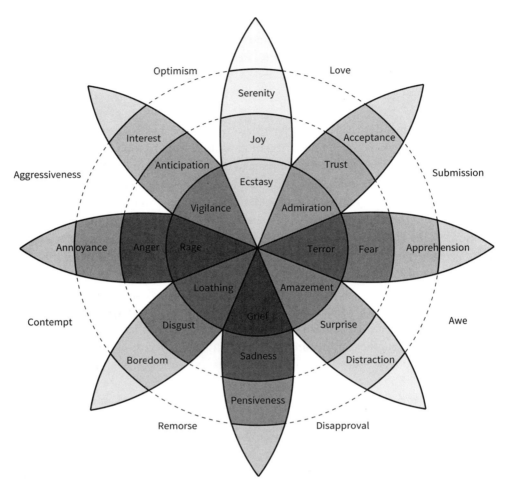

Figure 7.2
Dr. Robert Plutchik's "wheel of emotions." Image credit: Machine Elf 1735, Wikimedia Commons, Public Domain.

It's a good game design exercise to randomly pick an emotion from Plutchik's wheel and attempt to design a small game that elicits that emotion.

Social and Spiritual Experience

While experiences of thought, memory, imagination, will, and perception are common to almost every type of game, and emotional experiences are the drivers of most styles of game, the other types of experience I mentioned earlier could also be valuable for game designers wishing to innovate.

Social experience is a key factor in the design of any multiplayer game, from team-based eSports to massively multiplayer games. Spiritual and religious experience is a topic increasingly of interest to game designers. The early game theorist Johann

Huizinga saw the playground as a sacred space, akin to a site of religious worship, and James Carse, a historian of religious literature, discusses the spiritual aspect of play in *Finite and Infinite Games*.[4] Tracy Fullerton and Bill Viola investigated this frontier in their game *The Night Journey*. New game designers are appearing who are interested in meditation, mindfulness, ritual, and ecstatic religious states.

Writing Down Your Experience Goals

The experience goal is arguably the most important of our project goals. I strongly recommend that you focus on emotion, but you should choose the type of experience that works best for you and your creative intention.

Again, don't try to describe *how* your game will create this experience for your players. Just clearly isolate and focus on a core experience goal, describing it in language that is as clear and concise as possible. Try to make your experience goals specific and concrete, and summarize each one with a single sentence. Consider using words from Plutchik's wheel of emotions. Be bold in combining concepts to create new ideas, but avoid run-on sentences that pack too many different experiences together. Clarity and brevity are the keys here.

Don't include goals that are too loose or too vague, such as "create an interesting and entertaining experience for the player"—this kind of experience goal is too generic to guide your design successfully.

It can be useful to talk about the experience that a game gives its players in terms of role-playing, or the fulfillment of a fantasy—"be the ultimate spacefaring hero" or "be a doctor in a busy hospital." In the game industry, you'll sometimes hear experience goals framed as the "essence statement," "vision statement," "X statement," or "core fantasy" of a game. It can also be valuable to discuss the experience of the game in terms of a mixture of core game design and narrative elements: you'll hear people talk about the "pillars" or the "themes" of a game. All of this is fine. There are many ways to describe the experience that a game will give. Whatever you call them, choosing experience goals will guide you in the creation of your game.

Your Experience Goals Should Be Rooted in Your Prototypes

At the beginning of ideation, it's fine to just pick some game mechanics and a narrative theme and see what kind of experiences they produce. The best way forward from ideation is to pick the prototype we like best and spend the rest of the project working to amplify and enhance the experience that it gives.

It is risky to set an experience goal at the end of ideation without having *any* idea of how you're going to create the experience. If you want to be sure that your project will be a success, give it a goal related to an experience that one of your prototypes has

---

4. Huizinga, *Homo Ludens*; Carse, *Finite and Infinite Games*.

already begun to produce, even if only in an unrefined form. You can take the spark of an experience and work to amplify it during preproduction, our next project phase.

Design Goals

Your design goals complement your experience goal. They will probably be related to the hardware your game runs on, the genre of the game, the game's mechanics, or the type of interface it has. There might be a narrative style that you want to use, some subject matter that you want to address, something you want to accomplish with your game, or some other type of constraint that you want to set.

If, by the end of ideation, there's anything that you're 100 percent confident that you want to do with your game, then write it down in your design goals. Your design goals might overlap with your experience goal, or they might be totally separate.

Some common categories of design goals are:

- **The hardware your game will run on.** What platform will your game run on? PC or Mac? A mobile device? A game console? A fitness tracker, a watch, or some earbuds? A self-driving car's console, or a refrigerator? As digital technology makes its way into more of the objects and environments around us, your choice of hardware platforms is only going to increase. You don't *have* to lock in your hardware platform with your project goals, but doing so can help you move forward confidently and might save you design time later. This design goal also has an important relationship with audience and market. If you want to reach a particular group of players, you have to consider what hardware platforms they play games on.

- **Game mechanics, verbs, and player activities.** Think about the types of play in the game you're imagining and consider committing to at least some of those game mechanics, verbs, and player activities with your design goals.

- **Interface conventions.** How will the player control your game? Using a keyboard and mouse or a game controller? On a touchscreen, by tapping, holding, pinching, and swiping? Using a device that detects the position of their body in space, or the direction of their gaze in virtual reality? Locking in one or two interface conventions at the end of ideation can send your project in a good direction.

- **Special hardware or software you want to use.** You might decide to use a virtual reality headset, an augmented reality framework for mobile, or an "alt-controller" (a specially designed alternative controller) like those seen each year in the alt.ctrl. GDC festival.

- **Your game's genre.** If the game you're imagining fits into a genre of gameplay or narrative, say so in your design goals. Remember, the most creative works often subvert genre to bring us something fresh and lively.

- **Your game's subject matter.** In straightforwardly literal terms: what is your game about? It might be about a lost puppy, a presidential election, or lovers struggling to reunite.

- **Your game's theme**. Your game's theme is the central topic addressed by your game's narrative. Different authors have different opinions about when to set the theme of a story they're writing. Some do it at the start; others find it emerging as they work. Very early on in the development of *Uncharted 2: Among Thieves* we decided that our game would be about trust and betrayal, and that helped us to shape our story. If you can decide your game's theme at the end of ideation, set it in place with your design goals.

- **Your game's art direction goals**. You might have a strong idea by the end of ideation about the art direction of your game, possibly as a result of some research you've done or a prototype you made.

- **Your game's artistic goals**. If you are an artist using videogames as your chosen art form, you might have some artistic goals in mind for your game. Perhaps you are making a game to express something you feel or an idea you have. You might wish to be entertaining, or to make a serious point, or some mixture of both. If you are an artist interested in social or political interventions, this might overlap with . . .

- **Your game's impact goals**. You might decide to make a game that has some impact in the world—these kinds of games are often called impact games, serious games, functional games, applied games, or transformational games. Perhaps you want your game to be educational, to have a positive impact on the health of your players, or to make an argument about something political. Sabrina Culyba's book *The Transformational Framework: A Process Tool for the Development of Transformational Games* is an invaluable resource for those seeking to design and assess games that have the intention of creating lasting change in players.

Even though I've described many different types of design goal here, I think it pays to only set a small number of design goals at the end of ideation. What we want to do is to give ourselves a direction to move in, while still allowing ourselves plenty of room for maneuver as we go forward through our game's development.

Make a handful of design commitments to things that you're sure you will be happy to keep. By seeing the unique combination of your goals together in one place, written down as your project goals, you might see game design opportunities that others have missed.

Taken Together, Experience Goals and Design Goals Give Us Our Project Goals

Our project goals are a commitment to a direction. Once we've chosen our project goals, we hope to stick to them for the entirety of the project. So we should choose them carefully.

It's up to you to decide how you'll mix-and-match experience goals and design goals to create your project goals. The right number of individual experience and design goals will depend on your team, your project's duration, and its context—for example, whether it's a commercial game or a personal project. In my USC Games classes, I get my students to specify one or two experience goals, and a few (usually no more than three or four) design goals.

We occasionally jettison a project goal partway through development, in response to a discovery that we've made, and we will check in on our project goals again toward the end of preproduction to see if they need revision. But if we keep changing our minds about what our project goals are, we're likely just to spin in circles. By carefully choosing our experience goals and design goals, we give ourselves a clear direction for the work that's coming next. It's like choosing to navigate toward a lighthouse in the distance; if we keep the lighthouse in sight, we can always work out where we are and will never get lost.

Repertoire and Growth

When we're making a game, we shouldn't just consider what we want to make, we should also factor in what we *can* make: what we're able to build with the skills we have. That's not to say we shouldn't push ourselves and be ambitious.

Many creative groups have a repertoire: a body of work, in a particular style, that they know how to create skillfully or to perform well. For example, the Chicago Shakespeare Company performs the plays of William Shakespeare, but does so in modern settings and in modern dress.

The game designer Gary Penn, of the prolific Scottish game studio Denki, suggested to me in 2010 that game designers and game development studios also have repertoires, but that we often don't talk about them in these terms. For example, Naughty Dog's repertoire is made up of character-action games, and there are common game-mechanical and narrative themes uniting *Crash Bandicoot*, the *Jak* series, *Uncharted*, and *The Last of Us*, even though those game series are wildly different in other ways.

Repertoire is important because making art is hard, and making videogames is exceptionally hard. In his 2010 GDC Microtalk, Gary Penn said, "Don't think, talk, or write about it. *Do it*. Play-act. Visualize. Prototype. . . . Development is quicksand. Don't aim for perfect first time. . . . Chance favors the prepared mind. Expect trouble. Rehearse. Explore. Get perspective. Make informed choices. Do to build repertoire, like musicians and actors. Repertoire is applied muscle—the practiced and reusable."[5] A game development studio that is working well will both play to their strengths, using their repertoire—what they already know how to do—*and* learn new things with each project, growing in the process. While *Crash Bandicoot* and *The Last of Us Part II* share common DNA, Naughty Dog learned so much in making each series that every one marked an evolutionary leap forward.

On our game development teams, we should ask ourselves: What is our repertoire, and how do we want to grow? What are we already good at, and what do we want to

---

5. Gary Penn, *GDC Microtalks 2010: Ten Speakers, 200 Slides, Limitless Ideas!*, https://www.gdcvault .com/play/1012271/GDC-Microtalks-2010-Ten-Speakers, 17:01.

learn or improve upon? What do we want to try? We might want to work in a new game genre or with new game mechanics. We might want to try a new narrative genre, or a new story style. We might want to try new tools, new hardware or software, a new audience demographic or a new monetization plan.

The simplest takeaway here is: don't try to run before you can walk. As we choose areas for growth, we can work to find a balance between what we already know how to do, and the areas in which we will push ourselves. By finding balance, we can take risks and excite ourselves with new game styles, mechanics, and stories, while making sure that we don't expose ourselves to too much risk.

Considering the Possible Audience for Our Game

Whatever kind of game you're making, thinking about the audience of people who will eventually play your game will almost certainly help you to design it. And most game designers can benefit from spending some time thinking about how they will find and communicate with an audience that would like to play their games. The time when we lay out our project goals is the perfect moment to give some thought to the audience for our game.

You can do this with a very simple exercise, by writing just a few words at the end of your project goals, completing the sentence: "The possible audience for our game is . . ." Some examples might be:

- "The possible audience for our game is anyone who likes playing games on their phone while standing on the subway, and who likes watching funny videos on social media."
- "The possible audience for our game is core gamers who love 3D 'Soulslike' action games and 2D 'Metroidvanias,' and would enjoy a combination of the genres."
- "The possible audience for our game is made up of people who enjoy Sudoku and the novels of Jane Austen."
- "The possible audience for our game is people who enjoy gardening and are aged eighty years of age and older."

By looking at your game through the lens of the people who would enjoy it, you might get new design ideas that lead you in interesting and productive directions. Perhaps you'll realize that something is missing from the way you were thinking about your game, or that something you were considering isn't such a good fit after all.

In the business world, the process of connecting with people who might want a product is called marketing. I realized early in my career that considering our audience and having good marketing is an important part of making games. Now, as a game designer you can and should think about your audience without necessarily being beholden to a market. But even if you're going to give your game away for free, I hope that you would like people to see your work. If you are someone who plans to make their living from making games, then it's crucial that you—or someone you work with—can figure out how you're going to connect with people who might give you money for the opportunity to play your game.

I don't think that we need to approach marketing cynically. Marketing can help us reach people who wouldn't even consider playing a certain game, perhaps because of their preconceptions. As Mark Cerny told me, "I think we succeed most dramatically when a larger audience—that wouldn't be interested in the game pitch—comes into contact with and falls in love with the game." Creative marketers can help us to reach audiences by showing what there is for them to love about our game.

These "possible audience" descriptions are a simple form of positioning statement, a tool used by marketing professionals which I learned about from my colleague Jim Huntley. Jim is a marketing and brand management consultant with over twenty years of experience across multiple industries, including five years at game publisher THQ. He told me that the end of ideation is a good time to develop a positioning statement, which briefly describes a group that could make up your audience, their likes or needs, and how you want them to perceive your game, maybe in terms of its brand identity. You can find information online about creating a positioning statement, or reach out to a marketing professional.

You can also think about the audience for your game in terms of community: finding, communicating with, and positively cultivating a community around your game. Community management is now a mature and well-respected part of the game industry. It exists at the intersection of marketing, social media, online moderation, and game development. As games become less like boxed products and more like live services with an active, engaged community, the role of community managers becomes ever more important, and for players blurs into their experience of the game itself.

You can learn more about the possible audience for your game using demographics, psychographics, and something called market sizing. You can read about these on this book's website, playfulproductionprocess.com. It's also useful to consider comparables when imagining audiences for your game—"This will appeal to people who like (a certain game, movie, TV show, book, or comic)." Many creative people do this by considering prior art when they're doing research for a new piece of work.

At the end of ideation, it's sometimes enough just to imagine the potential audience for your game. Actually finding and talking with your audience will come later. Each time throughout development you complete the sentence "The possible audience for our game is . . ." you will know more about your game and what your playtesters enjoyed about it, and the exercise will flow more easily for you.

There are books about all the marketing work that needs to be done in parallel with a game's development, in order to launch a game successfully. Joel Dreskin's *A Practical Guide to Indie Game Marketing* and *Video Game Marketing: A Student Textbook* by Peter Zackariasson and Mikolaj Dymek are two good references.

Becoming a Developer for a Specialized Game Platform

If one of your design goals is to create a game for a console made by a platform holder like Sony, Microsoft, or Nintendo, or which is to be released on a mobile platform in the Apple ecosystem, then you must apply to become a developer for that platform toward the beginning of your development process. Developing a console game usually requires a special development kit—a version of the console hardware that can be connected to a computer for development and debugging purposes—so the relationship between a developer and a platform holder begins when the developer applies to develop for the platform and to receive the "dev kits" they need.

The end of ideation is a good time to start planning for this, and you should be aware that the process of getting approved can be long and complex. The details vary from platform to platform, and you should do plenty of research to find out exactly what you need to do to get approved as a developer for your platform. The platform holders have worked hard to make the application process friendly, but start early, and start even earlier than you think you need to.

In order to be approved as a developer, you submit a proposal for the game you want to release, along with some information about your team. Once you've been approved, you will gain access to the resources you need to develop for the platform, including development kits, technical documentation, and information about the release approval and publishing process. We'll return to the subject of specialized game platforms in chapter 34. Use what you learn from the platform holder about developing for their hardware, fold it into the processes described in this book, and you should be on track for releasing your game on the platform of your dreams.

Advice about Forming Your Project Goals

Think carefully about your project goals and try to follow what you learned from making your prototypes. Don't ignore a successful prototype! It's often good to follow something in a prototype that players reacted to in a positive way, even if it leads you away from your original ideas. You're not selling out on those ideas: *you* made the prototype that got a good reaction, and even if you stumbled upon it, the new direction is an authentic part of you.

Go back to your initial brainstorms and research if you're having a hard time choosing your project goals. The first sparks of an idea often look different once you've built some prototypes. Write a rough draft of your project goals, and then ask for feedback on them from your team and bosses, your peers and friends, or your professor and classmates. Iterating on your project goals at least once or twice is a great way of arriving at a very clear high-concept view of the game you want to build.

You may well have to collaborate with business partners when setting your project goals. Game designers rarely have complete independence unless they're self-financed or on a student team. Bring your best collaborative skills to the table to find project goals that the people putting up the money can be excited about, and that you're excited about too.

Setting the goals for a project is an important responsibility of a game team's leadership. Hopefully everyone will have a voice in contributing to the game's project goals, but it's the role of the team's leadership to help identify what's interesting in the blue sky thinking and research, to synthesize seemingly conflicting ideas into new ideas that everyone can get behind, and to help identify what's working in the prototypes. It's also leadership's role to help the team find a way through the challenges along the path to realizing the project goals and to stay focused on the creative direction they set. As Mark Cerny reminded me: "A great creative director (or game director) will constantly challenge the team, pushing them in that special direction."

Your project goals will guide you throughout your project, but don't overthink them. We'll check in on them again at the end of preproduction, to see if they need revision. Even when you've committed to a decision, you can remain flexible in your approach. We're almost done with the ideation phase of our project, and we'll wrap things up in the next chapter.

8   The End of Ideation

At the very start of the ideation phase, our emphasis should be on free exploration expressed through blue sky thinking, research, and prototyping. By halfway through ideation, we should start getting oriented to our favorite ideas and our biggest prototyping successes. Maybe that means leaving some promising things behind because it will soon be time to set a direction. By the end of the ideation phase, we must choose: which of our ideas do we like the most, and which of our prototypes have shown us a path forward for our game?

How Long Should the Ideation Phase Last?

We didn't have a formal ideation phase at the studios I worked at, but we certainly had an informal ideation phase at Naughty Dog, usually in the three or four months between shipping our previous game in late summer and getting back from the winter break in January.

This gave us the chance to do some R&D (research and development) in a relatively low-pressure atmosphere. People across every discipline had time to play around freely with ideas they were excited about, and it was a good time to try new tools and techniques. You often get a lot of good ideas as you're shipping a game that aren't useful right then but could be great for your next game. The next game's directors would begin to work up some core ideas and would quickly draw other people from around the team into that work.

Uncharted 2 and *Uncharted 3* were two-year projects, and I estimate we spent about 15 percent of their total project timelines in a phase that felt like ideation. In my classes at USC, I have my students spend around the same amount of time in ideation. How much ideation time is right for your project will depend on you. If you have the luxury of time, then perhaps spending longer in ideation could be good, especially if you're trying to do something truly innovative.

I would recommend that you "timebox" your ideation phase, though. Give yourself a limited and fixed amount of time for ideation. Don't let it drift on forever. The time limit will help you stay focused and will give an energetic boost to the beginning of the project. I'll talk more about timeboxing in chapter 11.

Some Final Advice about Prototyping

Make as many prototypes as you can, and explore your ideas as widely, as deeply, as quickly, and as radically as you can, with physical prototypes, playacting with toys, and fast, focused digital prototyping. Explore the ideas that you brainstorm up from as many different angles as you can, by making, building, creating, and constant, constant playtesting.

If you're just setting out in your game design practice and want more instruction, you can learn a lot more about paper prototyping and digital prototyping in Tracy Fullerton's book *Game Design Workshop*.[1] I'll talk more about how we can use the physical and digital prototypes we make during the ideation phase in the next section, on preproduction.

A Summary of the Ideation Deliverables

Figure 8.1 shows a short summary of the deliverables due throughout the ideation phase of a game project, to help you to stay on track.

Deliverable	When Due
Blue sky thinking results	The start of ideation, and possibly throughout ideation, as needed
Research notes	Throughout ideation
Prototypes	Throughout ideation
Project goals	The end of ideation

Figure 8.1

---

1. Fullerton, *Game Design Workshop*, 4th ed.

Phase Two: Preproduction—Designing by Doing

9 Gaining Control of the Process

Properly gaining control of the design process tends to feel like one is *losing* control of the design process.

—Matthew Frederick, *101 Things I Learned in Architecture School*

The first original game that I worked on, *Tinhead* for the Sega Genesis (or Sega Mega Drive, depending on where you live) had only one project phase: production. To be honest, I'm not even sure we called it that, but that's what it was. We just started building the game and worked until we finished it. We guessed that the game would take us six months to build—we finally finished it after eighteen months, and we had to crunch to finish it, working late nights and weekends. Sadly, this would be the first of many crunches in my career. A few years later, the first project I worked on that had more than one project phase was *Soul Reaver*, which also marked the first of my many collaborations with *Uncharted* game director and creative director Amy Hennig.

Inspired by what we'd read about the development of movies, we attempted to bring *Soul Reaver* under better control with a planning period called preproduction. We did a lot of good preparation during preproduction, making concept art and test levels, and starting to plan our game's design on paper and with prototypes. But we still struggled with our game's overall timeline—we'd missed some key aspects of preproduction that would have helped our project stay on track. Eventually, we figured out that preproduction is the most important phase of a game project, and that a good preproduction phase will set a project up for success.

The Assembly Line and Waterfall

Building on the ideas of Ransom Eli Olds (of Oldsmobile fame), Henry Ford revolutionized the industrial production of the automobile by inventing the moving assembly line (sometimes called a production line). A plan for a car is devised by engineers, and each car is built on the assembly line in stages, starting with the chassis and then adding an engine, fuel tank, wheels, bodywork, and everything else needed to make the car complete.

Over time, the idea of the assembly line found expression in the world of computer science with the "waterfall model," an approach to software design that appeared in the mid-1950s (although the term *waterfall* didn't appear until the 1970s). The idea behind waterfall is essentially the same as that of an assembly line: designers and engineers think carefully and then write a comprehensive specification ("spec") for the software that will be built. They then create a plan for implementing the spec, and both documents are passed to a team of software engineers who create the finished program in stages, piece by piece, carefully following the instructions they've been given.

Beginning in the late 1980s, people tasked with the project management of games looked toward these waterfall development methods, which were widely used in the world of business software development, as they desperately sought to bring their projects under control in terms of time, person-power, and money. The "bedroom developers" of the 1980s game scene, the indie game developers of their day, were often very young and were busy inventing an art form. They worked freely, intuitively, but often dysfunctionally, brute-forcing their projects to completion with sustained crunches, working every waking hour for months on end without a day off. Sometimes the projects came in on time and to high quality—and very often they ran wildly over time and budget, or never reached completion at all. In many cases, the projects burned their creators badly, shattering their mental and physical health.

So perhaps it's not surprising that the game producers of the day started to dream about comprehensive game design documents, grand monolithic specifications that would define everything up front, ready to be turned into lists of assets and tasks, so that a game could be created on an assembly line like a car or a washing machine, predictable in terms of the time, money, and number of people needed.

Nice dream. But in most videogame cases, waterfall just doesn't work, at least not for the early stages of game creation. Of course, predictable budgets and schedules are very important for the full production phase of a project, but the good planning intentions contained in a waterfall approach are often hijacked by the uncertainties of the process of discovering what's good about the game that you're trying to design.

Making Something New

If you're making a game in a reliable pattern, with well-established game mechanics that you already know work well, then elements of the waterfall approach could work. But what about when you're struggling to do something new? Something where you're not yet sure how all the pieces of your game fit together—which parts will prove to be great and need amplifying, and which parts don't work so well and need backgrounding or removing from the game altogether?

It's my belief that the right way to make games has a lot in common with the way a painter makes a painting. We do preliminary sketches, we expand our original ideas, we stick our noses in books and do research, and eventually we're ready to grab a canvas and draw sketches in charcoal. We then start to use oil paint over the sketches to create a finished painting. Sometimes, when we're halfway through the painting, it takes on a life of its own and leads us in new directions that we hadn't anticipated.

We already looked at the research and sketching parts of the creation of a videogame in our section on ideation. Now it's time to take a look at the process of developing beyond the charcoal sketches of our prototypes, fleshing them out with oil paint during the preproduction phase of a game project, using an iterative design process.

Planning during Preproduction

Good planning contributes to success in many—maybe most—acts of creativity. But a game's design is made up of an uncountable number of decisions, involving a vast number of assets, pieces of code, and other moving parts. We couldn't possibly list them all and plan for every contingency. Good planning doesn't necessarily equate with *more* planning. How can game designers do just enough planning to set themselves up for success with a game design that they understand, and a project plan that is realistic and realizable?

Preproduction is the phase of the project when we plan our game's design and production—what the game is going to be and how we plan to manage the project. But planning can be a trap, sucking away our valuable development time as we ponder and discuss, as we hesitate to commit and repeatedly change our minds. We get caught up in imagining details of things that we'll later discover we don't need, and we completely overlook things that are beyond our imagining but will prove to be essential.

In *101 Things I Learned in Architecture School*, a book beloved by game designers, the author and architect Matthew Frederick says:

> The design process is often structured and methodical, but it is not a mechanical process. Mechanical processes have predetermined outcomes, but the creative process strives to produce something that has not existed before. Being genuinely creative means that you don't know where you are going, even though you are responsible for shepherding the process. This requires something different from conventional, authorization control; a loose velvet tether is more likely to help.[1]

This is great advice; it's very much in the spirit of this whole book, and it's highly informative when we're talking about planning. We need to plan, but how can game designers find a balance between too much planning and not enough? I got the answer to this question at Naughty Dog from my friend and mentor Mark Cerny.

Mark Cerny and Method

Mark Cerny is a game designer, developer, and executive who began his career in the early 1980s, joining Atari at the age of seventeen. Inspired by miniature golf, racing games, and M. C. Escher, Mark designed and coprogrammed the wildly innovative

---

1. Frederick, *101 Things I Learned in Architecture School*, 81.

arcade game *Marble Madness*. Next he worked at Sega in Japan, creating games for the Sega Master System and Sega Genesis, before returning to the United States to found the Sega Technical Institute and become project leader on *Sonic the Hedgehog 2*. He later became vice president and then president of Universal Interactive Studios.

At Universal Interactive, Mark met two young game developers called Jason Rubin and Andy Gavin. Jason and Andy had founded a game studio while still in high school—they called it JAM Games (for "Jason and Andy Magic")—but it wouldn't be long before they renamed themselves Naughty Dog.

Mark recognized Jason and Andy's talent—they had already created a respectable number of successful digital games, including *Keef the Thief* and *Rings of Power*. Naughty Dog collaborated with Mark to create their first international smash hit, *Crash Bandicoot*, and Mark brought healthy development processes resulting in high-quality games to his future work with Naughty Dog, Insomniac Games, and many other teams.

Somewhat unusually for a game executive, Mark has remained hands-on as a developer, helping to create levels and mechanics for games as well as guiding their development process, and he helped me with much of my work on the *Uncharted* series. Mark now works as a senior consultant for Sony Interactive Entertainment and was the lead architect of the PlayStation 4 and the PlayStation 5.

In 2002, at the D.I.C.E. Summit in Las Vegas, Mark Cerny gave a history-making talk that began a quiet revolution in the games industry. Simply titled "Method," the talk is a wellspring of game design wisdom, good practice, apt criticism, and planning advice.[2] It clearly lays out a process for making great games in a better way. Every game developer and game student should watch this talk at least once.

Method is an approach to making games that Mark and his colleague the game designer and educator Michael "MJ" John had codified as they observed best working practices in their collaborations with game studios. Several of the things proposed by Method were radical, even heretical, and you can hear the gasps, laughter, and applause from the game directors and business leaders in the auditorium as Mark asserts that preproduction *can't* be scheduled, or it won't work.

It's interesting to note that Mark gave the Method talk in 2002, just a year after the Agile Alliance published their "Agile Manifesto for Software Development."[3] There are many philosophical correspondences between Method and Agile, in that they both recommend a "loose but structured" approach to making great software. As such they are easy to pair, as we'll see in later chapters.

The Value of Preproduction

I believe that preproduction is the most important project phase, and in his talk Mark Cerny says that when a project gets into trouble, it's most often because preproduction

---

2. Mark Cerny, "D.I.C.E. Summit 2002," https://www.youtube.com/watch?v=QOAW9ioWAvE.
3. Ken Schwaber, "Manifesto for Agile Software Development," 2001, https://agilemanifesto.org/.

was done improperly or skipped altogether. "I believe that 80 percent—I'm not exaggerating—of mistakes in game development are a direct result of things that were done, or not done, in preproduction."[4] Mark goes on to say, "Preproduction does not require a large team, but it does require your best and probably your highest paid staff. This core team will determine everything that's important about your game, and most likely become your team leaders in production. So get the best people you can possibly find and get them early."[5]

We work out all the most essential aspects of the game partly by thinking but mainly by *doing*. Just as in ideation, it's building things that helps us to develop our ideas. We'll come back to the philosophy and practices of Method several times, but now let's get down to brass tacks: what are we going to *do* during preproduction? We're going to create three key deliverables: a vertical slice, a game design macro, and a schedule.

4. Cerny, "D.I.C.E. Summit 2002," 3:40.
5. Cerny, "D.I.C.E. Summit 2002," 6:26.

10   What Is a Vertical Slice?

The concept of a vertical slice has become widely known throughout the game industry over the past fifteen years or so, and it's a valuable one. Simply put, a vertical slice is a high-quality demo of your game.

A vertical slice has been polished to the point where the game design, graphics, sound design, control scheme, visual effects, and *all* of its elements are of high enough quality that we can consider them finished. It's called a vertical slice because it includes something of everything that's significant. Imagine a cake with alternating layers of sponge, whipped cream, raspberry jam, and chocolate ganache. When you eat a slice of the cake, the flavors mix, creating a unique aesthetic experience. You don't have to eat the whole cake to know what the cake tastes like.

The vertical slice of a videogame includes a sample of all (or most) of the core features, assets, and narrative that are essential to the experience of the whole game. It's a cross-sectional snapshot of our game's design, and demonstrates, in playable form, exactly what kind of game we're planning to make (figure 10.1).

The Core Loop

Many games are built around a repeating pattern, as described by Jaime Griesemer in his famous concept of the "thirty seconds of fun" underlying the gameplay of the *Halo* series. In the single-player game of *Halo*, there's a repeating pattern of player activities that you cycle through over and over again. You enter an area, notice where the enemies and loot are, and take cover. You take aim at the enemies, defeating them one by one, and work your way around and through the map until you finally reach the exit—only to enter a new area, beginning this basic pattern of player activities again.

However, that doesn't mean that *Halo*, or any well-designed game, is repetitive. In an interview with Engadget in 2011, Jaime said,

> I talked about taking that thirty seconds of fun and playing it in different environments, with different weapons, different vehicles, against different enemies, against different combinations

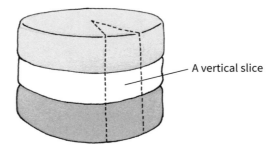

A vertical slice

Figure 10.1
A vertical slice.

of enemies, sometimes against enemies that are fighting each other. No thirty second stretch of *Halo* is ever repeated; the missions are constantly changing the context on you.[1]

Game designers often refer to this as the "core loop" of a game. Built on top of this underlying pattern of repetition is endless variation, appearing through a collaboration between the game's designers and players. The designers present ever-changing combinations of game elements. Players are free to approach each part of the game in many varied ways.

A vertical slice will include at least one section that represents the core loop of the game and shows the type of experience we'll be having most of the time while we're playing.

Depending on the style of game, this core loop might be "run/jump/climb" in a character-action game like *Uncharted*, or "choose-type/select-area/build" in a city-building game. It might have a lot of moment-to-moment control—"move-left/move-right/rotate/drop" in *Tetris*—or it might be at more of a distance from the action, like "select-unit/issue-command" in *StarCraft*.

As I'm sure you realize, creating a demonstration of these core loops requires the creation of a lot of different game mechanics, input methods, game entities, and assets. For a character-action game, we won't just need "run/jump/climb," we'll need some things to run on, jump over, climb onto. For a simulation game, a real-time strategy game, or a multiplayer online battle arena, we'll need some entities to build, control, and fight. In a narrative game, we'll need some characters to talk to, some places to visit, and some events to have happen. To really get a sense of our gameplay, we'll have to see some of the most interesting moments that can arise from our mechanics.

Special Sequences

In our vertical slice, we should also attempt to show something representative of any special sequences in our game. This can be very challenging for contemporary

---

1. Ludwig Kietzmann, "Half-Minute Halo: An Interview with Jaime Griesemer," Engadget, July 14, 2011, https://www.engadget.com/2011/07/14/half-minute-halo-an-interview-with-jaime-griesemer/.

videogames, which often feature a mind-boggling number of special-case missions and one-off moments.

To give a simple example of what's desirable: the vertical slice for *Crash Bandicoot* (created long before my time at Naughty Dog) featured two levels (a game design term meaning environments). One level showed side-scrolling gameplay, where Crash jumps over pits, smashes open crates to collect the Wumpa fruit inside, and spins into enemies to knock them out of play. The other level featured one of the special sequences of gameplay that can be found throughout the finished game, where Crash runs toward the camera with a panic-stricken look on his face, pursued by a giant boulder.

These two playable levels, taken together as a vertical slice, told everyone at Naughty Dog, their publisher Universal Interactive, and anyone else who had a stake in the project just what to expect from the full game.

The Three Cs

There's another way to look at how the vertical slice helps us to figure out our game's design. It involves a consideration of the "three Cs" of a videogame: character, camera, and control.

Character

We need to decide who or what the main player-character of our game will be. What do they look like and how do they sound? How do they move? How do they represent the game mechanical verbs that the player will use in the game? What narrative-shaping emotional qualities does the player-character bring to our game? (It's important to note that some of the finest videogames don't have anything that we could easily identify as a player-character—more on that in a moment.)

The player-character is the avatar that enacts the player's actions in the game world. Game designers will sometimes refer to this character as the "player," but be wary— there is another player to consider and to talk about in our design discussions: the person holding a game controller, hitting a keyboard, or guiding a mouse, full of ideas and feelings, plans and misapprehensions. You'll have more ability as a game designer if it's always completely clear whether you're referring to the human player of the game or the player-character within the game.

Many digital games have at least one player-character, and some have more. For games that *don't* appear to have a player-character—whether it's *Pong*, *Tetris*, *SimCity*, or *StarCraft*—we usually don't have to look far to find an analogy. It could be the paddle in *Pong* or the tetrominos in *Tetris*. Perhaps it's the cursor, zone-selection, and build options in *SimCity*, or the cursor and its ability to select units and buildings in *Star-Craft*. Whatever assemblage of audiovisual elements is most directly under moment-to-moment control by the player we should consider to be the player-character, and we should figure out what ours is going to be by building a vertical slice.

Camera

The camera for a game is sometimes hard for new game designers to discuss, and difficult to describe in all of its complexity and nuance. It's "out of sight, out of mind"—we look through its lens, and we have such a close identification with it that we're probably not aware of everything that it's doing as we play. Different games have radically different camera considerations.

- **First-person cameras.** First-person games give us a seemingly simple case, where we're looking through the eyes of the player-character and the mouse controls the direction of our view. But anyone who has tried to code—or even alter the premade settings of—a first-person camera will soon discover that it's not that simple. The proportional relationship between mouse movement and direction of view, the motion of the camera if it bobs along with the player-character's footsteps, the camera's field of view—these elements and more make up this "simple" case.

- **Third-person cameras.** A more complex case is a third-person camera that is placed at a distance from the gameplay, as in a 2D side-scrolling game like NES *Super Mario Bros.*, 2D isometric games like *Bastion* or the original *StarCraft*, a 3D character-action game like *The Witcher 3: Wild Hunt*, or a 3D city-building game like *Cities: Skylines*. This camera will move either because it tracks the player-character, in *Super Mario Bros.*, *Bastion*, or *Witcher 3*, or because it's under the direct control of the player, in *StarCraft* and *Cities: Skylines*.

Both these options require finesse. For example, side-scrolling action games set up a "dance box" for the player-character: a limited field of free movement where the player-character can move without moving the camera, creating smoother camera behavior. Itay Keren's 2015 GDC lecture and Gamasutra article "Scroll Back: The Theory and Practice of Cameras in Side-Scrollers," provides an excellent discussion of the many different approaches that 2D action games have tried in their search for the perfect camera.[2]

The third-person cameras in 3D character-action games like *Witcher 3* and *Uncharted* give us very complex cases. Here, the camera is placed close to the player-character, like a camera drone that follows their progress closely. The camera is usually under the player's direct control (maybe using a thumbstick) and oftentimes it's *also* under the control of invisible trigger volumes in the environment. These trigger volumes move the camera to a certain elevation, direction, and angle of pitch in order to show the most relevant, most interesting, or most beautiful parts of the environment, all the while keeping the player-character on-screen. Sometimes they jump the camera to a particular position with a cut.

Here, there is a large and complex suite of algorithms determining the behavior of the camera, and many of the behaviors that result from a setup like this can easily

2. Itay Keren, "Scroll Back: The Theory and Practice of Cameras in Side-Scrollers," Gamasutra, May 11, 2015, https://gamasutra.com/blogs/ItayKeren/20150511/243083/Scroll_Back_The_Theory _and_Practice_of_Cameras_in_SideScrollers.php.

make the player feel like they're fighting the camera. If we don't set things up just right, the camera's motion will feel jerky or sluggish—the opposite of the elegant, energetic, graceful camera moves that we're used to seeing in feature films and on television.

There are many other camera problems lying in wait for us in a 3D character-action game, relating to our environments. What happens when the player-character backs up against the wall or goes behind a column? The camera usually can't go inside a wall, or it will show us "outside" the graphics of the game, breaking the illusion of our computer graphics world and shattering the player's suspension of disbelief. Moving the camera in closer or rotating it around might offer solutions, but usually at the cost of a bunch more problems: moving the camera too close, giving us nothing but a view of the back of the player-character's head, or moving the camera to point in a new direction, when the player wanted to look somewhere else.

I bring these problems up so that you can prepare for the preproduction of your first 3D character-action game, but they are solvable. The talented developers of the games we love have shown us time and again that there are many excellent and elegant solutions to these challenges. It just takes time and effort.

So, by the time we've finished our vertical slice, we must know a lot about how our game's camera is going to work, if the vertical slice is going to do its job of telling us essential things about our game's design.

Control

Control is the mechanism by which the player interacts with the game, making choices that express their agency. Determining the controls of a game partly has to do with deciding what button presses, mouse motions, and thumbstick gestures will result in certain actions in the game, but there's more to it than that.

The agency that the player uses when they engage with the controls of a game is part of another loop that is very important for game designers to think about. It's the loop involving both the player and the game's hardware and software. We'll use the example of someone playing a console game with a controller. As with any loop, we could examine it starting anywhere, but let's start with the player's perceptions of the images and sounds that the game is putting out through a screen and speakers.

The player's perceptions lead them to some thoughts and feelings about what they see and hear, and to a decision-making process about what to do next, all of which we can file under "cognition." Then they take an action; in this example by pressing a button or moving a thumbstick on the controller.

The game console receives this input and folds it into the computation that the game is constantly performing. It decides what happened in that split second and sends some new output to the screen and speakers, and so the loop begins again (figure 10.2).

In that the player's agency is based on what they understand about the game, the mental model they have of the systems on the game, and what they anticipate will happen if they take a certain action, we might see control as woven into the fabric of every aspect of the game. From the way that the game's current state is represented in

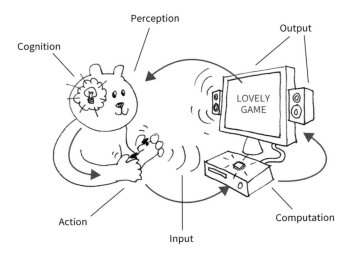

Figure 10.2
The perception-cognition-action-input-computation-output loop.

its graphics and sound, to what the player has learned through trial and error about what they can do in the game, to what goals the player thinks that the game wants them to achieve and what it will reward them with should they meet those goals—these questions of control are scattered everywhere through the game's design and aren't just about which buttons do what.

In his book *Game Feel*, game designer Steve Swink takes this thinking one step further when he discusses the "perceptual field," a concept from the world of psychology. Attributing the idea to psychologists Donald Snygg and Arthur Combs, Steve says:

> The idea of the perceptual field is that perception is carried out against the backdrop of all previous experience, including our attitudes, thoughts, ideas, fantasies and even misconceptions. That is, we don't perceive things separately from what's come before. Rather, we experience everything through the filter, against the background, and within the structure of our own personal vision of the world.[3]

I find this fascinating, and it can be helpful when we're trying to figure out how to design games that players can engage with in rich and satisfying ways. It reminds us that as players, we bring a lot to the games we play that is personal, cultural, and even political.

Each individual game will have specific considerations for the design of its controls. Focus on creating controls that players can discover and use easily, and where player actions are acknowledged immediately by some reaction in the game. Think about game feel and juiciness, concepts that you may already know about, and that I'll briefly describe in chapter 22. Think about the control conventions used by other

---

3. Swink, *Game Feel*, 50.

games: they might help players pick up your game more easily, if that's what you want. Consider accessibility for players with a disability.

By iterating on the design of your game's controls as you make a vertical slice, you can ensure that your game is easy to use, fun to play, and challenging in an interesting way—or that it's expressive, meaningful, and intriguing.

So, the three Cs: *character*, *camera*, and *control*. We must get a good handle on these elements of our game during preproduction by creating a vertical slice with a polished player-character or -characters, their core abilities, and the core mechanics of the game.

Sample Levels and the Blockmesh Design Process

The vertical slice will also include one or more sample levels (environments) from the game, so that we have a place to play in and can get a sense of what the finished game will look and sound like.

Most level design for games starts with work on paper or a whiteboard. At Naughty Dog, we would start by discussing our ideas for the gameplay and story beats in the level, and what the level needed to accomplish. Then, we would sketch out the sequence of gameplay we were imagining for the level as a rough flowchart, as shown in figure 10.3.

Using this flowchart, we would make some loose diagrams for the level, in plan view (top-down) and also in elevation (side view) if necessary, as shown in figure 10.4.

On my earlier projects we would spend many hours making detailed architectural plans for our levels, on paper or in Adobe Illustrator. As our level design process matured at Naughty Dog, we began to spend less time on detailed paper layout and would move quickly from our loose whiteboard sketches to a blockmesh level layout process.

Blockmesh, also known as blockout, whitebox, or graybox level design, is low-resolution three-dimensional geometry, usually of two types: renderable (visible) geometry that can be seen, and invisible geometry used for collision. Using these two types of geometry, designers can quickly and easily sketch in a level in its most basic form. It's best when the designer can collaborate at this stage with the artists, programmers, animators, audio designers, and anyone else who will contribute to the level's design.

Over time, the blockmesh will be refined with successive iterative passes to improve the level's design. At some point artists will begin to develop the level's visual look, first with rough draw-overs to begin to lend definition to the level, and then with successive passes of finished art, as shown in figure 10.5. Designers, artists, and everyone else will continue to collaborate, each lending their skills to improve the level until it is complete.

Blockmesh is sometimes color-coded to show important elements like climbable edges or water. If you're interested in this process, be sure to look at the inspirational

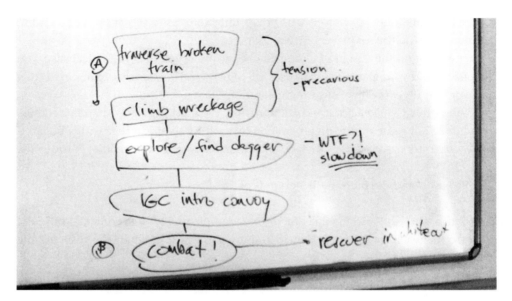

Figure 10.3
A whiteboard flowchart sketching out the gameplay and story sequence at the beginning of
Uncharted 2: Among Thieves. Image credit: UNCHARTED 2: Among Thieves™ © 2009 Sony Inter-
active Entertainment LLC. UNCHARTED 2: Among Thieves is a trademark of Sony Interactive
Entertainment LLC. Created & developed by Naughty Dog LLC.

#blocktober Twitter hashtag (figure 10.6) that was started by Naughty Dog game
designer Michael Barclay in 2017 to honor blockmesh, because, in Michael's words,
"level blockouts are art."[4]

There's an analogous process to 3D blockmesh level design for 2D games, where we
sketch in the level in the engine's level editor using simple primitives. Exactly how that
would be done depends on the game style and engine, but the basic principle is the
same: quickly rough in something playable and refine it through iteration.

Building sample levels using a blockmesh design process is an important part of the
creation of a vertical slice for many games, although other level design methods—for
example, using procedural level generation—might also be appropriate.

In addition to these simple pointers in level design, I recommend these resources:

• You can find many good talks about level design that were originally given at the
GDC Level Design Workshop if you search for "level design workshop" on the GDC
Vault (gdcvault.com).

• Christopher W. Totten's book *An Architectural Approach to Level Design* has high-
quality and comprehensive coverage of the subject.

4. Michael Barclay (@MotleyGrue), "What's Up Level Designers," Twitter, October 1, 2017, https://
twitter.com/MotleyGrue/status/914571356888371201.

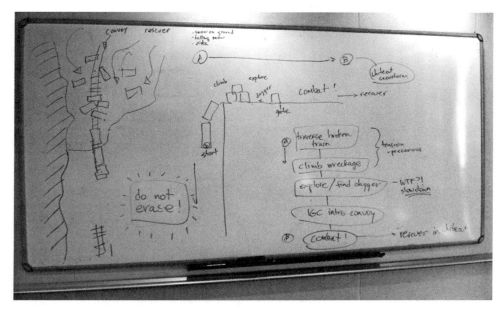

Figure 10.4
Whiteboard diagrams showing the way that we moved from flowchart to rough level layout for
the beginning of *Uncharted 2: Among Thieves*, in plan view and elevation. Image credit: ©2009 SIE
LLC/ UNCHARTED 2: Among Thieves™. Created & developed by Naughty Dog LLC.

- *Level Up! The Guide to Great Video Game Design* by Scott Rogers has many great
  sequences about level design.
- *101 Things I Learned in Architecture School* by Matthew Frederick contains a lot of
  wisdom aimed at architects but valuable to level designers.
- The article "Defining Environment Language for Video Games" by Naughty Dog lead
  game designer Emilia Schatz is a must-read.[5] Emilia is an extraordinarily insightful game
  designer, and her superb article integrates level design thinking with more general
  game design philosophy.

The Size and Quality of Vertical Slice Sample Levels

The sizes of the sample levels in a vertical slice will ultimately be up to the designers of the game, although the stakeholders in the game (such as its producers or
financiers) will probably ask for levels of a certain size. The sample levels should be
long enough that we can play for a while, to get a sense of how the finished game
will play.

---

5. Emilia Schatz, "Defining Environment Language for Video Games," 80 Level, June 27, 2017,
https://80.lv/articles/defining-environment-language-for-video-games/.

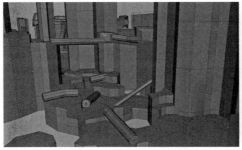

(a) Game designers create blockmesh level layout and begin to refine it through an iterative process of playtesting, notes, and changes.

(b) An artist or designer makes draw-overs of sample parts of the level, to begin to visualize how the blockmesh might look in the finished game.

(c) When the blockmesh is considered sufficiently well developed, artists begin with a pass of visible low-polygon renderable geometry. Game designers continue to maintain the invisible collision geometry, so that the game remains playable, and the iterative process continues, as the team solves problems and finesses the design.

(d) In successive passes of more detailed work, artists finalize the renderable artwork with more detailed geometry. They are already collaborating with the texture artists who will add textures to the level to plan ahead.

Figure 10.5
The blockmesh (aka blockout, whitebox, or graybox) process of level design and art creation. Images credit: Erick Pangilinan and ©2009 SIE LLC/ UNCHARTED 2: Among Thieves™. Created & developed by Naughty Dog LLC.

On a commercial game team, we'd expect to make everything in our sample levels as complete and as polished as their art, animation, design, code, sound, and music would be in the finished game, so that our vertical slice is truly shippable.[6] However,

---

6. Game developers and other types of creative people often talk about "shipping" and "shippable." Shipping means releasing or publishing a game so that it's available to the public, and shippable means that something is good enough to be released. These words come from a time when software was put onto physical media and placed in boxes to be shipped to distant places.

(e) Texture artists, lighting artists, and visual effects artists complete the level using the skills of their discipline. 3D artists, game designers, and others continue to problem-solve and finesse the design.

Figure 10.5
(continued)

for many smaller teams, including student teams, it's often not possible to design and "art up" even a single level by the end of preproduction. This is where the concept of the beautiful corner comes in.

The Beautiful Corner

Simply put, a beautiful corner is a part of a level, enough to fill a single screen on the player's computer, where the art and audio have been polished to look and sound as good as they will in the finished game. It's a little corner of the game which has been made beautiful (or if your game doesn't conform to traditional notions of beauty, which has been worked, refined, or crafted).

In a 3D game, we might point the camera into the corner of a space, where two or more walls intersect with the floor and ceiling. The camera's "view frustum" is the wedge-shaped volume of space that is visible from the point of the view of the camera, given its field of view, aspect ratio, and depth-culling settings. Everything that we see of the beautiful corner inside the camera frustum should look great. That includes not just the background but the objects that are present too. We should beautifully animate anything that will be moving in the finished game, and everything there should *sound* great. Never overlook sound design at any stage of the game design process.

If we turned the camera a few degrees away from the beautiful corner, we could see the low-detail blockmesh that makes up the rest of the level. But by pointing the camera into our beautiful corner, we can vividly visualize what the finished game will be like. I've drawn an example for you in figure 10.7.

We can also use the concept of a beautiful corner in the design of a 2D game, whether it's a side-scrolling, top-down, or isometric game. Again, we should be able to position the player-character and camera in a place where everything on the screen looks and sounds great. The concept of a beautiful corner can even be applied to nondigital

---

When someone thinks that something they're working on is *finally* good enough, they might exultantly cry, "Ship it!"

 **Michael Barclay**
@MotleyGrue

What's up level designers. Level blockouts are art.
#blocktober should be a thing. #leveldesign #gamedev
#gamedesign #inktober #animtober

12:22 PM · Oct 1, 2017 from Los Angeles, CA · Twitter for iPhone

Figure 10.6
Michael Barclay's Twitter post, which started the #blocktober hashtag.

games and parts of games. You could polish a part of a board game or card game, or a part of an "alt-controller" game with a novel or innovative control interface.

I picked up this concept of the beautiful corner somewhere in the game industry, but I haven't been able to discover who coined it. (The term has historically been used to describe a home altar.)[7] The concept serves small teams and students incredibly well when building a vertical slice. If we use a beautiful corner, it doesn't matter if big parts of the levels in our vertical slice are blockmesh and not shippable: we can still use the vertical slice to come to an understanding of our core mechanics in action. The

---

7. "Icon Corner," Wikipedia, https://en.wikipedia.org/wiki/Icon_corner.

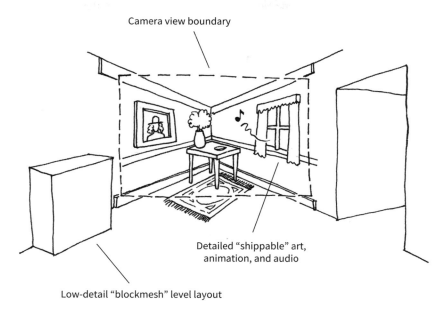

Camera view boundary

Detailed "shippable" art, animation, and audio

Low-detail "blockmesh" level layout

Figure 10.7
A beautiful corner for visualizing how a completed game level will look.

beautiful corner will show how our game's levels will look and sound when they are complete and finished with final visual art, animation, and audio assets.

As we'll see later, the work that we have to do to bring a vertical slice to a shippable level of quality, whether by creating a beautiful corner or whole shippable sample levels, will help our process in a number of different ways.

The Challenge and Reward of the Vertical Slice

Building a vertical slice can be a daunting task. So daunting, in fact, that many people doubt whether it's even possible to build a true vertical slice for a large contemporary commercial videogame. The sheer number of game elements that we could consider "core," and the huge amount of time it takes to create and polish assets to the standard of the high production values we see in games today, makes the challenge of the vertical slice ever more daunting year by year.

Indeed, because of various production setbacks that we'd encountered on the first *Uncharted* game, we weren't able to make a true vertical slice and instead made a concept movie, cut together from tech demos, key art, animatics, and a rough playable level, which helped us illustrate the design of our game in the same way that a fully playable vertical slice does.

If we stay flexible in our thinking about the vertical slice—using beautiful corners, supplementary concept movies, and other presentation materials to visualize the experience of our game—then the vertical slice becomes a realizable goal and does a huge amount to prepare us to make the rest of our game.

Making the vertical slice is when we have to take our next steps in committing to the design of our game. As we've previously discussed, committing to ideas is hard. It always feels too early to commit, and we're always second-guessing our decisions. But the design commitments we make during preproduction allow our game to stay on track throughout the rest of the project, and we must learn to have the courage to make them.

Designing-by-making is the best way that I know of to design and develop a game, and the satisfaction of creating a vertical slice, to show ourselves and everyone else that we're on to something, pays dividends in terms of our team's morale. In the next chapter, we'll look in detail at how we should go about building this excellent thing.

11 Building a Vertical Slice

Okay, so we've decided to build a vertical slice. How do we go about building it? I've talked about "iterating" a lot so far in this book, so it won't surprise you to learn that we will use an iterative design process to make our vertical slice.

Inexperienced game developers may think we build a game like this:

Initial ideas → Design → Develop → Finished game?

. . . on an assembly line, like the old-fashioned "waterfall" technique we discussed in chapter 9. They don't understand that, in order to make our game great, we need to build and revise it over and again—and that's why they run out of time.

This is how a game actually gets built:

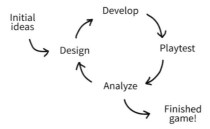

Iterative game design happens when we come up with a design based on our original ideas, develop (create) something playable based on that idea, playtest what we built, analyze the results of the playtest, revise the design, build something new—and so the iterative cycle continues, until we eventually finish making our game.

Iterative design takes place in a loop. But how do we stop ourselves just going around in circles? That's where our project goals come in. When, at the analysis stage, we can see that our game is meeting the experience goal we set, then we know we are heading in the right direction. If we're not, our next piece of design work should help get us back on track. In this way, we're prevented from spiraling around aimlessly trying different things and are guided toward a goal.

Work from a Prototype

In his D.I.C.E. 2002 discussion of Method, Mark Cerny describes the "publishable first playable," his term for what would come to be known as a vertical slice. Mark says that we should start where we started in ideation: with prototypes.

> I don't have to tell you how much you learn from making prototypes. Specifically, the team is making lots of successive prototypes. It's important not to wait before you start making these prototypes. Take the pieces that you have, however sketchy, and build the best you can. Because prototypes are where you learn. . . . [These] prototypes eventually become indistinguishable from game levels. . . . Each prototype brings together artwork, game mechanics and technology to show an entire level of a game that could be.[1]

So, we can begin making a vertical slice by taking the prototypes we made during ideation, looking at them through the new lens of our project goals, and continuing to iterate. We can go with the strongest single prototype or combine two or more of them to make something new.

Maybe we'll start over with a new prototype that serves our project goals better than any of our previous prototypes, but as I mentioned in chapter 5, that can be unwise. It's your choice: I trust you to make the best decision for your project.

Create an Early Sequence from the Game—but Don't Make the Very Beginning Yet

As you work from your prototypes to build a vertical slice that represents the core of your game, you'll probably find yourself creating an early sequence of your finished game. The basics of a game are usually shown clearly toward the start of the game, so this is a natural development.

However, don't design the *very* beginning of your game into your vertical slice. Give yourself permission to jump a little way forward into the game, assuming that the player will have learned the very basics of the game and its narrative by the time they get there. This will help you come to grips with the core of your game more effectively and with less difficulty. You can always use a controls cheat sheet to get your playtesters into your game, like the one we'll discuss in chapter 12.

You can read more about the philosophy behind this thinking, under "What Order Should a Game Be Built In?" in chapter 22.

Iterate on the Core Elements of Your Game

Just as we did while we were prototyping, we should start building our vertical slice by focusing on the small set of game mechanics, verbs, and player activities that form the

---

1. Mark Cerny, "D.I.C.E. Summit 2002," https://www.youtube.com/watch?v=QOAW9ioWAvE, 7:21.

core of our game as we're imagining it. If we had a slightly sloppy approach to development while we were prototyping, now it's time to tighten everything up before we move forward.

Make everything solid in terms of gameplay, graphics, audio, control, interface, and usability. This vertical slice should be fun to play with, easy to learn, and bug-free. Polish out the problems as you go along. We'll talk about this more in chapter 13.

Notice Mark Cerny's emphasis on successive prototypes in the quote above. This means building and then discarding the thing that will eventually turn into our vertical slice, maybe several times in a row. In his talk, Mark says that we'll probably throw away about four different versions of our vertical slice before we're eventually happy with it. He recently told me, "It was the fifth vertical slice that successfully demonstrated what Naughty Dog was trying to achieve [with *Crash Bandicoot*]; once this was in hand we headed into production. Kudos to Andy [Gavin] and Jason [Rubin] for the patience to iterate so many times at five or six weeks per iteration."

If we only have a few weeks for preproduction, we probably won't have time for five full iterations on our vertical slice—but we will probably start over at least once. Most of the levels in every game I've ever worked on got junked and restarted at least once during their development, and that's just the nature of game development. There are many reasons to start over: design and technology discoveries, notes from a team leader, and playtest feedback.

It's good general game development practice to save your work "early and often," to avoid losing work. Make successive saves with incrementing version numbers so that you can backtrack if you need to. If you're already using a version control system (a tool used to manage the changes made to computer files), make frequent commits. You could also save to an online storage service that lets you go back to an earlier version if needed. If you do ever lose work and have to start over, don't sweat it. It will take you much less time to build the thing you lost the second time around.

Throughout our work on the vertical slice—and indeed, throughout our entire development process—we should constantly be playtesting our game. We'll look at this in detail in the next chapter.

Commit to a Game Engine and Hardware Platform

At some point during preproduction—the earlier the better—you should make a firm decision about the game engine you will be using to make your game, and what operating system and hardware platform it will run on. It could be that, very early in preproduction, you are building your vertical slice using whatever game engine you have to hand. However, your decisions about game engine and platform will impact many things to do with the creation of your game, from the tools that you use to the audience you're considering, and so you should not delay in deciding.

If you choose a hardware platform like a game console that will require you to pass a certification process before you can release your game, you should immediately begin to familiarize yourself with the requirements for certification. You will read more about this in chapter 34.

Practice Good Housekeeping

"Housekeeping" is the quaint term that software developers use to describe a set of practices around keeping our code base and our project folder tidy, organized, and well-maintained. We do this to make things easier for ourselves later on, as our project grows in size and complexity.

It is good project folder housekeeping to:

• Organize your files into a hierarchy of folders, storing like with like, so that you can find things more easily.

• Use subfolders when a folder fills up with enough items that the list of files becomes hard to read through quickly (usually ten or so).

You can find a simple project folder hierarchy to use as a housekeeping starting point on this book's website, playfulproductionprocess.com.

It is good code housekeeping to:

• Structure and comment your code in a way that makes it easy to read and understand when you haven't looked at it for some time, or when others need to work on it.

• Choose variable names that are descriptive, but not too long.

• Use "camelCase" to make variable names more readable.

• Follow naming conventions (determined by the team) to give extra information about variables. For example, use a _leadingUnderscore to denote variables that are local in scope.

Other good housekeeping practices include:

• Document your work where necessary, with documents and lists that capture any important information that would be missing otherwise.

• Use a version control system to create an online repository of code and assets that can be shared among team members and used to roll back to a previous version if you ever need to.

Every team has its own set of best housekeeping practices, based on past experience and refined over time. If you weren't already using good housekeeping practices during ideation, then you must start during preproduction, in order to lay a stable foundation for your game and to speed up your process.

By the way, you aren't working on a prototype or test version of your game anymore. Don't ever call an asset, folder, or script "tempSomething." I've lost count of how many projects I've seen where the player-character object in the shipping game is called "playerTest." Entities that go into a game have a tendency to stick around and evolve. It's usually a hassle to rename things and doing so might even break the game. Your vertical slice is now your real project, so choose names accordingly.

Start to Add Debug Functions

Preproduction is a good time to start adding debug functions to your game that will help you develop it efficiently. Debug functions might come in the form of special on-screen menus, cheat key combinations, or commands typed in at a prompt. They are usually only accessible to the game's developers and allow us to do helpful things as we build the game. These might include teleporting to any level, making the player-character invulnerable to damage, or showing numerical and state-based information about elements of the game that is usually hidden from the player.

The first debug function that many designers add to their game is a reset key combination. Very often, when playtesting a vertical slice, the game will get stuck in some state, or the player will reach the end and want to start over. To avoid having to close and restart the game, wasting valuable time, the developer can simply hit the cheat keys to reset the game, putting it into a state that is identical to a freshly launched version of the game. Make sure that you choose some obscure combination of keys or gamepad buttons that the player is unlikely to hit accidentally—for example, holding "R" and "=" on the keyboard at the same time.

Fail Early, Fail Fast, Fail Often

Failure is an inevitable part of the iterative process. A lot of what we'll try isn't going to work out. That means that failure isn't bad, and we should adjust our mindset accordingly. If something we try fails, we should pick ourselves up and have another go.

You may have heard the saying "Fail early, fail fast, fail often," which comes from the world of rapid prototyping, a group of iterative industrial design techniques. This credo encourages us to start building things early in our process and to try to understand as soon as we can what the "deal breaker" problems are with what we're building. That will leave us more time to have as many different attempts as possible at building something that doesn't have any major problems.

This fits in well with this book's philosophy of design iteration and constant playtesting. Remember, try not to work for more than an hour or two before playtesting what you've built on someone.

Work in the Same Physical Space or Together Online

If you're working on a team, try to work together in the same physical space as your teammates whenever possible, or work together online using videoconferencing, audio calls, or instant messaging. There is something about working together at the same time that makes everything run more smoothly when designing games. Not everyone can be in the same physical space—many teams are globally distributed—but even small amounts of real time coworking can make a big positive impact on the smooth running of a game project, if they happen frequently and regularly.

This is partly practical: it's easier and faster to communicate effectively about the highly complex game development process when we're working together at the same time and can quickly chat about an issue. But it's also related to emotion and team morale. It's hard to tell how another person is doing when we're communicating asynchronously through email. Did something we said make them tense up? Do we need to fine-tune the way that we're communicating, so that our teammate knows we respect and trust them?

We have to prevent small misunderstandings and miscommunications from building up into bigger problems if we want to keep collaborating effectively. Working in the same physical space or online at the same time is the best path to the good team morale that is essential in the creation of an excellent game.

Save and Categorize Your Design Materials

Every design process generates a large volume of design material: documents, images, movies, and original game assets, much of which will go unused in the finished game. As you work on your game, you should save and categorize everything that you make.

This will take a little extra effort when you're working. It's tempting to dash forward and leave our unused design materials scattered behind us, dumped in some random folder with poorly chosen names. But just as we practice good housekeeping in our engine's project folder, so we should practice good housekeeping with our design materials. Again, you can find an example folder hierarchy for your design materials on this book's website, playfulproductionprocess.com.

At the end of every day or every week, take a moment to sort your design materials into the correct folders, making sure that the files have well-chosen names that you'll understand easily later when you're searching for something. Then, whenever you need any of your design materials, whether you're looking for a piece of game design that you'd set aside or are searching for some unused concept art that would be perfect for your social media campaign, you'll be able to find it easily.

Be Guided by Your Project Goals

At the start of preproduction, our project goals are fresh in our minds: after all, we only just wrote them down. But as we get caught up in building our vertical slice, our project goals can quickly fade from our memories. So print them out and put them up somewhere on the wall in your workspace to keep them fresh in your mind.

As you work on your vertical slice, allow your project goals, your experience goal in particular, to guide and focus your design. Does each thing that you add support the experience that you wanted to create or detract from it? Asking that question can be helpful in providing direction to keep us on track.

When to Modify Your Project Goals

Sometimes, as we work on a vertical slice, it might lead us in a new direction. We might serendipitously hit on a combination of elements that doesn't exactly line up with our project goals but that everyone loves. Our playtesters from inside and outside the team don't want to stop playing at the end of the playtest, and we, the development team, are excited about what we're making.

This is a time when you should consider modifying your project goals to bring them into line with what you've discovered. Tracy Fullerton says, "I call this crafting or honing the goals—as you understand them better, through iteration, you are not changing them, so much as honing them down, getting to the essence of your goals. I think it is actually quite an important part of 'meeting' your goals—to hone them to the point where they are achievable."[2]

There's some risk in this, of course—if you keep changing the direction that you're moving in, you might end up going around in circles. Think carefully, and rather than constantly making many small changes to your project goals, get clear about your new direction, and change them so that they align with the game that has emerged from your iterative cycle of design, implementation, playtesting, and analysis. Then stick with them.

What We Are Doing by Building the Vertical Slice

Okay, let's move on to look at what building a vertical slice will get us. By building the vertical slice, we're doing four important things.

Designing by Building

In chapter 9, I talked about the early days of game development and attempts to use the waterfall model to manage game projects. Under this model, game designers were asked to imagine a game in as much detail as they could and then write a huge game design document, describing the imagined game in intricate detail.

The resulting paper document was often several inches thick, and getting anyone on the team to read it was incredibly difficult. The document might have had a lot of thought put into it, but within a few days of starting to build the game discoveries would be made to lead the design in a better (and previously unimagined) direction, making all of that hard work obsolete.

Today, games are designed iteratively, by creating something playable: first prototypes in ideation, and now a vertical slice. We playtest, evaluate, and make changes that boost the parts that are working and downplay or remove the parts that aren't. We think about the "three Cs"—character, camera, and control—and we start to become

---

2. Private communication, May 25, 2020.

confident about how each "C" is going to work for our game. Gradually, our game begins to appear before our eyes, as we get our ideas out into the world and shine sunlight on them.

Making Something That Communicates Ideas

It is very important, throughout the course of the project but perhaps particularly during preproduction, that we can communicate about the emerging design of our game. Building a vertical slice helps us to communicate that design.

Within our game development team, we have to communicate the essential features of our design to every last person who will work on the game, from the team leads to the most junior new hire. We have to ensure that everyone understands what we're building, so that they can contribute effectively to the project. We also have to be able to communicate what we are making to people outside of our team. Early in development, this is often the stakeholders in our project: our immediate bosses, our studio heads, the publishers who are bankrolling the project, or the investors in our company.

The team needs to feel good about this project that they're going to sink their precious time into, and the project's stakeholders need to believe in the project so that they will back it. A vertical slice that someone can pick up and play communicates game design ideas more quickly, efficiently, and truthfully than any game design document, and nothing gets people more excited about a game than a playable early version that shows how great it's going to be.

Learning about Our Tools and Technology

Alongside figuring out our game's design, we also need to figure out the tools and technology that we will use for our game. This is easier than it used to be now that we have great off-the-shelf game engines. Still, the best way to make solid, detailed plans for tools and technology is to build a vertical slice, in order to see what works well from the start and what will need more effort. Perhaps we'll have to buy some middleware to achieve a special technological need of our game. Maybe we will need to write a special tool from scratch.

Not every last technological innovation that will go into your game needs to be figured out during preproduction, but the core of your tools and technology should be. The more that you can avoid or anticipate problems, the better.

Gathering Information about How Long Things Take Us and Who We'll Need on the Team

Our vertical slice has many elements that will be brought to a good level of polish. That means that, as we build it, we can gather concrete information about (a) how long it takes our team to build things and (b) how many cycles of iteration we have to go through, on average, to get to a level of quality that we're satisfied with. This information will be very valuable when we're scheduling full production. Track the time you spend, and where you spend it, using one of the many free time-tracking tools available online.

It's not sensible to track exactly how long it takes you to create each individual entity in the vertical slice—avoid getting bogged down in too much detail. Just starting to track your time in chunks of one or two hours each will help you get a handle on how quickly you work. Making games takes patience and perseverance; everything in game development takes much longer than you initially think it's going to. Hard-to-solve problems can suddenly arise, even in types of work that you've done easily in the past. As creative director and writer Mel MacCoubrey pointed out on Max and Nick Folkman's excellent *Script Lock* podcast, in games "the firefighting hat and the creative hat *are the same hat.*"[3] So it's your responsibility to build up a realistic picture of the rate at which your team can make progress.

Making a vertical slice can also help us realize how many people we're going to need from each of the traditional disciplines of game development (art, engineering, animation, audio, and so on) and whether we're going to need any specialist help.

In chapter 5, I mentioned that we should keep a running list of attributions for any found and third-party assets that we're using, along with a list of credits for everyone who works on the game. Make sure you continue to do both as you work on your vertical slice.

Preproduction Cannot Be Scheduled Conventionally

In his D.I.C.E. 2002 talk, Mark Cerny declared that the idea that "it is possible to plan and schedule the creation of your game" is a myth, receiving a round of applause from his audience in response.[4]

Every experienced game developer knows that creativity in our field is like riding a bucking horse. It pulls us this way and that, always leading us in unexpected new directions as we make discoveries about the realities of our gameplay, our story, and our development methods. That's part of the beauty of creativity, and it's what makes every development experience a unique journey, where we can learn new things about the design process, about games, and about ourselves.

When Mark Cerny says that we can't plan and schedule the creation of a game, he isn't saying that we won't schedule any part of our project. Having worked closely with Mark, I know how much he values good scheduling for the full production phase of a game project. He is explaining that during preproduction, when we're figuring out the basic template for what we're going to make, the project can't be run according to task lists and milestones.

---

3. Jon Paquette and Mel MacCoubrey, *Script Lock*, ep. 46, February 18, 2019, https://scriptlock.simplecast.com/episodes/ep-46-jon-paquette-mel-maccoubrey.
4. Cerny, "D.I.C.E. Summit 2002," 3:40.

When we're designing-by-building a vertical slice, we're looking for that *eureka!* moment when, like Archimedes noticing his bathwater rise, we finally understand something theoretical about our game's design because of the practical work we're doing. Many people feel that the best way to reach this moment of revelation is to work freely and intuitively—and that you can't schedule your way there. In his talk, Mark Cerny calls this the "vital chaos" of preproduction and says that we must allow it to be chaotic or it won't work properly.

Of course, every designer will use some kind of structured process during preproduction—the iterative design loop, for example—and you should use whatever methods work for you, to help you find the right amount of vital chaos for your team. Just do your best to keep things loose and adaptable.

Timeboxing

Just because preproduction can't be scheduled conventionally, that doesn't mean we should allow it to run on indefinitely. Timeboxing is a well-known concept from project management that is used a lot in agile development. When you timebox your work, you give it a set amount of time. If you start to run out of time, you have to reduce the scope of the task you're working on, because the length of the timebox is fixed. In this way, timeboxing is like playing speed chess—you get some time to think, and then you must act to make a decision.

A constraint is a designer's best friend, because constraints bring out our creativity. They give us concrete problems to solve and force us to think beyond our usual ways of doing things. Constraints can help us overcome the "blank-sheet-of-paper problem" by giving us a starting point in the form of a challenge, and they can give us motivation and focus. Timeboxing is a constraint in time, and so it can help us stop procrastinating. It nudges us into action, helping us to make ever more specific decisions about the design of our game. In practical terms, being able to deliver work within a set time is important for securing funding for a project and for getting paid at milestones.

The trick of timeboxing is to keep one eye on the clock and understand when you have to start wrapping everything up. We could all keep fiddling forever with something we're making, especially if we're enjoying making it. But there comes a time when you're not really polishing anymore; you're just making more changes. A good maxim to keep in mind is one often attributed to Leonardo da Vinci: "Art is never finished, only abandoned." Each creative person has to decide when their work is good enough. Game designers can often look to their playtesters to tell them, and as you gain experience you will find it easier to know when something is done.

Sometimes you get close to the end of a timeboxing period, and the work is simply not finished or not yet good enough. That's the time to have a discussion with your collaborators and stakeholders. Talk about what you're trying to achieve, how much time you think it will take, and whether you should change your plans to try and achieve fewer things or different things.

Software developers call this list of achievable things the scope of a project, and we'll be talking about project scope, rescoping, and scope creep throughout the course of this book. Of course, it is better to have this discussion about scope *before* we reach the end of a timebox. Most game designers, as they gain experience, become more and more comfortable with rescoping on the fly as they approach the milestone marking the end of a timeboxed period.

Here's one way to think about scope. The 1938 screwball comedy *Bringing Up Baby* famously had a big influence on the design of *Uncharted: Drake's Fortune*. Game director Amy Hennig took inspiration from the rapid-fire banter between Katherine Hepburn and Cary Grant in writing the characters of Elena Fisher and Nathan Drake. The director of *Bringing Up Baby*, Howard Hawks, was once asked to define what made a great movie. His answer was, "Three great scenes, no bad ones."

And so it goes for games. I learned back at the start of my career that players won't miss the things you don't put into your game for want of time, but they *will* notice things in your game that are bad because you ran out of time to make them good. As a game designer, you're a systems thinker, so you know that a small set of rules can create a huge and fascinating "possibility space" (the abstract space of all of the different things that might happen when a game is played). So, when you start to run out of time, instead of racing to cram everything into your game, cut some things from the design, work with what you have, and make the parts that are present interact in more systemically interesting ways. You may need to take note of the time-tested writing advice and "kill your darlings," letting go of ideas that don't truly belong in the game, even though they might mean a lot to you.

When you're timeboxing work on your vertical slice, remember that not everything needs to be completed by the end of preproduction. Mark Cerny says, "You can't schedule the date when you will have worked out all of your seemingly intractable problems."[5] Focus on the core of your design and use your skill and judgment to figure out which issues you can wait to resolve later during full production (the project phase that comes after preproduction).

Use timeboxing to help you break your bad habits of procrastination and commit to your ideas through action. Timeboxing each project phase, not just preproduction, reliably helps us to move forward through the project, committing to the right decisions at the right times. It's easier to do this when you have a game design professor like me setting you assignments, but if you're on a professional team, remember how important your producers are in holding you accountable to getting things done on time.

Be kind to your team and to yourself during the creation of the vertical slice. Sometimes preproduction is easy, and sometimes it's hard. Designing-by-making is challenging

---

5. Cerny, "D.I.C.E. Summit 2002," 5:23.

work, with many different factors in play: intellectual, emotional, aspirational, and artistic. Make sure that you and your team get the help and support you need and deserve, from your mentors, your friends, and your professional peers.

Remember that great game design does not necessarily come from innate genius or outstanding technical ability. More usually, it comes from simply committing to a decision, thinking flexibly about how to achieve an experience goal, and taking careful note of what is succeeding with players. Don't overlook successes that seem modest or trivial. By seizing on even the simplest positive reaction from a player and amplifying it with more design work, we can make truly great, deeply emotional, and highly memorable games.

Remain patient with each other as you struggle through this challenging process. If you nurture each other's efforts, and guide each other through your travails, you will come to see the vertical slice in the same way that I do: as an essential tool in the practice of healthier game production processes, and as embodying the unison of design, craft, and art.

In the next chapter we'll look at a rigorous playtesting method, inspired by the process we used at Naughty Dog, that will help you get the best results from the iterative design process used in building a vertical slice.

12 Playtesting

Playtesting is at the heart of our playful production process. I already gave you some simple guidelines for playtesting in chapter 5. This chapter will explore a healthy playtest practice you can use throughout the whole course of a project, and lays a foundation for the "formal" playtesting processes that we'll discuss in chapters 24 and 25.

Of course, as we implement things, we should playtest them ourselves. Most game developers do this automatically as they work, running the game now and then to see how it looks, sounds, and plays. It's also very good to regularly do quick playtests with someone else—a teammate, friend, or passerby—to help check that the game is landing with other people in roughly the way that you intend.

I like this term, *landing*, which I picked up somewhere down the line. Creative people of all kinds use it to talk about the ways that other people receive their work. When something lands, it creates an experience. That experience might be welcome: if my game lands well with you, I see you enjoying it, picking up on how it works, being able to gradually improve your skill or your interest, and wanting to play more. I assume that you're having experiences that you like or appreciate. If my game is landing badly with you, I might see any number of things that lead you to want to stop playing. You might find it frustrating because you don't understand it, or you might think you understand it but are mistaken. It might be too difficult and you can't see any way to grow the skills you need to do better. It might not be to your taste, or it might make you feel something you don't want to feel. This wide, deep realm of subjective experience is one of the things we're looking at when we run a playtest.

The game designer Tanya X. Short talks about the "legibility" of systems. Most games are systems of rules, resources, procedures, and relationships, and for a game system to be understood, it must be legible: it must be presented in such a way that its meaning is clear. "Legibility as in allowing the player to decipher this new language that the game is trying to teach them."[1] The legibility of our games is another thing that we're checking for when we run a playtest.

---

1. Tanya X. Short, "How and When to Make Your Procedurality Player-Legible," Game UX Summit 2018, https://www.youtube.com/watch?v=r6rTMGFXktI.

The Designer's Model, the System Image, and the User's Model

I like to use the concepts of the designer's model, the system image, and the user's model to help me think about the legibility of a game. They come from *The Design of Everyday Things*, a highly influential book by the usability designer and psychologist Donald A. Norman. This book is beloved by game designers and interaction designers for the insights it offers about how people perceive and interact with systems.

In Don Norman's thinking, the **designer's model** is how the designer sees the game (or some other kind of interactive system) in their head. It's "the designer's conception of the look, feel, and operation of a product."[2] The **system image** is how the game actually presents itself to the player. "The system image is what can be derived from the physical structure that has been built (including documentation)."[3] The designer hopes that this is close to their model, but it might actually be quite different, especially in an early iteration of the design.

Finally, the **user model** is what is going on in the head of the person playing the game. "The user's mental model is developed through interaction with the product and the system image."[4] But the user brings their own experience, biases, and ability to interpret the things that the system image shows them (the "perceptual field" that Steve Swink talks about in *Game Feel*).[5] This can create a gulf of understanding between the user model and the system image. And if the system image doesn't quite match the designer's model, then the user model can drift even further away from the designer's model, like a game of "telephone" warping and distorting a message. As Don Norman says: "Designers expect the user's model to be identical to their own, but because they cannot communicate directly with the user, the burden of communication is with the system image."[6]

Experienced game designers often have a shock of recognition when they hear about this for the first time, because they've already learned how difficult it is to communicate effectively with the players of their games. The concepts and mechanisms in our games and stories are often complex and abstract, and getting them across to our players in a reliable way is extremely tough. The situation is made even more challenging by the indirect methods of communication we're using.

To address these issues, we often have to communicate the same concept to the player through many channels at once: the way the system looks, what shape and color its elements are, what we see it do, what we explicitly say about it through text or speech, and the training sequences we set up. We have to layer the information we deliver, communicating redundantly (communicating the same thing through multiple channels at once) until everyone who plays our game can get it.

---

2. Norman, *The Design of Everyday Things*, 32.
3. Norman, *The Design of Everyday Things*, 32.
4. Norman, *The Design of Everyday Things*, 32.
5. Swink, *Game Feel*, 50.
6. Norman, *The Design of Everyday Things*, 32.

Affordances and Signifiers

Don Norman describes how the system image gets communicated to the user through "affordances" and "signifiers." The concept of affordances comes from the psychologist James J. Gibson, who, in his book *The Ecological Approach to Visual Perception*, outlines a "theory of affordances" related to the way animals use their environment. Norman refined this idea into a theory of **affordances**, which "define what actions are possible," and **signifiers**, which "specify how people discover those possibilities: signifiers are signs, perceptible signals of what can be done."[7]

The classic example of affordances and signifiers is that of a door which can swing open in one direction but not the other. A well-designed door will have a handle on the side that must be pulled toward you to open it, and a metal push plate on the side that must be pushed. The signifiers of the handle and push plate convey the affordance of the opening, as well as its direction.

People often run these two concepts together under "affordance," but it's important to recognize affordance and signifier as distinct. A videogame might have a feature whereby if I stand still in a certain place in a level for more than five seconds, I automatically and instantly get moved to another place in the level. This feature is an affordance: a mechanism that, when used, leads to an outcome. But if that place in the level isn't marked in any way, this is a pretty weird feature. We have no way of finding this auto-move spot except by accident, and it would be disorienting to find myself elsewhere in a level without any explanation. If I know that it's there somewhere, but I don't know where, then maybe I can find it by a tedious process of trial and error. It would probably seem like a bug, rather than a feature.

However, if we place a platform at this auto-move spot, and the platform has a glowing floor panel to stand on which hums quietly to itself, which begins to hum more loudly when I stand on it, perhaps with a number counting down on the panel, "5, 4, 3 . . . ," a glow that appears around my player-character, and a zapping, crack-of-thunder sound effect when I'm moved to the new location—then we have designed a teleporter. The signifiers of the platform, the glowing panel, the sound effects and visual effects, and the countdown readout, all clearly convey the functioning of the affordance. The affordance is functionally the same in both cases. It is the signifiers that turn something useless as a game mechanic into a part of our stock-in-trade as game designers.

Playtesting for Legibility and Experience

Hopefully you can start to imagine how we can investigate these relatively objective issues of legibility through playtesting. Just by watching people play, we can look at the overlap or disconnect between the designer's model, the system image, and the user's

---

7. Norman, *The Design of Everyday Things*, xv.

model, and the way that affordances are communicated through signifiers. By asking follow-up questions, we can refine *our* understanding of our playtesters' understanding.

We can also use playtesting to investigate the experiences that people have when they play our games, and while this process can be rather more complex because it's much more subjective, we can learn a lot by using the same techniques of watching people play and talking to them afterward. In order to look at how our games land with people—in terms of both the legibility of our games and the experiences they create—we should adopt some best practices to help guide our playtest process.

Best Practices for Playtesting

Over the course of my professional practice, I developed a set of best practices for playtesting, based on what I learned from my mentors and my reading, and things that I saw working well in the studio. Best practices for playtesting will always be dependent on the game and its context, but these basic ground rules are flexible and adaptable, while also being appropriate for most situations. Let's dive right in.

Minimize Your Conversation with Your Playtester before and during the Test

Before the playtest starts, be polite: say hello to your playtester, and invite them to sit down and get ready to play. Beyond that, speak to them at a bare minimum. Definitely do not tell your playtester anything about your game before they start to play or while they play it. At all costs, you must avoid even accidentally giving away any information that will prejudice the feedback that you get about your game.

Use Headphones for Both Playtesters and Designers

As you watch the playtest, you must hear what your players hear, as well as seeing what they see. A game's audio is as important as its visuals and plays a huge role in shaping players' emotion. In a room where many games are being tested at once, the only reliable way for the game designer to hear what the playtester is hearing is to have them both wearing headphones that are connected to the game. A simple way to approach this is to use a stereo audio splitter to connect multiple pairs of headphones, and an audio extension cable for the designer, who is usually sitting a short distance behind the playtester. Wireless headphone technology makes this even easier and more convenient, although at a higher cost.

Prepare a Controls Cheat Sheet if Necessary

A well-designed game will usually teach its players how to control it by introducing the control mechanisms one at a time, and letting the player practice each one. However, a game early in its development often won't yet include any such training. Some designers just explain the game's controls verbally, introducing variability and bias into their playtesting process. Experienced game designers will make things more objective by quickly preparing a controls cheat sheet that shows the control scheme,

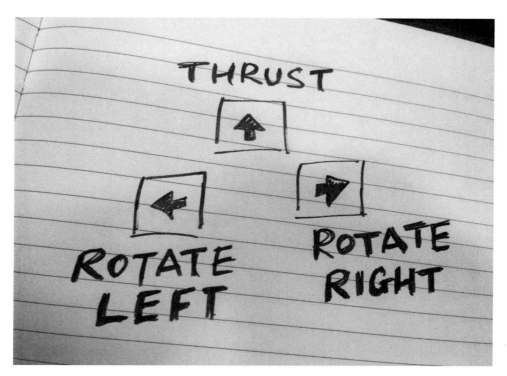

Figure 12.1
A controls cheat sheet.

and by showing the same sheet to every playtester (see figure 12.1). It can either be shown once at the start of the playtest or left on the table nearby for ongoing reference. Again, the goal is to avoid talking to your playtester at all until after the playtest.

Prepare a Written Hint or Helper to Help Players with Any Known Gameplay Issues or Functional Issues

Very often, a game that we're testing will have an issue we know about, and which interferes with our ability to get good feedback from our players. Maybe we relit the level just before the playtest, and now a doorway that should be easy to see is completely and accidentally hidden in shadow. (This happened to us a lot on *Uncharted*.) Maybe there's a bug that means that the playtester can only proceed if they're told what to do. That's the time to use a written hint or helper (see figure 12.2). Write down the information the playtester needs in order to deal with the known problem, and then show it to them at the appropriate time, without speaking. Just like a controls cheat sheet, this gives every player exactly the same information, making our playtests uniform. But be careful: this approach is only for use in emergencies when you know that the player is definitely going to get stuck, and couldn't possibly work out how to proceed on their own.

Figure 12.2
A written "hint" or "helper."

Suggest That Your Playtester Thinks and Feels Out Loud

"Thinking out loud" when playtesting a game—talking about your perceptions and the ideas that you're having while playing—is a good way for a playtester to give the game's designer information about the experience they're having that the designer couldn't get just by watching. "Feeling out loud" by talking about the emotions the playtester is having does the same. Some people are better at this than others. Designers should just ask their playtesters to think and feel out loud and let them start to play. If a playtester doesn't start to speak as they play, the designer could suggest one more time that they do so, and then leave them alone. You can learn almost as much by watching your playtester carefully as you can by listening to what they say, and you will notice that most everyone has a hard time talking during intense sequences of gameplay, when all of our attention is occupied by the game.

As a game designer, you should practice your own skills of thinking and feeling out loud. These are very powerful abilities to have when collaborating with your teammates and other professional peers. If you start by telling a game's designer in detail about the ideas you have and the emotions you feel as you look at and listen to *even just their game's title screen*, that can set the frame for giving them a very rich and full picture of how their game lands with you when you start to play.

Use Content Warnings if Appropriate

Content warnings are valuable because they free us to make any kind of work we like, and they help us to present it only to people who consent to see the kind of thing we're making. Perhaps because of the historical associations that games have with children's culture, game designers have sometimes been reluctant to engage with so-called adult subject matter. But videogames, as a maturing entertainment medium and art form, are an entirely appropriate way of looking at every kind of subject. By using a content warning at the beginning of a playtest, which acts just like an age rating on a movie, we can alert people to the presence of any type of content that they may wish to avoid. Search online for "content warning" to get more information about what kind of content to use warnings for, and how to deliver the warnings.

Be Observant of Your Playtester's Experience of the Game

Watch your playtester closely to see what they do in the game. Notice their reactions and behaviors. What do they seem to understand about what they can and can't do in the game? What do they fail to understand? What do they try to do, and what don't they try to do? What emotions do they show?

Observe What the Playtester Does and Says and Note It All Down

As you watch your playtester, carefully write down your observations in as much detail as you can. Note down what they do in the game, what they seem to be thinking and feeling, and anything they say about their thoughts and feelings. Many of us, young people especially, imagine that our memories are infallible total-recall devices like the hard drives of our computers. In fact, as psychologists and cognitive scientists have proven many times, memory is highly fallible, and is strongly shaped by emotion. The way that you feel about a playtest session and your game will strongly skew your memory of what players do. That's why you should write down *everything* that you notice during a playtest. You should have filled a page with notes within the first few minutes of watching your playtester, writing or typing as fast as you can in an attempt to record every last detail of what the tester does. Every time that you see a good thing or a problem, write it down, once for every time that the good thing happens or the problem occurs. Then, when you review your notes after the playtest, the best things about your game and the biggest problems will jump out at you. You will know what is really working about your game, and what to fix first.

Don't Help Your Playtester at All

This is one of the most fundamental principles of playtesting and is also one of the hardest to follow, even for experienced game designers. Watching someone play a game that is mid-development can be excruciating if you're not allowed to give them any help. Your playtesters will butt up against the problems in what you've built, misunderstanding the mechanics and story, struggling to proceed, or getting stuck altogether. As a game designer, you must steel your nerve and remain silent, diligently resisting the temptation to help your playtester in any way during the test. You have to learn to take the pain that you feel as you watch a playtester struggling and transform it into motivation for making fixes in your next round of design iteration. If your playtester asks you questions while they're playing or appeals to you for help, apologize and tell them politely but firmly that you can't help them, and that you'd like them to keep trying to proceed in the game on their own. This is the only way to clearly see how your game is landing with people, and the only exception to this is covered by the use of a written hint or helper, above.

Keep an Eye on the Time

Remain aware of the passage of time during your playtest, as a part of your general heightened state of awareness about what is happening with your playtester and your game. If you're not gathering metrics data (see chapter 26), you should make notes about how much time passes as your player progresses through your game. How long did they take to get through the first level, and the second? Depending on the context of your playtest, the time for each test might be limited. It's good to keep an eye on the time if there's something—a level perhaps—that you want to be sure your playtester sees. You also need to reserve some time to ask them questions afterward.

After the Playtest, It's Time for an Exit Interview

When the time for playing is finished, guide your playtester through what is known as an exit interview. The form that this conversation takes is always up to you, but I have some general guidelines to help you. Start by asking your playtester an open-ended question that focuses on some aspect of your game that you're interested in. Avoid questions that can be answered with a yes or no answer, or with another kind of short, simple answer (like a number). The videogame project director and artist Marc Tattersall created a list of five excellent open-ended questions to ask playtesters, which were reported by Alissa McAloon on the game industry community site Gamasutra:

- What was your favorite moment or interaction?
- What was your least favorite moment or interaction?
- When did you feel the most clever?
- Was there anything you wanted to do that the game wouldn't let you do?
- If you had a magic wand and could change any aspect of the game or your experience, what would it be? Unlimited budget and time.[8]

These questions go straight to the heart of some important aspects of your game's design. What stays in the player's memory, for good reasons or bad? When did the

---

8. Alissa McAloon, "5 Questions You Should Be Asking Playtesters to Get Meaningful Feedback," Gamasutra, October 10, 2016, https://www.gamasutra.com/view/news/283044/5_questions_you _should_be_asking_playtesters_to_get_meaningful_feedback.php.

player most feel that their agency was given expression or was too restricted? What creative ideas does the player have that you're overlooking? Using these questions as a model, what open-ended questions would you ask?

Capture everything that your playtester says during the exit interview (with their consent), either by taking notes or by making a recording of the conversation. As your conversation with the playtester unfolds, try not to lead them to express any particular opinion, but do follow up on things that they say—when they make a comment that you find interesting but don't quite understand, try to draw more out of them.

A note about playtesting games for children from game designer and producer Alan Dang: "When asking questions, testing with kids can be hard since they tend to want to please adults and don't want negativity associated with them. One way around that is to ask kids how they would describe this game to a friend or a person at their age, or what they think someone else would think."[9]

Don't Be a Game-Explainer

During the exit interview, many game designers are seized by a powerful urge to explain their game to their playtester—how it works, what the storyline means, and what the player misunderstood. Resist this temptation. You might be trying just to fill in a few details about how you intended the design to work, so as to get better feedback (and there may come a time for that, eventually). The problem is that within seconds, the playtester's head is swimming with concepts and questions that they *didn't get from playing the game*, and they are left with a clouded impression of their experience. It doesn't matter that your playtester didn't understand your game. What matters is that you come to understand their user model, in Donald Norman's terms, and how it differs from your designer's model and the system image, so that you can improve your game's design with the next round of iteration.

Don't Get Discouraged

Playtesting is often a very emotional process for designers. Creative people typically invest a lot of themselves into the things they make. When we make something and show it to other people, we might feel exposed, anxious, or even panicked, even before we have seen how our game is landing. We might become overwhelmed by the often-contradictory feedback that we get from different playtesters and end up feeling lost in the maze of our design. These difficult feelings can be powerful even when testing a game that is refined and working well—imagine how much stronger, messier, and more complicated they are with something new and full of problems. If we don't deal with the emotions that come up during a playtest, they can be destructive. They can make us want to give up, to throw away our game, and start on something new. They can even make us want to quit game design altogether.

---

9. Private communication, May 10, 2020.

One good way to deal with this is to anticipate your emotions and to get ready to deal with them, in whatever way works for you. You might remind yourself that the game is not the designer, to give yourself some emotional distance. It's never okay to express difficult emotion toward a playtester, but I think that rather than "stuffing your feelings" it's better to find a healthy way to express them. I encourage groups of game designers to offer each other emotional support after a playtest: to complain and moan if necessary, expressing frustration or sadness about the fact that the playtest didn't go the way they would have liked. To do this in a way that isn't toxic—not nasty or mean, and not focused on an individual—can help us to let go of the emotion and allows it to move into the past. Once you've worked through the emotion, then review the notes that you took during the playtest. Mine them for knowledge about what is working in your game and what is not. Be honest with yourself and own the successes of your project as much as the failures. Start to make a plan to address the problems, and trust that the next playtest will be better. It almost always is. Follow the advice that Matthew Frederick gives in *101 Things I Learned in Architecture School*:

> Engage the design process with patience. Don't imitate popular portrayals of the creative process as depending on a singular, pell-mell rush of inspiration. Don't try to solve a complex [problem] in one sitting or one week. Accept uncertainty. Recognize as normal the feeling of lostness that attends much of the process.[10]

I hope that you find this list of best practices useful for playtesting your games. Should they be treated as guidelines or rules? I think that they're important enough that I use them as rules and follow them strictly. Just remember: rules are made to be broken and should never outlive their usefulness.

Running Regular Playtests

In most every type of game design process that I can imagine, it's important to run regular playtests, either with people who haven't played the game before or with people who haven't played it in a while. In a professional context, these playtests could take many forms: teammates testing with each other, friends and family playtests, early access playtests with members of the game's fan community, and so on—our imagination is the only limit. In an academic setting, in a class focused on making creative work, I think that it's appropriate either to run in-class playtests almost every week or to require students to playtest every week outside of class. It takes work to make playtesting into an ingrained part of one's game design practice, and teachers can support students in developing this healthy habit.

Mark Cerny once told me that perhaps you need as few as just seven different playtesters to understand how your game is landing with people in general, and it should be

---

10. Frederick, *101 Things I Learned in Architecture School*, 81.

quite easy to get close to this number of new impressions of your game every week. Test whatever you have at each stage of the project: prototypes during ideation, builds that are on the way to becoming a vertical slice during preproduction, and games that are in some stage of build-out during full production. Learn to see the different types of design insight that you can gain through playtesting at each stage.

By running regular playtests throughout the course of the project, good playtesting practice will become deeply ingrained in everyone on our team, and by the time we're ready to run formal playtests during full production, the extra tools that we'll use won't be overwhelming, and things will run smoothly.

Evaluating Playtest Feedback

Making sense of the results of a playtest can be difficult, and we must be disciplined in the way that we approach the process. It's almost impossible to make a coherent evaluation of playtest feedback based on memory alone, since memory is skewed by emotion. That is why it's important to take lots of notes during the playtest and the exit interview, to create an objective record of our observations.

In reviewing my notes, I find that a lot of them fall easily into one of three categories:

1. **Broken: Must Fix.** These are problems of design or implementation that keep the player from having the kind of experience we want them to have. The possible fixes are usually quite obvious.

2. **Question: Maybe Fix.** These are things that might not be working, at least not as intended, and that warrant further investigation. These problems could be in the design (the designer's model), in the game (the system image), or in the player's comprehension of the game (the user model). We must look more closely at these issues because the solution is not yet clear.

3. **Suggestion: A New Idea.** A lot of new ideas will bubble up during playtests, and they might be game design gold, or they could be totally irrelevant to what we're trying to achieve. By discussing the suggestions, accepting some and rejecting others, we can finesse our game's design.

Once you've reviewed and sorted your notes, open up the document where you wrote down your project goals. For each note, ask yourself: would acting on this feedback help us meet our project goals, and our experience goal in particular? This should be particularly helpful when you're trying to evaluate notes in the question and suggestion categories. You can often expose the true nature of hidden problems by asking a playtester open-ended questions about them in an exit interview.

Remember that while what playtesters say about the game is very valuable (whether they're thinking out loud or talking in an exit interview), it can also be misleading. The player might misunderstand why they were acting in a certain way: perhaps something in the game was miscuing them. This is why simply watching players play is very important. Great game designers learn how to interpolate between what players say and what they do, to build up an accurate picture of how their game is working.

However, be very wary of falling into a trap when someone struggles to play your game in a playtest. Never say, "They're not playing it right." To say this is to misunderstand something fundamental about digital game design, and about your responsibilities as a game designer. A well-designed digital game teaches itself to the player: sometimes overtly, through tutorials, and sometimes discreetly, by just letting the player mess around and make discoveries. Every game, because of its interactivity, empowers the player to express their agency within the constraints of the game. If your player isn't having a good time, it's either because of your design or because your game just isn't right for that player.

You should also resist the urge to dismiss playtest feedback because "they just don't get it." Instead, try to understand why they're not getting it. What is missing or not working that is preventing the playtester from having the kind of experience you want them to have? Is it something in the game or is it something in the player? If it's the latter, then again, not every game is for every person, and the same is true for all art and entertainment. But saying "they just don't get it" too quickly is a mistake. Be certain that you've learned everything you can from the feedback your playtesters give you before you dismiss it.

A cardinal rule for the evaluation of playtest feedback is that we must resist the impulse to become defensive. You know that feeling: someone says something critical—or that *sounds* like a criticism—and your feelings flare up. In your mind you yell, "That's nonsense!" and you begin to make a mental list of all the reasons why it's nonsense. You think that your reasons are rational, but when you look at them later you can see how skewed by emotion they were.

Notice when you get defensive and cool yourself down before you engage. It can be helpful to sleep on feedback—getting some distance from it can help you evaluate criticism more rationally. If you try to talk about an issue when you're feeling defensive, you might soon find yourself in an argument rather than a discussion.

Becoming defensive in response to criticism—whether it's reasonable or not—is the curse of many human endeavors, from our professional and creative lives to our personal lives. It can do damage to relationships, which is a real problem for people collaborating on a project. Defensiveness also denies us access to the wisdom that constructive criticism offers, wisdom that would help us to make our games excellent.

Don't ever engage with any criticism that isn't constructive—that just tears down or denigrates your work. Turn away from destructive criticism and look elsewhere for the kind of helpful and useful constructive criticism that we discussed in chapter 6.

The thing I find most useful when I'm trying to evaluate playtest feedback is simply discussion with someone else who knows my game well. It could be a teammate, a peer, or a mentor. Just getting a second opinion about some contentious, troubling, or confusing piece of feedback will often immediately clarify whether it's worth spending more time on or whether we can safely dismiss it.

Playtest Feedback Evaluation Checklist

✓ Watch and listen.

✓ Write everything down.

✓ Take the feedback seriously—don't get defensive, and don't dismiss it too quickly.

✓ Can the feedback be easily categorized as (1) must fix, (2) maybe fix, or (3) a new idea?

✓ Plan to fix the must-fixes.

✓ Investigate the maybe-fixes and evaluate the new ideas, checking against your project goals.

✓ Carefully interpret what players say, using what you saw them do in gameplay as a guide.

✓ Discuss the feedback with a collaborator.

"I Like, I Wish, What If . . . ?"

"I Like, I Wish, What If . . . ?" is a technique for giving feedback effectively, developed by the design and consulting firm IDEO. It's related to the "sandwiching" we discussed in chapter 6. I learned the technique from game designer and researcher Dennis Ramirez, and it's a staple in the USC Games program. Designers can use this technique when they are playtesting each other's work, and it works for effective communication about almost any subject, including discussions about game development process or relationships between team members.

The "I Like, I Wish, What If . . . ?" technique is so simple that it barely needs any explanation. Having reviewed some creative work—maybe having playtested a game, or looked over a design document—we frame our feedback using the phrase, "I Like, I Wish, What If . . . ?" For example: "I like the game feel that this character's jump has—it controls well in the air. I wish that they got up into the air a little more quickly when the jump button is pressed. What if you shortened or removed the beginning of the jump animation?"

With "I like," we present something that we appreciated about the work. Just as in sandwiching, this opens the channels of communication and establishes a basis for respect and trust. As in sandwiching, we should choose something that we authentically like, and take the time to reflect on it, so that the person we're talking to understands that we genuinely respect them and appreciate their work. It's also useful for designers to hear what *is* working in their design.

Then, with "I wish," we begin to open up a line of constructive criticism, by saying what we would like to be different about what we are reviewing. I think that "I wish" is a clever formulation, because it accurately frames the comment as one person's opinion, and also expresses a desire rooted in an appreciation of the work. If we understand that an opinion is being given, perhaps we'll be less likely to get defensive. "I wish" is a positivistic way of saying, "I want this to be better," and appeals to designers in their ongoing and iterative work.

Finally, with "What if . . . ?" we have an opportunity to be constructively critical by offering an idea that might fulfill our wish. We might propose a solution to a problem or suggest a different design direction. Saying "What if . . . ?" and offering one of our own ideas to a designer is a generous act, and one that underlines the respect and appreciation that hopefully are present. Maybe the designer will choose to accept our idea and try it out in a future iteration. Maybe they won't accept it directly, but it will give them another idea that proves to be the right solution. Or maybe they'll reject it— it might be in conflict with another of their design goals or game mechanics.

Whatever the outcome, "What if . . . ?" is a good way to conclude a particular piece of feedback; it opens up room for a conversation about the work, since it very naturally prompts a response from the designer receiving the feedback.

IDEO, the design agency that created this technique, recognizes that communication is a key aspect of the design process, and that we need to get along well together— even during difficult conversations—if our designs are going to turn out well. The authors of the Stanford Design School *Bootcamp Bootleg* say:

> Designers rely on personal communication and, particularly, feedback, during design work. You request feedback from users about your solution concepts, and you seek feedback from colleagues about design frameworks you are developing. Outside the project itself, fellow designers need to communicate how they are working together as a team. Feedback is best given with I-statements. For example, "I sometimes feel you don't listen to me" instead of "You don't listen to a word I say." Specifically, "I like, I wish, What if" (IL/IW/WI) is a simple tool to encourage open feedback.[11]

So try "I Like, I Wish, What If . . . ?" and see how it works for you. It's a simple but sophisticated tool for becoming a more effective communicator, and for helping to create an environment of respect and trust on a team.

Playtesting for Designers and Artists

The distinction between art and design is an interesting one. Many creative people are both designers and artists, and the boundary between the utility of design and the transcendence of art is blurry at best or even nonexistent. A beautifully designed typeface, for example, certainly seems to warrant our consideration as a work of art, and many contemporary art museums house design collections.

There's a place in artmaking for an attitude of "This is my work: I do not need to explain or justify it." But contemporary artists seem increasingly interested in the ways that their work lands with people. Design and art are increasingly engaging in social advocacy, political activism, and ethical intervention. In her book *Design as an Attitude*, design critic Alice Rawsthorn highlights *integrity* as "a nonnegotiable ingredient

---

11. Thomas Both and Dave Baggeroer, "Design Thinking Bootcamp Bootleg," accessed December 10, 2020, https://dschool.stanford.edu/resources/the-bootcamp-bootleg.

of desirable design." She says, "If we have any reason to feel uncomfortable about the ethical or ecological implications of any aspect of a design project—from its development, testing, and manufacturing, to distribution, sales, marketing . . . we are unlikely to find it desirable."[12] Beyond that, art has opportunities to effect positive change in the world by highlighting injustice and suggesting more equitable futures.

I hope it's clear that playtesting has great utility as part of a game design process, whether we're designing a game that is entertaining, interesting, artistic, or driven by impact-related considerations. But I hope that the practices described in this book, including playtesting, are not just useful for game designers, interaction designers, and experience designers. I hope that they will prove equally useful to artists of all kinds, and will lead toward a richer, fuller creative practice, by fostering a deeper connection between artist and audience.

---

12. Rawsthorn, *Design as an Attitude*, 123.

13 Concentric Development

Why the Universe Is Organized into Hierarchies—a Fable

There once were two watchmakers, named Hora and Tempus. Both of them made fine watches, and they both had many customers. People dropped into their stores, and their phones rang constantly with new orders. Over the years, however, Hora prospered, while Tempus slowly became poorer and poorer. That's because Hora discovered the principle of hierarchy. . . .

The watches made by both Hora and Tempus consisted of about one thousand parts each. Tempus put his together in such a way that if he had one partly assembled and had to put it down—to answer the phone, say—it fell to pieces. When he came back to it, Tempus would have to start all over again. The more his customers phoned him, the harder it became for him to find enough uninterrupted time to finish a watch.

Hora's watches were no less complex than those of Tempus, but she put together stable subassemblies of about ten elements each. Then she put ten of these subassemblies together into a larger assembly; and ten of those assemblies constituted the whole watch. Whenever Hora had to put down a partly completed watch to answer the phone, she lost only a small part of her work. So she made her watches much faster and more efficiently than did Tempus.

Complex systems can evolve from simple systems only if there are stable intermediate forms. The resulting complex forms will naturally be hierarchic. That may explain why hierarchies are so common in the systems nature presents to us. Among all possible complex forms, hierarchies are the only ones that have had the time to evolve.[1]

What Is Concentric Development?

Concentric development is a game development strategy that helps us find solutions to a number of difficult problems that most game developers face. We have a long list of things we want to implement to make this game, but:

- What order should we build them in?
- Is this even the right list of things we need to make this game great?

---

1. Herbert A. Simon, *The Sciences of the Artificial* (Cambridge, MA: MIT Press, 1969), paraphrased by Donella H. Meadows in *Thinking in Systems: A Primer*, and by Richard Lemarchand; Meadows and Wright, *Thinking in Systems: A Primer*, 83.

- What happens if some of these things take a lot longer to build than we think? (In game development, most of what we create will take a lot longer to build than we think, because of hidden assumptions we have, things that go wrong, limits on our skill, limits in the tools, or unexpected limits on our time, like getting sick and missing a week of work.)
- What happens if we need to make major changes based on playtesting or other feedback?
- Is the game going to come together at the end? If we run out of time, are all the pieces that we have going to knit together into a coherent whole?

I first heard the term *concentric development* during a conversation with Crystal Dynamics' then–studio head John Spinale, sometime around 2002. John is best known today as managing partner and cofounder of JAZZ Venture Partners and has a background as an investor and entrepreneur in media and entertainment technology.

One day, John and I were discussing healthy approaches to building games, and how effective it is to build the core elements of a game first and then work outward. I had seen this working well as a best practice of many of the smartest teams I'd come into contact with, and John volunteered that he called this concentric development. When I got to Naughty Dog, I discovered that they too worked in this way and had been doing so for years.

What does it mean to develop games in a concentric way? Let's start with a basic definition. Concentric means starting at the center and working outward to the things that surround and support that center.

Think about a keep, the structure in the very center of a castle, where the rulers and riches are hidden away, surrounded by successive layers of curtain walls, moats, and barricades, as shown in figure 13.1. As we develop concentrically, we're going to build the keep first, to make sure that we have something worthy of support by the things that surround it. That means implementing the fundamental elements of the game

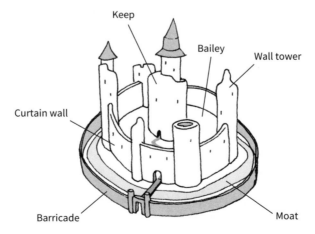

Figure 13.1
The concentric structure of a castle.

first and working on them until they are complete. These fundamental game elements are sometimes referred to by developers as the primary mechanics of the game.

Implement Primary Mechanics First until They Are Complete

It's tempting to think of a game's primary mechanics as the game elements that make up the core loop that we discussed in chapter 10. But when we're talking about concentric development, it's useful to consider an even smaller set of elements than those in the core loop, and to really focus in the one or two most fundamental mechanics in the game.

For games with a player-character that is directly controlled by the player, the three Cs of character, camera, and **only the controls that relate to movement** give us a good picture of the primary mechanics. This could be:

- The controls for movement and camera in a first-person game.
- The algorithms to move the player-character and camera around in a side-scrolling point-and-click adventure.
- The controls to move the player-character and camera around in a third-person action game.

For games without a player-character, I usually look at the mechanics that the player is directly interacting with to help me determine the game's primary mechanics. These could be:

- Moving the camera view around a map, and a single, simple click-to-interact mechanic, in a real-time strategy game.
- The most commonly used single interaction in a puzzle game.
- The basics of the text parser in a text adventure.

It's up to you, the designer, to determine what the primary mechanics are for the game you're building. Choose whatever you think will provide a solid foundation for your gameplay. It's usually not too hard to figure out your primary mechanics. For example, in *Tetris*, the primary mechanics consist of a tetromino that is falling until it comes to rest at the bottom of the screen, and the ability to move it left and right and to rotate it clockwise and counterclockwise. For *SimCity*, it could be the ability to lay either a road tile, a building tile, or a zoning area. For *The Sims*, perhaps it's just a single Sim walking around a room and interacting with a single object in the environment. For *Dance Dance Revolution*, it might be just the simplest part of the main game loop: a beat coming down a track toward you, and the ability to stamp on a pad (or press a button) just as it reaches the bottom of the screen.

Central to the philosophy of concentric development is the idea that we don't just slap these primary mechanics together, as we would do when we are prototyping. Instead, we take the time to work on them until they are complete and polished. That means creating finished art, animation, sound effects, and visual effects, and knitting them all together with good game design and code.

For a game with a player-character, there's a lot to implement to get character, camera, and controls for movement into the game. For a 2D game, we have to design a character and create frames of animation for idling and movement. For a 3D game, we have to build a model for the player-character, texture it, rig it, and create animations for idling and walking or running. We have to hook up the game's controls so that our inputs result in movement in the game, and we have to create camera control algorithms. For games without player-characters, there's similar work to do in creating art and animation assets and setting them up for controls and camera.

Even then, we're still not done if we're developing concentrically. We must also complete the sound design and visual effects design for the primary mechanics. For a game with a player-character, we'll need to add audio for footsteps, and perhaps visual effects, like puffs of dust thrown up by the footsteps. If some part of our character emits light, we'll need to set up light sources that move with them. We might need special shaders on the character model, if some aspect of their skin or clothes has an unusual or distinctive appearance.

In addition, we'll need to build some context for our primary mechanics. For games with a player-character, this is usually a place to stand and to walk around in. We could just create a blockmesh (whitebox/graybox/blockout) test level to serve this purpose. If we have time, it's better to create some background graphics that are representative of what a small part of our game might look like when it ships, and to maybe make a "beautiful corner" of the kind we discussed in chapter 10.

Again, using concentric development, we don't start implementing any secondary mechanics until the primary mechanics are *completed* to a good degree of polish and we've iterated on their design, improving the controls, animation, and game feel until this small group of primary mechanics is shippable (good enough to be released). Secondary mechanics need a solid foundation to rest on and can't be evaluated properly if they're based on primary mechanics that are still unfinished. The longer you wait to polish each mechanic, the more degrees of uncertainty creep in, and the less stable your overall design becomes. As the game designer George Kokoris once said to me, to implement secondary mechanics before the primary mechanics are properly finished would be "like putting up walls before the foundation has dried."

Once we have finished implementing the primary mechanics, we can work outward through a concentric hierarchy of mechanics, implementing and iterating on secondary mechanics and then on tertiary mechanics.

Implementing Secondary Mechanics and Tertiary Mechanics

I think of secondary mechanics as the one or two most important player activities or verbs of the game. These are often the verbs that complete the core loop of the game. For games with a player-character, these would most commonly be:

- Jumping and climbing in a game about traversal.
- The main combat actions in a game about combat.
- Speaking with other characters in a narrative game.

For games without a player-character, these might be:

- Selecting and creating buildings and units in a real-time strategy game.
- The mechanics that make it possible to complete a level in a puzzle game.
- Advanced aspects of the text parser and text presentation in a text adventure.

We implement, iterate on, and complete all the associated art, animation, audio design, visual effects, controls, and algorithms for each of our secondary mechanics, bringing them to a ready-to-ship level of polish. We work through each of our secondary mechanics in this way, one at a time, until they're all complete. Then (and only then) we can move on to implementing and iterating on our tertiary (third level) mechanics.

These tertiary mechanics will make up the "next layer out" of our game's mechanics. They are usually dependent on the primary and secondary mechanics in some way, and they flesh out the game's design. There will probably be a long list of them to implement. For a game with a player-character, they relate to everything that the player can interact with in the world: characters both enemy and friendly, tools and weapons, switches and doors, treasures and traps. Depending on your game's design, you could continue creating a hierarchy of game mechanics, down through quaternary, quinary, and senary (fourth, fifth, and sixth level) mechanics, each tier being dependent on the mechanics in the tier above it.

Only take this as far as is useful for your game's design. You may (rightfully) be suspicious of hierarchical thinking as simplistic and even oppressive, and the mechanics of some games might not have any hierarchical structure, though they will likely still be modular. The goal is to implement your game's mechanics in a rational order, always bringing things to a good level of completion, working outward from something that can provide the foundations of your game.

Concentric Development and Design Parameters

Many of the games we play have some kind of design parameters built into their design, like an invisible grid in space (sometimes also in time) that game designers use to plan their levels well. For example, how tall is the player-character? How far can they jump, both horizontally and vertically? When they throw a punch or reach out to pull a lever, how far forward can they reach?

In a 2D or 3D platform game, the placement of the platforms in a level has a critical relationship with the distances that the player-character can jump. Place the platforms too far apart, and the player won't be able to jump from one to the next. Game designers will sometimes spend a long time laying out their levels and then change their minds about how far they want the player-character to jump. Perhaps they've decided that they want to make their player-character look a little more superpowered, and so they extend the height and the horizontal distance of the jump. Suddenly, the player can easily jump to places that were previously inaccessible and can skip past whole sections of carefully designed gameplay. The designer then has to start over with the gargantuan task of level layout.

This commonly encountered problem makes a very clear argument for concentric development. The design parameters of our game's mechanics—the measurements that determine their fundamental properties—must be locked in firmly before we move on to build what we hope are the final levels of our game. Using concentric development helps us figure out these important aspects of our game's design before we move too far ahead.

Test Levels

During preproduction, create blockmesh test levels that you can use to dial in your game's design parameters and check over your mechanics. Anyone on the team can run, jump, and climb around in the test level to try out the mechanics and polish whatever they're working on.

In a character-action videogame (like the games in the *Uncharted* series), a traversal mechanic test level contains boxes, ramps, grabbable ledges, and ropes. These elements are laid out in grids showing the possible spatial relationships that they might have in the game. For example, we would place boxes to jump between, with gaps between them of 1.5 meters, 2 meters, 2.5 meters, 3 meters, and so on. You can imagine test levels for other types of game mechanic and other genres of game.

These test levels can be used as a lab or gym to fine-tune and confirm our game's design parameters as we work on our vertical slice. They can also be used as we work on the game feel and juiciness of our game's mechanics (described in chapter 22). They help us decide the degree of fun and difficulty of different arrangements of elements. Importantly, they also help us detect if something goes wrong somewhere in the code and our design parameters change slightly without our knowing—for example, if the player-character can now jump across a gap of 6.1 meters rather than 6, breaking the game.

Polish as You Go

In the world of film and theater, production value is the quality of a production in terms of the money spent on its staging, set, and appearance. (I'd argue that it's more the attention spent on these things, rather than just the money.) We can apply the term *production value* to games, too, to talk about the quality of the graphics and audio design, the visual effects and lighting, even the haptic design of the rumbling, vibrating controller or phone. When you're prototyping, production values usually don't matter much, but they do matter for a vertical slice. A quick path to good production values in a vertical slice is to polish as you go, working concentrically, completing and polishing everything in stages, working from primary to secondary to tertiary mechanics.

As the legendary UCLA basketball coach John Wooden is quoted as saying: "If you don't have time to do it right, when will you have time to do it over?"[2]

Don't Use Defaults

As you work on your vertical slice, use concentric development and make everything you build good from the get-go. Use light and sound to create an evocative sense of time, place, and mood. Don't leave any aspect of your game set to the defaults provided by your game engine, if they can be changed in a few seconds to something deliberately chosen by you. This particularly applies to the settings for the skybox or the camera background, and to the ambient lighting settings. Good designers don't use defaults. Quickly change default values to contribute something to the world you're shaping, to build context, convey information, or offer opportunities for interaction.

Polish Can Be Punk

It's a mistake to think that "polished" or "shippable" necessarily equates to "slick," "high-fidelity," "bland," or "boring." I've been critical of the game industry's historical reliance on photorealism over style. Happily, things are changing for the better, and we see a lot more variation, stylization, and experimentation in the visual aesthetics of videogames today. Beauty and interest don't come from high-end computational performance—they come from having something beautiful and interesting to express, using whatever tools are at hand.

By my definition, polished games don't have to look shiny or tidy. They can be rough, loose, abrasive, glitchy, blurry, or tarnished. People of my generation would call this a punk aesthetic. You'll have your own names for styles that make artistic, social, or political statements by rejecting mainstream aesthetics. I believe that punk styles can still be polished. Maybe "worked," "crafted," or "tooled" are better terms.

Artwork that has been worked and crafted over time, created by many iterations of systemic process at the hands of a person or a machine, often has a special quality that's hard to name but easy to recognize. It has depth and interest. Attention has gone into it, drawing and holding attention from others. So, go beyond your first implementation of your art and audio, to the second, third, or fourth iteration. That's usually when the vital stuff arrives.

---

2. "The Wizard's Wisdom: 'Woodenisms,'" ESPN, June 4, 2010, https://www.espn.com/mens -college-basketball/news/story?id=5249709.

Concentric Development, Modularity, and Systems

You might already have realized that when we practice concentric development, we are building our games in a modular way. A module is a component of a larger or more complex system. Most videogames are modular, whether we're considering the game's entities and rules or the code in which the game is written. As game designers, programmers, and architects all know, the more that a creative process can be adapted to honor the modularity of the end result, the more efficient the creative process will be, and (usually, though not always) the better the outcome will be too.

It's my belief that you can't truly evaluate a digital game or a piece of interactive media without all of its details having been implemented, because the details inform so much of what makes a game work or not. Remember industrial designers Ray and Charles Eames's advice that "the details are not the details. They make the product."[3] Think about all the detailed work that goes into creating good game feel and juiciness. It seems clear that in game design, as in all design, every last detail matters, impacting the audience's understanding, perception, and appreciation of the work. Even a single minor detail that has a negative impact can spoil the whole experience. One colorful (and profoundly gross) example of this idea is the saying, "How much poop do you mind having in your soup?"

The benefits of building in a modular way are made clear by the parable about watchmakers at the start of this chapter. If we build in modules, we can create stable intermediate forms for our project that empower us to do things like test (and then iterate on) a small part of the game early, rather than having to wait until the end to see whether what we've made is working.

In his book *Advanced Game Design: A Systems Approach*, game designer and educator Michael Sellers gives us some extra context for understanding the importance of modularity in game design. He introduces the concept of metastability, which means "stable but always changing." He says, "Something that is metastable exists in a stable form across time (typically) but is nevertheless always changing at a lower level of organization."[4] Mike goes on to say:

> The word *synergy* means "working together." It . . . was originally brought into modern usage by Buckminster Fuller, who described it as "behavior of whole systems unpredicted by the behavior of their parts taken separately" (Fuller 1975). This is another way of describing metastability, where some new *thing* arises from the combination of parts at a lower level of organization, often resulting in properties not found in the parts themselves. . . .
>
> The idea that systems are metastable things with their own properties and that they contain other, lower-level metastable things within them is one of the key points to understand for both systems thinking and game design.[5]

---

3. Daniel Ostroff, "The Details Are Not the Details," Eames Office, September 8, 2014, https://www.eamesoffice.com/blog/the-details-are-not-the-details/.
4. Sellers, *Advanced Game Design*, 42.
5. Sellers, *Advanced Game Design*, 43, quoting Fuller and Appleton, *Synergetics*, 3.

One key idea here is Buckminster Fuller's observation that "behavior of whole systems [is] unpredicted by the behavior of their parts taken separately." As we connect the modules of our game, new patterns emerge in our game's design, often coming at us out of the blue. This can cause problems—we didn't know that if we put this and that together, an undesirable thing would result! We usually give these unexpected issues names like "bug," "design problem," and "exploit," and we'll be talking about all three throughout the remainder of this book.

However, these unexpected behaviors are also sources of creative opportunity. Even if our game design seems not to be working, changing one small thing at a low level might transform it. Sometimes, something that starts out looking like a bug can become a game's best feature. The very best cases give us "emergent gameplay," where fun and interesting situations unimagined by the designer are discovered by players as they explore the possibility space of the game.

Iteration, Evaluation, and Stability

Iteration is important in the design of our games but is often challenging. It's easy to get lost in your iterative cycles if you don't go slowly and carefully. George Kokoris says he believes that "the most important thing to do when testing and iterating is to reduce the number of moving parts in each test case, the better to identify the cause-effect relationships in your changes."[6]

When we build in a modular way, we can take rests or breaks at regular intervals throughout the project, perhaps to pause and evaluate where the project is at. In addition, as the game designer Marc Wilhelm reminded me, we should consider that "on medium and especially large, industrial-scale teams . . . working modularly also allows for 'feature teams' to divide up work and contribute more focused efforts and less daunting deliverables. This can increase a sense of ownership and therefore (a sense of) commitment and pride in an individual's work and contribution to a project."

In order to work most effectively, we need to have everything in our game ready and able to be evaluated at every stage of the project, whether that evaluation is a daily playtest in our studio, a formal playtest with members of the public, or a presentation to our project's stakeholders and financial backers. For us to be able to evaluate any module of our game, every submodule has to be stable and working healthily. This is very much in line with the agile development way of doing things. As game developer and producer Alan Dang says, "By being able to evaluate at every stage, you can implement changes or change priorities to help make the game better, and make it come into line with everyone's vision."[7]

---

6. Private communication.
7. Private communication.

Concentric Development Helps Us Manage Our Time

Building in a concentric, modular way can help us get a better handle on the overall passage of time for our project. Arriving at the alpha or beta milestones, game designers often face a challenge in having to reconcile the modules of their game into a complete, coherent whole, having scoped their project down during full production. Rescoping is an inevitability for most projects—we all eventually run out of time and have to cut something from the game.

The big questions for every smart developer are: When will I realize that I'm running out of time? Will I have time left to respond to my realization? Working concentrically will help you realize sooner when things haven't come together and that time is running out. While a watchmaker might not be able to ditch a submodule of their watch, games are remarkably plastic (in the sense of being easily shaped or molded). If we discover that implementing the basics of our game unexpectedly ate up half of our overall project timeline, we still have time to think in a smart way about what we're going to include or exclude in the overall game, and how we might shift the focus of our design to draw everything together at the end.

When we build in a concentric, modular way, we are able to see earlier and more clearly when a particular module of our game isn't working, supporting the rapid prototyping credo that I mentioned in chapter 11: "Fail early, fail fast, fail often." If we think in terms of modules, not just in terms of the interconnected whole, then we're better able to ditch stuff that's failing, or that isn't so important, as early as possible. This lines up with a thought from Pixar director Andrew Stanton (*Toy Story*, *A Bug's Life*, *Finding Nemo*), which Ed Catmull and Amy Wallace describe in their book about Pixar's process, *Creativity Inc.*

> Andrew is fond of saying that people need to be wrong as fast as they can. In a battle, if you're faced with two hills and you're unsure which one to attack, he says, the right course of action is to hurry up and choose. If you find out it's the wrong hill, turn around and attack the other one. In that scenario, the only unacceptable course of action is running *between* the hills.[8]

Even if we "attack the wrong hill," and end up having to throw away some work, concentric development ensures that we've done so in a productive way, uncovering facts about our project, rather than unproductively noodling on something that didn't teach us anything.

The Switch to Concentric Development

During ideation, we usually work in a rough-and-tumble, quick-and-dirty way, slapping together prototypes to stand up working examples of the ideas that we have for

---

8. Catmull and Wallace, *Creativity, Inc.*, 97.

our game. Remember, I stressed that during ideation we're not making a little demo of our game: we're just testing individual ideas.

However, in the playful production process described in this book—when the ideation phase is complete and the preproduction phase begins—we switch to concentric development, and it can be a tough transition to make. It requires us to change both our mindset and our practical approach almost overnight.

One thing we can do to ease the transition is to make the last few prototypes that we build toward the end of ideation a little more polished. This often happens quite naturally. One of our ideation prototypes will usually have been more successful than the others. Polishing that prototype (and maybe bringing in elements from other successful prototypes) can provide a very smooth transition to working concentrically on a vertical slice.

Concentric Development and the Vertical Slice

I hope that you can now see clearly how concentric development supports our overall progress toward the end of the preproduction, when the vertical slice is due. If we work in this way, we always have a game made up of complete (or nearly complete) features, that is always playable, that looks and sounds great, and that we can easily playtest.

If we get to the date by which we had planned to complete the vertical slice, and all of our mechanics are still half-assembled, unfinished in terms of their looks and sound, and not working well, then we miss the milestone and are left struggling to make something good out of a broken mess. If we work concentrically, everything that we've managed to make when we get to the date that the vertical slice is due will be working well, and will give us a solid foundation to work with as we move into full production.

This is very much the way that we created the first three *Uncharted* games. We started to build a vertical slice, beginning with a list of features that we wanted to implement. Some came together quickly, and some took more time than we'd expected. At the end of preproduction, we had to leave some of our ideas by the wayside, for want of time. But because we worked concentrically, everything that we did build came together, giving us the basis for a good game. The ideas that we didn't use went into our mental back pocket and often made their way into our next project.

In this way, concentric development prevents us from having to go through the stressful process of rushing everything together at the very end. Less stress means better physical and mental health for the developers on our team, and it also means that our game is much more likely to be of excellent quality when it finally ships.

Concentric development isn't just useful during preproduction. It's valuable throughout full production, the next project phase after preproduction, and will support us as we progress toward the alpha milestone, when the game is "feature complete," and the beta milestone, when it's "content complete." We'll talk more about these milestones in later chapters.

Concentric Development and Agile

Concentric development was a radical idea in game development circles when I had my conversation with John Spinale in 2002. Perhaps because of the legacy of rapid prototyping—"slap it together, just make it function, leave it rough and unfinished!"—(a philosophy that is valuable during our ideation phase) it was hard for people to understand the value of shifting to this approach at the beginning of preproduction.

However, though the approach isn't always called concentric development (many people work this way without having a name for what they're doing), it's used by increasing numbers of developers, and it's become much more widely adopted since the rise of development approaches like Mark Cerny's Method and Agile.

You might already know something about Agile software development, since it's used by many game and software developers around the world. Like Method, agile development was a progressive reaction to the assembly-line ideas embodied in the "waterfall" approach to building software. It emerged via other processes like rapid application development in the 1970s and 1980s, and the rational unified process in the 1990s.[9] Agile is an approach to software development in which the design of the software being built—and the decisions about how best to build it—evolve over time through a collaboration between the development team and the project stakeholders.

Agile is an effective, creative way to approach software development. "It advocates adaptive planning, evolutionary development, early delivery, and continual improvement, and it encourages rapid and flexible response to change."[10] As summarized in "The Manifesto for Agile Software Development," Agile emphasizes:

Individuals and interactions over processes and tools

Working software over comprehensive documentation

Customer collaboration over contract negotiation

Responding to change over following a plan[11]

A rule of thumb for Agile developers is summarized by a saying older than Agile: "Treat change as an opportunity, rather than a crisis."

Modularity is built into the philosophy of Agile, as teams pick the most important modules of functionality and content and work on them in a focused way during a sprint, before stopping and reevaluating the overall course of the project in light of the things that did and didn't turn out well.

---

9. "Rapid Application Development," Wikipedia, https://en.wikipedia.org/wiki/Rapid_application_development; "Rational Unified Process," Wikipedia, https://en.wikipedia.org/wiki/Rational_Unified_Process.

10. "Agile Software Development," Wikipedia, https://en.wikipedia.org/wiki/Agile_software_development.

11. Ken Schwaber et al., "Manifesto for Agile Software Development," 2001, https://agilemanifesto.org/.

Maximizing the Amount of Work Not Done

Concentric development forces you to have an ongoing discussion about what's most important to the design of your game, as you see it on your screen today—a very Agile outlook. This not only helps your project improve but it minimizes the amount of uncontrolled overwork you might otherwise do and helps you run a more stress-free project. As my colleague in the USC Games program, interaction designer and educator Margaret Moser, says, "This frequent revisiting of priorities is how you maximize the amount of work not done (my favorite Agile principle)."[12]

What Margaret is describing here comes from one of the twelve principles behind the Agile manifesto, namely, "Simplicity—the art of maximizing the amount of work not done—is essential." This concept of "the work not done" is a tricky one. Don't we want to maximize the amount of work that we actually do? What is being said here is that we should keep a focus on what has been shown to add something to our game in terms of our project goals, our experience goal in particular. We should also remain aware of when something is not adding anything that contributes toward our project goals. If it's not adding anything, we shouldn't work on it. This is an aspect of Agile that we could summarize as "work smarter, not harder."

Referring to your project goals and experience goal regularly helps you to maximize the number of tasks that you *didn't* work on, because you realize you don't need to do them—they don't contribute to the kind of experience you're trying to create. By keeping our experience goal in mind and playtesting our game regularly, we have a good basis for evaluating each feature or piece of content as soon as it goes into the game, and for deciding if we should keep it or ditch it.

Maximizing the amount of unnecessary "work not done" should clear your decks of unneeded tasks and can help you focus on getting rested for the next day's work, or spending time with your friends, partner, or children. The time that you spend in leading a happy, fulfilling, connected life—and the good physical and mental health that results—is also an important part of your overall game design practice.

The Pace of Concentric Development

When you're working concentrically, you have to go somewhat slowly, and it might feel frustrating at first. You're doing a lot of detailed work on the boring primary mechanics, while you really want to start playing with the exciting secondary mechanics. The primary mechanics are so *basic*—surely they're going to work!

However, this enforced slowness usually (and perhaps counterintuitively) gives us more of a sense of urgency to get the primary mechanics finished, details and all, so that we can get to those other mechanics that are usually the interesting and fun parts

---

12. Private communication.

of our game. Because of this, when you're working concentrically, you're less likely to waste time noodling on insignificant aspects of your primary mechanics and are more likely to spend the right amount of time on making them good.

.ఴ   ❀   ఴ.

If you're working in a team, concentric development and modular building will require some extra effort in communication and information sharing, so that you and your teammates can evaluate what you're making, decide who will do which task next, and discuss any blockages that are preventing you from making progress. This emphasis on communication is built into agile development, with practices like the stand-up meeting, which we'll discuss in chapter 22. It's also important to discuss your game-making process on an ongoing basis. Sometimes it's not just about how your game is turning out; it's about how your process is turning out. As Alan Dang reminded me, "Being able to discuss best practices or development, ways to be efficient, etc., are part of the core principles of Agile."

You've probably realized that concentric development, and the process of ongoing scoping that it entails, might demand that you renegotiate a contract partway through development, to change its details to reflect the new scope of your project. If you'd agreed with a publisher that you'd deliver some list of features, and then realize that you can't deliver them all, you might be in hot water. Fortunately, and partly thanks to the rise of Agile, smart game publishers are increasingly realizing that a polished game with a shorter list of innovative, integrated, playable mechanics is more entertaining (and sells better) than a game that has lots of features but is buggy, unpolished, and all over the place in terms of its design. I hope that your publisher has this kind of progressive attitude, and you should try to build some reasonable degree of flexibility into your contracts. If you get into difficulty around this, you should seek out advanced project management and contract advice.

You can use concentric development for any kind of project, large or small, years-long or hours-long. It works well when you only have a fixed amount of time to make what you're making, and it also works well when your project timeline is open-ended. If you use it, it's almost guaranteed to bring your development process under better control, and to lead to games and interactive media of higher quality and more innovation made under less stress.

14 Preproduction Deliverable—The Vertical Slice

Let's talk about the vertical slice as a deliverable. (Remember, a deliverable is something that must be provided by the developers as part of a development process.) The vertical slice is one of three major deliverables that are due at the end of the preproduction phase of the project, the other two being a game design macro and a schedule. Taken together, the vertical slice and the game design macro will allow us to construct a schedule for the full production phase of the project. In our playful production process, we can't truly be said to have left preproduction until we have a vertical slice.

Delivering a Build of the Vertical Slice

We deliver the vertical slice by creating a build (see chapter 5). When delivered, the vertical slice should be relatively free of major bugs and other technical problems: the polish that we give the vertical slice should extend beyond our game design and production values to the stability of the game. No one can expect a vertical slice to be perfectly bug-free, but it would be embarrassing to have it crash repeatedly during a demo to an important group of collaborators or stakeholders. That means making time as we work on the vertical slice to keep the code healthy and working well, which is in line with the concentric development that we just discussed.

Any superfluous assets not used by the game but present in the project folder should be excluded from the build, to minimize its size. This is sometimes a pain to achieve and can involve learning new technical aspects of one's engine, but it is good to do this by the time the vertical slice is due, to help get us into the kind of optimization-oriented mindset that characterizes good game-making process. It also means there's one less thing to learn toward the end of the project, when minimizing the size of the build will be very important.

Supporting the Vertical Slice with Other Materials

If you've created your vertical slice using concentric development, it might not take long to play through, and that's okay. Quality matters more than quantity. It's often difficult to create an ideal vertical slice where all of the core elements of the game are present, playable, and polished. Whether it's because of the scope of your game's design or because you just ran out of time, you can support your vertical slice with other materials like concept art, movies, and documentation. Deliver them alongside the vertical slice in a nicely presented package, so that it's easy to understand how they represent the essential things that are missing from your vertical slice. This will be an exercise in professionalism—you want to communicate clearly and make a good impression.

Learning about Scope from the Creation of the Vertical Slice

It's wise not to ignore what we learn during preproduction about how long it takes us to build things. Attempting to build the core of our game in a timeboxed preproduction phase (see chapter 11) gives us our first major opportunity to look at the scope of our project. How much are we planning to make overall for our game? Is that realistic, based on what we've just learned about how many iterations it takes us to get to a level of quality that we're happy with? Is it already time to cut some things from the design and focus on using our game's core elements to realize our project goals in innovative new ways? In the next few chapters, we'll look at how to make a realistic plan for a game we can build in the time we have for full production.

Playtesting the Vertical Slice

Once we've delivered the vertical slice, it's time to playtest it. Run a playtest with at least seven individuals, using the guidelines and techniques that I lay out in chapter 12. Capture all the information that you can from the playtest by taking notes based on your observations of the play sessions and the exit interviews. Evaluate the feedback and iterate on your design from there.

Focus Testing Our Game's Title and Early Key Art

The end of preproduction is a good time to do some more work in figuring out how we might connect with the potential audience for our game. We can do this simply by running a focus test to research what might be a good title for our game and get some feedback on a prototype for the first piece of key art. (Key art is a single image that conveys a lot of information about your game and is used in marketing.) If you'd like to do this, you can find detailed instructions on this book's website, playfulproductionprocess.com.

Well done! You've delivered—or are well on your way to delivering—a vertical slice, which is one of the most important things you can make to define the design of your game. In the next chapter, we will take a break from our discussion of the deliverables due at the end of preproduction, to talk about a serious issue that most game developers will encounter at some point in their careers: the problem of crunch.

15   Against Crunch

Crunch, as you probably know, is the term that game developers use for a time during a project when they're working extra-long hours to hit a major milestone or to finish a project. They will often work late into the night and might work six or seven days a week. Sometimes people set out to crunch for only a few weeks but end up doing it for months or even years at a time.

I'm not proud of it, but I took part in a number of crunches during my time in the game industry, and I saw firsthand the toll that crunch can take. Extended crunch is very harmful to the health of individuals, teams, and organizations. It can damage both the physical and mental health of game developers, it can cause teams to lose morale, stop communicating, and eventually split up. It can, in the long term, destroy studios and companies.

Now, don't get me wrong: I like to work hard, and I believe that some amount of extra-hard work is needed to make most anything excellent. But there's a difference between a healthy period of pushing oneself harder in order to get things done or to hit a high bar of quality, and the kind of uncontrolled overwork that characterizes game industry crunch. It's my belief that crunch is often a symptom of a game design process that isn't working well, and this book is designed to help game developers minimize the amount of uncontrolled overwork they do, while maximizing the excellence of their game.

Managing the scope of our game, using the project phases and milestones in our playful production process, gives us a partial solution to the problem of crunch, and in the next two chapters we'll look at using a thing called a game design macro to plan a project well. Another partial solution is the attitude to our work that we hold as we progress through the project, and that's what we'll discuss in this chapter.

At the start of a project, many of us set out with good intentions, meaning to put all our energy into the full hours of a normal week, whether that's the forty or so hours of a full-time employee, or the dozen hours that a student might put into a major class project. We focus on getting the most out of our time, but for one reason or another, perhaps because of the illusion of infinite time that we have at the start of a project, the temptation is to start to take it easy, and we become less focused on making every hour productive. Also, it's hard to feel the urgency of a project when so much about what we're going to build is still unknown.

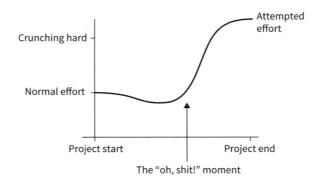

Figure 15.1
Attempted developer effort for many typical game projects.

Then, somewhere around halfway through the project, we reach what is known in the trade as the "oh, shit!" moment (figure 15.1). This is the point when we realize that we now have less time remaining for the project than has passed. We start to work harder.

And, if we're passionate but inexperienced game developers, and we're not sure how to bring our project under control, we keep working harder and harder, desperately trying to claw back the time we need to get all our planned features and content into the game. Soon we're crunching hard, working until midnight night after night and on the weekends too.

We can probably keep this up for a little while. But research shows that our productivity falls off rapidly when working extended hours, as described in a CNBC article by Bob Sullivan: "Employee output falls sharply after a 50-hour work-week, and falls off a cliff after 55 hours—so much so that someone who puts in 70 hours produces nothing more with those extra 15 hours."[1]

Losing sleep makes things worse. People who are tired are cognitively impaired: they can't find solutions to the problems they face, they make mistakes that take time to fix, and they get distracted by things that are inconsequential in the big picture of the project. In an excellent article in the *Harvard Business Review*, Sarah Green Carmichael quotes research in saying, "Most of us tire more easily than we think we do. Only 1–3% of the population can sleep five or six hours a night without suffering some performance drop-off. Moreover, for every 100 people who think they're a member of this sleepless elite, only five actually are."[2]

---

1. Bob Sullivan, "Memo to Work Martyrs: Long Hours Make You Less Productive," CNBC, January 26, 2015, https://www.cnbc.com/2015/01/26/working-more-than-50-hours-makes-you-less-productive.html.
2. Sarah Green Carmichael, "The Research Is Clear: Long Hours Backfire for People and for Companies," *Harvard Business Review*, August 19, 2015, https://hbr.org/2015/08/the-research-is-clear-long-hours-backfire-for-people-and-for-companies.

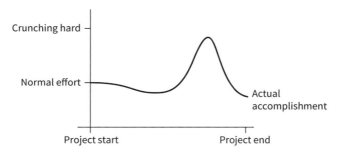

Figure 15.2
Actual developer accomplishment for many typical game projects.

So, while a crunching person is attempting to work hard, pretty soon their efforts become self-defeating. After a brief spike of productivity, most people's actual accomplishment falls to below where it would have been if they'd just kept working regular hours (figure 15.2).

There's a better way of working. If we make sure that we keep up our effort from the beginning of the project, and gradually ramp it up so that we're working hardest in the middle, instead of trying to go flat-out at the end, then we can start to bring the work under our control. If the project is special to us, we may choose to work harder than we would under regular working circumstances. But if we plan things right, we might never have to work harder than around 125 percent of normal effort and won't fall off the productivity cliff of the fifty-five-hour-plus workweek.

If we bring the scope of our project under control, we can start to combat the damage that crunch does. It takes self-discipline and is complicated by the realities of game-making, but even just setting this as a goal can be helpful to the health of teams and individuals. I feel strongly that working a little harder than normal in a controlled, sustained way leads to greater overall productivity than trying to expend a huge burst of effort in the second half of a project. Maybe it's like the fable of the hare and the tortoise: slow and steady wins the race.

In addition, if we don't slack off in the first half of the project, work as hard as we're ever going to work in the middle third of the project, and gradually ramp our effort back down again toward the end, then we won't be totally shattered as we try to ship our game. Shipping a game takes a huge amount of extraordinarily difficult, complicated work in solving design problems, fixing bugs, and overcoming technical challenges. We need to arrive at the end of the project relatively fresh and well rested.

So, figure 15.3 shows the ideal path. It's not easy to pull off in practice—it's hard to overcome the temptations of procrastination. In figure 15.4, you can see the path that many of us will probably take as the project unfolds. It's natural to increase our effort as a milestone approaches and to need a rest when a milestone is passed.

I hope you'll agree that the effort shown on the "probable effort" path, which only rises to a reasonable amount of extra intensity, is better than the flame-out of huge attempted effort and consequent burnout that most of us associate with crunch.

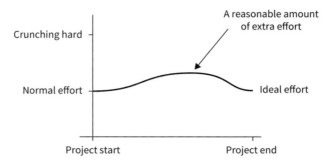

Figure 15.3
A better way for developers to expend any extra effort.

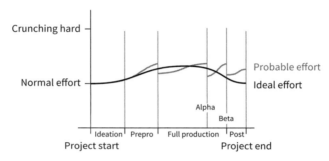

Figure 15.4
The probable effort path for developers, as they try to work in a healthier way, in relation to the major milestones of the playful production process.

   In summary, gradually increase effort throughout ideation, enter preproduction with good momentum, and maintain a calm but tangible sense of urgency. Try to keep it up through to the alpha milestone. After that, if everything goes well, and if you remain in control of your project's scope, you may be able to bring your effort down in stages as you reach each milestone. While I can't promise that you'll coast across the finish line, you should have energy left to finish, submit, and promote your game.

Even though we've made great improvements over the last ten years, the game industry still has a difficult problem with crunch. The adrenaline and excitement of crunch, and the joy of making something amazing at the end, makes it very addictive. Just like any addiction, it comes with a terrible cost of negative effects on physical and mental health, strained intimate relationships, parents not being present for important moments in their children's lives, and, ultimately, people leaving the game industry, taking with them all their hard-won wisdom and expertise.

   Crunch comes in many forms, most of them damaging. Among the worst is the problem of "moving goalposts," when the final milestone of a project gets repeatedly postponed. This kind of project management strategy—of giving a project more time when it's clear that not everything will get done—is a natural response when you're trying to finish a project. Trouble comes with the fact that our team members simply can't pace themselves. We work hard to hit the milestone, which then gets moved further away, and we work even harder to try to hit it. If it gets moved again, we become trapped in a cycle of exhaustion and effort. Our tiredness leads us to make increasing numbers of mistakes and bad decisions, ultimately slowing the project down even further. It's a vicious cycle, and one that underlies a lot of game industry crunch.

But there is cause for hope. We can overcome the problem of moving goalposts by using timeboxing and by checking the scope of our project early and often throughout development. As Alan Dang reminded me, we have to admit when our estimates about how long things would take were wrong, and rescope as early as possible. The techniques and methods described in this book are designed to help us to avoid crunch in all its forms, and Agile methodologies serve the same goal.

I want to acknowledge that it's easier to argue against crunch or reject a working lifestyle that involves crunch when coming from a position of privilege, like the privilege that I've enjoyed throughout my life because of my gender, ethnicity, and socioeconomic background. People who are marginalized often have to work twice as hard to receive the same rewards as someone with unearned privilege. That's why I see it as my duty to speak out about crunch and try to effect some change.

Crunch is not a problem confined to the game industry. You'll find it across the tech industry and the entertainment industry, in other industries, in medicine, and in government. Perhaps the best way for us to approach the problem of crunch is to think philosophically about our lives. What do we want? What makes us happy? What makes us healthy? How can we benefit the world (and ourselves) without doing harm?

I believe that balance in all things is important, and that while hard work is usually needed to make excellent art, we also need a diversity of life experience to draw on, if our art is to have meaning. Work has given my life great meaning, but there's more to my life than work. Devote yourself to finding the right balance in *your* life, so that you can work hard without crunching, and achieve excellence without harming yourself or those around you.

I was around in the game industry when the problem of crunch was at its worst. And I've seen things start to get better, as people simply began to discuss the problem and to figure out how to address it. You can contribute to a future with less crunch by talking about it with your teammates, your professional peers, and your friends, and by adopting better and more sustainable development practices that don't burn people out, but that still lead to great games.

Storytelling is the study of change.
—Irving Belateche[1]

I'm fascinated by the relationship between games and stories. In my career, I chose mostly to work on storytelling games, like *Uncharted* and *Soul Reaver*. I never really met a form of storytelling or play that I didn't like, and when I joined the game industry in 1991, part of my excitement about game design as an emerging art form was focused on the possibility and promise of interactive storytelling, from the reality of *The Secret of Monkey Island* to the fantasy of the *Star Trek* holodeck.

Not every game has or needs a story. But most games have some kind of narrative shape or arc, if you accept that our minds make sense of the world by telling stories about it. We mentally order events into sequences of cause and effect, even when some of the events seem random. Looked at in this light, a round of chess and a basketball game both have a narrative aspect.

In the following chapters, we're going to discuss the process of planning a game's design using a game design macro. A consideration of the narrative shape of games is a useful way to get into this planning, so in this chapter we'll take a look at some story structure fundamentals, with an eye to reconciling our views of story and games.

Aristotle's *Poetics*

The Greek philosopher Aristotle lived from 384 to 322 BCE. Around 335 BCE he wrote a treatise on dramatic performance in the theater called the *Poetics*. This is the earliest known work of dramatic theory and was lost to the Western world for over a thousand years, being reintroduced thanks to a twelfth-century translation by the Spanish-Muslim philosopher Ibn Rushd.

---

1. Irving Belateche, "Film Script Analysis: *Back to the Future*," class lecture, John Wells Division of Writing for Screen & Television, USC School of Cinematic Arts, Los Angeles, June 11, 2018.

In the *Poetics*, Aristotle writes that a story first states a position, then explores that position, and then reaches a conclusion, to create "a representation of an action that is whole and entire," with a cause-and-effect relationship between the parts. Put more simply, "A whole is something that has a beginning, a middle, and an end."[2]

For Aristotle, the heroes of stories face some problem, which he characterizes as a "knot." He divides stories into two halves: complication and unraveling. In the complication phase, the hero either learns about the problem or watches the problem appear. In the unraveling half, the hero tries to deal with the problem, leading to some ultimate outcome.

The three-part structure of Aristotle's *Poetics* fits well onto the three-act structure of many contemporary screenplays and novels. Act one, the beginning, sets up the story by introducing us to the characters and world; act two, the middle, is usually twice as long as act one and shows us how the story becomes more complicated as it unfolds; act three, the end, is often the shortest act and shows the climax and resolution of the story. A two-hour feature film might have a three-act structure, but so might an hour-long episode of a television series. Even a ten-minute short film might be set up in three acts.

This simple construction of beginning-middle-end seems directly applicable to games, whether they're competitive games like those we've been playing for thousands of years, or the storytelling "campaign" mode of modern single-player digital games (and most every game between these two poles). A game has a beginning when the teams kick off or the player-character sets out on their journey. Things become increasingly complicated in the middle part of a game, as the teams vie for the lead or the player-character progresses along their journey. All games—unless they're abandoned—reach an end, when time's up and one team wins, or when the player-character reaches the end of their quest (for now, at least).

Freytag's Pyramid

In 1863, the German playwright and novelist Gustav Freytag wrote a book called *Die Technik des Dramas* (Technique of the drama), in which he laid out a theory of a five-part dramatic structure. The diagram that accompanies his theory is familiar to students of drama and cinema and is known as Freytag's Pyramid (figure 16.1).

Freytag's theory builds on Aristotle's three-part structure and gives us some extra equipment to work with. For Freytag, a story consists of five parts.

1. The **exposition** or introduction, where the world and the main characters of the story are explained or set up. This is when the time and place of the story are established, along with its mood or tone.

---

2. Aristotle, *Poetics*, 26.

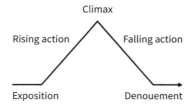

Figure 16.1
Freytag's Pyramid.

2. The **rising action**, where the unfolding complications of the story take place. This is a very important part of the story, because its events need to logically flow so as to carefully set up the next part.

3. The rising action peaks with a **climax**, where all of the complications come to a head, providing a turning point where the characters' fates are fundamentally changed.

4. The climax is followed by the **falling action**, where the results of the climax are played out. The falling action will often contain one last moment of suspense, where the final outcome seems uncertain.

5. Finally, we reach the **denouement** or **catastrophe**, where we see how the world of the story has undergone lasting change, because of the events of our tale. The characters begin to get used to this change, and this results in catharsis, an emotional release of all the tension and anxiety that built up in the audience during the story.

Like Aristotle's *Poetics*, Freytag's five-part structure fits with the way that many stories are written and told. Most of Shakespeare's plays take place in five acts, and in his book *Into the Woods: A Five-Act Journey into Story* the television producer and script editor John Yorke argues that a five-act analysis is useful for stories across all dramatic forms, including games.

Game Structures Mirror Story Structure

This focus that both Aristotle and Freytag have on the importance of a beginning, middle, and end is a good starting point for our discussion of story structure through a game design lens. As Ellen Lupton points out in her book *Design Is Storytelling*, we all recognize this fundamental structure in our own lives, which inevitably have a beginning, a middle, and an end.[3]

A well-designed game is undeniably dramatic, with moments of excitement, elation, and despair, and with patterns of rising tension and cathartic release. In addition, many videogames are structured around missions or quests, all of which have, by necessity, a beginning, middle, and end. At the beginning, the player-character might

---

3. Lupton, *Design Is Storytelling*, 21.

receive either an explicit mission from a nonplayer character (NPC), or an implicit mission in the form of a locked door with a conspicuous keyhole (exposition, in Freytag's terms). The player (via the player-character) sets out into the world of the game, looking for the object or information that will fulfill the mission; obstacles arise, and must be overcome (rising action).

Eventually, things come to a head: a monster must be defeated or a problem solved in order to gain the thing needed to fulfill the mission (climax). There's sometimes a journey back to the NPC that issued the quest, or to the door that needed a key, and events continue to unfold: maybe a surprise attack by more monsters or a rockfall that blocks the way, necessitating the discovery of a new path (falling action). Finally, the mission is complete (dénouement). The NPC hands over some valuable trinket, or the door opens, revealing the path forward to a new quest.

Stories and Gameplay Are Fractal

So, a story can be broken down into three or five acts. Similarly, acts can be broken down into sequences. Frank Daniel was a film director, producer, screenwriter, and a dean of the USC School of Cinematic Arts. He is famous for teaching a "sequence structure" approach to screenwriting, which sees a film as made up of eight sequences: two for the first act, four for the second act, and two for the third act.

In his book *Screenwriting: The Sequence Approach*, Paul Joseph Gulino, who learned screenwriting from Frank Daniel, says, "A typical two-hour film is composed of sequences—eight- to fifteen-minute segments that have their own internal structure—in effect, shorter films built inside the larger film. To a significant extent, each sequence has its own protagonist, tension, rising action, and resolution—just like a film as a whole. The difference between a sequence and a stand-alone fifteen-minute film is that the conflicts and issues raised in a sequence are only partially resolved within the sequence, and when they are resolved, the resolution often opens up new issues, which in turn become the subject of subsequent sequences."[4] Or as Tracy Fullerton puts it: "A sequence asks a dramatic question and answers it, but does not necessarily resolve it. Will the detective take the case? Will she find any clues at the murder site?"[5]

Similarly, a sequence can be broken down into a number of scenes, each of which usually takes place in a separate location or focuses on a particular constellation of characters. Like a sequence, a scene is its own kind of stand-alone story that shows characters going through changes as they act and react to the unfolding events and to each other.

But a scene is not the smallest unit of dramatic action in a story: we can break a scene down into a number of beats. A beat is a concept from the theater and from

---

4. Gulino, *Screenwriting*, 2.
5. Private communication, May 25, 2020.

filmmaking, relating partly to the timing of the unfolding drama, but also referring to an event, a decision, a discovery, or just an exchange between two characters. Beats push a story along on a moment-by-moment basis.

It can be useful when thinking about scenes and beats to think about the emotional valences of the characters as they enter and leave the scene or the beat. *Emotional valence* is a term used in psychology to discuss the up-ness or down-ness of emotions. Emotions like anger, sadness, and fear have negative valence, while joy has a positive valence. A scene or a beat usually has characters come together with certain emotional valences—say, one happy and the other sad—and then they bounce off each other, having an emotional interaction and changing their valences in the process—the one that was sad is now happy and vice versa. If a scene leaves the characters with the same valences they had when they entered it, then perhaps that scene isn't serving the story.

So, stories, acts, sequences, scenes, and beats. It seems clear that the shapes of whole stories that Aristotle and Freytag describe also apply to the subparts of stories, and their sub-subparts, right down to the level of the beat. Each beat in a scene has a rising and falling pattern of complication and unraveling, of call and response. This undulating pattern keeps us interested from moment to moment and hour to hour, just as we might be transfixed by the flickering flames in a hearth or the waves on the shore.

In this way, stories are *fractal*, a concept from mathematics that describes structures whose parts and subparts are similar in shape to the whole structure. As the action rises and falls across the story, so it rises and falls across each act, sequence, scene, and beat (figure 16.2). (This idea probably originates with the "Dramatica" model of story structure developed in the 1990s by Melanie Anne Phillips and Chris Huntley.)[6]

It only takes a small leap of imagination to see that games are fractal in their structure too. We just looked at how a game mission has the same structure as Freytag's Pyramid. Now you can probably imagine the same rising and falling pattern in a subsection of the whole mission or in a sub-subsection, in a way that is reminiscent of Jaime Griesemer's concept of the thirty seconds of fun in *Halo*, which we talked about in chapter 10.

Jaime's thirty seconds of fun describes a number of different individual gameplay beats. Enter a new level and hunker down behind cover. Fight each enemy. Work between cover spots, collecting power-ups as we go. Each of these beats rises and falls, adding up to overall progression through each part of the game, and eventually through the whole game.

We can easily see this fractal pattern in competitive games and sports as well, which are structured around halves and quarters, sets and matches, rounds and series. We can even use the fractal concept to reach upward toward the "meta" of competitive digital gaming and of sports: a metagame of tactics, strategies, and player or team relationships.

---

6. Phillips and Huntley, *Dramatica*.

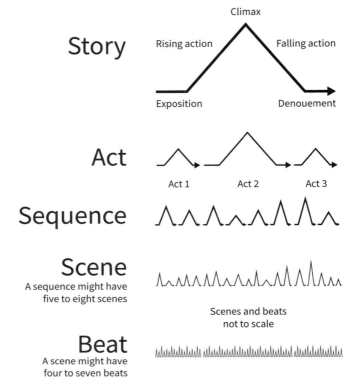

Figure 16.2
The fractal structure of a feature film story.

Everywhere we look at story structure, we can find correspondences that are valuable to our thinking about the design of our games.

The Components of Story

Now that we've looked at some story structure basics, let's take a slightly deeper dive into the components that make up most of the stories we know and love.

Most stories have a **protagonist**, the hero of the story, whose viewpoint we are closely aligned with from a practical and emotional standpoint. The storyteller uses techniques of **empathy and sympathy** to get us to resonate with the hero of the story, and those techniques are many and varied. A filmmaker uses close-ups of facial expression and emotive music to build an emotional bridge between us and the protagonist. A novelist often uses the inner voice of the protagonist. Game designers are free to choose how to bring us emotionally close to player-character protagonists, but we have to work hard at it, since facial close-ups and inner monologues are often hard to incorporate elegantly into our designs. Many great stories have more than one protagonist, and some video-games have more than one player-character.

Most stories also have an **antagonist**, perhaps an enemy, who does something to provide the **main tension** or **core conflict** that will drive the story. Many games pit the player against enemies that must be defeated, but the core conflict need not come from people or monsters; it could be a state of affairs in the world, like a race against time. The main tension can have a very positive impact on both story and gameplay, focusing the player's mind and building excitement.

Conflict's relationship to storytelling can be a hot-button topic. The author Ursula K. Le Guin wrote, "Modernist manuals of writing often conflate story with conflict. This reductionism reflects a culture that inflates aggression and competition while cultivating ignorance of other behavioral options. . . . Conflict is one kind of behavior. There are others, equally important in any human life, such as relating, finding, losing, bearing, discovering, parting, changing."[7] This list of behaviors is a gift to any game designer seeking to explore new frontiers of gameplay.

I agree that conflict's role in storytelling has been overemphasized and brings baggage with it. But I also believe that people who want to deemphasize conflict in their storytelling have to work *very* hard to create interest in other ways if they're going to hold their audience's attention.

The through line of a story is often provided by something that the protagonist longs for, which some storytellers term an **external desire** or a **want**. The steps that the protagonist takes to get that thing, set against the greater context of their **life's dream**, propels them through the story, bringing them into contact with the interesting characters and scenarios that will make up the body of the story. In the course of trying to achieve their goal, the protagonist usually struggles with something harder to see or to name, something to do with their character, their limitations, and their personal growth. Some storytellers call this an **internal desire** or a **need**, and the ways in which the protagonist deals with this hidden desire, to grow, to get past something, to become someone new, often contain the true meaning of the story.

The first part of the story usually sees the protagonist at home, amid the **status quo** of whatever is the **ordinary world**, for them. Then something happens that begins to propel them into the story: this is known as the **inciting incident**. The protagonist might resist at first, but eventually they embark on a **journey** that sees them encounter novel or challenging situations and **characters**, which they move through and relate to in ways that we find interesting to see or hear about. They're on this journey trying to get to their external desire, of course, but as they move along, their internal desire is tested or activated in various ways, diverting their journey in new and interesting directions. The storyteller will use techniques like **foreshadowing** to prime us for what's to come, and **plants and payoffs** to string us along through the story. They'll use **reversals** to surprise us and **reveals** to satisfy us. They might occasionally

---

7. Le Guin, *Steering the Craft*, 146.

use **red herrings** to divert our attention or a **MacGuffin** to create story impetus and continuity.

In many stories, the protagonist's situation eventually reaches a **crisis**. It seems like all is lost; the protagonist's external desire can never be attained. But often the protagonist's personal growth in relation to their inner desire is pushed to the fore in this moment, and their actions cause a **climax** to be reached. We see everything come to a head at this point of great dramatic intensity and discover how things will play out. The final result of the protagonist's journey is shown in the **resolution**, as it affects the people in their lives and the world they live in.

This brief summary of story structure uses terms from a variety of sources, and I'm indebted to my colleagues Irving Belateche and Jack Epps Jr. for many of them. There are many approaches to story structure that you can read about and use. Perhaps the most famous of them is the hero's journey, originated by Joseph Campbell in his book *The Hero with a Thousand Faces* and popularized by Christopher Vogler's *The Writer's Journey: Mythic Structure for Writers*. The hero's journey is a good starter story structure for game designers, since it maps easily onto the quest-based structure of many of our games. Be warned that inexpert use of the hero's journey can lead to clichéd and hackneyed stories, rife with the problems that any "savior myth" smuggles on board. In the right hands, it can also lead to great artworks, like thatgamecompany's *Journey*.

Blake Snyder's *Save the Cat!* is a good beginner's guide to structuring stories, and Jack Epps's book *Screenwriting Is Rewriting: The Art and Craft of Professional Revision* will teach you a lot about the iterative nature of good writing. You can discover many more excellent books on story structure and writing through your own research. To see the very many terms used by different story structure experts, refer to Ingrid Sundberg's "Arch Plot Structure" which you can find online, and which includes a diagram clearly showing the many different names used to refer to the elements I've described above, along with their sources.[8]

You might feel skeptical and wonder where we get this set of storytelling fundamentals from. Many great storytellers don't care for discussions of story structure. They just sit down and start writing, relying on their abilities to describe people and events in a clear and interesting way, to get us to feel things for imaginary people, to make us laugh or cry, and to keep us riveted to their unfolding tale.

But for game designers, it's my belief that we need some basic understanding of the structures of story if we are to line up the rising and falling energies of gameplay and story in a successful way. The components that I've described above offer a jumping-off point for your own game design and storytelling practice. Like every storyteller, you are free to pick and choose, to mix and match, to try new things. You may advance in your storytelling craft more quickly if you follow this tried-and-tested pattern, or

---

8. Ingrid Sundberg, "What Is Arch Plot and Classic Design?," June 5, 2013, https://ingridsundberg .com/2013/06/05/what-is-arch-plot-and-classic-design/.

maybe you'll find amazing new ways of holding your players spellbound that have not yet been considered.

How to Improve the Stories in Your Games

There are whole books dedicated to the craft of storytelling and the narrative design of games, and you should certainly strive to hone your own skills as a writer, storyteller, and narrative designer. However, the best thing that you can do in the short term to improve the stories in your games is very simple: collaborate with a writer.

Unless you have a history of successful creative writing, don't make the mistake of hubris that many game designers (including me) have made, and try to write your game without expert help. Writing well is incredibly difficult. It requires the insight of a psychotherapist, the detail-orientation of a sociologist, the lyricism of a poet, and the joke-writing ability of a stand-up comic. The chances are that, wherever you live in the world, you're within a mile or ten of not just one great writer but a whole community of them—people with a good ear for dialogue (one of the hardest things to write, in my experience), a love of videogames, and monthly rent to pay.

It used to be hard to find writers who understand game design or could learn to understand it. Nowadays, both things are much easier because so many of us have grown up playing and loving videogames. You should expect to spend some time working with your writer to help them understand how your particular game works, what its needs are, and how they can fit into your creative process. But usually that investment of time pays dividends not only in terms of great characters, plot, and dialogue but also yielding fresh new game design ideas.

Find your writer very early—ideally, at the beginning of your project. The more that a writer is embedded in the design team and integrated into the overall design process, the better everything will be for everyone on the team and for the resulting game. Games that have story retrofitted onto a preexisting game design only occasionally turn out well. That said, don't panic if you only find your writer late in development. Great writers can work magic, and a "punch up pass" just to polish a game's dialogue can be completely transformative.

You should expect to work with your writer or writers throughout the entire development process. There will be times when they are very busy, and other times when there is little for them to do. Depending on the type of game that you're developing, there may come a time well before the project is complete when the writer's work is finished. But in my game development experience, new writing jobs appear all the time throughout development, in environmental narrative (the text on a poster or billboard in a level, or the writing on an in-game object), in interface design (the names and descriptive "flavor text" of collectible objects), and in materials outside of the game but related to the player's experience, like development blog entries and social media posts, advertising copy, and trailer voiceover dialogue.

Perhaps most importantly, your game's writer should be empowered to make creative decisions. A game writer who isn't invested with some clout on a team will always have their wise decisions stomped on by others, which leads to a game where gameplay and story don't hang together well. The game's director should support the writer—not blindly or unconditionally, but in a way that lets everyone on the team know that their work is to be respected, because it impacts the player's experience in a fundamental way.

When in Doubt . . .

Storytelling is a complicated business. Some people devote their whole lives to its craft. As a game designer, you might not be at all interested in story, and that's fine. Game design is a vastly expansive cultural form, and not every game needs a story.

However, I stand by my thought that our minds, in much of their regular functioning, make sense of our lives by creating narratives. Even if a game doesn't have a story, it certainly has some kind of narrative. Chess doesn't have a story, but the fact that a knight is shaped like a horse is a narrative element, and the push and pull between two players or two teams has a narrative shape.

So, when considering the narrative structure of your game, look to Aristotle, and when in doubt, just give your game (and every part of it) a good beginning, a good middle, and a good end. This might sound obvious, but you'd be amazed at how many games I play (and some that I've made) whose stories have a great beginning and middle, but a weak ending. You'd be unlikely to create a competitive game whose matches had a beginning and middle but no end (even though that sounds like a great prompt for a piece of experimental game design), so show the same respect to your storytelling games.

That's not to say that great stories must have a tidy ending that resolves completely. Open endings in stories, where the audience is left to draw their own conclusions about what ultimately happens, can be just as interesting and satisfying as closed endings, where there is no doubt as to the outcome. Just make sure to close your game in a way that fits what came before and respects the time that your audience of players has given you.

In the next chapter, we'll look at how we can plan the rising and falling patterns of gameplay and story using a kind of lightweight game design document called a game design macro. We can then use this macro to schedule the creation of the game in the phase of our process called full production.

17 Preproduction Deliverable—The Game Design Macro

A game design document is a record of the planned design of a game. In the early days of the game industry, great emphasis was placed on the game design document as *the* source of a game's design. Game designers spent time writing huge game design documents before much game development work had been done by the rest of the team. Hardly anyone read these slabs of paper, and they would eventually get thrown out once the realities of the game revealed themselves during development. These days, games are generally designed in tandem with the creation of a vertical slice, with designers creating just enough documentation as they go along. This works much better.

Game design documentation *is* necessary and important. In particular, during preproduction we do need to make a plan for the project phase that comes next: full production. The challenge is to create a game design document that has just enough detail but not too much. In this chapter, we'll look at Mark Cerny's conception of the game design macro and how it can be used by designers to get a handle on the scope of their games.

Making a Map for Full Production

> I wisely started with a map, and made the story fit. . . . The other way about lands one in confusions and impossibilities.
> —J. R. R. Tolkien, *The Letters of J. R. R. Tolkien: A Selection*, 177.

Tolkien wrote *The Lord of the Rings* by first devising a map of Middle Earth, the setting for his epic fantasy, with "meticulous care for distances."[1] The story of the quest to return the One Ring to Mordor hinges on how quickly people, animals, objects, and information can move across the land. By setting a map into place before he began writing, Tolkien was able to be certain about a crucial aspect of his tale—distance—and was able to create his complex and highly structured story.

---

1. Tolkien, *The Letters of J. R. R. Tolkien*, 177.

Consider an overview map of the whole British Isles. You can see the big cities and larger towns, some mountains and forests, and the motorways and major roads—but you can't see Big Ben, or Edinburgh Castle, or the little town in north Gloucestershire where I grew up. However, you can plan a journey across Britain using a map like this, and you can figure out the details of your travels as you go along.

The game design macro is like this: it's an overview map of our game's design that we can use to navigate through full production. Using a game design macro, we can find the best path to our goal of an excellent, polished, finished game. It will help guide our creativity and prevent us from going around in circles.

Why Use a Game Design Macro?

A game design macro is a stripped-down game design document. It's a matrix of ideas that represents an overview of our game's design. It lists all the important aspects of our game in a compact way, giving us enough information to be able to steer the project. It doesn't dwell on details, because they are prone to change as we make discoveries while working on our game. We should be able to see at a glance from the game design macro important quantitative aspects of the project: how many levels or locations the game has, how many characters, how many major object types, and so on.

The concept of the game design macro comes from Mark Cerny, who discusses it in his 2002 D.I.C.E talk about the approach to digital game development that he dubbed Method.

> In Method, traditional design documentation is completely discarded. Instead, the design is split into macro and micro designs. The macro design is a five-page document that gives the framework that your game fits into and is a deliverable at the end of preproduction. The micro design is what your game is and is created on the fly during production. By separating these two, you can make a creative game that is still coherent and fun to play.
>
> The macro design is completed by the end of preproduction. The micro design is created during production. . . . This methodology is the result of one of the most dangerous myths in game development: "The more defined your initial vision, the better."[2]

Mark goes on to criticize the idea that we need to write a hundred-page game design document before we start making our game. He tells us that not only do we not need this document to start our game, we don't need it *ever*. Writing such a document is a waste of resources and lulls you into thinking that you know more than you actually do. And, as Mark Cerny says, "No matter how great it is, I guarantee you: no player will ever enjoy your game design document."[3]

We do have to create some documentation, though—we can't fly blind into full production. We need a map. We base the macro on what we discover when we create

---

2. Mark Cerny, "D.I.C.E. Summit 2002," https://www.youtube.com/watch?v=QOAW9ioWAvE, 28:51.
3. Cerny, "D.I.C.E. Summit 2002," 28:58.

our vertical slice. It contains the design information and design decisions that we need to enter full production, and no more.

Mark Cerny told me that the idea of the game design macro was invented for *Crash Bandicoot 2: Cortex Strikes Back*. I learned about the game design macro in detail by studying the one that had been written for *Jak 3*, a project that I worked on toward its end. I then went on to contribute to the macros as a lead game designer for *Jak X: Combat Racing* and for all three of the *Uncharted* games that I worked on. I believe that the good quality of the games created by Naughty Dog, Insomniac Games, and other studios that use the technique clearly shows the usefulness of the game design macro.[4]

The Game Design Macro and Our Project Goals

The game design macro has an important relationship with the project goals that we discussed in chapter 7. You can consider the macro to be an expansion and a more detailed definition of the experience goal and design goals that we set out in our project goals.

Sometimes, our project goals can change partway through preproduction. This might happen because the game that emerges from our work on the vertical slice didn't exactly match our project goals but was compelling enough that we wanted to follow a new direction. When that happens, it's important to revise your project goals before starting work on the game design macro. At the very latest, if you're going to lock in new project goals, you should do so by the end of preproduction, at the same time as you complete the macro. We always want to keep our vision coherent by having our project goals and game design macro line up nicely as we head into full production.

The Two Parts of a Game Design Macro

In his D.I.C.E. talk, Mark Cerny describes the game design macro as having two parts. The first part is a short game design overview summarizing the core elements of the game: the fundamental elements of gameplay, the most important of the game's special mechanics, and a brief outline of the game's plot.

The second part of the macro is a macro chart, which is a spreadsheet or table that gives a step-by-step breakdown of the levels of the game, and the action, activities, and story beats that take place within each level. This second part typically takes a lot more design effort to create, and at Naughty Dog, the terms *macro chart* and *game design macro* became pretty much synonymous.

---

4. Ted Price, "Postmortem: Insomniac Games' *Ratchet & Clank*," Gamasutra, June 13, 2003, https://www.gamasutra.com/view/feature/131251/postmortem_insomniac_games_.php.

The Game Design Overview

Professional game development teams should create a game design overview document during or after the creation of their vertical slice. Again, it should be a relatively short document: between five and twenty pages depending on the scale of the project. It should contain an introduction to all the most important game design and narrative elements in the game, along with other important aspects of the game's direction.

It should describe the "three Cs" of character, camera, and control that we discussed in chapter 10, and should discuss the major game mechanics, verbs, and player activities of the game. For a game that has them, it should introduce the important characters in the game along with an overview of the game's plot (if it has a story). It should show or describe the art direction, sound design, music, and graphic design planned for the game, and should set out the tone and mood of the game.

The game design overview is an important part of the game design macro and helps the creative leadership of the team represent their ideas to their team members, their project stakeholders, and any other interested parties. As such, it represents a kind of social contract about the design elements that we see in the vertical slice.

(In my fifteen-week, single-semester classes, I do not have my students create a game design overview. We can easily see, hear, and play the three Cs, core gameplay, and aesthetic direction of their games in their vertical slices, and I don't want to make busywork for them during what is likely to be one of the most intense phases of their game's development. However, if my class lasted a full academic year, I would certainly have my students write a game design overview document as an exercise in creating clear, compelling game design documentation and in setting direction for their game.)

The Game Design Macro Chart

The game design macro chart is made by thinking through the experience flow of a game in detail and writing it down in a spreadsheet. This is the most difficult part of creating a game design macro and also the most valuable. It helps us to reach an agreement about what's going in our game and is an important step toward bringing the scope of our project under control.

The game design macro chart is made up of ten or more spreadsheet columns and as many rows are needed to describe the game in just enough detail.

In this spreadsheet, we have to describe (in Mark Cerny's words) "what sort of gameplay goes where in the game." We also have to take note that "every mechanic that you intend to use should be in this chart." What we're aiming for in creating the game design macro is "a knowledge of the planned variety of the game, the scope of the game, its high-level structure."[5]

---

5. Cerny, "D.I.C.E. Summit 2002," 31:54.

The vertical axis of the spreadsheet represents time, with the earliest part of the game at the top, and the end of the game at the bottom. (Later in this chapter I'll talk about how to use a macro to handle nonlinear games.) The columns along the horizontal axis of the spreadsheet are used to list out information important to the design of each part of the game.

The game design macro for *Uncharted 2: Among Thieves* was a spreadsheet around seventy rows long, and it showed the structure of the game that we shipped a year and a half later almost exactly, to within 5 or 10 percent. So, the macro chart is more concrete than any hundred-page game design ever written during preproduction. It pins important details into place, but it has enough of a level of abstraction that you don't waste time devising design elements that later get changed.

The Rows and Columns of the Game Design Macro Chart

Let's start to break down the game design macro chart in greater detail. We'll start with an example that Mark Cerny gives in his D.I.C.E. talk.

Each row describes one of the levels. The relevant information changes from game to game, but in (one possible) case, it's the locale of the level, whether it's a 3D or 2D level, what "exotic" gameplay it contains, what the player must have collected in order to enter the level. And finally, what objects can be collected in the level.[6]

Mark's example comes from a time when games were smaller. Today, a single row in a game design macro chart would only describe one small part of a level. But Mark gives us a good starting point to think about each row of the macro.

Each row should describe:

- The environment of that part of the game
- The objects and characters in the environment
- The type of gameplay taking place there
- What the player has to do or could do there

For games with a narrative component, the row should also describe what happens from a story point of view.

Every game is different. When I joined USC, I knew that I wanted to bring the game design macro to my students as a better way of making game design documentation. But I was hesitant at first: could the macro be used to describe a wide variety of games, not just the kind of character-action storytelling games that I had worked on?

Happily, I've discovered that the answer to this question is a resounding yes. The design of most every type of game benefits from being summarized in a spreadsheet at

---

6. Cerny, "D.I.C.E. Summit 2002," 31:54.

the end of preproduction. Creating a game design macro chart is a great way of examining any game's structure and getting a handle on its scope.

A Game Design Macro Chart Template

Figure 17.1 is a template to help you get started in creating a game design macro chart. The template is really just a spreadsheet, with a heading for each column. Add as many rows as you need to describe your game.

Different styles of game might need different game design macro chart headings, but this set is a good starting point. Feel free to create headings that match your needs. Here's a description of most of the columns, apart from Player Goal, Design Goal, and Emotional Beat, which I'll describe in detail in their own section at the end.

Location/Sequence Name
The leftmost column gives us a title for this row, by describing where the events of the row take place. It might be "at the bottom of an old well" or "inside the airlock." I can imagine a game without locations or where gameplay events aren't strictly tied to locations, which is why I offer the alternative "sequence name" for this heading.

Time of Day/Weather/Mood
Daybreak, morning, afternoon, dusk, or night? Fine, sweltering, or stormy? Otherwise, what is the mood of this row? This column is useful to art directors creating "color scripts" to plan the color palette and mood progression through a game.

Location/ Sequence name	Time of day/ Weather/ Mood	Brief description of events	Player mechanics	Player goal	Design goal	Emotional beat	Characters encountered (including enemies)	Objects encountered	Other assets needed	Audio notes	Visual effects notes

Figure 17.1
A game design macro chart template.

Brief Description of Events

In a nutshell, what happens here, from both a gameplay and story perspective? This is a place to give a very brief overview that will be supplemented by the other columns in this row.

Player Mechanics

What mechanics are available for the player to use in this part of the game? They should be listed out for every section where they're available, even if you don't expect the player to use them all. Listing the player mechanics will act as a reminder of what the player has learned to do and *could* do. It might also suggest design opportunities for that part of the game.

Use color-coding or bolding to show when mechanics are being newly introduced. You could even list new mechanics in their own separate column. It's very useful to see whether this part of the game has to spend time introducing and practicing something new. Some games take away game mechanics after they've been introduced, and you could indicate that here too.

If a game jumps between multiple player-characters over time, you could indicate which player-character is being used in this column or—even better—break out that information into a separate column.

Characters Encountered (including Enemies)

What characters will the player encounter in this part of the game? Remember, enemies are characters too! If it's useful to you (as it was for us on *Uncharted*), break friendly or neutral nonplayer characters and enemies out into two or three different columns.

Objects Encountered

What objects are to be found in this part of the game? Doors that can be unlocked? Keys and switches? Breakable jars with a penny inside? Bouncy platforms? Arcane scrolls? Cell phones that play a voicemail message? Puzzle items, power-ups, weapons, armor, potions, and trinkets should all be listed here, along with any objects that deliver narrative, like letters, books, or audio recordings.

Other Assets Needed

Assets here means elements of visual art, animation, audio, and haptic (controller vibration) design that will be needed to make this part of the game complete. They are often things that are present just for aesthetic value, maybe in the background. If they're going to be even slightly time-consuming to create, list them here.

Audio Notes

Game designers often fail to think about the sound design of their games early enough. That's a big mistake—we make the best games by thinking about sound design from the beginning. The inclusion of this column is a nudge to think through the audio needs of the game in macro-level detail. Does the game have music or just ambient sounds? Will any of the sound effects be particularly difficult or time-consuming to create? Will the soundtrack be adaptive (will it change based on events in gameplay)?

Make enough notes here to indicate the scale and scope of the music and sound design work that you plan to do. The process of walking through a game with a sound designer or composer is called "spotting" for sound or music, so seize the opportunity to collaborate with audio talent and start spotting your vertical slice early to help you write your macro.

Visual Effects Notes

Similarly, game designers often fail to think early enough about the visual effects their game is going to include. Visual effects can be time-consuming to create, and so you should list out at least the major visual effects for each part of the game in the game design macro.

Player Goal, Design Goal, and Emotional Beat

Influenced by the character-action game design ideas of my friend Amy Hennig, I developed these column headings to help us to think through the layered nature of a game's design.

Player Goal

When someone plays a game, they set goals for themselves within the game, based on what the game tells them, what they want to do, what they understand about how the game works, and what they've experienced in other, similar games. This process of self-goal setting is described by Mihaly Csikszentmihalyi as "autotelism," and he associates it with persistence, curiosity, positivity, openness to experience, and a willingness to learn.[7] (Csikszentmihalyi is a psychologist well-known to game designers for his concept of "flow," a highly focused mental state found in athletes, surgeons, and game players alike.)

Simply put, the player goal for each part of your game is what the player holding the controller (a) wants to do or (b) thinks they're meant to be doing. Use all the creative means at your disposal, along with your understanding of human psychology, to make your best predictions about the goals your players will set for themselves. If you're familiar with the idea of user stories in Agile or the user journey in user experience design, then player goals encapsulate something from both.

A good game designer never loses sight of the fact that when a player first approaches a game, they have no idea what they can do or how they're meant to do it. The player might bring some preconceptions with them and will quickly jump to conclusions

---

7. Csikszentmihalyi, *Flow*, 67.

based on even the faintest traces of information the game gives them. But it's up to us as designers to shape our players' understanding of what this game holds in store and how it can be played. Soon, by experimenting with the controls and observing the game's environment, they start to figure it out.

Anna Anthropy and Naomi Clark give us a great example of this when they discuss the level "World 1–1" of *Super Mario Bros.* in their book *A Game Design Vocabulary: Exploring the Foundational Principles behind Good Game Design*. In talking about how good game design can teach a game's mechanics and elements simply through play, they say:

> *Super Mario Bros.*, 1985, didn't need a tutorial. It used design, a communicative visual vocabulary, and an understanding of player psychology—gained from watching players play the game, changing it, and watching them again—to guide the player to understanding the basics of the game. Those first screens teach everything the player needs to know: Mario starts on the left of an empty screen, facing right. The floating, shining reward object and the slow but menacing monster—set in opposition to Mario by walking in the opposite direction—give the player an incentive to jump.[8]

As the player continues to play, they set more and more goals, making discoveries and learning skills as they go. They might decide that they have to go to a certain place in a level, collect some objects, or find a key to unlock a door. As a designer, it is your job to guide the player's experience as they set goals. Under "Player Goal," write what you want the player to understand as their goal (or possible goals) for this part of the game. During playtests, you can track how players set or don't set goals for themselves and adjust your design accordingly. (It might help you here to think back to the designer's model, system image, and user's model we discussed in chapter 12.)

The designers of a game might set explicit goals for their players. We can tell them in a text bubble at the start of a level, "Collect a hundred stars and get to the finish line before the timer runs out!" Or maybe we'll let the player work out for themselves what they have to do to progress. In this case, we will have to decide how (and to what extent) we want to coax players into understanding the goals of the game.

Design Goal

Game designers often want to achieve other goals with a part of the game, beyond simply getting the player to set *their* goal. We want to teach the player something, give them an opportunity to practice something they've already learned, test their skill, or set them a puzzle. We might want to introduce a new character into the game's story, develop a relationship between preexisting characters, or show an event happening that marks an important plot point. We might have other, more complex, goals.

The design goal for each part of the game is what the designer is trying to accomplish in practical terms in that part of the game. It might be as simple as introducing

---

8. Anthropy and Clark, *A Game Design Vocabulary*, 5.

the player to the "jump" mechanic, or it might be as complex as having them discover a new way to use an existing ability to defeat a boss. (The *Zelda* games do this a lot.)

Sometimes the player's goals and the game designer's goals line up in a simple way: "Get to the end of the level and collect a hundred stars before the timer runs out, and have fun doing it!" But very often, the interplay between what the player wants and what the designer wants is more complex—and can create some excellent creative opportunities for designers, as we'll see in a moment.

So, under "Design Goal," write what you, the game's designer, wish to achieve in this part of the game. During playtests, you can track how well you achieve this goal. Did you teach the player the new mechanic you wanted to introduce? Did you get them to feel fond of a friendly NPC? Did they set a player goal for themselves that you wanted them to set?

Emotional Beat

When someone plays a part of a game, they have a subjective experience of that part. Think back to how we set an overall experience goal for our game at the end of the ideation phase of the project. In chapter 7, we talked about experience in terms of thought, memory, imagination, will, perception, and emotion, with a particular focus on emotion. We're now going to focus even more closely on emotion in determining the "emotional beat" that accompanies each part of our game. You can think of emotional beats as a sequence of sub-experience goals.

Each part of a game has an opportunity to shape the player's emotional and intellectual experience during the time they spend playing it. It's usually best to focus on emotion, which is why this column of a game design macro chart is titled "Emotional Beat." For games with a story—or any kind of narrative element—the unfolding of the player's emotion as they move through the game is critically important. Each moment in the game might make the player feel happy or excited, lonely or sad, or anything shown in Dr. Robert Plutchik's "wheel of emotions" (figure 7.2).

(If it's useful to think beyond emotion to other types of experience, then do so. Maybe your game will convey new ideas in a memorable way: the practical teaching applications of games are immense. Maybe it will give your players a purely perceptual experience: a vivid new appreciation of the color orange, or the chills people get from ASMR videos. If you want to focus on nonemotional types of experience, consider adding appropriate columns like "Perceptual Beat" or "Conceptual Beat.")

Planning a sequence of emotional experience is a key skill for any storyteller and, increasingly, for game designers too. Matthew Luhn is a writer and former Pixar storyteller, and during the creation of *Uncharted 2* a group of us from Naughty Dog attended one of his workshops in order to improve our storytelling ability. In his book *The Best Story Wins: How to Leverage Hollywood Storytelling in Business and Beyond*, Matthew describes how contrasting patterns of dopamine-producing upbeats and oxytocin-releasing downbeats can create powerful emotional effects. He uses the example of the beginning of Pixar's *Up*, which moves many audience members to tears within the film's first five minutes. Matthew reveals that this sequence is so moving in part because of its rapid-fire pattern of happy and sad moments. He says, "When we place these sad and happy moments next to each other in a story, we build an amusement park ride for people's hearts and minds. Ups and downs, tension and release, you've created a story that keeps an audience sitting on the edge of their seats."[9] It's easy to see how the ups and downs of gameplay also keep a player gripped by the flow state of an excellent game.

Psychology and personal experience tell us that the strongest emotional experience builds over time. Think of the deep love we feel for old friends, our parents, or a long-term partner. Think of the profound grief we might feel at the loss of one of these. The happenstance of life produces emotional heights and depths, but the huge emotional payoff at the end of an excellent movie or game doesn't happen by accident: the film-makers or designers have moved you there beat by beat. Chapter 16 of Jesse Schell's excellent book *The Art of Game Design* describes how designers, artists, and entertainers can use "interest curves" to plan sequences of compelling experience.[10]

The lasting emotional experiences that we set our sights on with our project goals are made up of patterns of contrasting emotion. This is something that people often overlook: in order to tell a story about one emotion, you have to use *many* emotions. A sad story can't be all sad: if we don't experience some happiness along the way, we won't feel the sadness in a profound way.

So, in our game design macro, the "Emotional Beat" column describes what the designer would like the player to be feeling at that point in the game. Game designers have many techniques for shaping emotion. One of the most powerful of these is sound design (including musical composition), but game writing, color palette, visual composition, lighting, character design, and—of course—game mechanics all play a role in shaping the player's emotion.

Of course, it's wrong to think that we can completely and predictably shape the emotions of every person. Each of us responds emotionally to an artwork in a personal way. The possibilities and ambiguities around the emotion shaped by an artist are a part of what makes art great. It's what makes an outstanding artwork appear fresh and new each time we approach it, and it's what makes it possible for us to have different emotional reactions to an artwork over time.

Articulating each emotional beat of our game in the game design macro chart helps designers to make better, more emotionally impactful games. It also helps us in our macro-level planning by requiring us to think through the structure of our games from the player's subjective perspective, as viewed through the lenses of both gameplay and narrative.

---

9. Luhn, *The Best Story Wins*, xxv.
10. Schell, *The Art of Game Design*, 297.

An Example of the Relationship between Player Goal, Design Goal, and Emotional Beat

This complex relationship between (a) the goals that the player perceives or sets for themselves, (b) the goals that the game designer has for a part of the game, and (c) the emotional experiences that the game produces for the player is a key part of the art of game design. Let's look at an example of the relationship between player goals, design goals, and emotional beats.

At the beginning of *Uncharted 2: Among Thieves*, our protagonist, Nathan Drake, wakes up in a wrecked train car which is dangling over the edge of a cliff above a fatally deep drop in the frozen Himalayan mountains. The player is introduced to Drake through a brief cinematic, and they see that he is wounded. Hopefully, the close-up of his pain-wracked face is enough to begin to elicit the player's sympathy.

Moments later, Drake tumbles from his seat, falls a hundred feet through the vertically suspended train car, and—managing to grab on to a twisted railing as he painfully bounces off it—is left hanging on to the very bottom of the car. Now that the player understands Drake's predicament, hopefully we've inspired them to help him get out of this mess. This very naturally sets up a **player goal**. The player can see clearly that there's no way down for Drake: the drop below him is too deep. The only way to escape is to climb upward.

Many (though not all) videogame players will naturally deflect the left thumbstick on the controller, and Drake begins to move. The design of the railing suggests that he can only move to the left, and when he does so, he moves around a corner. The player can now see, again from the visual design, that they can make him climb upward. The player is beginning to achieve the goal they set for themselves.

Of course, one part of our **design goal** was to have the player get Drake to safety. But a bigger design goal was to teach the player our game's core mechanics. As the player helps Drake climb the ruined train car, we put them through a carefully staged sequence of moves, traveling up, around, and through the train car, using on-screen prompts to introduce new button presses that will activate Drake's various climbing, jumping, and swinging abilities. The player will use these abilities throughout the rest of the game, and this is where they learn them first.

So, our design goal here is to provide the player with a tutorial. Many videogames start with a tutorial level, and you might be wondering what the big deal is here. The finesse of this sequence comes with the **emotional beats** for this part of the game. Unexpected and near-disastrous things happen as Drake climbs: a chunk of debris plummets past him, a train seat gives way as he hangs from it, a pipe that he's clinging to swings around in an unexpected direction. All of this creates surprise, fear, and excitement, and ratchets up the tension for the player in a pattern of upbeats and downbeats. Even if our rational minds know that our protagonist will make it through, our emotional minds can be tricked into doubting it by staging the scene dramatically, and both parts of our mind are keen to see what happens next. This is how storytelling works.

By combining the player goal of "get Drake to safety" with our design goal of "teach the player the core traversal mechanics of the game" and the emotional beats of "surprise and fear," we were able to create a tutorial level that drew the player into the game and taught them things without them even realizing that they were learning.

At the beginning of *Uncharted 2*, players typically just think they've been launched into the middle of an exciting adventure. They may not ever think about what we, the designers, have just taught them, or how they will use that knowledge in later parts of the game. Designers never run the risk of alienating the player by making them go through a heavy-handed tutorial sequence before they can really start to play the game.

Every game has this kind of opportunity to teach its new players in elegant and playful ways, and the extended possibilities here—for creating great moments throughout the entirety of a game—are endless. By breaking down our understanding about and planning for each part of our game into a consideration of player goals, design goals, and emotional beats, we can come to a deeper understanding of what we're trying to do in our game and can invent clever new ways of creating unique gameplay and storytelling experiences.

The Advantages of a Game Design Macro

There are two chief advantages to writing a game design macro instead of a lengthy game design document. The first is in communicating game design ideas, and the second is in assisting in the scheduling of the full production phase of the project.

The Game Design Macro as Communication

The hundred-page documents that I was asked to write at the start of my career were never warmly received by my teammates and gathered dust, unread, on their desks. But the game design macros I worked on at Naughty Dog were always eagerly anticipated by most everyone on our teams and were pored over for the information they contained. Why the big difference?

A game design macro has great readability. If it's written well and laid out clearly, with short easy-to-scan sections of text, then top-level details can be taken in at first glance, key pieces of information jump out on a second look, and important details can easily be discovered with a closer reading.

Using information design techniques like color-coding the cells in the macro chart, bolding and italicizing certain keywords, sizing their column widths carefully, and freezing the top row of the spreadsheet (so it never scrolls off the top of the screen) all make the macro easy to read.

The macro can be made even clearer and easier to read with the use of flowcharts, like those described by Insomniac Games director and designer Brian Allgeier in his book

Directing Video Games: 101 Tips for Creative Leaders.[11] In a blog post titled "Provide Structure: How Macro Documents Keep a Project on Course," Brian uses examples from the design of *Ratchet & Clank Future: A Crack in Time* to illustrate techniques that supplement a spreadsheet-based game design macro chart. He shows how concept art and screenshots can be used to develop a "visual macro," and how the macro can be used, as I mentioned earlier, to create a color script, "an image used for mapping out the color palettes, mood, and emotions across the experience."[12]

The game design overview part of the macro is very useful for pitching the project to stakeholders like senior producers, studio leadership, publishers, and other financial backers. It's also useful for pitching the project internally to the development team.

The spreadsheet-based macro chart part of the macro is particularly valuable to the game development team, who are eager to know about the structure and content of the game they're going to make. What characters feature in the game? What locations does the game take place in? What kind of gameplay does the game include, and how does the story unfold? On a large development team of up to several hundred people, it can be hard to transmit this information to everyone who needs it, but a game design macro chart helps everyone get some answers to these critical questions with just twenty minutes of reading.

Presenting game design information in a macro form makes it easier to understand not just the content but the planned sequencing of the game. As Mark Cerny says, the macro chart allows us more easily to see:

> Is all gameplay of a certain type bunched at the end or the beginning? Are abilities and moves introduced and trained in a smooth distribution? Do my barriers to level entry progress properly?[13]

The game design macro has great power to communicate game design ideas. At first, we can use it to solicit feedback about the overall game's evolving design as we're iterating on it during preproduction. Later, once the game's design has been locked in at the end of preproduction, we can use the macro to communicate the design decisions that we've committed to. We'll come back to this idea in a moment.

The Game Design Macro as Scheduling Aid

The preproduction phase of a project is a free-form time and can't be scheduled conventionally. But we'll need a schedule for the full production phase of the project if we want to get everything done on time. The game design macro, taken together with the experiences we have during preproduction, is an excellent starting point for making that schedule. Since it's a macro list, we should be able to find a level of granularity for

---

11. Allgeier, *Directing Video Games*, #33.
12. Brian Allgeier, "Provide Structure: How Macro Documents Keep a Project on Course," Directing Video Games, August 10, 2017, http://www.directingvideogames.com/2017/08/01/provide-structure/.
13. Cerny, "D.I.C.E. Summit 2002," 32:53.

our schedule that has just enough detail, without bogging us down in trying to list out each and every one of the many small assets we'll need to make.

During preproduction, while we're writing the macro, we are also spending time building a vertical slice, making things and iterating on them until they are good enough to call them done. As we discussed in chapter 11, that means we can gather information about how long it takes our team to make things, and how many iterative cycles it takes us to get to a level of quality that we're satisfied with. Capturing this information by tracking our time during preproduction will help us build a schedule for full production. We'll talk more about scheduling techniques in chapter 19.

The Game Design Macro Is Set in Stone

The game design macro is delivered at the end of preproduction and represents a definitive commitment by the game team's creative leadership to an upper limit for the size of the project, and to its content and structure. Nothing significant in terms of features or content should be added to the game design macro after the end of preproduction without taking something else out.

This means the game design macro is an excellent way of combating "scope creep," the age-old game development problem where developers get excited about new ideas and add them into the game's design during full production. Scope creep—and the type of scope creep known as "feature creep"—extends a project in an uncontrolled way and can sometimes prevent it from ever being finished. We'll look at feature creep again in chapter 28.

This is not to say that design changes can *never* happen during full production: we'll look later at the ways in which we can (and must) keep thinking flexibly during full production. But by taking the game design macro seriously, and reminding ourselves that it's set in stone, we take a major step toward bringing our project under control. Exciting new ideas will always come along after the end of preproduction, but unless our design is failing in a major way, we should stick with what we have and work to make it superb. We can save those new ideas for our next project.

Furthermore, because the macro only specifies the design in a macroscopic way, there is still a huge amount of room for creativity on the part of the developers doing the *micro* design. The opportunities are endless: we get a constraint from the macro, to be sure, but as every good designer knows, a constraint spurs creativity, rather than blocking it. In the words of Mark Cerny:

> As good as your preproduction may have been, you'll still learn things in production. Certain techniques, cameras, gameplays, may work better than others. So, so long as you don't violate your macro design, you can advance the state of the art in the game during production with confidence that you will not break the continuity or consistency of the experience.[14]

---

14. Cerny, "D.I.C.E. Summit 2002," 35:55.

While nothing should be added to the macro after the end of preproduction, except under very special circumstances, things *can* be removed or moved around, since that shouldn't impact the schedule much. By simply changing the order of the elements in your game, you might find creative solutions to game design problems or ways of improving your story. The *in medias res* train wreck sequence that opens *Uncharted 2: Among Thieves*, which chronologically takes place in the middle of the events of the game, was not moved to the beginning of the game design macro chart until sometime after the end of preproduction.[15]

Is the Game Design Macro a Game Design Bible?

You'll sometimes hear game developers talk about a "game design bible," but be wary, and check to make sure you understand what they're talking about. They might be talking about an old-fashioned, too-big-to-be-useful game design document. Or they might be referring to a game design macro: either just the game design overview, or the whole two-part macro including a macro chart.

Also, be careful not to confuse the game design macro with the "writers' guide" or "story bible" used in the worlds of film, television, comic books, and fiction. These are large worldbuilding documents laying out the canon, lore, and tone of an expansive fictional universe. A famous example is the "*Star Trek: The Next Generation* Writers'/ Directors' Guide" that Gene Roddenberry wrote in preparing to make the series.[16]

Story bibles are essential in the planning of intellectual property franchises and have something in common with a game design overview in the way that they summarize story, characters, and world, but their size and scope make them quite different from the focused design macro used to plan a single game project. That said, if you are working on a game that is part of the creation of a major new entertainment franchise, you and your colleagues should of course create a story bible for the new world you're planning.

You might be feeling intimidated right now, by the seemingly gargantuan task of creating a comprehensive plan for your game. In the next chapter, we'll look at some easy and practical techniques that you can use to get started in the creation of a game design macro chart.

---

15. "A narrative work beginning *in medias res* (Classical Latin: "into the middle of things") opens in the midst of the plot. . . . Often, exposition is bypassed and filled in gradually, through dialogue, flashbacks or description of past events." "In Medias Res," Wikipedia, https://en.wikipedia .org/wiki/In_medias_res.

16. Gene Roddenberry, "Star Trek: The Next Generation Writers'/Directors' Guide," September 8, 1987, https://www.roddenberry.com/media/vault/TNG-WritersDirectorsGuide.pdf.

In the previous chapter, we discussed what goes into a game design macro chart, the spreadsheet part of a game design macro. Having read about it, you might be feeling overwhelmed. How can I possibly begin to put together this grand, macroscopic plan for my game? Where do I start?

Don't worry. First, I'll tell you about a technique that Amy Hennig developed at Naughty Dog, and then I'll connect you back to the work that you did in the ideation phase. Soon, the bones of your game design macro chart will begin to appear.

The process that Amy and our group of collaborators used to assemble the lengthy and complex game design macros for *Uncharted 2* and *Uncharted 3* began with a stack of humble index cards. Amy would look at the list of ideas that we'd had for locations, characters, gameplay set pieces, and story beats, and write each one on an index card, color-coding the ideas for clarity: a pink card for a location, a blue card for an event, and so on.

We would lay out the cards on a desk and begin to shuffle them, looking for good combinations: a collapsing bridge sequence and a Himalayan monastery; some cornered journalists and a war-torn city. Pretty soon, constellations of ideas that seemed to hang together particularly well would emerge and we'd pin them up on a cork board in Amy's office (see figure 18.1). Gradually, sequences of the game would start to come together, and—with enough thought and discussion—whole acts of the macro appeared.

This playful, tactile method of arranging and rearranging ideas, coupled with Amy and the team's knowledge of game design and storytelling, meant that eventually we were able to figure out a plan for the whole game. As soon as a sequence that we felt confident about appeared on the cork board, we wrote it up in our macro chart spreadsheet. Eventually, we had our game design macro chart (see figure 18.2), ready to pass on to the interested parties.

First, we'd show it to the discipline leads and team members at Naughty Dog to get their feedback. These folks had contributed ideas to the process and would put this grand plan into action, so it was important to get their input. Then, after some more revisions, we'd send it to our producers and executive producers at Sony Interactive Entertainment (Naughty Dog's parent company), as part of our "end of preproduction" milestone review process.

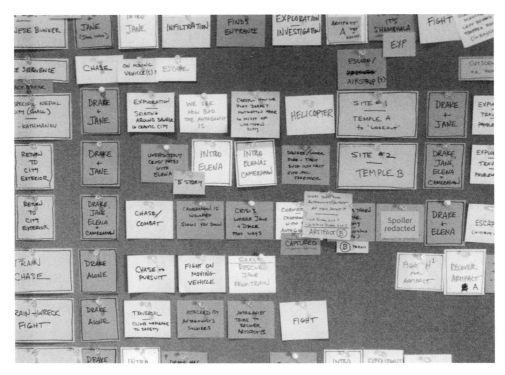

Figure 18.1

The cork board index card planning that led to the game design macro chart for *Uncharted 2: Among Thieves*. Note that Chloe Frazer was called "Jane" at this stage in development. Image credit: ©2009 SIE LLC/ UNCHARTED 2: Among Thieves™. Created & developed by Naughty Dog LLC.

You could use this index card method, or you could do something similar in a digital document. Remember the lists of ideas that you made in a spreadsheet during ideation? Those lists are the right place to start in assembling your game design macro. Copy-paste your ideas for locations, gameplay, story events, and characters, mixing and matching them in search of combinations that work well together. Soon, you'll be able to start assembling them into the rows of your game design macro chart.

The Granularity of the Macro Chart

The granularity of a macro chart refers to the level of detail that it has. Every game designer will have to make a decision about the granularity of their macro chart, trying to make it detailed enough but not too detailed.

A shorter game could have a more detailed macro chart; a longer game will require a lower level of detail. Exactly what level of detail you use for your macro chart is up to you, but remember, don't get bogged down in details that might change later.

For example, each row in the macro charts for *Uncharted 2* and *Uncharted 3* represent about ten to fifteen minutes of gameplay. By contrast, in my classes, where students are making a ten-minute game, each row in the macro chart represents about thirty seconds to one minute of gameplay. It's a useful design exercise for my students to get a little more micro in their planning than they would when designing a larger, longer game.

A good rule of thumb to use when writing a macro chart is to avoid piling too many different events into the same row in the spreadsheet. Break discrete events out into separate rows in the macro whenever you can. If you find that you've written a short paragraph in any given cell, that's probably a sign that that row should be broken out into two or more rows.

Do your best to keep the macro chart concise. Brian Allgeier advises: "The Macro Design should stay high level and leave more detailed information to supporting documents like the story scripts and design documents. Team members need to be able to easily reference it and quickly understand how the elements of the game are structured together."[1]

Sequencing the Game Design Macro Chart

Writing a game design macro chart gives you a chance to plan out your game's flow in terms of the sequencing of the game, which we usually consider in three ways: the sequence of gameplay events, the sequence of narrative events, and the sequencing of place (of your levels, the spaces in which both the gameplay and narrative take place).

Sequencing Gameplay

A good place to start when considering the sequence of gameplay events is the order in which the game mechanics are introduced and how the player learns them. Creative opportunities immediately arise out of this. Let's say that your character can run and jump. Most games teach a player to run before they jump, but would it feel fresher and more interesting if we somehow taught the player to jump first and then to run?

As we introduce our game mechanics, we combine them in setups to create the interesting variety of gameplay that will sustain the player throughout the course of the game. A setup is a collection of game elements, arranged in such a way as to create interest for the player. Setups are logical units of gameplay. A very simple setup might be a pit with some spikes in it. If you fall into the pit, you restart the level; if you jump over the pit, you can proceed through the game. A more complex setup could involve a platform carrying an enemy moving up and down, with some poison darts being shot across the path ahead. You have to time your moves carefully, so as to make the jumps, defeat the enemy, avoid the poison darts, and move onward.

We can clearly understand what a setup is by looking at the very nicely designed setup at the very beginning of *Super Mario Bros.* World 1–1, shown in figure 18.3.

---

1. Brian Allgeier, "Provide Structure: How Macro Documents Keep a Project on Course," Directing Video Games, August 10, 2017, http://www.directingvideogames.com/2017/08/01/provide -structure/.

UNCHARTED 2 Macro Design

LEVELS	LOOK DESCRIPTION	TIME OF DAY/ MOOD	ALLY-NPC	ENEMY MODELS	MACRO GAMEPLAY	MACRO FLOW	PLAYER MECHANICS																
							Free Climb/Dyno	Wall Jump	Free Ropes	Pendulum	Monkey Bars	Monkey Swing	Balance Beams	Carry Objects Heavy	Carry Objects Light	Traversal Gunplay v.1	Forced Melee	Puzzle	Stealth	Swim	Moving Objects	Push Objects	Bino colars
Train Wreck																							
Train-wreck-1	Train Wreckage, Dangling cars	Snowy, Transitioning to White out	Bloodied Warm-weather Drake		Stay alive - injured	Highly scripted moments of Injured Drake traversing injured through wreckage.	X																
Museum																							
Museum-1	Istanbul, Turkey Museum	Night	Drake-1 Flynn-1 Chloe-1 (cut Only)	Museum Guards	Infiltrate - Stealth - Co-op	Co-op w/Flynn to infiltrate the museum. Helping him steal/decipher an artifact there	X			x	x	x	x			x	x		x		x		
Museum-2	Roman Sewers Below the Museum	Night	Flynn-1	Museum Guards	Escape	Flynn dicks you over, Run from the authorities through an ancient sewernetwork. Flynnprevents you from escaping - BUSTED!	X									x	x		x		x		
Dig																							
Dig-1	Lush, Wet Jungle/Swamp Lazaravic's dig & campsite structures	Dawn - misty (rainy)	Chloe-2 Sully	Laz Diggers Laz Army HOT Lazaravic Flynn-2	Sabotage - Infilitrate - Fight	Enter Laz dig sight w/Chloe & Sully on radio. Start causing trouble for guards & workers	X									x	x		x	x			x
Dig-2	Lush, Wet Jungle/Swamp Lazaravic's dig & campsite structures	Dawn - misty (rainy)	Chloe-2 Sully	Laz Diggers Laz Army HOT Lazaravic Flynn-2	Sabotage - Infilitrate - Fight	Explosions - Chaos distracts pulls Laz away from "treasure" - Gives Drake clue to find Dagger	X			x	x	x	x			x	x		x	x	x		
Dig-3	Follow a stream up a mountainside.	Dawn - misty (rainy)	Chloe-2 Sully	Laz Diggers Laz Army HOT Lazaravic-1 Flynn-2 MP'sDeadCrew	Sabotage - Infilitrate - Fight	Get to higher ground after scoping Laz's tent - towards mountain in wide world. Stumble onto a temple																	
Warzone																							
war-1-market	Nepalese city broken & burning	High Noon -War-torn & smokey		Laz Army HOT Freedom Fighters	Explore Traverse Minor Gunfights	Basic Gunplay Traversal Gunplay	X	x			x	x	x			x		x					x
war-2-streets	Nepalese city broken & burning	High Noon - War-torn & smokey	Chloe-2	Laz Army HOT Freedom Fighters	Explore Traverse Minor Gunfights	Basic Gunplay Traversal Gunplay	X	x			x	x	x			x		x					x
war-3-inside war-4-highrise	Nepalese city broken & burning	High Noon - War-torn & smokey	Chloe-2	Laz Army HOT Freedom Fighters	Explore Traverse Minor Gunfights	Basic Gunplay Traversal Gunplay Get to higher ground (hotel)	X	x			x	x	x			x		x					x
city	Nepalese city broken & burning	High Noon - War-torn & smokey	Chloe-2	Laz Army HOT Freedom Fighters	Explore Traverse Minor Gunfights	Skirt close to Laz Army	X	x			x	x	x			x		x					x
city-2	New area unlocked of City	High Noon - War-torn & smokey	Chloe Elena-1 Cameraman	Laz Army HOT Freedom Fighters	Traverse Major Fight	Basic Gunplay Traversal Gunplay	X	x				x				x		x					
temple	Temple complex built in the middle of the city	mysterious	Chloe Elena-1 Cameraman	Laz Army HOT Freedom Fighters Dead Expeditions	Explore Problem Solve Escape	Portable Objectsuse for fending off bugs w/Fire Water Currents	X	x		x	x	x	x	x	x			x			x	x	
city third pass	City + Train Yard	high tension	Elena-1	Laz Army HOT Freedom Fighters	Escape/Fight Chase			x				x				x							

Figure 18.2
Part of the game design macro chart for *Uncharted 2: Among Thieves* (see also appendix C). Image credit: ©2009 SIE LLC/ UNCHARTED 2: Among Thieves™. Created & developed by Naughty Dog LLC.

This particular arrangement of gameplay elements creates a playful situation that provides a challenge without too much danger. As Anna Anthropy and Naomi Clark describe in *A Game Design Vocabulary*, this *Super Mario Bros.* setup creates a learning opportunity for the player, where the learning is natural, free form, and fun.[2]

The player can bash into a "question mark" block or a "bricks" block from below to find out what happens. They can collect a mushroom and become big and more powerful. They can bash into the Goomba monster from the side and take some damage or bounce on it and destroy it. The placement of the elements that the designers carefully

---

2. Anthropy and Clark, *A Game Design Vocabulary*, 17.

GAMEPLAY THEME (FOCUS)	WEAPONS																					ENEMIES											NON-PLAYABLE VEHICLES	CINEMATIC GAMEPLAY SEQUENCES	Vistas
	Tranq-gun	Pistol-semi-a	Pistol-semi-b	Pistol-full-a	Pistol-revolver-a	Pistol-revolver-b	SMG-a	SMG-b	Assault-Rifle-a	Assault-Rifle-b	Shotgun 1	Shotgun 2	Sniper-Rifle	Cross bow	Grenades	RPG	Rocket Launcher	Turret 1	Pillbox Turret	Mobile Turret	Museum Guards	Light	Medium	Armored	Shotgunner	Sniper	Shield	RPG	Heavy	SLA Easy	SLA Hard			
Highly scripted - traversal L1 + R1 Lock sequence																																		Exploding Tanker - Washing machine sequence	X
Train Traversal L1 + R1 Tranquilizer guns Intro Stealth Attacks Cover as Stealth	X																				X													X
	X																				X													
Train Traversal Train Shooting Introduce Stealth Attacks Cover as Stealth Forced Melee	X	X																			X													X
Forced Melee Basic Gunplay IntroTraversal Gunplay Grenades		X							X				X								X													
		X							X				X								X													
Basic Gunplay Traversal Gunplay		X							X				X								X											Helicopter		X
Basic Gunplay Traversal Gunplay		X							X				X								X					X						Helicopter		X
Basic Gunplay Traversal Gunplay		X							X				X								X											Helicopter		X
Basic Gunplay Traversal Gunplay		X							X				X								X											Helicopter		X
Basic Gunplay Traversal Gunplay		X							X	X			X	X	X						X	X										Helicopter		
Portable Object suse for fending off bugs w/Fire Water Currents		X							X	X			X								X	X											Collapsing statue	
		X							X	X			X								X	X												

Figure 18.2
(continued)

arranged has a relationship with the design parameters of the character's abilities—how long, high, and quickly they can jump—so that the space is neither too constrained nor too open. Depending on where and when you choose to run and jump, you'll sail through this setup gracefully or get into a pickle.

Designers create sequences of successive setups to gradually increase and decrease the difficulty of gameplay over time, creating the "rising sawtooth" pattern of difficulty regularly used by game designers, and described by Ernest Adams in his book *Fundamentals of Game Design*. "Start each game level at a perceived difficulty somewhat lower than that at which the preceding level ended, and increase the difficulty during the course of each level as well. . . . This sawtooth shape creates good pacing over the course of the game."[3]

---

3. Adams, *Fundamentals of Game Design*, 424.

Figure 18.3
The setup at the beginning of *Super Mario Bros.* World 1–1. Image credit: Nintendo.

A mistake that game designers sometimes make is to increase the difficulty of their setups too quickly. Because we're so familiar with the elements of our game's design, and so skilled at playing our own game, we have a tendency to jump ahead to setups with a degree of complexity beyond what our players can handle. Methodical planning, using a game design macro chart, is a good way to counter this tendency, and regular playtesting with new players allows us to be sure that we're gauging our difficulty correctly.

There are other gameplay sequencing considerations. Are there bosses in your game, and how are they used? How do other special sequences of gameplay fit into the game? Can the player move freely around an open world, or are they constrained to a linear path? If the player-character can accept missions, can they only choose and accept one at a time, or can they have multiple missions? If they earn a resource like money or experience points, can these be spent at any time, or only at key moments in the game? We're invited to come up with answers to these important questions when we write a game design macro chart.

Sequencing Narrative

Narrative is another good place to start when considering the sequencing of a game. In his D.I.C.E. talk Mark Cerny says about the macro chart: "You should count on having a pretty solid story that you don't intend to change."[4] This idea, that the game design macro is an important place for planning the story of your game, became more and more important at Naughty Dog as the stories of our games became more complex and more emotional.

---

4. Cerny, "D.I.C.E. Summit 2002," 33:47.

The words *story* and *narrative* have similar meanings but are interpreted in different ways by different people. I have my own definitions that I think are useful when talking about games. For me, a narrative is a report of events that are connected in some way, presented in a sequence that starts somewhere and ends somewhere else. It gives you some information to do with what you will. By contrast, a story is a narrative sequence that has a particularly strong coherence, usually following one or just a few characters, and with a meaning or theme implicit in what happens to those characters. The story starts somewhere meaningful and ends somewhere more meaningful. Taken as a whole, a story communicates something to you in a way that a narrative may not.

So, for me, story is a subset of narrative. Narrative is looser, and story is more specific. For me, almost everything is narrative, because the mind is a narrativizing mechanism. So, I might spin you a narrative about how my afternoon went or what happened in my last online game session, but it might not be much of a story. If I sharpen my narrative with characters, tone, theme, meaningful drama, and a particular conclusion, then it becomes a story.

Your definitions of story and narrative might be different from mine, especially if you have some training in a specific technical field like literary theory, dramaturgy, or narrative design. Whatever terms you choose, it's useful for game designers to be able to tell when we're talking about narrative as a collected sequence of events, or something more like the traditional story that we would find in a novel or a film.

When thinking about sequencing narrative in a game design macro chart for a game that has less in the way of traditional story, the narrative of the game is implicit in the description of the gameplay events in the macro. Reading down the macro chart will be like reading a narrative about a game as it unfolds through its gameplay. A lot of the narrative of the game will be contained in the Player Goal, Design Goal, and Emotional Beat columns.

For a game that has a traditional type of story, you first have to introduce your player-character, their world, and one or two key relationships. You might establish some of their motivations, needs and goals, a reason for them to go on a journey through your game, and some forces of antagonism that will create interest along the way. Or you might create interest for your story in some other way, by having the player uncover fragments of prose-poetry, as in *Dear Esther*, or discover musical experiences, as in *Proteus*. As we discussed in chapter 16, not every interesting story need be driven by conflict. You'll introduce characters to meet, places to go, and plot points that send the story in a new direction. Eventually, you'll need to wrap up your story by having the events come to a climax, a resolution, and a dénouement.

Whether your game has a story or not, think about the rising-falling, beginning-middle-end structure of Aristotle's *Poetics* and Freytag's Pyramid that we discussed in chapter 16. Those simple models of drama will help you bring structure to the experience of your game.

Narrative game designers like me are often asked, "Which comes first: the idea for gameplay, or the idea for story?" The answer is that either can come first, but what counts is that pieces of story are matched well with the gameplay that accompanies them, and vice versa. I think about the relationship between gameplay and story as if they were two kids playing leapfrog: the first jumps over the second, then the second jumps over the first, and on and on.

Each moment of gameplay, even a very simple moment like learning to move left and right, presents a narrative opportunity. Similarly, every story beat might find a match with some element of your gameplay. Don't squander these creative opportunities! A tight correspondence between gameplay and story is where the magic of game storytelling lies; in sequencing them together, we can draw play and narrative tightly into a harmonious, resonant braid.

Sequencing Place

In sequencing most types of game, you'll need to think through the places in which the events of the gameplay and story happen. Level design for videogames is a fascinating art. A well-designed level is a kind of spatial materialization of the events that will, or could, take place within it.

Think through your levels and sublevels and how they connect. Many great game levels are made up of open areas connected by narrower paths—does your game have that kind of structure? How large or long is each part of the game? How many places does the game have in total, and how do they fit together overall? Are they strung together in a linear order, do they branch, or are they arranged around a hub? Where do the bosses and other special sequences of gameplay appear?

The creation of the places in which your game takes place will likely be among the most labor-intensive (and hence costly) work that your team does. Using the game design macro chart to plan the places that you'll visit in your game is an important step in bringing the scope of your game under control. In addition, considering how you can reuse the same place for different sequences in your game can help you work efficiently, making the most of those costly environmental assets, and may lead to the best creative decisions. As Tracy Fullerton says: "Re-lighting an existing environment for the climactic moment may actually be a more dramatic decision than creating an entirely new environment."[5]

Contrast and Continuity in Sequencing

In sequencing the gameplay, narrative, and places in your game, think about contrast and continuity. Yes, you want the continuity of a good flow from one thing to the next, but you also need contrast to create the variety that will hold the player's interest.

---

5. Private communication, May 25, 2020.

Follow a sequence of relaxed exploration with some intense action. Follow the establishment of a character as likable or funny with a dramatic revelation about that character. Contrast a wide-open space with a labyrinth of narrow passages. These contrasts create a modulation of the player's experience which feels like a journey rich with interest and meaning. A pattern of more-less-more, smooth-rough-smooth, active-passive-active is a great basis for your sequencing. The idea of contrast comes in part from Bruce Block's excellent book *The Visual Story*, which we used to unite gameplay and story in the *Uncharted* series.[6]

Making the Macro Chart Complete

The macro chart should include *every single part of your game*, including the **front end** and all its **menus and interfaces**. This includes the **title screen** for your game, your team's animating **logo**, and any other "bumpers" (logos) that you want to include to show the name of your publisher, creative partners, technology licensors, or university program. It includes the **pause screen**, **options screens**, **loading screens**, and any **"game over" screens** you want to include. It also includes a screen or sequence showing the **credits** for your game.

To reiterate: *all these things belong in your game design macro chart*. People are sometimes startled when they realize how long it's going to take to create all these essential, easy-to-overlook parts of their game. It's better to have this realization at the end of preproduction than at the end of the project, while there's still time to plan and build everything needed to make the game complete.

Micro Design

This macro design work that we're doing is contrasted with the micro design, which is all of the detailed work we will have to do later to build out our game. We'll base our micro design on the framework laid out by the macro design. If we're on a larger team, this work will be done by our game's designers, working together with the artisans in the other disciplines. If we're on a small team, we'll do it ourselves.

Creating micro design usually proceeds by taking a single line from the macro and expanding it with details about level layout, object placements, enemy descriptions and behaviors, puzzle designs, and narrative mechanisms. In the 1990s and 2000s, the teams I worked on would do this by creating detailed level layout maps on paper or in Adobe Illustrator, but today it's more usual to do some quick sequence planning on a whiteboard, and then build blockmesh (whitebox/graybox/blockout) levels directly in the tools, using placeholder gameplay elements. More detailed supporting game

6. Block, *The Visual Story*, 234.

design documentation, usually in the form of flowcharts and lists, can then be created as necessary.

The micro design is usually created on a just-in-time basis, so that we don't waste time developing details that will later get changed. What just-in-time means for your team is up to you. Generally, we want to get far enough ahead with our micro design so that we don't create a bottleneck for other parts of our team, especially if the micro design teams get slowed down for some reason.

Nonlinear Games and the Game Design Macro Chart

Let's discuss the creation of a game design macro chart for a nonlinear game. Obviously, the two-dimensional space of a spreadsheet is good for planning out linear games, which flow in a one-way sequence from A to B to C. However, a macro chart can also be used to plan out branching games that might flow from A to B *or* C, or open-world games that could take place in any order of B, C, or A.

I've been pleased to see students in my classes adapt the macro to many different types of games, with different types of game progression. The advantage of the macro is its two-dimensional space, where elements can be gridded to list them comprehensively in a compact way on the page and to show relationships between them.

For a game with a branching structure, A to B or C, it's easy just to list the various branches one below the other and find a way to indicate how they link together. The content of each branch can be described, of course, just as it would be for a linear game.

For a game with an open-world structure, where you might encounter levels A, B, and C in any order, you have a slightly bigger challenge on your hands, but there are usually logical groups that you can organize things into in the macro chart. A good approach is to break the macro chart into two parts. The first part contains a list of game mechanics and the objects they interact with. The second part contains a list of places and the objects those places contain. Correlating the two parts of the macro will reflect the way that the world opens up to the player when the player-character gains certain abilities.

Planning Holistic Games

Open-world action-adventure games where parts of the game world are gated by abilities that the player-character earns throughout the game present a particular challenge during preproduction. These are sometimes known as "holistic" games, because every part of the game's design is connected to every other part. Metroidvania games are holistic games, as are most games in the *Zelda* series.

Writing a game design macro chart for a holistic game presents a considerable challenge, because a lot more of the game's micro design needs to be completed during preproduction. As Mark Cerny says, "If later level construction depends heavily on abilities learned in earlier levels—for example, you learn a gliding mechanic or how to use explosives—then the designers will need a lot of information in order to make levels or areas which properly interrelate with each other."[7]

All the abilities need to be designed in detail before the layout of *any* level can take place, so that small changes to the design parameters we discussed in chapter 13 (for example, the distances that a traversal action will carry the player-character) don't lead to impossibly huge amounts of level layout rework later. For smaller projects, this isn't usually a problem, but for larger games, the preproduction phase of the project should be extended appropriately, so that the level design team can enter full production confident in the quality and finality of the mechanics they are designing for.

Example Game Design Macros

I'm often asked to provide example game design macro charts, and those that I have secured permission to share can be found on this book's website, playfulproduction-process.com.

I hope I've sold you on the idea of the game design macro. It's not a very glamorous or world-shaking game design concept, but it's practical and pragmatic. People often wonder what the secret ingredients are that make Naughty Dog's games so good. One of the chief ingredients is not so secret: it's just the game design macro.

Creating a good game design macro takes some thought, hard work, and experience. Toward the end of my time at Naughty Dog, some of the team making *The Last of Us* vanished into a meeting room for the better part of eight months, eventually emerging with the cork board full of index cards seen in figure 18.4. If you're familiar with *The Last of Us*, you'll be able to see its macro structure in this image. The team had no way to imagine every last detail that would eventually go into the game, but they were able to think through the macro sequencing that would make the experience of playing through their game so impactful.

Making a plan for the whole of your game might seem like a lot to ask at the end of preproduction, but just give it your best shot. Trust your instincts, focus on the ideas you liked best during ideation, and don't worry about making your macro perfect. The important thing is simply to try to create a plan that you can commit to, which has enough detail that you can make a good schedule for full production but that leaves you some wiggle room to exercise your creativity. Don't overthink it. An imperfect plan is much better than no plan at all. Trust your gut and get your macro down in a spreadsheet.

You should aim to create a first draft of your game design micro some time before the end of the preproduction phase of your project. That way, you can get feedback about its length and quality and have time for at least one and preferably two rounds

---

7. Cerny, "D.I.C.E. Summit 2002," 34:55.

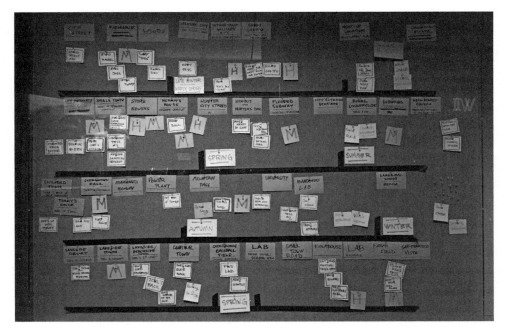

Figure 18.4
Cork board macro planning for Naughty Dog's *The Last of Us*, in the "Videogames" Exhibition at
the Victoria and Albert Museum, London. Image credit: The Last of Us™ ©2013, 2014 Sony Interactive Entertainment LLC. The Last of Us is a trademark of Sony Interactive Entertainment LLC.
Created & developed by Naughty Dog LLC.

of iteration. External feedback from design peers and mentors will help you to create
the best game design macro possible in the time you have.

Try to get feedback about problems in the macro chart: places where either the gameplay or the story doesn't flow well; places where too many different things are happening
in a single row of the chart; any parts of the macro that are unclear.

In particular, try to get feedback about the scope of the project. **The moment of the
creation of the game design macro chart presents a critical opportunity to get the
scope of a game project under control**. It's vanishingly rare for game developers to
under-scope their projects. Less experienced developers are particularly prone to over-
scoping, because they haven't yet come to understand what a long time it takes to build
a game and how many problems and obstacles they'll encounter during development.
Experienced developers come to acquire an intuitive sense of whether a game's planned
design will fit into the time available for development. Check in with your experienced
peers and mentors and do your best to make sure that your project's scope is under control by the end of preproduction.

The tension between the quality of a game and the length of the experience it provides is an enduring challenge for every type of game developer, and one that we should
always be discussing. It's my belief that players would rather have a shorter experience

that they're excited to play over and again than a longer, lower-quality experience that they'll play only once. Of course, the truth or wisdom of that is dependent on the player in question, and it is part of a game designer's job to understand the values and preferences of their particular community of players.

You can't learn to create a great game design macro overnight, but you can begin to hone your macro skills by starting with a small project and trying out the technique. As you progress as a game designer, and as you get to know the design opportunities and pitfalls of the style of games you like to make, writing a game design macro will get easier and easier, and eventually you'll come to value this practice as one of the most essential parts of your craft.

19 Scheduling

The preproduction phase of our project hasn't been tightly scheduled. We've been designing-by-making, playtesting and iterating on our game's vertical slice, and using a mixture of rationality and intuition to smoke out the excellent core of the design of our game. Now it's time to shift gears. Since we have a finite amount of time to work on our game, we need to keep track of what's going to go into our project, by scheduling it.

This doesn't mean we suddenly change from working in an enjoyable, liberated way to toiling under some bureaucratic management system. Our creativity will perish if we try to corral it too rigidly. But we do need to find a way to be confident that we won't run out of time as we enter the full production phase of our project, where we are going to build out the whole game. The two basic methods of game scheduling that we'll look at in this chapter will give you the best of both worlds. First, we'll look at a simple but effective approach to scheduling, and then I'll describe my favorite advanced method: the burndown chart.

Since these methods break down the work into tasks measured in hours, they work best for shorter projects with relatively few team members. Breaking the work down so finely may not be practical for larger, longer projects with more team members—it might just create too much bureaucracy. Some game studios schedule the work to be done by breaking it down into tasks measured in days or even weeks. You'll have to decide what is best for your project.

If you are just moving beyond beginner status as a game designer and producer, or if you're already at intermediate level and want to brush up your skills, then I recommend trying out the methods below. They can also be used for longer projects if you break the project down into sprints of two to four weeks. Sprint is a concept from agile development, where a team works toward a focused set of goals for a relatively short amount of time, before regrouping to evaluate their progress.

Simple Scheduling

Let's look first at a very simple scheduling method. Because we wrote a game design macro chart, we now have a document that describes everything important that's going into our game. Not only does the macro give us a blueprint for our game, it gives us the perfect starting point for scheduling the full production phase of our project. Now that we know how much work there is to do, we also need to know how much time we have to do it.

How Many Person-Hours Do We Have to Make Our Game?

Professional game developers need to make sure they get their project finished and are usually rigidly bound by time and money, whether they're funding their project themselves or it's being funded by someone else.

Running out of time to finish the game is the single greatest problem that game developers face. If the game isn't complete enough or good enough as the end of the project gets closer, we're faced with a choice: spend more time (and more money) to finish it properly or finish it more quickly but compromise on quality or length.

We can deal with this problem in a better way if, rather than realizing that we're running out of time near the end, we understand earlier in our process that we're over scope. Almost every tool that we've discussed this book—from our project goals to concentric development, the vertical slice, and the game design macro chart—is oriented toward this goal. The sooner we can understand that we're over scope, the sooner we can reallocate our resources and rescope our game, so that the finished game still feels complete and high quality.

The core resource available to game developers is the person-hour. This is a unit that measures the undivided attention of a single person working on the game. Money can be equated with person-hours, since one can pay for the other. It's good to see your time as financially valuable, especially if you are not used to valuing your time and the way it's spent. It's important that people should be compensated properly for their time.

So, as you reach the end of preproduction, work out how many person-hours you have available to create your game during full production. You can do a simple calculation to figure this out. First, decide how many weeks you will spend in full production to bring your project to the beta milestone when it is effectively finished and ready to be polished. You'll need to know how many team members you have on your project, and how many person-hours each of them will spend on the project in an average week. If you figure this out, you'll then have:

N = Number of team members

P = Person-hours that each team member will work in an average week

W = Number of weeks between the end of preproduction and the end of full production

To calculate T (for time), the number of person-hours that your project has available to take it from the end of preproduction to the end of full production, you can then use this formula:

$T = N \times P \times W$

So, for a two-person team ($N=2$), each of whom decides to work on the project for ten hours a week ($P=10$), with six weeks between the end of preproduction and the end of full production ($W=6$):

$T = 2 \times 10 \times 6 = 120$ person-hours

If the team members have different numbers of hours available to work each week, you'll have to adjust the calculation, but it's still pretty simple. For a two-person team in one of my classes, if one team member can work eight hours a week, and the other can work ten hours a week, with six weeks between the end of preproduction and the end of full production:

$T = (8 + 10) \times 6 = 108$ person-hours

The number of person-hours gives us a concrete starting point for figuring out whether our game is roughly in scope. Simply doing this calculation is an eye-opener for many people, and it's very grounding for anyone laboring under the illusion of infinite time. As we'll see in a moment, when we start to list out all the things we need to do during full production, these person-hours will soon get gobbled up.

Now that we know roughly how many person-hours we have at our disposal, we can start to work out how many person-hours we need to do everything listed in the game design macro chart.

The Simplest Schedule

I'm a fan of simple scheduling methods for games. Making games is a complicated business, and the reality on the ground of what we have to do and how long it takes to do it changes very rapidly. A simple schedule lets us know if we're roughly in scope without bogging us down in a lot of bureaucracy.

The simplest schedule starts with a straightforward list in a spreadsheet of tasks that we need to complete during full production to finish our game. The best way that I've found to do this is to list out the objects and characters that will go into the game, the environments that will make up the game, and all the other parts of our game that we mention in the game design macro chart. Sometimes making this list is as simple as copy-pasting from the macro chart into another spreadsheet.

It's also important to add other tasks to the simple schedule that don't correspond to an object, character, or environment in the game, but that we know we'll have to complete during full production, like the time taken for weekly planning meetings, for writing scripts for in-game dialogue, or for organizing and running playtests.

When we start to list out the tasks that go into making our game, it's easy to run into a challenge around how granular—in other words, how detailed—we should make our list. My advice is to use the completion time for each task to guide us. We'll talk more about that in a moment.

Simple Schedule Information for Each Task

Now that we have a list of tasks in a spreadsheet, we can move one step closer to a simple schedule by adding some information to each task.

Add four column headings to your spreadsheet, as shown in figure 19.1. Above your list of tasks add the label Task. One column over, add the label Priority. Next to that, add Hours Estimated. And to the right, add Team Member Assigned.

Priority

First, set a priority for each of the tasks. I recommend using three levels of priority. The most important things, which your game absolutely couldn't live without under any circumstances, should be set as **priority one**, the highest priority. For example, in a character-action game, that would be the player-character model, its traversal animations (and their audio and visual effects), its most basic control code, and the most simple and important pieces of environment art.

The things that the game needs but that you could possibly make some cuts from are **priority two**. I put the secondary elements here, like the verbs that the player-character uses to interact with the world, such as "pick up," "throw," and "talk." I also list the most basic objects that the player-character will interact with. That might be a coin to collect, a character to talk to, or an enemy to defeat. I also list the next-most important parts of the environment art here. Don't forget to list the audio and visual effects components too.

The things you could possibly cut under some circumstances should be set as **priority three**. Game verbs that it would be nice to have, but the game doesn't absolutely need. Variety in the objects and environment art. Bonus levels you want but could make do without.

Many game designers find it very hard to consider any of their tasks to be anything other than priority one. The game designs we've created hang together in our imagination with a kind of perfect crystalline integrity—all their parts seem equally important; none could exist without the others. How can we set any task to priority two or three?

Task	Priority	Hours estimated	Team member assigned
Game Object A - Model	1	4	Xavier
Game Object A - Textures	1	4	Yvette
Game Object A - Programming	1	8	Yvette
Game Object A - Animation	2	4	Xavier
Game Object A - Sound Design	2	2	Yvette
Game Object A - Visual Effects	3	1	Xavier

Figure 19.1
The beginnings of a simple schedule.

If we can bring ourselves to set some priorities for our work now, while we're making our first schedule, then later, when we have to make cuts for the sake of our project's scope, we'll have a clearer view of what we might be able to do without. I like to see this priority-setting as a kind of strategy game I'm playing with myself against the project scope.

I sure hope that I'll get to put everything into this game that I think it needs. But I trust myself enough as a game designer—and you should too—to know that if I have to cut something, I'll still be able to find a way to use the design elements at my disposal to make the game great. I've seen enough games developed to know that they are not born complete—they become complete through an iterative process of addition, subtraction, and refinement. So take a few moments to consider what your game absolutely needs and what it could possibly do without. Do you absolutely need all those levels or characters to tell your story? What if you had to make your game fun with just a single enemy type?

Of course, setting a priority for your tasks will also tell you what order to tackle them in. Priority one tasks should be completed first, then priority two tasks, then priority threes. Think back to our discussion of concentric development to help guide your hand when setting these priorities. I try to strike a balance in the finished list of around 40 percent priority one tasks, 30 percent priority two tasks, and 30 percent priority three tasks. That requires me to think just enough about the concentric order that I should do the work in and what I might have to cut.

(You can use the SUMIF function in your spreadsheet to work out how many hours' worth of tasks you have in each priority. Refer to your spreadsheet's documentation to see how to do this. It will take you a few minutes to figure it out, but SUMIF is an easy and useful function to learn.)

Don't worry: under most circumstances, you'll get to complete all of your priority one and priority two tasks, and most of your priority three tasks. However, while you've used your best instincts to imagine a game's design of the right size, you don't yet know if you are in scope. We're on the way to helping you to figure that out.

Hours Estimated

In this column, you should list out your best guess about how long it will take you, in a whole number of hours, to complete each task. By adding up the numbers in this column, you'll see how many hours of work you're planning to do in total during full production. If the number is bigger than the total number of person-hours you have available to your team for full production, you have a problem on your hands.

It's very difficult to estimate how long it's going to take to complete the tasks that go into making a game. It's doubly difficult if we're doing tasks of that type for the first time, in a new game engine, or with a new hardware platform. The difficulty of estimating how long things will take us is *the* reason why game projects are so difficult to bring under control. It's the reason for crunch at triple-A and indie studios; it's the reason for late projects and canceled vacations; it's the reason for the damaged physical and mental health of game developers who are being harmed by uncontrolled overwork. It's a nasty, thorny problem.

However, help is at hand in the form of a simple and clever scheduling trick. Under Hours Estimated, limit yourself to these numbers: 1, 2, 4, and 8. You can give a task one hour, two hours, four hours, or eight hours. Ninety minutes is not allowed. Neither is seven hours. Just 1, 2, 4, or 8.

I picked this trick up from the game designer, educator, and author Jeremy Gibson Bond, who taught me about the burndown chart technique we'll look at later. Jeremy explained that people are better at accurately estimating the length of short tasks than they are with longer tasks. The longer the duration of a game development task, the worse we become at making an accurate guess of how long it'll take us to complete.

Why is one hour the shortest task length we're allowed to put down? This is to help control the granularity of our list—if you have a lot of five-minute tasks that you're sure are five-minute tasks, put them down in your schedule grouped together under a single one-hour task. That way your task list won't get wildly long and difficult to read.

What about a bigger task that we think is only going to take us thirty minutes but is of a type that we haven't tackled before? Give it an hour in the schedule. As you know if you've spent any amount of time making videogames, a task that seems like it should be quick and easy will often take double the amount of time to complete that we thought it would, usually because of some unexpected problem that requires half an hour's detective work to solve.

Eight hours is the longest task that is allowed in our simple schedule. Because of the uncertainty that they introduce into the schedule, it's better to limit the number of eight-hour tasks that you put in your schedule. A job might seem like it's going to take eight hours but can easily end up taking half that time or, more likely, double it. Only use eight-hour tasks if you are completely confident that a task can be completed in eight hours. Tasks that are mechanically repetitive and won't need much creative thought or problem-solving, or tasks that can be timeboxed and wrapped up effectively when the eight hours are up, are good candidates.

It's best to break longer tasks down into shorter tasks. If you have a single task that you think will take sixteen hours, break it down into two separate tasks of eight hours, four tasks of four hours each, or eight tasks of two hours each.

Using the 1, 2, 4, 8 constraint helps us to write a schedule with tasks that we can be confident we will get done in the estimated time. It also gives us a good level of granularity in the way we list our tasks, with neither too many tasks listed out nor too few.

Team Member Assigned

Use this column to plan out which team member will tackle each task. You should assign the tasks based on who has the skills to do each job, but also by considering who is *excited* to make each part of the game. During my time at Naughty Dog, studio president Evan

Wells always encouraged the discipline leads to assign tasks to people who felt passionate about doing them, whenever possible. It's clear to me that the enthusiasm of individual team members creates a direct path to excellence in the resulting work.

Again, you can use the SUMIF function in your spreadsheet to keep a running tally of the number of hours of tasks that have been assigned to each team member. Of course, you should try to make sure that you're dividing up the work fairly, according to how many hours each team member can contribute. It's okay if any individual team member decides to do more or less work than their teammates each week, as long as we reach a prior agreement about this, so that our shared responsibility is consensual and well-negotiated. Different people are able to make different levels of contribution, based on the circumstances of their lives and the other responsibilities they have.

Scoping with a Simple Schedule

We now have all the information we need to check that our goals are likely to be achievable and that our project is probably within scope. We already calculated the number of person-hours, T, that our project has available to take it from the end of preproduction to the end of full production.

We can now use the SUM function in the spreadsheet to add up all the time in the Hours Estimated column of our simple schedule, to calculate how much work we're currently planning to do during full production. Let's call that number W (for work).

If we have more work than time, our project is over-scoped, and we're in trouble! If we have more time than work, we're fine.

if $W > T$ then we're over scope!

if $W <= T$ then we're in scope

The calculations involved here are inexact, of course—this method gives us a best guess, and if W is greater than T by less than 10 percent or so, we might still be in scope. But if W is significantly larger than T, we can be certain that we are over scope. We either need to bring on more team members or increase the duration of full production to increase T, or we must cut some features and content from our game to reduce the number of tasks and decrease W. That means going back to the game design macro chart and seeing what we can do without.

If W is much smaller than T, then either we have time to include some more things in our game, or we can use the extra time for polish. But it's much more common that, when people make their first schedule, W is larger than T—sometimes much larger—and we have to reduce the scope of our game. Sometimes simple decisions can bring things back into scope. Just cutting one level, and strategically moving parts of it to another level, might be enough. Sometimes the job of reworking the plan in the game design macro chart is harder.

This, right here, is the essence of project scoping. There's no arguing with this process. No matter how much you love your game design macro chart, if your simple schedule tells you that you don't have time to make all that game, then you have to find a better plan.

Living in denial, planning to just put in overtime, or hoping that things will go more quickly than you estimate is very unwise. Living in denial is clearly irrational. Hoping that things will go more quickly than you estimate is unrealistic, as every experienced game developer knows. Planning to put in overtime is more complicated but easily leads to the kind of crunch we discussed in chapter 15.

If you do plan to bring your project into scope by working longer hours, bear in mind that the number of consecutive weeks that people can work long hours is very limited, and that productivity loss and burnout quickly ensue. As Sarah Green Carmichael says, backed by research, in her article for the *Harvard Business Review* that I mentioned in chapter 15: "Even if you enjoy your job and work long hours voluntarily, you're simply more likely to make mistakes when you're tired. . . . Work too hard and you also lose sight of the bigger picture. Research has suggested that as we burn out, we have a greater tendency to get lost in the weeds. . . . The story of overwork is literally a story of diminishing returns: keep overworking, and you'll progressively work more stupidly on tasks that are increasingly meaningless."[1]

Another reason to scope a project well is the uncertainty of the future, and the days or weeks that every project loses to unforeseen events like ill health, family emergencies, expired software licenses, or broken hardware. Crucially, when we come to the critical last third of the project, when we're trying to draw all the strands of the game together with the last few important design decisions, we must not be exhausted, bad tempered, and demotivated, as crunching people quickly become. We need to arrive at the end of the project with good physical and mental health, so that we can make the right decisions and have the game turn out well.

Ironically, when people's passion drives them to try to make a game of greater scope than they have the person-hours to make, they often end up making a bad game, or no game at all. Scoping often boils down to a simple choice: you can make a forgettable larger game that no one wants to play, or you can make a smaller game that people love, remember, and enjoy playing over and over again.

Tracking a Project Using a Simple Schedule

You can use the simple schedule we've built to track your project as you move through full production by simply checking tasks off the list, as shown in figure 19.2. Each time you complete a task, use the strikethrough formatting in your spreadsheet to cross that row off the list.

---

1. Sarah Green Carmichael, "The Research Is Clear: Long Hours Backfire for People and for Companies," *Harvard Business Review*, August 19, 2015, https://hbr.org/2015/08/the-research-is-clear-long-hours-backfire-for-people-and-for-companies.

Task	Priority	Hours estimated	Team member assigned
~~Game Object A - Model~~	~~1~~	~~0~~	~~Xavier~~
~~Game Object A - Textures~~	~~1~~	~~0~~	~~Yvette~~
~~Game Object A - Programming~~	~~1~~	~~0~~	~~Yvette~~
Game ObjectA - Animation	2	4	Xavier
Game ObjectA - Sound Design	2	2	Yvette
Game ObjectA - Visual Effects	3	1	Xavier

Figure 19.2
Striking tasks off a simple schedule.

If you also change the Hours Estimated to zero for the completed tasks, that will update any calculations you've made using SUM and SUMIF, for the total hours remaining for each priority, team member, and in total.

But tracking your progress with a method this simple can be risky. Some weeks, things will go better than expected, and you'll race ahead of schedule. Other weeks, things will go slow, and you'll fall behind. Wouldn't it be great if you had a tool to help you work out whether you're ahead or behind overall? Good news: you can have one, and it's called a burndown chart.

The Burndown Chart

Ken Schwaber is a software developer and product manager who helped formulate the agile development framework Scrum. Ken invented the burndown chart as a scheduling tool to help Scrum teams predict the course of their projects, and he first described them on his website in 2000.[2]

During my time teaching in the USC Games program, I have seen burndown charts help over one hundred projects reach successful completion. I have watched as ambitious game developers have realized their dreams, without burning themselves out, simply by watching a line on a graph over the course of a few weeks.

A burndown chart creates a graphical representation of (a) the work left to do on your game before it's finished, (b) how quickly you're getting work done on average, and (c) whether you're going to run out of time. As such, it is extremely useful for helping us to get a handle on our project scope amid the uncertainties and unknowns involved in the complex creative process of making a videogame.

Setting up a burndown chart from scratch can be challenging, but you can find many examples and templates online, including on this book's website, playfulproductionpro cess.com. Many online project management tools offer an automatic burndown chart system, making burndown charts much easier to use.

---

2. "What Is a Burndown Chart?," Agile Alliance, accessed December 12, 2020, https://www .agilealliance.org/glossary/burndown-chart/.

Using a Burndown Chart

A burndown chart usually has two parts: (a) a spreadsheet or table, where data about the project tasks is entered, and (b) an infographic, where we can see at a glance whether we're likely to hit our milestone.

Entering the data about the project tasks is a lot like creating the simple schedule that we made in the previous section. We fill out the spreadsheet or table with a list of the tasks we have to complete in this project phase or sprint. (If a project phase is longer than four weeks, we can divide it up into shorter sprints.) We give each task a priority, using exactly the same criteria I described for our simple schedule, aiming for a roughly even split between priority one, two, and three tasks. We estimate the number of hours that we think each task will take to complete, and we only assign task lengths with values of 1, 2, 4, or 8. We assign each task to a team member, trying to apportion the work fairly, and in line with the time that each team member can commit to the project for this sprint. Most burndown charts will show us how many hours of tasks we have in each priority and assigned to each team member.

The burndown chart is set up so that it knows the date when we plan to start the sprint. In the example in figure 19.3 the sprint is due to start on 7/20 (July 20—you can see this date in the eighth row down). This example burndown chart is set up for a two-week sprint, from July 20 to August 2.

As we move forward through the sprint, we update the burndown chart to say how much work we have left to do to complete each of the listed tasks. We do this by finding the column that corresponds to today's date, by looking along the dates (again, in the eighth row down, in the example in figure 19.3). This burndown chart is set up so that we can update it every day, and it was only updated on 7/21 and 7/22.

As we work down the column for today's date, we look across at each of the tasks listed in the leftmost column. If we've done some work on that task, and now we think there are fewer hours than our original estimate remaining to do, we plug in our new best guess about how many hours are remaining in the same row as that task, and in the column corresponding to today's date. Some people choose to stick with the 1, 2, 4, 8 restrictions when updating their hours remaining, and some loosen the restriction to use any whole number. If a task is complete, we put a zero into the spreadsheet in the corresponding cell.

This is where part of the brilliance of the burndown chart comes into play. The burndown chart doesn't care about how much work we *did* on a task this week—it only cares how much work there is *left to do*. That's not to say that you shouldn't keep a record of how much work you do each week, to prevent you from working too hard and getting burned out, but the burndown chart is not the place to keep that record.

The Infographic

Once we've updated the spreadsheet for today's date, we're ready to look at the other part of the burndown chart. This is an infographic that will help us know whether we're on track to get everything done before the end of the sprint or whether we've fallen behind.

	Nickname	TOTAL (by dev)		Priority	TOTAL (priority)
Xavier	X	21		1	18
Yvette	Y	22		2	14
		43		3	11
					43

																	31
																	6
																	14
																	11

Features & Content	Priority	Hours est.	Assigned	7/20	7/21	7/22	7/23	7/24	7/25	7/26	7/27	7/28	7/29	7/30	7/31	8/1	8/2	Remaining
Example Feature 1	1	4	Y	4	0	0	0	0	0	0	0	0	0	0	0	0	0	0
Example Content 1	1	4	Y	4	4	2	2	2	2	2	2	2	2	2	2	2	2	2
Example Feature 2	1	2	X	2	0	0	0	0	0	0	0	0	0	0	0	0	0	0
Example Content 2	1	8	X	8	8	4	4	4	4	4	4	4	4	4	4	4	4	4
Example Feature 3	2	4	X	4	4	4	4	4	4	4	4	4	4	4	4	4	4	4
Example Content 3	2	4	Y	4	4	4	4	4	4	4	4	4	4	4	4	4	4	4
Example Feature 4	2	4	Y	4	4	4	4	4	4	4	4	4	4	4	4	4	4	4
Example Content 4	2	2	X	2	2	2	2	2	2	2	2	2	2	2	2	2	2	2
Example Feature 5	3	4	Y	4	4	4	4	4	4	4	4	4	4	4	4	4	4	4
Example Content 5	3	1	X	1	1	1	1	1	1	1	1	1	1	1	1	1	1	1
Example Feature 6	3	4	X	4	4	4	4	4	4	4	4	4	4	4	4	4	4	4
Example Content 6	3	2	Y	2	2	2	2	2	2	2	2	2	2	2	2	2	2	2

Figure 19.3

An example burndown chart spreadsheet. Image credit: Jeremy Gibson Bond, Richard Lemarchand, Peter Brinson, and Aaron Cheney.

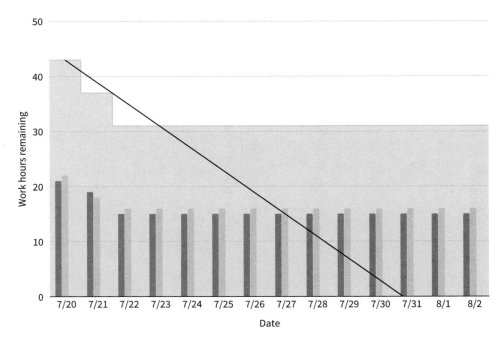

Figure 19.4

An example burndown chart infographic. Image credit: Jeremy Gibson Bond, Richard Lemarchand, Peter Brinson, and Aaron Cheney.

A burndown chart infographic usually looks something like the one in figure 19.4. This is the infographic for the spreadsheet in figure 19.3, and it shows several key pieces of information.

In our example, there is a pale gray area in the background, a group of vertical bars side by side, and a diagonal line. You can see that the horizontal axis is labeled along the bottom with the same dates that we saw earlier. The vertical axis is a representation of the number of hours of work remaining before we complete every single task in the burndown chart. Figure 19.5 takes a closer look at our infographic, this time with some explanatory labels.

The bars show the total number of hours of work that each team member has on their plate. (In this example, there are just two team members.) You can see those bars get shorter as we go along the horizontal axis to the right, as tasks are marked as underway or completed.

The gray background shows the total number of hours of work left to do. Its height at any given point along the horizontal axis is equal to the heights of the team members' bars combined. As we go through the project, marking tasks as complete, the gray background will march down and to the right across the graph in a stairstep pattern. Eventually, when we've completed all the work, the bars for the team members and the stairs of the gray background will reach the bottom, where the vertical Work Hours Remaining axis is equal to zero.

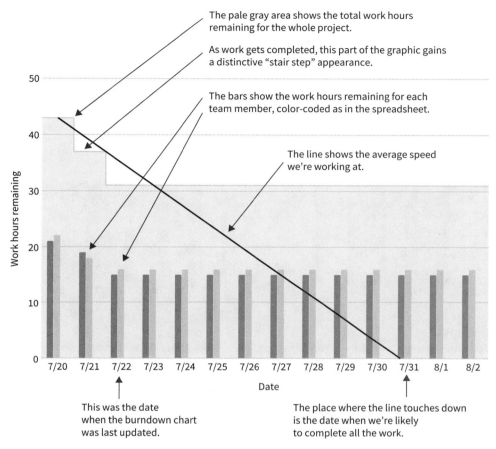

The pale gray area shows the total work hours remaining for the whole project.

As work gets completed, this part of the graphic gains a distinctive "stair step" appearance.

The bars show the work hours remaining for each team member, color-coded as in the spreadsheet.

The line shows the average speed we're working at.

This was the date when the burndown chart was last updated.

The place where the line touches down is the date when we're likely to complete all the work.

Figure 19.5
An example burndown chart infographic, annotated. Image credit: Jeremy Gibson Bond, Richard Lemarchand, Peter Brinson, and Aaron Cheney.

Now let's talk about that diagonal line, because it's the most important thing on the infographic. This line is an expression of the rate at which we're working, compared to how much work there is left to do. The place where the line reaches the horizontal axis, where the vertical axis is equal to zero, shows us the date on which our burndown chart predicts that we are likely to complete all our tasks.

I'll let that sink in for a moment. The burndown chart knows how much time has passed—it has a formula that references today's date—and it knows how much work we've managed to get done so far in total. It also knows how much work we have left to do. So, the chart can do a calculation to project into the future to show us when we are likely to get everything done by if we keep working at roughly the same rate we've been working so far. It averages out our better weeks, when we got more done, and our slow weeks, when we got less done. The date where the line touches the bottom of the graph gives us a pretty good guess about when we're going to be done.

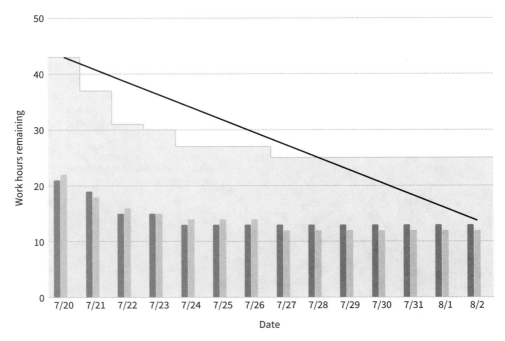

Figure 19.6
The same example burndown chart infographic, a few days later. Image credit: Jeremy Gibson Bond, Richard Lemarchand, Peter Brinson, and Aaron Cheney.

That means that as we move through a sprint or even a whole phase of the project, we can know on an ongoing basis whether we're behind schedule or ahead of schedule, on average. We can then make informed decisions about the scope of our project. Do we need to reduce our scope further? (That's when the priorities that we set for each task become very useful.) Should we bring more people onto the team? Are there other steps we can take—acting earlier, rather than later—to ensure that we have the time to get everything done to a good level of polish?

In figure 19.6 you can see the same burndown chart infographic a few days after figures 19.4 and 19.5. Both team members have managed to get some more work done, but their rate has slowed significantly. You can see that the stair steps in the gray background get a lot shallower as they head to the right. Maybe each teammate faced unexpected problems in the work that made each task take a lot longer than expected, or perhaps something else in their lives prevented them from having much time to work on the project.

Now the line no longer touches down at the bottom of the infographic. That means it's not likely that all the work due to get done during this sprint will get done. If we look over to read the vertical axis at the point when the line reaches the right side of the infographic, we can see that if the team keeps working at the same average rate, there will be about twelve hours of work remaining on 8/2, the last day of the sprint.

This team now has to make a plan to bring the project back on track. Their project is currently over scope for this sprint. They're likely to need to cut some tasks from the sprint. They could wait a couple more days to see if their working rate somehow increases. Perhaps they've overestimated the amount of time that the next few tasks will take, and their average working rate will increase again. Nonetheless, they should start to make a plan for what they can cut to get them back on track.

Deciding What Can Be Cut

Almost every game project runs into scoping problems during full production. Cutting features and content in order to bring a game back into scope is a key skill that every game designer must learn. When we're deciding what to cut, the lower-priority tasks are our first candidates. Having thought through our game's design when we were setting priorities, we began to figure out what we could possibly do without. (Please note that, depending on how we've structured our project, we might be completely cutting things from the game, or we may only be cutting things from the current sprint and could possibly include them in a future sprint.)

However, not every low-priority task will be easy to cut. Some will be more cuttable than others. Some relatively low-priority tasks might actually be firmly cemented into the design of the game by their relationship with other parts of the game, and others might be more independent of the overall design. As Mark Cerny recently reminded me: "What's important here is that you be aware which portions can be removed and which cannot. If the locale is needed for narrative or character progression, it can't be removed . . . so continuously reviewing project status and adjusting the design with knowledge of what has to be kept is quite important. That way you'll still be able to make adjustments late in development without doing harm to the game." Every type of game has its own considerations around what can easily be cut and what must remain, and as your game design practice develops, you'll get better at discerning one thing from the other.

Rescheduling in a Burndown Chart

When we realize that we're over-scoped for the current sprint (the period of the project covered by the burndown chart) and have decided what we're going to cut, we should remove the cut tasks from the chart. The best way to do this is to mark the task in the spreadsheet with strikethrough formatting and reduce its Hours Estimated to zero. (In some burndown charts, deleting a row will break the chart, and I like to be able to see what was cut; strikethrough achieves that.) This will remove the tasks from the calculations that the burndown chart is making and should make the line touch down further to the left, because there is now less work to do before the end of the sprint.

If you discover that you've grossly underestimated the time needed for the tasks, or that you need to do new tasks you hadn't anticipated before you can proceed, then you have a choice to make. It is generally not good to add tasks to a burndown chart or increase the Hours Estimated numbers during the middle of a sprint, because it can throw off the calculation. You *could* just keep working until you finish the tasks you underestimated, setting their hours to zero, having cut enough other tasks from the sprint to get you back on track. This leaves you flying blind, though. It is generally better to start a new sprint at the end of the week, with a better list of tasks and better estimations.

The burndown chart is a ready-reckoning device. It's not a way of knowing the future for certain, but it is an incredibly powerful tool for becoming better informed about what is likely to happen as we work to complete our game. In my experience, game developers (including me!) are not great at predicting when work will be completed. The mathematics tucked away inside a burndown chart give us an excellent handle on our progress. I've never found a scheduling method that works as well as the burndown chart, especially for scheduling relatively short projects or short sprints of work.

Many thanks to Jeremy Gibson Bond, who developed the original burndown chart that these examples are drawn from, and who taught me how to use this valuable tool. You can find more insight into the use of burndown charts in his excellent book *Introduction to Game Design, Prototyping, and Development*.[3] (In the interests of full divulgence, I wrote the foreword!)

Burndown Charts Create an Atmosphere of Trust and Respect

Production methods and scheduling tools can sometimes feel oppressive. Personally, I never do my best work when I feel like my performance is being scrutinized in an unfeeling way. Good project managers run teams using methods that help individual developers to work confidently, and they avoid setting up systems that prevent developers from feeling trusted and respected.

Because a burndown chart only records how much work we have left to do, rather than how much work we've done, it never feels like it's being used to check up on how many hours team members are putting in each week. If a team's leadership has a feeling that someone isn't living up to the commitment they made to the project, that's a special problem that needs addressing in its own way. But most game developers are well-intentioned, conscientious, and excited to do creative work.

The way to get the best out of people is to trust them and to demonstrate that trust by showing them respect. To believe that someone has put in their hours each week, even if it seems like they didn't make much progress, is to show them respect. The burndown chart is a scheduling tool that demonstrates respect to the developers on a team and builds trust as a consequence.

I've given you two approaches to scheduling a project here, one of them simple and one of them more complex. For creative people who are just starting to get to grips with

---

3. Bond, *Introduction to Game Design*, 227.

the challenge of bringing their time under better control, and who are learning to take responsibility for scoping their projects, these simple methods are a good place to start.

Once you have mastered the basics discussed in this chapter, there is more to learn about scheduling a digital game project. Professional producers on large teams often use complex scheduling systems, and you might want to learn about Gantt charts, which are used to track dependencies between tasks. You can find advanced ideas about project scheduling in books like *Agile Game Development: Build, Play, Repeat* by Clinton Keith and *The Game Production Toolbox* by Heather Maxwell Chandler.

You could also look at the scheduling tools included with software project management packages like Asana, Basecamp, HacknPlan, Jira Software, Monday, and Trello. Meredith Hall discusses these tools, and more besides, in her Gamasutra article "Choosing a Project Management Tool for Game Development."[4] You can also find low-cost or free project management tools for Agile teams online, like the "Top 7 Open Source Project Management Tools for Agile Teams" listed on opensource.com.[5]

It's my belief that everyone on a game development team should be involved in managing the team's time, not just producers and project managers. The time that we take to make a game is inextricably bound up with our playful, iterative, creative process. If everyone participates in looking ahead thoughtfully, then together we will ensure that we are running our project in a way that achieves our project goals.

Whatever scheduling methods you adopt, I wish you luck. Try to figure out as early as you can when your project is over scope and continue to keep an eye on scope as you move forward through full production. Keep your methods oriented toward a team culture filled with trust and respect, and on tracking the realities of the project with as little bureaucracy as possible. If you do so, you will be fulfilling a key job responsibility of an effective producer: helping your teammates to do their jobs as well as they possibly can.

---

4. Meredith Hall, "Choosing a Project Management Tool for Game Development," Gamasutra, June 29, 2018, https://www.gamasutra.com/blogs/MeredithHall/20180629/321013/Choosing_A_Project_Management_Tool_For_Game_Development.php.
5. "Top 7 Open Source Project Management Tools for Agile Teams," Opensource.com, January 13, 2020, https://opensource.com/article/18/2/agile-project-management-tools.

20   Milestone Reviews

Game culture is full of what I call communities of review at every level of the creation and enjoyment of videogames. Professional game reviewers publish reviews that inform game buyers' purchasing decisions. Game players publish user reviews on review aggregation and game distribution sites. Social media personalities talk about games as they play them live in a video stream. Publishers review game projects that they're paying to have developed, and there are many different ways that publishers and other stakeholders give feedback to a development team. Game development teams hold internal reviews of their in-progress projects. A process of review is built into the iterative cycle of design-develop-playtest-analyze-design that we've been discussing throughout this book. (It's the "analyze" part.) For example, everyone on a team constantly reviews their work as they build out their parts of the game, as we'll discuss in chapter 23.

In this chapter, we'll focus on the kind of project-wide review that happens at major milestones throughout a project. We'll look at a type of review that brings together the game development team (or certain members of the team, including its most senior members) with a group of people from outside the team who look at the game and give some steering advice.

When to Run Milestone Reviews

In our playful production process, milestone reviews happen at these major milestones:

- The end of preproduction
- The alpha milestone
- The beta milestone

These milestones offer good points to pause and review the work in a comprehensive way. The end of preproduction, when the deliverables of vertical slice, game design macro, and schedule arrive, is an excellent moment to look at the game that is materializing. It's often very clear whether a strong design has emerged and is barreling forward, or if the core design of the game still needs some figuring out. We'll look at the alpha and beta milestones in future chapters. There's also a special kind of review that happens when the project is complete, the post-project review. We'll look at that in chapter 36.

On longer projects, where there are more than a few weeks between each milestone, we should hold additional reviews between these milestones. In my experience, it's usually helpful to a game development team to have a project-wide review every three or four months, to help make sure things are staying on track. In some cases, such as games-as-live-service, you should continue to hold milestone review meetings beyond the game's release, to discuss the responses of the game's community of players and as the game's design continues to evolve with patches and updates.

Internal and External Milestone Reviews

This chapter is going to focus on external milestone review meetings that bring people in from outside the team to give their opinions about the game, but at each major milestone, the whole team should also get together to discuss the project with each other. By having an internal milestone review meeting, the team can gain additional consensus and clarity about what is working well in the game and in their development process, and what problems they need to address. Each individual or group will also come to understand their teammates' perspectives on the game in a deeper way.

If a team is too large to have an internal review with everyone present, then multiple meetings could take place, with discipline meetings (the art group, the engineering group, and so on) and with interdisciplinary groups made up of members from every discipline. The deep specialization of a discipline focus *and* the collaborative, synergistic mindset of an interdisciplinary viewpoint are both very valuable at each milestone.

Holding a Milestone Review

Holding a milestone review requires some preparation from the development team and from their leadership in particular. If a project is running well, the work that has been done to meet each milestone naturally dovetails with the work needed for the review. Some additional work will be needed from the people who will present the work for review but maybe not much.

A milestone review begins with setting some time aside for the review. For a short game, this could be as little as fifteen or twenty minutes. For a big game, it could take a whole day or longer. Choose a comfortable meeting room or classroom with good video and audio, and be sure to have water available—there's going to be a lot of talking in the review, and mouths will get dry. Then, the development team (or their leaders) will prepare to present the work. We'll look at what they should prepare in a moment.

Next, a group of people to review the work should be assembled. This review group will give advice about what's working and what isn't in the emerging design of the game. Very often in the game industry, a milestone review group will be made up almost entirely of project stakeholders, the people who are putting up the money to create the game. We'll look at this in greater detail under "Presenting to Project Stakeholders," below.

The heads of the studio will usually be present, as will other members of leadership and other developers from around the studio. People from outside the studio might be brought in too—board members or consultants. The review process works best if the people reviewing the game are game developers themselves, who know the ins and out of the game-making process. In a class where multiple games are being developed, the team's classmates, instructor, and student assistants make excellent review group members.

When the date and time of the milestone review arrives, everyone meets, and the review process begins. A typical milestone review meeting will run something like this:

1. The developers briefly introduce their game and summarize where they're at with the project.

2. The game is demoed or playtested in front of the review group.

3. If appropriate, a senior member of the review group starts the process of giving notes.

4. The other review group members pitch in with their notes, making remarks about the game. Lively conversation between them might ensue.

5. When the time allocated for the review is up, the game developers thank the group for their feedback.

6. In a setting where multiple projects are being reviewed, like a quarterly business meeting or a game development class, we move on to the next project.

Let's dive more deeply into this process.

1. **The developers briefly introduce their game and summarize where they're at with the project.**

   a. The team will typically use presentation slides to help them introduce their game in an effective way.

   b. Introduce the project by its current name. If it's only a working title, say so.

   c. The team describes who they consider to be the audience for their game. They could use the simple positioning statement we created in chapter 7, "The possible audience for our game is . . ."

   d. The team briefly describes the state of the project as it currently stands. They might describe a major piece of work that was recently completed, or the content of what they're presenting that day. If the work corresponds to a milestone, they say whether they met or exceeded the requirements of the milestone. If they didn't hit the milestone, they say what's missing.

   e. They describe any known issues with the game, including any big problems that they know will jump out at the review group. Depending on the nature of the problem, this can help the review group decide whether to give advice or to not waste time on a known issue.

   f. If appropriate, they say what kind of feedback it would be useful to receive from the review group.

g. This initial presentation part of the review is kept as short as possible—we want to start looking at the game as quickly as we can.

2. **The game is demoed or playtested in front of the review group.**

a. Depending on the game and its state, the game team will either show the game by playing it themselves, or they'll ask for a playtester to play it in front of the review group.

b. It's often better to demo the game when it is in a relatively early state, with known problems that new players will stumble over. It's also better to demo the game when there is a lot of content that the team wants to be sure that the review group sees.

c. Sometimes a game will have a twist or surprise ending that the presenters might be reluctant to reveal for fear of "spoiling" the experience. While the game's eventual audience of players should be shielded from spoilers, the review group should not be. They're there to help, and so need to know everything about the structure of the game in order to give a good analysis.

d. When seeing a game for the first time, a review group may choose to hold back its comments until the end. However, as a review group gets more familiar with a particular game over successive review meetings, it may begin to offer their comments "live" while the game is still being demoed.

e. This kind of live commenting is more appropriate for some types of games than others. If the live comments affect the way that other members of the review group receive the game—for example, in a particularly tense or emotional game— then it's best to hold comments until after the game has been shown.

3. **If appropriate, a senior member of the review group leads off in the process of giving notes.**

a. At a studio, the most senior non-team member present—the studio president or a design director—might give their notes first. In a classroom setting, the instructor might do the same. This can be useful to set a tone for the discussion or to immediately identify any major issues that seem (to the senior member, at least) particularly worthy of discussion.

b. This moment presents an opportunity for the senior review group member to use "sandwiching" (chapter 6) and "I Like, I Wish, What If . . . ?" (chapter 12) to set a tone of confidence in the designers, respect for their work, and collegial, constructive criticism.

c. The senior member should keep their remarks relatively brief, framing the big issues they see. The goal is to open things up for conversation and even debate among the other review group members as quickly as possible.

4. **The other review group members pitch in with their notes, making remarks about the game. Lively conversation between them might ensue.**

a. The review group members might either start speaking spontaneously or will raise their hand to be called on by the game team, or whoever is leading the meeting.

b. The conversation about the game often develops quite naturally. Members of the review group will build off—and sometimes disagree with—each other's comments. It can be very productive when members of the review group disagree with one another, and when some (polite, respectful) debate ensues, digging deeply into the issues that they see in the game.

c. One of the presenting team members takes notes (or, with the permission of the review group, makes an audio or video recording) to capture the review group's comments.

d. The developers might reshow sections of the game that the review group are particularly interested to discuss. If the game is short, they might show the whole thing again. This can prompt in-depth discussion about this or that part of the game.

e. During the discussion, the game's designers quickly get a quite clear picture of the strengths and weaknesses of their work, as the review group sees it. They also find out if there are any aspects of their game that different people see in different ways.

5. **When the time allocated for the review is up, the game developers thank the group for their feedback.**

a. It's a matter of common courtesy for the game developers to thank the review group for their time, attention, and expertise.

b. This act also creates a good end cap to the session and builds an implicit bridge to the next time that the review group will look at the game.

6. **In a setting where multiple projects are being reviewed, like a quarterly business meeting or a game development class, we move on to the next project.**

a. In my classes, we divide up the time we have available for review evenly among the projects, in the interests of fairness. Some games take longer to play than others, and we deal with this on a case-by-case basis.

b. The development team and review group members can follow up with each other outside the meeting if time is up but there's more useful conversation to be had.

c. The amount of time we spend looking at each game usually increases as development progresses.

   i. At the end of preproduction, we spend fifteen minutes looking at each game. The vertical slices we're looking at are often quite short and may only take two or three minutes to play through. This leaves us plenty of time for discussion.

   ii. At the alpha and beta milestones, we spend progressively longer looking at each game, increasing to at least thirty minutes.

The Pixar Braintrust

This process, or some variation on it, works well for most types of milestone review. It's partly inspired by the Braintrust process discussed by Ed Catmull and Amy Wallace in their book *Creativity, Inc.* Variations of this method can be found in creative communities around the world.[1]

An interesting and important thing about the Pixar Braintrust is that it has no direct authority over the creative people whose work is being reviewed: it is a peer review group, where directors, storytellers, and artists from different projects come together to review works in progress in a collegial way, without having the authority to give notes that *must* be acted upon. It's up to the team to listen to the feedback they're given and decide how to address it.

At the same time, the creative people whose work is being reviewed do have a responsibility to solve the problems that are identified. If the same problems come up over and over again in successive milestone meetings, that's a red flag about a bigger problem with the project that will eventually need to be addressed, maybe by canceling the project or changing its leadership.

Of the Braintrust, *Creativity, Inc.* says that "its most important characteristic was an ability to analyze the emotional beats of a movie without any of its members themselves getting emotional or defensive."[2] It goes on to say,

> Because of the way the Braintrust is structured, the pain of being told that flaws are apparent or revisions are needed is minimized. Rarely does a director get defensive, because no one is pulling rank or telling the filmmaker what to do. The film itself—not the filmmaker—is under the microscope. You are not your idea, and if you identify too closely with your ideas, you will take offense when they are challenged. To set up a healthy feedback system, you must remove power dynamics from the equation—you must enable yourself, in other words, to focus on the problem, not the person.[3]

Too often, games don't get good feedback at a milestone review, because of a power dynamic around the game team: a studio president or publisher wants certain features or content and might raise hell if they don't get it. Especially in a commercial context, a game team's leadership will often have to deal with reviews of this type, as we'll discuss in "Presenting to Project Stakeholders," below.

So, the more that we can bring the Pixar Braintrust mindset into our process of reviewing our games as we work on them, the better. Removing power struggles from the review process allows us to focus on the objective qualities of the game and the ways in which it is or isn't meeting its project goals.

---

1. Catmull and Wallace, *Creativity, Inc.*, 86.
2. Catmull and Wallace, *Creativity, Inc.*, 70.
3. Catmull and Wallace, *Creativity, Inc.*, 93.

What Makes a Good Note?

A *note* is a piece of feedback, and you'll find this term is used in many different creative fields. A note that I give you about your work, whether it's a videogame, a screenplay, or a painting, is some remark of mine about my perceptions, thoughts, feelings, and theories about your work in progress, that I hope you'll find useful. Depending on whether I'm your peer, your boss, or your friend, my notes might have a certain flavor or strength. Great game designers are always on the lookout for the good notes that will help them to improve their games.

A milestone review group gives lots of notes, about almost anything that they see in the game. They might mention things that they like. They might ask a question about something that wasn't clear or give a suggestion to make something good even better. They might identify things that they perceive as weaknesses or problems in the game. Some notes are helpful, full of insight into ways to make the work better, and some are not. So, what makes a good note?

Directness

First, a note should be direct. It should honestly deliver the useful information it has to give. Sandwiching and "I Like, I Wish, What If . . . ?" are both excellent techniques for framing a note in a kind and respectful way, but don't beat around the bush: say what you have to say.

Most people value honesty and aspire to be honest. But honesty brings difficulties with it. You might be unsure how someone else is going to react to hearing what you think, and total honesty can be brutal. It can wound, anger, or demotivate. At one time in my life, I found the need to be compulsively, reflexively honest, but it often didn't help me or anyone else very much.

I still wanted to be direct—to speak my truth, as I see it, in a straightforward way—and over time, I found better ways to be honest, by choosing my words thoughtfully, by focusing on compassion for everyone involved, and by choosing the right moment to say what I have to say. Sometimes it's important to speak privately with someone about a sensitive topic, for example. *Creativity, Inc.* talks about this in terms of "candor."[4]

By shifting my approach from total, brutal honesty toward a kinder, considerate kind of directness, I became much more useful to others, and I helped myself, too. I am now much better at being direct in my communication in a way that can be received well. If you focus on tactful directness as you communicate, you won't go too far wrong—in giving a note or in life.

---

4. Catmull and Wallace, *Creativity, Inc.*, 86.

Constructive and Timely Criticism

For a note to be useful, it must be both constructive and timely. *Creativity, Inc.* lays out some thoughts about this very clearly when the authors say:

> A good note says what is wrong, what is missing, what isn't clear, what makes no sense. A good note is offered at a timely moment, not too late to fix the problem. A good note doesn't make demands; it doesn't even have to include a proposed fix. But if it does, that fix is offered only to illustrate a potential solution, not to prescribe an answer. Most of all, though, a good note is specific. "I'm writhing with boredom," is not a good note.[5]

There's a lot of wisdom crammed into this short paragraph. Let's unpack it.

"A good note says what is wrong, what is missing, what isn't clear, what makes no sense." The milestone review group is looking for problems in the game they're reviewing: things that they can see but the developers can't. It might be that something is wrong or is missing: the game gets too difficult too quickly or doesn't get difficult enough, or maybe the game doesn't give the player an opportunity to learn how to play it. In game design, problems are very often related to a lack of clarity: I can't understand how those game systems work, what that resource does, or who this character is. It might be that the game doesn't create the emotional experience that the designer intends. It might come off as unintentionally funny when the designer wants it to seem deadly serious.

As you can see, most of these possible problems are dependent on what the designer intends. Review group members will often ask about the designer's intent before they give a note. Sometimes the designer's intent will be relevant, and sometimes not. I can imagine situations where a designer would be wise to hear a note, irrespective of their intent.

"A good note is offered at a timely moment, not too late to fix the problem." The closer we get to the end of the project, the more important this aspect of note-giving becomes. It's less of a consideration during the earlier milestone reviews, when all issues are up for grabs. It's crucial to talk about almost every issue that the review group sees in a vertical slice, because we want the design foundations of a project to be strong. But we can't add any more features beyond the alpha milestone (see chapter 28) and we can't add any more content after the beta milestone (see chapter 31), so the notes from the review group should keep these production realities in mind.

"A good note doesn't make demands; it doesn't even have to include a proposed fix. But if it does, that fix is offered only to illustrate a potential solution, not to prescribe an answer." Some people think that for criticism to be constructive, it *must* offer a solution to a problem. But sometimes it might be enough just to identify a problem. At Pixar, the Braintrust review group doesn't have authority and isn't trying to tell anyone what to do, and *Creativity, Inc.* says that that's what makes it work so well. What is most useful for artists of all types is to understand what *isn't* working for the people

5. Catmull and Wallace, *Creativity, Inc.*, 103.

who encounter their work. This opens up a space of communication about solving the problem, where we can iterate until we eventually find the right solution.

"Most of all, though, a good note is specific. "I'm writhing with boredom," is not a good note." I recognize this principle from my time at Naughty Dog, where we would always try to keep our feedback focused on what we saw on the screen, heard through the speakers, and felt through the controller in our hands. Making a note concrete and specific, avoiding abstracts or generalizations, and only ever critiquing the game design, never the designer, is the most constructive way to move a game design conversation forward.

Creativity, Inc. sums up good note-giving and constructive criticism by quoting the director Andrew Stanton:

> There's a difference between criticism and constructive criticism. With the latter, you're constructing at the same time that you're criticizing. You're building as you're breaking down, making new pieces to work with out of the stuff you've just ripped apart. That's an art form in itself. I always feel like whatever notes you're giving should inspire the recipient—like, "How do I get that kid to want to redo his homework?" So you've got to act like a teacher. Sometimes you talk about the problems in fifty different ways until you find that one sentence that you can see makes their eyes pop, as if they're thinking, "Oh, I want to do it."[6]

What Should the Presenting Game Developers Do during a Milestone Review?

As we discussed in chapter 12, our memories are generally faulty and strongly colored by emotion. So the developers who are presenting their game should do what every game designer should do in every context when they are receiving feedback: *write it down.* (Or make a recording, with the review group's permission.) By recording every note we receive during a milestone review, they are readily at hand for later analysis, when the game designers on the team are discussing how to react to the constructive criticism of the review group.

When any game designer is presenting their game, they should try not to get defensive. Receiving feedback can be an emotional process but becoming heated and starting to argue in defense of one's work never helps. Designers should always stay emotionally cool while a critique of their work is unfolding, and instead of arguing a point, should ask for clarification.

The time for discussion will come later, when the team is trying to figure out how to respond to the feedback from the review group. For the presenting designers to argue too much during the meeting would waste valuable time when they could be getting a lot of high-quality notes. There are moments when it's appropriate and useful for a game's designer to explain something in the game, to help a review group member refine their feedback. I encourage people to explain just enough to bring the note on point.

---

6. Catmull and Wallace, *Creativity, Inc.*, 103.

Presenting to Project Stakeholders

So far, we've been discussing a Pixar Braintrust–style milestone review, which works very well for teams who can bring in trusted peers to help give perspective on a game, and in game design classes where students are contributing constructive critique of their classmates' games. However, as we've mentioned a few times in this chapter, a very common type of milestone review in the game industry happens when a project's stakeholders—the people funding the project—review a game as a work in progress. In the past, game project stakeholders have usually been game publishers. Today, money might come to game projects from a variety of financial and creative institutions, as the game industry grows and diversifies.

At a milestone review meeting, the stakeholders might want to check in on a game's progress toward completion, or they may have concerns about the direction that a game's design has taken since the last milestone review. There could have been a change in strategic plan or leadership on the part of the stakeholders, and there may be new questions about the game or its marketability. Future funding for the game—and therefore the livelihoods of the people working at the studio—may very well be dependent on the outcome of the milestone review, with a bad review possibly leading to a delayed milestone payment, slashed budgets, or a canceled project. Because of the costs of the overheads associated with running a game studio with a bricks-and-mortar location, a single delayed milestone payment might lead to the bankruptcy or closure of a studio without much in the way of cash reserves.

A milestone review meeting to project stakeholders has a different dynamic than a Braintrust-style review. Accordingly, the development team's leadership may be called on to explain or justify the design decisions that the team have made so far. Setting a clear agenda for a milestone review meeting could be useful to help keep the meeting on track and to make sure there aren't any difficult surprises in store during the meeting. A pre-review discussion between members of leadership on both sides could help with this. Bringing empirical data about positive feedback that a game has received during playtests can also help developers to show their game in its best possible light.

A full discussion of everything that might happen during a milestone review meeting with project stakeholders is outside the scope of this book. The key players in any conflict that takes place around a milestone review presentation to project stakeholders will need strong skills of negotiation, excellent business acumen, and extensive knowledge of contract law, in order to be able to navigate the terrain in a way that creates the best outcomes for everyone.

The more that can be done to cultivate a relationship between the development team and the stakeholders based on trust and respect, the better the milestone review process will be. Healthy relationships are precious and take time to develop, which is why developers and publishers will often work with each other from project to project. If you are a game developer, seek out financial backing for your projects from stakeholders who have a reputation for fair dealing and who are known to support—rather than work in opposition to—the game developers they strike deals with. Scrupulously avoid any publisher that has a track record of withholding or denying milestone payments on trumped-up grounds. Such practices are a simple "smell test" for business integrity. In addition, game developers should avoid overpromising in terms of their milestone deliverables, to avoid creating an inaccurate impression in their business partners of what they should expect to see at a milestone review.

Don't hesitate to seek out expert advice from experienced members of game industry leadership teams when you find yourself faced with the challenges around milestone review presentations to your project's stakeholders. Mentors and board members are often happy to help when difficult situations arise.

Emotional Aspects of the Milestone Review Process

When we present our work to others, it can feel like there's a lot at stake—and if our game's future funding is dependent on a milestone review, there may actually *be* a lot at stake. Showing work that isn't finished or that has problems can be emotionally exposing because of the relationship we have with the creative things we make and because of the financial risk that might also be involved.

As a result, we should take a moment to consider the emotional aspects of the milestone review process. First, I want to acknowledge that the emotions you feel as a part of a milestone review are real. I would never tell you that you should just suck them up, stuff them down, or tough it out. In my experience, that just shunts the emotions away into a hidden place where they can curdle and ferment, gaining strength. Stuffed emotions will inevitably creep up on you later and give you a nasty surprise at an inappropriate moment.

Throughout the development process, it is helpful to keep our emotions under control—not to suppress them, but to manage them so they don't negatively impact the game design work that we're doing. Strong emotions like anger or fear that are expressed in an uncontrolled way can be damaging to groups of collaborators, though you shouldn't feel like you have to completely hide your feelings from your teammates. They'll know if you're upset; just do what you can to moderate your feelings. If it helps you to let go of difficult emotion by venting—letting out anger or fear by giving voice to them—then find an appropriate time and place to vent, where you have some distance from your teammates. Your nonwork friends or family members might be able to offer you this kind of support, so you can come back to your work feeling better and ready to focus on your game.

On the teams I've been on, I've always made it a point to remember that we were all working together toward the greatness of our game. Working in a way that builds strong collaborative relationships between team members is a reliable path to excellence in game design, and there is nothing as satisfying as the feeling that you're working at your optimal capacity among peers who respect and trust you. This good feeling can extend to the members of a milestone review group, if we keep this same attitude of openness to input and gratitude for the ideas that are being given to us.

Milestone reviews work best when they are founded on trust, respect, and empathy. The more trust that can develop between the game developers whose work is under review, and the group that is giving notes, the better. Some review processes can be brutal or even cruel. I'm sure you've heard of critique sessions in the creative arts that reduced people to tears. In my experience, that kind of process is rarely constructive. As reviewers we should work to be kind, respectful, and supportive. Making art is tough enough, and we should present our critique in a way that can be heard. In my professional life, I had to learn to get my ideas across so that the design could be improved, but I also needed to choose my words—and sometimes, my timing—carefully, so my feedback would make it across to the person who needed to hear it and not get blocked by a wall of their defensiveness.

As game designers and developers, we need to look deeply at our work in order to improve it, and that might mean being exposed to opinions that are difficult for us to hear. The tension between humility and ego is an important one for every creative person. We need an ego—a point of view—to make creatively interesting work, but we also need to be humble and remain open to new ideas, opportunities, and solutions if our work is to excel.

Despite whatever attempts we make to have our milestone review process be collegial and free of power dynamics, the process of critique is often explicitly or implicitly hierarchical. It's naive for a studio head or a professor to ignore the authority they hold as an aspect of their role or the power held by review group members who are very senior, charismatic, or popular. There are also questions of social equity to consider, as people from marginalized communities might receive critique in a fundamentally different way from those with privilege. Every creative community and review group will have to find their own way through this. Returning to the grounding principles of respect, trust, and consent might help.

Game designers today, from indie to triple-A, will regularly reach out to their friends and peers, sending them builds of their games or bringing them into the studio to get their feedback. It's very healthy for game designers to get a large amount of informed feedback on a game by game design experts who don't have any kind of stake—financial, emotional, or social—in their games.

When a review group gets to know a developer, as the individuals in the review group get to know each other, and if bonds of mutual respect and trust are set up, that review group becomes one of the most powerful resources that the game development team has at their disposal. Don't miss the opportunity to receive this valuable input throughout the lifetime of your project, and particularly as you reach each of your project's major milestones.

21 The Challenge of Preproduction

The preproduction phase of a project offers us a significant challenge. Three big deliverables come due at the end of preproduction: the vertical slice, the game design macro, and a schedule. They must be created in a relatively short amount of time—usually about a third of the total project length—and during that time we have to make a large number of important decisions about our game.

However, taken together, the ideation phase and the preproduction phase create a good on-ramp to this decision-making process. As we discussed in chapter 15, it's best to work hardest in the middle of a project. The increased amount of effort that it takes us to get to the end of preproduction very naturally maps onto a gradual ramping up of our momentum as we move through ideation and preproduction.

Most creative projects gather momentum as we work on them. The more work we do, the more committed we become to our ideas, and the more we understand the design elements that we're working with. The plan for what we're making becomes clearer and clearer to us, we get used to our tools and workflow, and we figure out how to communicate effectively with our teammates. Some creative people get so caught up in their momentum that they forget to figure out whether their project is in scope. That's why we make a macro and a schedule, and it's appropriate to do this well before we hit the halfway mark of our project—to plan our time while we still have a good chunk of it left.

As we'll see in this book's next section, where we'll discuss the full production phase of the project, even though we write the macro and schedule at the end of preproduction, it'll probably take us a little while to settle down into a firm, final plan. So don't be paralyzed by the challenge of creating a game design macro, or mistake it for something bureaucratic, inflexible, and intractable. There will still be room for maneuver in full production.

Committing to a Design

I'm a fan of "yes, and" styles of communication and design collaboration, where we build constructively on each other's ideas to move a design forward. I try to say "yes, and" whenever I can throughout every creative interaction and in every phase of a project.

However, designers in every field—not just game design—do have to say no a lot as part of their process. A designer has to be able to recognize when an idea has a fatal flaw in it. It's an inevitable part of the design process that, when we're entertaining a particular design idea, we have to think the idea through from many different perspectives and identify any obvious reasons why it won't work. Perhaps the interaction between two design elements will undermine the experience we're trying to create. It could be the case that the design will create a situation that is physically unsafe, like causing someone to run into a wall in virtual reality or wander into traffic while looking at their phone. Maybe a particular design approach will be too expensive in terms of time or money.

We have to find design ideas to commit to that we can't imagine any major problems with. It's likely that we'll still find problems when we begin to work with those ideas, but if we start with ideas that seem okay, then at least we're setting out down a good track. So, at the start of preproduction, you might be saying no a lot in conversations about your game's design. Of course, you want to make sure that the reasons for your disagreements are grounded in reason and rationality, rather than differences in taste, attempts to gain power, or contrariness.

By halfway through preproduction, you want to make sure you're reaching more agreements than disagreements about your game's design. You have to shift into a mode where you are committing to ideas rather than rejecting them. A good way to do this is to synthesize seemingly differing concepts into new ideas that hang together well. As designers, we all have a natural tendency to want to defer a final decision until later when we have more information and have had more time to think. That's not how we become better designers, though.

We become better designers by making a few solid decisions that we trust and then running with them, committing to even more ideas that build on that foundation. Even if we make mistakes, at least we are designing, not spinning our wheels.

Canceling a Project if Preproduction Doesn't Go Well

In Mark Cerny's D.I.C.E. Summit talk, he spends some time discussing a difficult but important aspect of the preproduction phase: canceling a project if preproduction doesn't go well. In Method, preproduction culminates in a greenlight process, where the results of preproduction—the vertical slice and the macro—are presented to the project's stakeholders: the people who will put up the money for the completion of the project. It's up to the stakeholders to evaluate what they see and to decide whether this is a game that they think will be successful in the marketplace.

If the stakeholders believe the project will be successful, then it will be granted additional funds and can move forward into full production. If the stakeholders have reason to doubt that the project will be a success, then either the development team will be given some more time and money to address the issues that the stakeholders see, or the project will be canceled, and the team will go on to work on something else.

It's not cheap to create a vertical slice. In 2002, Mark Cerny estimated that preproduction could cost a million dollars, and today it could cost a *lot* more than that. Mark acknowledges that spending a large sum of money on preproduction for a project that might not get greenlit might sound like a license just to blow a lot of cash, but maintains that this is an important and ultimately money-*saving* part of the process.

> By being cost inefficient during preproduction, you are in fact being cost efficient vis-à-vis the actual production of the game. That's because if it's not going to work out, you only blew a million dollars. You could blow a lot more, believe me.[1]

At the time of writing, a commercial videogame might cost anywhere between fifteen and one hundred and fifty million dollars to develop, and might cost an additional equivalent amount in marketing spend. How much better would it be to spend a fraction of the development and marketing budget of a big game in building a vertical slice, to prove whether or not we can make something good, than to bring a game to market only to have it flop? We could explore risky but exciting new game styles and story subjects, instead of relying on the same familiar, tried-and-true approaches. Happily, publishers finally seem to be coming around to this way of thinking, though we still have a long way to go.

Of course, this greenlight sink-or-swim process can lead to disappointment and even frustration on the part of the developers. It is certainly hard to put your heart and soul into a project only to have it seemingly rejected. Mark Cerny has some words of consolation for a team whose project does not receive a green light, which he offers them by way of dispelling a myth:

> "A canceled project is a sign of bad management or a bad team." Well, no, actually! A canceled project is sometimes something to be very proud of. Regardless of the talent of the team, if you can't reach a compelling first playable [vertical slice], it's time to kill the project and move on. Folks, you just saved yourself several million dollars and a year of the team's lives.[2]

The respect that Mark shows here for the development team's time is admirable and an often-neglected aspect of the cultures around game creation. Showing respect for each other's time, whether we are game developers or game players, game marketers or game businesspeople, is something that ultimately benefits everyone in terms of increased trust and better games.

Onward into Full Production

Now that we've (a) used a vertical slice to create a design for our game that we know has a solid core, and (b) begun to bring the scope of our project under control using a game design macro and a schedule, we're ready to move into full production.

---

1. Mark Cerny, "D.I.C.E. Summit 2002," https://www.youtube.com/watch?v=QOAW9ioWAvE, 6:26.
2. Cerny, "D.I.C.E. Summit 2002," 26:48.

In the next section of this book, I'll look at how we shift gears as we move from preproduction to full production. I'll describe stand-up meetings, a simple technique to keep our team in sync as we work together. I'll discuss ways to further formalize our playtesting process so we can become more and more confident that the game we're making is turning out okay, and I'll tell you about game metrics, where we build tools that give us deep insights into our players' experiences and our game's design. Then I'll discuss the two important milestones that will help us bring our project home: alpha and beta.

A Summary of the Preproduction Deliverables

Figure 21.1 shows a short summary of the deliverables due during the preproduction phase of a game project.

Deliverable	When Due
Game design macro - first draft	Enough time before the end of preproduction to be able to have a few rounds of iteration.
Vertical slice	Close to the end of preproduction, but before the final draft of the macro, so that the design of the core of the game is clearly understood when the macro is finalized.
Game design macro - final draft	Close to the end of preproduction.
Schedule	At the end of preproduction, after the final draft of the macro, which the schedule is based on.

Figure 21.1

Phase Three: Full Production—Building and Discovering

The full production phase of a game project is the time when we build out the game. It has two major milestones: the alpha milestone and the beta milestone. Each of these is preceded by a phase with the same name: the alpha phase leads up to the alpha milestone, and the beta phase leads up to the beta milestone.

The alpha milestone typically arrives about two-thirds of the way through full production, and, in an interestingly fractal way, it also usually comes about two-thirds of the way through the whole project. The beta milestone marks the end of full production in our playful production process (see figure 22.1). We'll talk more about alpha and beta later in this chapter, and each milestone has its own chapter later in this book.

Presenting the Vertical Slice and Game Design Macro

It's typical to begin the full production phase by presenting the vertical slice, game design macro, and schedule that the team has created. Depending on the context, the team's leadership may have already presented these deliverables to the project's stakeholders (executive producers, publishers, or other financial backers) in order to receive feedback and to be given the green light to enter full production. Depending on the total team size, it's good to then re-present the deliverables to the team itself to make sure everyone is on the same page as full production begins.

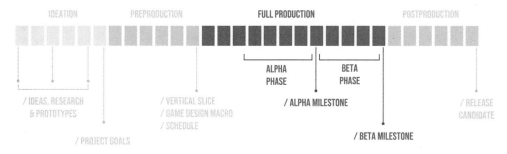

Figure 22.1
The full production phase and its milestones. Image credit: Gabriela Purri R. Gomes, Mattie Rosen, and Richard Lemarchand.

Sharing our work is a good way to kick off full production. We can see what we have accomplished in the first two phases of the project—and it's usually a lot. We create a shared understanding of the game that everyone on the team is building, and we start to understand what's already working well and what needs more attention. We are now ready to begin implementing the remaining parts of the game and to engage in the ongoing playtesting and design review that characterizes our playful production process.

Working through Your Task List

The preproduction phase was a freewheeling time of unstructured, relatively untracked time and intuitive designing-by-making. The full production phase is different. Remember the assembly line that we talked about in chapter 9? Full production is a little more like that. Thanks to our macro and schedule, we now have a list of tasks that we have to complete in order to build out our game, and we can start to work down it. We'll do the step-by-step work to create the mechanics, characters, and levels we need, checking off tasks from our list until our game is complete.

But we shouldn't switch our brains off and follow our plan blindly. We need to stay engaged and alert about our game's design. Games are holistic systems—every little thing we add or remove will affect the game as a whole. Our game design macro is a commitment to a certain design, and we need to follow it, though maybe not to the exact letter. We've made enough decisions about our game's design that we can move forward with confidence, but those decisions are only macro decisions. We still have plenty of room to shape the game as we complete the detailed micro design work that goes into it.

I'm not giving you permission here to change your mind about your game halfway through full production. If you change your macro a lot as you pass through full production, your game probably won't come together. You'll be like a puppy in a meadow chasing butterflies this way and that. As delightful as it would be to be that puppy, during full production we want to be more like an energetic dog dashing toward a frisbee that it's about to catch.

Sometimes things that you put in the macro will reveal themselves to you in new ways as you move through full production. You might discover some wise design intuition in your macro, the impact of which you hadn't fully realized when you wrote it. Or you might make discoveries during full production that will transform the whole player experience of your game, and which don't derail the design work you've done but instead enhance it. We'll look at this phenomenon in "When to Take a Risk during Full Production," below.

Changing Gears in the Transition from Preproduction to Full Production

It can be hard to suddenly change your way of working, and this shift in attitude between preproduction and full production may take some time to adjust to. Notice how your work habits adapt as you begin to work from a list of tasks. If you're a more intuitive developer who likes to make decisions on the fly, it may take some effort. It might be helpful to think about simple aspects of your process, such as how you like to track your progress through a list of tasks. You might like to look at the task list at a regular time every day, whenever you finish a task, or even more frequently than that.

One common thing that often happens at the beginning of full production is that the game design macro chart (the part of the macro in the spreadsheet) needs some extra attention. This has been true for just about every project I've ever worked on. I used to get stressed out about it, thinking that it meant we had failed at preproduction in some way. Nowadays, I just accept it as a part of the process of changing gears from preproduction and full production. I try to deal with it gracefully, by accepting that the game design macro needs some more care and attention to bring it up to a high level of quality, and giving it that attention as quickly as possible. Use the milestone review feedback and seek out additional advice about whether your macro needs more work.

However, avoid the pitfall of just fiddling with your macro chart when you should be getting on with building out the rest of your game. You might be familiar with the saying, "The perfect is the enemy of the good." One of the keys to becoming a successful creative person is learning to know when you've done enough work on a task and should move on to something else.

Checking In on Your Project Goals

Whenever you have to make a call in interpreting your game design macro, or if you ever get stuck when trying to solve a design problem, refer back to your project goals. Your experience goals and design goals will almost always guide you toward a solution. In my experience, projects whose goals drift radically from their original conception only occasionally turn out well; it's a healthy part of most every design process to stay in touch with what you were originally planning to do. However, there's a difference between drifting away from your project goals and refining your goals to make them more specific as you learn more about your game. One is counterproductive, while the other is at the core of the design process.

In chapter 11, Tracy Fullerton talked about the value of honing and crafting our project goals as we make discoveries about the design of our game through playtesting and iteration. Tracy told me that, as she sees it, "locking [your project] goals and never reconsidering them in light of the reality of your game . . . is a rigid process that will thwart [development]. . . . As the game emerges from the work you are doing, it begins to illuminate and illustrate more clearly the essence of your originally stated goals. Like rewriting a sentence or a paragraph as you work through an idea, honing your experience goals can bring better and better focus to the production process."

Back in chapter 11, Tracy told us that keeping our project goals achievable is an important part of their usefulness. So, the beginning of full production presents a great opportunity to hone and craft our project goals, to bring them into line with everything we've discovered. This will keep them current, so that whenever we need them to guide our future design work, they will still offer us good advice.

Stand-Up Meetings

If you're not already running stand-up meetings as a regular part of your game development practice, the beginning of the full production phase of a project is a great time to start. A stand-up meeting is a group-based communication activity designed to help teams of people stay in regular touch about their responsibilities, goals, accomplishments, and problems, with the aim of keeping the project moving forward smoothly.

Stand-up meetings are important and ubiquitous in the world of Agile software development, where you'll sometimes find them called the morning roll call meeting, the daily scrum, or just the daily meeting. The meeting is held standing up, which is intended to keep the meeting short. It's a clever hack, since people naturally want to sit back down, and that reminds everyone to keep their comments in the meeting brief and to the point. The meetings are centered on three questions, which must be answered by every individual team member:

- What did you work on since we last met?
- What do you plan to work on before our next meeting?
- What problems are you facing that are blocking your forward progress?

It is easy for teams to drift apart in their understanding of who is doing what. People change their minds about what they're going to work on, get sidetracked, or hit a problem that they have to solve. Checking in about what you have just done and what you're about to do helps build team clarity.

The third question—what problems are you facing?—can be the most important of the three questions. When we quickly and concisely summarize the problems (sometimes known as impediments or blockers) that we're facing in completing our work, we do at least three things:

1. We identify that there's a problem.
2. We may get a little clearer about the exact nature of the problem simply by describing it out loud to somebody.
3. We create an opportunity to get some help with that problem.

Again, it's easy for even a very small team to fail to have ongoing discussions about the problems blocking their progress. People tend to struggle through, reluctant to ask for help, thinking that they should be able to figure out challenges themselves. The stand-up meeting forces us to put the problems we're facing on the table. If anyone in the group thinks they can help, they offer to do so, and the discussion will continue *after* the stand-up meeting has finished.

On professional teams, it's common for stand-up meetings to take place every working day. It's traditional that the meeting should take place at the same time and in the same place every single day, usually toward the beginning of the day, which promotes a regular, steady rhythm of continual discussion and update. Whatever your setting, hold stand-up meetings as often as you can, and note that the meeting should take place even if not all the team members are present.

Stand-up meetings are always valuable for keeping teams in sync, and you might want to run them from the very beginning of your project until the very end. You can read more about stand-up meetings on this book's website, playfulproductionprocess .com. When they're working well, stand-up meetings promote accountability and cultivate an atmosphere of respect, trust, and consent on a team, as we clearly communicate with each other about the work we're doing, recognize everyone's effort, and help each other through difficulties. This lays the groundwork for further discussions about our process, and helps make sure that we're all okay with the unfolding path of our shared endeavor. Stand-up meetings will supercharge the community of your team if you commit to this simple, time-efficient practice.

The Milestones of Full Production

So, there are these two major milestones during full production: alpha and beta. We'll look at them in detail in upcoming chapters, but it's useful to preview them now.

At the alpha milestone, our game will be "feature complete," when all of its moving parts are in place. Everything that does something functional in the game should be in there by alpha, at least in rough form. It's particularly important to get everything that is functionally unique into the game—for example, the abilities of the player-character and other characters, the mechanics and core loops of the game, the base behaviors of the objects in the world, and parts of the game like interface elements and options screens. In addition, at the alpha milestone we'll be using a technique we adopted at Naughty Dog, where all of the levels of the finished game should be present at alpha, at least in rough form.

As we approach the alpha milestone, we'll gradually have to move away from using concentric development and will start putting in placeholder content so that we can get the game built out. The alpha milestone is a good time to develop a plan for how we will find people who will want to play our game, and tell them about it. We'll discuss these in chapters 29 and 30.

At the beta milestone, our game will also be "content complete," when the whole game is now in place. All of the art, animation, and audio assets will be present with at least a first-pass level of quality, and every last part of the game will be built out and working. The game may be buggy and have balance problems, but by locking in its content at beta, we turn a moving target into something stable that we can then polish.

If you've done some theater, maybe in high school, it might be useful to think of alpha as a technical rehearsal, where we're not so worried about the quality of the performances, but we're focused on the actors being in the right places at the right times, and on getting the lighting and sound cues down. Then you can think of beta as the dress rehearsal, where we now do care about the performances and everything else, even though it's all still going to be a little rough. We go through these rehearsals in order to take something that isn't quite ready and make everything right for our first-night audience.

The alpha and beta milestones are markers along the path to our project's final release candidate milestone, when the game is finally done and done and is ready to be thoroughly tested before being released.

What Order Should a Game Be Built In?

As preproduction ends and full production begins, we face a decision about what part of the game to build next. We just built a representative chunk of the game for our vertical slice, a polished version of which will often end up as an early part of the game. Now we have to decide whether we're going to work on the beginning, the middle, or the end of the game next. Based on my experience, I'd advise you to use an act structure to think about your game in terms of four parts of roughly equal length:

1. Act one, the beginning
2. The first half of act two, the middle
3. The second half of act two, the middle
4. Act three, the end

And then build your game in this order (figure 22.2):

1. The first half of act two
2. Act one
3. Act three
4. The second half of act two

Building act one first is rarely successful (we touched on this in chapter 11). The beginning of your game has a lot of complex work to do in teaching the player how

Build the four parts of your game in this order:

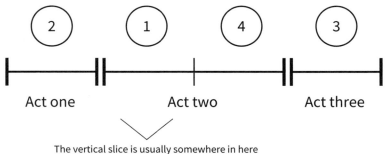

The vertical slice is usually somewhere in here

Figure 22.2

to play and in setting up the narrative and tone of the game. It also has to be fantastically good, to make a splash and grab new players. If you start with your vertical slice (which you hopefully can use in the finished game without many more changes) and then build out the rest of the first half of act two, you can continue to get to grips with the fundamental elements of your game—the core loop and secondary gameplay loops, and the important narrative elements—but you don't have to worry too much yet about how you're going to onboard the player. Once you've got the core of your game even more figured out than the vertical slice allowed, then you're ready to build a truly excellent opening sequence to perfectly catch and hold a new player's attention.

It's always tempting to leave the work needed for act three, the end of the game, until the very end of the project, but in my experience, that's a mistake. Endings are as important as beginnings—even more so, when considered from a dramatic point of view—and if we leave the end of the game until last, we're in danger of running out of time and creating an ending that is unsatisfying or unpolished. Of course, not every type of game has an ending, but many games have some kind of conclusion or resolution. I've met game designers who believe that the end of a game isn't that important, since not every player will reach the end. That seems cynical. My approach to game design is that I want to show respect and consideration to every last one of my players, and if even one of my players reaches the end of my game, I want there to be something excellent for them to play.

In my experience, the second half of act two is the most pliable and shapeable in terms of its content and its length. This is the part of a linear or narrative game experience that begins to draw together—or cut short—all of the strings of gameplay and story that we put into play in the first half of the game. We usually have opportunities to expand or contract this part of the game like a concertina, based on how much time we have left. If we have already completed the end of the game before working on the part that comes before it, then we have a destination in mind, and that's the kind of constraint that can be very useful for designers. I don't want to make this sound simple; shaping the "second half of the middle" so as to arrive at a particular ending might be some of the most exacting design work that you do on the project, and every game will bring a unique challenge.

Of course, there are no hard and fast rules here. Filmmakers often shoot and assemble movies out of order, and building anything nonsequentially creates unique challenges and opportunities, because of the interdependencies between the different elements. The ability to deal with these dependencies is another aspect of your growing skill as a game designer.

Game Feel and Juiciness

The beginning of full production is a good time to check in on the game feel and juiciness of your project. Game feel is "the simple pleasure of control, feelings of mastery and clumsiness, and the tactile sensation of interacting with virtual objects."[1] This is an essential aspect of videogame design, but was hard to discuss before the arrival of Steve Swink's groundbreaking book *Game Feel: A Game Designer's Guide to Virtual Sensation*, which I strongly recommend that you read. Steve very clearly breaks down the factors that go into making a game feel "floaty," "responsive," or "loose," and identifies the elements of real-time control, simulated space, and audiovisual representation that make a game feel good.

Juiciness is a concept that, to my knowledge, was first coined by Kyle Gray, Kyle Gabler, Shalin Shodhan, and Matt Kucic, the members of the Carnegie Mellon ETC Experimental Gameplay Project, in their 2005 Gamasutra essay, "How to Prototype a Game in under 7 Days." According to the group, juiciness is "constant and bountiful user feedback."

> A juicy game element will bounce and wiggle and squirt and make a little noise when you touch it. A juicy game feels alive and responds to everything you do—tons of cascading action and response for minimal user input. It makes the player feel powerful and in control of the world, and it coaches them through the rules of the game by constantly letting them know on a per-interaction basis how they are doing.[2]

Manifested through animation, sound design, visual effects, and interaction design, juiciness creates a rich experience for the player and feeds into game feel, emphasizing input, creating strong feelings of responsiveness, creating sense-pleasure, and encouraging further interaction. The principles and practice of juiciness, and its applicability to game design, are illuminated nicely by Martin Jonasson and Petri Purho in their GDC Europe 2012 Independent Game Summit talk, *Juice It or Lose It*.[3]

Concentric development helps to promote good game feel and juiciness in our games by having us attend to the details of implementation as we go along. Be careful not to vanish down a rabbit hole, though: both game feel and juice can easily eat up our implementation time if we're not careful. Learn to recognize when your game is good enough for the time being.

Focuses for Full Production

Once in full production, it's good to keep a laserfocus on what Tanya X. Short calls the "legibility" of our game, which we discussed back in chapter 12.[4] How easy is it for

---

1. Swink, *Game Feel*, 10.
2. Kyle Gray, Kyle Gabler, Shalin Shodhan, and Matt Kucic, "How to Prototype a Game in under 7 Days," Gamasutra, October 26, 2005, https://www.gamasutra.com/view/feature/130848/how _to_prototype_a_game_in_under_7_.php.
3. Martin Jonasson and Petri Purho, "Juice It or Lose It," GDC Vault, 2012, https://www.gdcvault .com/play/1016487/Juice-It-or-Lose.
4. Tanya X. Short, "How and When to Make Your Procedurality Player-Legible," December 21, 2018, https://www.youtube.com/watch?v=r6rTMGFXktI.

people to understand our game just by looking at it and listening to it? Can they figure out how to play the game just by experimenting with the controls? Do they pick up on the game's important concepts in both gameplay and story? This attitude helps us polish many different aspects of the game's design. It will help us create a game that communicates clearly and through multiple channels with the people who interact with it, just like any great piece of design does.

Consider the unity of form and function in a well-designed phone or chair; the same principles apply in a well-designed videogame. As we discussed in chapter 12, we understand how to use a thing by looking at it, by listening to it, by touching it, and we gather up meaning from these interactions. Holding this focus helps us think like a user experience designer, which is always a valuable way for a game designer to think. We'll look at this kind of approach in greater detail in the next few chapters.

Once we're in full production, we should continue to use concentric development. We should build the game in a way that continually makes it polished in terms of its gameplay and its production values, including its visuals, audio and tactile design, and usability. We will strive to make it so that our game always plays and controls well and has no usability problems. Keeping a focus on legibility will also help us plan ahead toward creating an entertaining and effective tutorial sequence for the start of the game—a sequence that is so interesting and well designed that, as we discussed in chapter 17, the player doesn't even realize that they're being taught something, but instead just has an experience of play.

Even though we're now in full production, it's still possible to continue to *fail early, fail fast, fail often* as we work on the detailed micro design of our project, with constant playtesting on people outside of our team and successive rounds of design iteration. Remember, don't do too much work without having someone playtest what you're making. This will create countless opportunities for you to make small adjustments to the direction of your design. In doing so, you can keep heading toward your project goals and experience goals, while dodging around any obstacles in your path. Again, whenever you get stuck, refer back to your project goals. The answer to your problem is probably lying in wait, if you simply refocus on your experience goals.

When to Take a Risk during Full Production

As I said earlier, occasionally you might need to diverge from your game design macro to make the best game you can possibly make. I have an example of this from the creation of *Uncharted: Drake's Fortune*, the first *Uncharted* game. Our aiming mechanic wasn't quite gelling, and game designer (now game director) Neil Druckmann had an idea to bridge the gap between the third-person auto-aiming system that we were using and the more deliberate aiming system used in first-person shooters. Well into full production, and just a few months before our alpha milestone, we prototyped a new aiming system and we were very happy with the results.

This single change to our game's design had a profound effect. Suddenly, the enemy encounters in *Uncharted: Drake's Fortune* came to life: they were a little more challenging, but not too difficult, and also—very importantly—they were more dramatic, because you always had to be looking straight at the enemy you were trying to defeat. The combat suddenly felt more intimate, more one-on-one than one-versus-many.

Even better: the change didn't break the game. There's always a risk associated with making a big change to your game's design during full production. Will the level layout need reworking? What other game systems now need changing in response to this change? Will that trigger a domino effect of further changes that eat up your valuable full production time? This particular change from auto-aiming to over-the-shoulder manual aiming didn't break our level layout, in most cases, and didn't have a bad knock-on effect with other game systems. For me, it was the perfect example of how sometimes you should take a risk during full production, when your game hasn't quite come together at the end of preproduction.

I've heard from other game designers that sometimes the design of their game didn't completely gel until quite close to the end of development, and that usually it was the addition, removal, or modification of one major element that made the game finally become really fun. Zach Gage said that this happened with Choice Provisions Inc.'s dice-based strategy game *Tharsis*.[5] Ryan Smith said that the same happened with the web-shooting mechanics of *Spider-Man* for the PlayStation 4.[6] These lessons show us that we should proceed methodically through our task list to build out our games, but we should always stay alert to the opportunities we have to radically transform the design of our game for the better.

Just exercise caution. In the case of *Uncharted: Drake's Fortune*, this was the only major change that we made to the game's mechanics during full production. If we'd given ourselves license to make too many big, late changes like this, our game would almost certainly have not come together at the end. Think of it like having just one or two wildcards in your hand. You want to save them for special occasions and not use them too impulsively.

⁊⁘ ❀ ⁘⁋

If the ideation phase was playtime, and the preproduction phase was a sprint, I like to think of the full production phase as a longer footrace, maybe even a marathon. We can't dash along at top speed anymore, or we'll burn out. We have to settle into a rhythm and work consistently and systemically, pacing ourselves so that we have

5. *The Spelunky Showlike*, "Episode 8: Designing *Tharsis* with Zach Gage," December 20, 2018, https://thespelunkyshowlike.libsyn.com/08-designing-tharsis-with-zach-gage .
6. Ryan Smith, "The 2019 GDC Microtalks," October 28, 2019, https://www.youtube.com/watch?v=66skmNruafI.

some energy left to jump over the hurdles we'll encounter in the last stages of the project.

We must keep our eyes open for obstacles in our path. Even small stumbles might cause us to crash out. And we have to stay on the lookout for opportunities—shortcuts or bonuses that will help our game's design take great leaps forward, even as we finish building the game. In the coming chapters, we'll look at a process of formal playtesting that will help us to notice both obstacles and opportunities to keep us on the path to an excellent game.

23 Types of Testing

Playtesting has a central role in healthy game design and development practice, as we've been discussing throughout this book. But there are many different types of testing that game teams use at different stages of development. It's useful to organize these into categories and subcategories:

- Informal playtesting
  - Informal playtesting by myself
  - Informal playtesting with my teammates
  - Informal playtesting with design peers
- Design-process testing
  - Formal playtesting
  - User testing
  - Focus testing
- QA testing
- Automated testing
- Public-facing testing

Let's look at these one by one.

Informal Playtesting

Informal playtesting is the playtesting that we developers do ourselves as we design and develop the game. We usually do it at our desks and in casual conversation, without the tightly controlled situations that characterize formal playtesting.

Informal Playtesting by Myself

As I'm working on some part of a game, I run the game every now and then to look at what I'm building. I play for a while, trying out what I just implemented, evaluating the gameplay, the controls, the graphics, the sound, and every other aspect of my design. Maybe I'm trying to get a sense of the overall experience of the game, or maybe

I'm focusing in on one small detail. This is a fundamental and time-honored way of playtesting.

But it's also prone to problems. It's almost impossible to tune the difficulty of a game this way. In the course of developing the game I—the designer—will probably play it for much longer than almost anyone else ever will, becoming a kind of super-player, with skills honed through repetition and an insider's view of the way the game works. This makes it very hard for me to properly evaluate the game's difficulty, along with other things like its legibility (how easy it is for people to understand the game mechanics or story).

Game designers can learn to overcome these obstacles to some degree. It's said that one of the great game design abilities of inspirational designer Shigeru Miyamoto is that every morning he's able to approach the game he's working on as if he has never seen it before. It takes great discipline of mind to do this, but whenever you succeed, you make a positive impact on the project. Great design in every field is about putting yourself in the shoes of someone who is encountering something for the very first time. Cultivate this habit of mind, and it will support you in the informal playtesting you do by yourself.

Informal Playtesting with My Teammates

When you're working on your game and you need a fresh pair of eyes, the natural person to call on for an informal playtest is the person sitting next to you. At most great game studios, it is accepted that part of everyone's day will be spent playing the things being built by their teammates. You chat about the game as you play it in a back-and-forth dialogue that wouldn't be appropriate during a formal playtest. Informal playtesting for our teammates is where an individual game designer's ability to think out loud comes to the fore. Giving feedback like this will also call on the foundational communication skills of sandwiching (chapter 6) and "I Like, I Wish, What If . . . ?" (chapter 12).

As a designer having my work tested by a teammate, I must resist any impulse to become defensive. I need to use my listening skills to hear what someone is really saying about my game, and I must not explain away someone's remarks as "they just don't get it" or "they're not playing it right." I must cultivate my ability to interpret the comments and root out the true sources of the problems in my design. Testing with a range of different people can help that process of interpretation.

Informal Playtesting with Design Peers

By design peer I mean someone who is an experienced game designer, and possibly someone who shares the same interests and sensibilities as you. Call on them and have them play your game. This type of playtesting is particularly useful when you are stuck on some design problem. Your design peer can look at your game with an impartial eye and give you some advice.

Design-Process Testing

I call the next three types of testing design-process testing because they relate to the design processes that we use to make our games as good as they can possibly be. You might find some overlap and even confusion between these three types of testing, even at professional studios, but I think it's good to acknowledge the distinctions between them.

Formal Playtesting

This is the type of playtesting where designers watch people who have never played their game before experiencing it under tightly controlled conditions, replicating the experience of a player playing a new game at home. The designers are trying to see how these brand-new players receive the game. Are they able to learn how to play it? Do they enjoy playing it? Does the game give them the experience that the designers hoped to create? What kind of problems do the players encounter, related to the design of the game, that prevent them from having the desired experience?

This kind of playtesting is as objective as we can make it within the bounds of all the complex human factors at play. Formal playtesting is used a lot at Naughty Dog, and I was closely involved in the process of running formal playtests of our games for most of my eight years at the studio. We'll be talking about formal playtesting a lot more in chapters 24 and 25.

User Testing

This is the type of testing that game designers inherit from the world of "usability" and "UX" (user experience). User testing centers on the design and use of interfaces (although it extends to much more than that), and in software engineering, "usability is the degree to which a software can be used by specified consumers to achieve quantified objectives with effectiveness, efficiency, and satisfaction in a quantified context of use."[1]

When viewed in a certain way, everything in a videogame is an interface. Not just the menus and head-up displays, but the design of the character, the view of the game world, and the control scheme—the "three Cs"—all communicate information, shape modes of interaction, and create experience.

So perhaps it's not surprising that you will often find the term *user testing* used to describe the formal playtesting we'll look at in chapters 24 and 25. The processes of formal playtesting that we use are partially derived from the worlds of usability and the academic discipline of human-computer interaction (HCI). Many game studios employ people with an HCI background to run their formal playtests, and many games programs have a usability class or faculty. USC Games professor emeritus Dennis Wixon

---

1. "Usability," Wikipedia, https://en.wikipedia.org/wiki/Usability.

helped to pioneer what *Wired* magazine called a "new science of play" at Microsoft Game Studios.[2] The scientific rigor and design process that Dennis and his colleagues used to improve the design of their games was an inspiration to the formal playtesting work that we did at Naughty Dog.

However, I think that it's a mistake to entirely conflate user testing and formal play-testing. As we'll see in the next chapter, formal playtesting is a somewhat subjective practice, where designers are often called on to make decisions based on their intuition or artistic sensibility. By contrast, user testing is a *very* rigorous, thorough, distinctly scientific practice, where we can be sure of achieving a particular design outcome by applying heuristics and measuring outcomes in an objective way.

Focus Testing

Confusingly, some game studios might call either their formal playtesting or user testing processes "focus testing." But focus testing is very different from either formal playtesting or user testing. Focus testing is a part of the professional and academic discipline of marketing, the business process of creating relationships with and satisfying customers.

A focus test is run by bringing together a focus group, the members of which are selected from the general public based on psychographic and/or demographic information that mark them as potential customers for the product, service, concept, or advertisement being tested. Focus group members are typically paid for their time. The focus group meeting is led by a specially trained researcher, who asks the members carefully designed questions under controlled conditions. The group's responses are recorded, and conversation between the group may be encouraged. They talk about their perceptions, opinions, beliefs, and attitudes toward the thing being tested. The results of the test are later analyzed by researchers and discussed by the stakeholders in the project.

Focus tests can be valuable early in a game's development, when we want to check that our ideas for the game are going to be received well by its possible audience. They are especially valuable if the budget for our game is very big, and we want to try to ensure that we're investing our money wisely. User researcher and game designer Kevin Keeker offers a lot of great advice about the effective use of focus tests in his essay "Getting the Most Out of Focus Groups" in Tracy Fullerton's *Game Design Workshop*.[3]

QA Testing

The vanguard of any game studio's testing effort is its QA (quality assurance) department, sometimes known simply as *test*. QA is a highly skilled professional discipline and has one of the most mature set of processes anywhere in game development. A QA

---

2. Clive Thompson, "Halo 3: How Microsoft Labs Invented a New Science of Play," *Wired*, August 21, 2007, https://www.wired.com/2007/08/ff-halo-2/.
3. Fullerton, *Game Design Workshop*, 4th ed., 191.

tester's job is, first, to look for bugs: technical problems and content problems that negatively impact the player's experience. These bugs might be hard to find because they only happen when some rare sequence of events unfolds in the game or when some unusual combination of elements comes together. QA testers are able to explore the vast possibility space of a game in a way that individual developers simply cannot. In doing so, QA makes it possible for us to have the games that we love.

QA tests the game by following a test plan that describes how the game will be tested and what kind of problems are being looked for. When QA finds problems, they document them in a bug database that is shared with the game's other developers. A QA manager passes the bugs to the discipline leads (the lead artist, the lead programmer, and so on) based on their evaluation of who will fix the bug. Maybe it's a problem with the code that an engineer will need to fix, it might be a design problem for a game designer, or it might be a badly mapped texture that an artist will correct.

The discipline leads then pass the bugs on to the individual developers in their group who fix them, check in their changes to the team's version control system, and mark each bug as fixed. (If they can't fix it, can't find the bug as reported, or disagree that it's a bug, then they can mark the bug appropriately, and it gets passed onward for further evaluation.) In the next build, the bugs marked as fixed go back to QA who then "regresses" them, checking again to make sure that the problem has indeed gone away.

The bug database eventually becomes an important part of every team member's life, and fixing the problems reported in the bug database will take up a large part of an individual developer's day. QA testers are much more than bug-finders and fix-checkers—they are a superb source of game design wisdom and gain great insight into the experience that a game is giving its players. The people who are drawn to games QA as a profession are usually highly passionate and vastly knowledgeable about games. They are often analytical thinkers with developed game design sensibilities and are brimming with excellent ideas. I have always made it a point to seek out the people working in QA at my studio, pay my respects to them, ask them about their work, and begin to learn from them.

QA is a development discipline, and people who work in QA are game developers. In line with this book's philosophy that everyone who touches a game is one of its designers (outlined in chapter 4), we should remember that the people who work in QA are game designers too. We should invite QA into the design and production process at every stage, working together closely and effectively to make the very best games that we can.

Automated Testing

Software developers have been creating mechanisms to automatically test the code they've written for almost as long as computer science has existed. In automated testing, special software is written to test other software, either to quickly and efficiently perform a repetitive human task in an error-free way, or to perform tests that would be hard for a human to conduct at all.

Unit testing, integration tests, and server load tests are famous examples of automated testing, where modules and groups of code and data are tested to see if they are working correctly. Automated tests of a game might simulate human input to the game through a controller, keyboard and mouse, or touchscreen. An automated test might use a programming interface to bypass the input system altogether, and interface directly with the code and content.

Automated testing is now an accepted and important part of the game programmer's toolkit. While I was at Naughty Dog, the studio's talented engineering team began to use "smoke testing" (also known as confidence testing, sanity testing, and build verification testing) to make sure that our overnight builds didn't have any problems related to memory and level loading. This ensured that our QA department would have a build to test every morning that didn't have any basic problems.

Given that game development is a human-centered, artistic field, I think that it's unlikely that automated testing will ever completely replace human testing, but it makes sense that code can check for certain kinds of problems and errors more quickly and thoroughly than a human being can, since computers are good at doing detail-oriented, boring, repetitive tasks with flawless precision. I expect that machine learning will help us test our games in new ways, just as it has begun to work magic in areas of our lives like speech recognition and image manipulation.

Public-Facing Testing

Public-facing testing is the kind of testing we do by releasing our game to the public before it's completely finished, perhaps in some limited form. This would include public beta testing, early access testing, and releasing a game into a small test market before its global release.

In public beta testing, a game developer or publisher allows members of the general public to download their game and play it after the beta milestone has been reached, but some weeks or months before it is completely finished. (It's more common in a public beta not to release the whole game but just a part of it, maybe a demo level.)

Developers receive a lot of different types of feedback from a public beta test. They can double-check the results of their server load tests to make sure their servers can handle the load of thousands—or hundreds of thousands—of players downloading and playing their game all at once. The developers can gather metrics data about the players' activities in the game, and in doing so can check to see if the game's design is working as intended. They can look for performance issues to do with frame rate or lag and for problems with security. Early users will often probe for security loopholes in a game, if only to see if they can hack their score. The developers can also get direct feedback from their public beta testers about their experiences in the game, just as we would in a formal playtest, using surveys or interviews.

In early access testing, the game is released—and maybe even sold—before it's either feature complete or content complete. This practice is now common in the world of professional game design, with Steam Early Access sales and platforms like Itch.io making it possible for game developers to use social media to bring their players into the design and development process earlier, more easily, and at greater scale than ever before. Public-facing testing can also help build community and excitement for a game.

Now that we've looked at some different types of testing, we will, in the next two chapters, take a deeper look at formal playtesting, which gives game designers a valuable tool for keeping their design process on track.

At the beginning of our playful production process, during the ideation and preproduction phases, our approach to designing and building our game is very free-form and artistic, and just structured enough to help us make the right decisions at the right times. Now that we're in full production, we don't stop working intuitively, but—following the plans that we've laid out with our macro and schedule—we do shift toward a more rational way of working.

We're now on our way to the major milestones of alpha, when our game will be feature complete (all of its major mechanisms will be somewhere in the game) and beta, when our game will be content complete (everything that's going to be in the game will be in and ready for polish during postproduction). How can we be sure that we're making this transition well, as we move from subjective to objective, from intuitive to rational? Formal playtesting can help us with this.

Formal Playtesting at Naughty Dog

I joined Naughty Dog with a passion for playtesting and was excited to work with Evan Wells and Mark Cerny, who had already helped institute a great set of formal playtesting practices at the studio. For much of its lifetime, Naughty Dog (and its parent company Sony Interactive Entertainment) had been running formal playtests where members of the general public are recruited through an online advertisement, brought into the studio, and paid to play a game under construction. These playtesters don't know ahead of time what game they are going to play or who is making the game they are going to test. We wanted people who would come to our game without preexisting biases, either positive or negative.

While I was at Naughty Dog, we worked with a third-party agent who reviewed the information given by everyone who responded to the advertisement and gave us ten playtesters for each formal playtest. The gaming experience and demographic information of the playtesters reflected the type of player we thought that our game would appeal to, within a spread of ages, genders, and gaming histories. Like many game developers, we would refer to these folks as "Kleenex" playtesters; like a paper tissue, we would only use them once. In a formal playtest, you need people who have never played your game before in order to get an accurate impression of its current state.

When I joined Naughty Dog to help finish *Jak 3*, we ran perhaps four or five playtests across the course of the whole project. For *Uncharted 3*, the last game that I worked on at Naughty Dog, we ran twenty-one tests over the course of the game's development, beginning around six months before the end of the project—about one a week. We ran our formal playtests in-house in a dedicated playtest room. Along one wall would be a row of ten playtest stations. Each station had a TV, a networked PlayStation with the build of the game we were testing, and a pair of headphones plugged into the TV, so that each player could only hear their station's version of the game. As the playtest ran, the game's designers would sit on the other side of the room, watching the playtesters play. Today, Naughty Dog has a dedicated playtest lab with a one-way mirror separating the playtesters from the designers watching them, a common feature of the "observation suites" built for user studies.

For the playtesting of *Uncharted 3*, we used networked digital video recorders that captured video of the game to our network as the testers played. We could review this video later to get a closer look at a particular player's actions in the game. We would do this when we'd either spotted a pattern of problems in a particular part of the game or to figure out what was going on when a particular player had encountered a specific problem, like getting stuck in one part of the game for an unusually long time. (It's important to note that these methodologies were invented by HCI (human-computer interaction) researchers working in user testing, who used them for some time before they were adopted by the game industry.) Today, Naughty Dog also records video of the faces, hands, and overall posture of their playtesters. This footage can be run alongside the gameplay footage to give an expanded sense of what the player is doing and feeling at each moment in the game, and the video can be streamed to the desktop of anyone in the studio who is interested to see what's going on in the playtest.

We put screens between the stations so that the players couldn't see each other's games, even accidentally. If your neighbor is further ahead of you in the game, your playthrough and your ability to progress could easily be affected by seeing them solve a puzzle, use a weapon in a particular way, or even just climb up onto a ledge.

We would ask our players not to talk during the playtest, and because we wanted to be as scientific as possible we would be ruthless about never giving them any help. As the players played, the game would record certain information about the gameplay session and post it to a database on our network. We called this our metrics data, and I'll discuss it in chapter 26.

At the end of the playtest, we would have the playtesters fill out a survey about their experience, and then we would conduct an exit interview, which we recorded for our later reference. The numerical information (quantitative data) that we got from the surveys helped us to track the changes in the players' perceptions of the game from test to test. We would almost always see a slow, gradual improvement, which helped us stay sane in the knowledge that the game was gradually getting better. We would also get some interesting, if rather less objective, game design perspectives (qualitative data) from the exit interview. The metrics data would give us even more objective information about how playable the game is.

In the remainder of this chapter and the next two chapters, I'll talk you through all these processes in greater detail, as I present you with a formal playtesting process that everyone can use to ensure that their games are as good as they can possibly be.

A Formal Playtesting Practice for Everyone

In chapter 5, we laid out a few guidelines to help us playtest. We expanded and tightened up these guidelines in chapter 12 to give us a rigorous playtesting practice to use throughout the course of our project.

When we reach a certain point in the creation of our game, usually just before the alpha milestone, it's important to transition into an even more rigorous form of playtesting, one that we can count on to give us clear information about our game. We want to get both objective facts and subjective points of view about the game, so that we can make any necessary final corrections to the course of our game's design. We can track these design changes over time to make sure that the last modifications we're making are improving the game, not making it worse. We will call this process formal playtesting, and we can use it to become ever more confident that our game is landing with players in the way that we wish it to land. We can complete our transition from intuitive making to objective evaluation and can prepare to ship the game.

Regular formal playtesting then becomes a vital part of the game development process, allowing us to work through smaller design issues in a methodical way, leaving us time to address more important game design topics. As Mark Cerny recently described it to me: "Once production is structured to have regular playtesting, the dialogue within and without the team is no longer 'Do you think the players will understand XYZ?' or 'Is the difficulty here appropriate?' or 'Is holding L1 and then pressing CIRCLE sufficiently intuitive?' These can be time consuming topics, but since we know that playtesting will quickly resolve them we are now free to spend our time on bigger structural issues in our game (for example, is the player building sufficient empathy with the player-character?) and not on these details."

So now it's time to add a few extra guidelines to the playtesting process described in chapter 12. The new guidelines are **in bold** in the list below.

- **Prepare a healthy build of the game to test, free of bugs and major gameplay problems.**
- **Use a formal playtest script.**
- **Use a pretest survey, if desired.**
- Use headphones for both playtesters and designers.
- Prepare a controls cheat sheet if necessary.
- Prepare a written hint or helper to help players with any known gameplay issues or functional issues.

- Suggest that your playtester thinks and feels out loud.
- Use content warnings if appropriate.
- Begin the playtest.
- Be observant of your playtester's experience of the game.
- Observe what the playtester does and says and note it all down.
- Don't help your playtester at all.
- **If desired, record audio and video of both the game and the playtester during the playtest session (with the playtester's consent).**
- **Use telemetry to capture metrics data about the playtest session.**
- **Keep an eye on the time: you need time for the survey and the exit interview.**
- **After the test, and before any conversation, give the playtester the formal playtest survey.**
- **After the survey, use your prepared exit interview questions.**
- **Either write down or record the exit interview answers.**
- Don't be a game-explainer.
- Don't get discouraged.

As you can see, we've been using a formal playtest process for most of the course of development of our game! This is good: it means that we've been rigorous all along in our approach to playtesting, and that has given us a solid foundation for this next stage of our work. Let's take a look at these new guidelines, which center on three new tools: a script, a survey, and some prepared exit interview questions.

Prepare a Healthy Build of the Game to Test, Free of Bugs and Major Gameplay Problems

Well in advance of the playtest—usually at least three days ahead—we should prepare a build of our game that is stable, healthy, and free of any issues that would prevent it from being playtested. This stage of preparation regularly creates a huge "gotcha" for less-experienced game developers. Developers are often tempted to keep making changes to their game right up until a playtest. Problems get introduced that break the game rendering it untestable and nullifying all the time, money, and effort that has gone into arranging the playtest. So it's imperative that a build of the game that is stable and healthy enough to be playtested is created and checked for major issues ahead of the playtest. If the developers wish to make small changes to the game in the days leading up to the playtest, then the stable, healthy build they previously prepared and checked becomes a "safety build" and must be installed and ready to use on the day of the playtest, as a fallback in case their late changes introduced playtest-destroying problems.

Use a Formal Playtest Script

In a formal playtest or a user research setting, it's traditional for the person running the test to use a written script to determine exactly what is said to each playtester. Having a script to follow means that every playtester receives exactly the same information. You can read more about this below.

Use a Pretest Survey, if Desired

Some researchers also use a pretest survey, to set a baseline for each playtester that can then be compared to the data received from the post-test survey. For example, we might ask a playtester how they're feeling, to see if they're in a different emotional state after the test. If you use a pretest survey, work what you say about it into your playtest script.

If Desired, Record Audio and Video of Both the Game and the Playtester during the Playtest Session (with the Playtester's Consent)

Software packages are available that allow us to capture the audio and video of our game while it is running, along with audio and video of the playtester as they play. The video of the playtester might be recorded through the camera built into a laptop or through another camera. Make sure that you gain the consent of your playtesters before you record them with audio and on video, to avoid invading their privacy. If you have the resources to do it, I recommend recording your playtest sessions this way. If you can't, don't worry—you can get a lot of good information by making observations and taking notes.

Use Telemetry to Capture Metrics Data about the Playtest Session

We create code in our game that captures information about what the player does in the game, how long it takes them to complete each part of it, and so on. We'll talk about this in detail in chapter 26.

Keep an Eye on the Time: You Need Time for the Survey and the Exit Interview

We talked about keeping an eye on the time during a playtest in chapter 12. We now have an extra reason for doing so: in a formal playtest, we have to use a survey and conduct an exit interview after the player is done playing but before the test is over.

After the Test, and before any Conversation, Give the Playtester the Formal Playtest Survey

As soon as our playtester has finished playing, but before we start asking them about their experience, we're going to give them a survey to fill out. This survey will ask them about their experience, but it will do so in a way that is controlled. Our survey will frame its questions using a technique developed by psychologists, so that we can get answers that are as objective as possible.

After the Survey, Use Your Prepared Exit Interview Questions

We've used exit interviews all the way throughout our playtesting process, and in chapter 12 I gave you Marc Tattersall's five open-ended exit interview questions to use as a starting point.[1] By the time we get to formal playtesting, we usually have some specific issues that we want to investigate in the course of our exit interviews. To get the best results, we should prepare and review the questions that we'll ask ahead of time and ask them of every playtester.

Either Write Down or Record the Exit Interview Answers

The things our playtesters say during an exit interview are often filled with wisdom and insight about our game's design, but our memories are fallible and biased by emotion—you'll remember some of what your playtesters say but often only the things that delight or depress you the most. To get a full picture of the nuanced ways that people respond to our games, we should capture everything they say. Take notes, or make an audio or video recording of the exit interviews for later review and maybe transcription to text. (Transcription services are increasingly affordable, especially automated services.)

Now that we've laid out our new guidelines, let's learn how to make the tools we're going to use: a formal playtest script, a formal playtest survey, and our exit interview questions.

Preparing a Formal Playtest Script

The script of a formal playtest specifies exactly what the person running the test will say at each stage of the playtest. A formal playtest script usually runs something like this:

- Greet the playtester. "Hello, and welcome to our playtest! Thank you for joining us today."
- Invite them to sit down. "Please sit down here."
- Show them the controls cheat sheet if you're using one. "You can use this sheet as reference for the controls of the game."
- Tell the playtester that you're testing the game, not their skill. However they play naturally will be fine. (Write your own script for this, and all the bullet points below.)
- Tell the playtester that the person running the test will not be able to give them any help during the playtest.
- Give the playtester any content warnings that are appropriate, to alert them to the presence of any type of content that they may wish to avoid.
- Give the playtester any health warnings that are appropriate: for example, a photosensitive epilepsy warning related to flashing imagery or contrasting light and dark patterns in your game, or motion sickness warnings for certain types of virtual reality game.

---

1. Alissa McAloon, "5 Questions You Should Be Asking Playtesters to Get Meaningful Feedback," Gamasutra, October 10, 2016, https://www.gamasutra.com/view/news/283044/5_questions_you _should_be_asking_playtesters_to_get_meaningful_feedback.php.

- Give the playtester instructions about how to give their consent if they are going to be filmed or recorded during the playtest.
- Tell them how to get ready to play (for example, putting on headphones and picking up a controller).
- Tell them to start playing, when everything is ready.
- The script should include something about what to say if the playtester asks for help, politely reminding them that the person running the playtest is not allowed to help them.
- The exception to this is when a written hint or helper is being used to help players deal with a known issue in the game. The development team should decide before the playtest when the written hint will be used. It could be given to every playtester by the coordinator whenever they reach a certain part of the game, it could be given to playtesters only if and when they encounter the problem, or it could be given only when a playtester requests help. Which of these is most appropriate will be dependent on the type of issue. A part of the script should be written that controls when the hint or helper is used, and what to say when it is used.
- The script should not tell the playtester anything else about your game.
- When the time for playing the game is over, use the script to ask the player to stop playing.
- Ask the playtester to fill out the formal playtest survey.
- Exit interviews usually start out tightly scripted but become less scripted as they proceed, as we'll discuss below.
- When the exit interview is over, the script is less important, but make notes in it about everything that you want to do at the end of the playtest, like thanking your playtesters.

Having written your script, read it out loud to make sure that it flows well and make changes as appropriate.

Preparing a Formal Playtest Survey

Immediately after the playtest, and before any discussion, we'll give our playtester a survey to fill out. (You'll sometimes hear surveys referred to as questionnaires.) I learned to make surveys for formal playtests while I was at Naughty Dog, using a template survey given to me by my friend Sam Thompson, our excellent producer at Sony Interactive Entertainment.

It was Sam who introduced me to the idea of the Likert scale survey, named for its inventor, the American social psychologist Rensis Likert (1903–1981). Likert scale surveys are used to measure people's attitudes and feelings toward something subjective in a way that creates a good degree of objectivity across different people's understanding of each question. Likert scale questions are commonly used in the social sciences, in conducting surveys for business activities like marketing and customer satisfaction, and in other attitude-related research projects. We create an individual Likert scale question by first forming a positive statement, perhaps something like:

"I like the QUALITY of the GRAPHICS in this game."

Notice that this is a very straightforward statement. The most important parts of the question are capitalized, so that they jump out at the reader. It's pretty clear that this question is asking you what you think about the QUALITY of the game's GRAPHICS. It does rely on some specialist knowledge: the reader has to understand what part of a game is being referred to as "graphics" and has to have a basis for forming an opinion about their quality. Make sure you use concepts that are well understood by the audience that you're designing for and playtesting with.

The person answering the question is then presented with a list of choices, which are usually presented in this way:

1	2	3	4	5
Strongly disagree	Disagree	Neither agree nor disagree	Agree	Strongly agree

The person answering simply chooses the number above the words that most align with how they feel about the statement.

At the very beginning of the survey, ask each playtester for their name (or another unique identifier, if the test is to be anonymous for some reason) so that you can correlate the results of the survey with the other information about that player's experience that you'll gather during the playtest.

You can also request other demographic data from the player, like their age or gender. (If you do ask about gender, remember that gender is a spectrum, not a binary!) I think that traditional demographic data like age, gender, and ethnicity is less useful than psychographic data about what types of games and other media a playtester enjoys. If you ask the player for demographic and psychographic information, ask for it at the end of the survey. This will help you to avoid bias associated with an implicit stereotype on the part of the playtester.[2]

At Naughty Dog, we would usually use a survey like this to ask between ten and thirty questions at the end of a formal playtest session. One great thing about a Likert scale survey is that people usually fill them out quickly. Because of the way the questions are phrased (as positive statements, which you've invited to agree or disagree with) people usually know as soon as they look at the question how they want to answer it.

---

2. "Implicit Stereotype," Wikipedia, https://en.wikipedia.org/wiki/Implicit_stereotype.

When creating a formal playtest survey, it's good to have a template as a starter kit. You can find a template survey over the next few pages, and you can find more templates on this book's website, playfulproductionprocess.com. Change the questions to suit your game, keeping the statements positive wherever possible, and capitalizing and bolding the keywords in the statement that forms each question.

You'll notice that question 4 in the template breaks the pattern of "Strongly disagree" to "Strongly agree" that the other questions have. Instead, it asks the playtester to rate the difficulty of the game on a scale of "Too easy" to "Too hard." It's acceptable in a survey like this to have some questions that break the pattern, if it would be too complicated to ask a certain question otherwise. Don't include too many questions that break the pattern in this way, though, or you risk creating a less-objective survey.

The survey can be printed and filled out by the playtesters with a pencil or pen, or it can be given digitally. If you search the Internet for "online Likert scale survey" you'll find many tools that allow you to gather your playtesters' responses using a computer or mobile device.

Preparing for an Exit Interview

After each playtester has filled out our survey, we'll conduct an exit interview. As part of the formal playtest process at Naughty Dog, we would create a prioritized list of questions that we would ask every playtester (or in our case, every group of playtesters—more on that in a moment).

The exit interview can be a challenging part of the formal playtesting process. The feedback that we receive about our game from a natural language conversation can be very difficult to interpret. We are usually looking for clear information related to the design problems we're trying to solve, but the information we receive in an exit interview might be far from clear.

In Naughty Dog's formal playtests, we would test our game on ten people at the same time. Since we didn't have the resources back then to be able to interview each playtester individually at the end of the playtest, we would interview them in one large group (or sometimes in two smaller groups). Doing this brought additional complexity to the feedback we'd receive, due to the social and psychological factors at play in a group discussion. We often found that the group would tend to agree with the most charismatic, forceful, and outspoken members of the group. That's natural, and it's part of a phenomenon known as social desirability bias, whereby people tend to want to give answers that will be viewed favorably by others.[3]

It's because of social desirability bias that it is best to have someone from outside your team run your exit interviews. If you, the game's designer, speak directly to the playtesters, and they know (or suspect) that you created the game they just played,

3. "Social-Desirability Bias," Wikipedia, https://en.wikipedia.org/wiki/Social_desirability_bias.

\<Game name\>

Playtest Survey

\<Date of playtest\>

Your name: _____

Please read each statement or question in the following survey carefully and give your feedback by circling a number on the scale.

For example, for a statement, you should indicate how strongly you agree or disagree with the statement. You should interpret the numbers as follows:

1: *I strongly disagree with this statement*
2: *I disagree with this statement*
3: *I neither agree nor disagree with this statement*
4: *I agree with this statement*
5: *I strongly agree with this statement*

This example shows how you should respond if you "Agree" with the statement:

I liked the **QUALITY** of the **GRAPHICS** in this game.

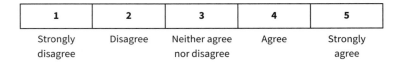

1	2	3	4	5
Strongly disagree	Disagree	Neither agree nor disagree	Agree	Strongly agree

*PLEASE REMEMBER TO ALWAYS **CIRCLE NUMBERS**, NOT WORDS*

When you're ready to begin, please turn the page.

(a)

Figure 24.1 a–d

they will be less likely to be candid with you regarding their thoughts and feelings about your game. This is why it's great to bring in a professional user research person to run your playtests.

Whenever possible, it's better to conduct exit interviews on a one-on-one basis or in small groups of up to four people, to get a clearer view of how our game landed with each playtester. For practical reasons, a member of the development team will sometimes have to run the playtest and conduct the exit interview for their own game. We should bear in mind that social desirability bias will be in play when a playtester is talking directly to the

1. I liked the **QUALITY** of the **GRAPHICS** in this game.

1	2	3	4	5
Strongly disagree	Disagree	Neither agree nor disagree	Agree	Strongly agree

2. I found the **GAMEPLAY** in this game to be very **ENJOYABLE**.

1	2	3	4	5
Strongly disagree	Disagree	Neither agree nor disagree	Agree	Strongly agree

3. Overall I felt the **CONTROLS** were **EASY** to use.

1	2	3	4	5
Strongly disagree	Disagree	Neither agree nor disagree	Agree	Strongly agree

4. Please rate the **OVERALL** level of **DIFFICULTY** of the game.

1	2	3	4	5
Too easy	Easy	Average	Hard	Too hard

5. Overall I **ENJOYED** playing at the level of **DIFFICULTY** I rated above.

1	2	3	4	5
Strongly disagree	Disagree	Neither agree nor disagree	Agree	Strongly agree

Continued overleaf

(b)

Figure 24.1 a–d
(continued)

person who made the game and we should give the information we receive less weight accordingly. Whenever we can avoid that situation, we should. For example, we could trade games in a classroom playtest setting, so that I run a playtest for a game that is not my own, and one of my classmates runs the playtest for my game.

As we create our list of exit interview questions, we should also decide how we will record the answers we receive. Maybe we will just make notes in a notebook or on a mobile device, if we can write or type quickly enough. In a professional setting, we would make audio or video recordings of the verbal responses that we receive from our

6. I thought that the **CONTROLS** of the game were **EASY TO LEARN**.

1	2	3	4	5
Strongly disagree	Disagree	Neither agree nor disagree	Agree	Strongly agree

7. The **CAMERA** always worked in a way that **SUPPORTED GAMEPLAY**.

1	2	3	4	5
Strongly disagree	Disagree	Neither agree nor disagree	Agree	Strongly agree

8. Overall I **ENJOYED** the **MAGIC SYSTEM** in the game.

1	2	3	4	5
Strongly disagree	Disagree	Neither agree nor disagree	Agree	Strongly agree

9. Overall I **ENJOYED** the **STORY** of the game.

1	2	3	4	5
Strongly disagree	Disagree	Neither agree nor disagree	Agree	Strongly agree

10. Overall I thought that the **UNICORN KITTENS** were **SUPER AWESOME**.

1	2	3	4	5
Strongly disagree	Disagree	Neither agree nor disagree	Agree	Strongly agree

Continued overleaf

(c)

Figure 24.1 a–d
(continued)

Your age: _____

Your favorite games: _____

Your favorite TV shows: _____

Your favorite movies: _____

Your favorite books: _____

Anything else you want to tell us about yourself: _____

Thank you for answering our questions!

Please tell the supervisor that you have finished,
and thanks for taking part in this playtest!

<Game name> Playtest Survey   Page 4 of 4

(d)

Figure 24.1 a–d
(continued)

playtesters in response to our questions, if we're able to conduct our exit interview in a quiet place. Of course, if we're going to record audio or video, that will require some additional preparation before the playtest, to acquire, set up, and test our recording equipment. Again, make sure that you gain the consent of your playtesters before you record them with audio or on video.

Devising Exit Interview Questions

The complexities of the exit interview make it essential that we go into the interview well prepared, with good questions to ask. The five open-ended exit interview questions of Marc Tattersall's that I gave you in chapter 12 usually work best earlier in development, when the design of our game is still being formed. By the time we get to the alpha milestone we should already be feeling quite confident that we know the answers to Marc's questions, and should instead be asking more pointed (yet still open-ended) questions about our game, seeking to check that it's working as we expect and to expose any problems that either we know about and want to explore further or that we don't yet know about.

As well as inventing the Likert scale, Rensis Likert developed open-ended interviewing in the 1930s, and the "funneling technique," whereby a researcher begins with open-ended questions and gradually moves toward more narrowly focused questions.[4] Funneling is the kind of advanced technique that an experienced exit interviewer can use to really dig down into the details of how someone experienced a game.

So, it's good to enter an exit interview with a list of thoughtfully prepared open-ended questions that will help you explore the experience of your game in a wide and deep way. Remember, an open-ended question is one that invites an expansive answer from our playtester, not just a simple yes or no. I usually prepare a list of five to ten questions, and maybe many more, depending on how much time we have for the interview. My questions focus on areas I am uncertain about or want to learn more about, and successive questions dive more deeply into particular areas. I might create conditional questions that I would only ask if my playtester gave a particular answer to a previous question.

I make my questions as specific and as concrete as possible—I try not to ask a question with too many ambiguous or vague concepts. I summarize each question in a single short sentence, and focus on clarity and brevity. It will be hard to interpret the answer that my playtester gives if they don't clearly understand my question. Each question is the beginning of a short conversation: I give myself permission to ask follow-up questions as the playtester replies (maybe questions that occur to me in the moment), to guide or funnel their responses in a direction that is useful to me.

4. "Rensis Likert," Wikipedia, https://en.wikipedia.org/wiki/Rensis_Likert.

Here are some example exit interview questions to get you started in writing your own list:

- How did (a particular sequence in the game) make you feel?
- Please describe how to (perform some action, e.g., unlock a door) in the game.
- Please describe how (some part of the game, e.g., the experience points system) works.
- Tell me about (a character in the game): who are they, and how do you feel about them?
- Please tell me about a part of the game where you felt confused or lost.

A playtest can be an intellectually and emotionally overwhelming experience for the designer of the game being tested. It's easy as a creative person to end up feeling lost or confused at any stage in the creative process, and this is especially likely to happen during a playtest, particularly one that isn't turning out as we'd expected or hoped. By asking each playtester a common set of questions we can be sure that we leave the playtest with a large amount of information about the things in our game that we care about and are focused on.

Focus Testing Our Game's Title, Key Art, and Logo Design

The formal playtesting that starts around the time of the alpha milestone creates a good opportunity to check in again on the title of our game, the game's key art, and our logo design, which we have probably been working on throughout development. We can focus test all three during the exit interview, using the techniques you'll find described on this book's website, playfulproductionprocess.com.

Preparing for the Day of the Formal Playtest

Exactly how you run your formal playtests will depend on the context you're in: whether you are a professional game development team, making games for fun, or studying game development in school; whether you have a location to test your game, and where that location is; whether you need specialized equipment or circumstances to run your game; how much time you need to test your game.

You will need to think through the practical details of your situation in order to properly prepare for the day of the playtest, to make sure that you arrive in the right place at the right time with the game ready to test and the playtesters you need to test it. I recommend that you appoint someone on your team to be responsible for all the details of the formal playtest, so that nothing gets overlooked.

Whoever is running the formal playtest will need to keep an eye on the clock to move things along, so make sure to go into the playtest with a timepiece that is separate from the computer or device being used by the playtester, so that you can regularly check the time. Anyone observing should record the time when the events they're noting down take place, so they need a timepiece too.

To prepare for the playtest, make sure that you have everything that you need from this checklist:

✓ A healthy build of the game to test, free of bugs and major gameplay problems

✓ A computer or device to run the game on, with any special hardware required (for example, a game controller or virtual reality headset)

✓ Cleaning wipes for controllers and virtual reality headsets

✓ A screen large enough for both playtester and observer to see

✓ Headphones for the playtester

✓ A method for the playtest observer to listen in on the game (for example, headphones, a stereo audio splitter, and an extension cable)

✓ A method for recording your observations during the playtest (a paper notebook and pen, or a digital device)

✓ If desired, a method for recording audio and video of the screen and/or the player's face and hands

✓ Paper or digital copies of the playtest script

✓ Copies of the controls cheat sheet, if you're using one

✓ Copies of the written hint or helper to help players with any known gameplay issues or functional issues, if you're using one

✓ Paper or digital copies of the survey

✓ Pens or pencils for paper surveys

✓ Paper or digital copies of the exit interview questions

✓ A method for recording the exit interview answers

✓ A timepiece

Now that we have everything we need, we're ready to run the playtest.

25 Running a Formal Playtest

Formal Playtesting in an Informal Environment

In an ideal world, we would run every formal playtest in a specialized usability suite, with an environment designed for naturalistic play sessions, audio-video feeds of the player and their screen, and with the game sending metrics data to a central server.

But with just a meeting room or a classroom, and with many different games being tested in the same space at the same time, we can capture the spirit of a formal playtest in even the most informal, crowded, noisy environment, using the guidelines that I lay out in chapter 12, "Playtesting," chapter 24, "Preparing for a Formal Playtest," and in this chapter.

By being careful about how we engage with our playtesters and by making sure that we don't accidentally give them what I call "privileged" knowledge of the game (special ahead-of-time or behind-the-scenes information), we can create a "bubble of objectivity" around them. We can then get a lot of clear, high-quality feedback about our game from our playtesters, just as we would in a scientifically controlled usability testing environment.

Finding Playtesters

Finding "Kleenex" playtesters for a formal playtest can be challenging, even at a game studio or in a game program full of people eager to play games and help their designers. The right way for your team to find playtesters will depend on your circumstances. If you are a professional company or an academic research project with a budget, and you have the resources to be able to pay your playtesters, then do—I believe that people should be compensated for their labor, even if that labor is enjoyable. If you have very little budget, payment in kind might work—perhaps a copy of the game when it is released, or food on the day of the playtest.

In a game program, there's an argument to be made that being a playtester in a formal playtest is a good learning experience for an upcoming designer. Every game designer needs to cultivate their thinking-out-loud skills as a basic part of their professional practice, and the experience of being stuck in a game and having the game's designer refuse to help you can be a valuable memory when it's your turn to be the designer.

I've used many methods to bring Kleenex playtesters into my classes for formal playtests. I've used posters and mailing list announcements to invite people from our university's community, and I've asked the students whose games will be tested to each invite a friend or two. People seem more committed to coming along when I ask them to sign up for the playtest using an online form, and providing snacks before or after a playtest can help guarantee that people show up. When students bring a friend, I try to avoid having them playtest the game that their friend made. This can lead to some disappointment, but I think there's too much social desirability bias present otherwise.

Remember that if any of your playtesters are below a certain age (depending on the law in your area) you will need their parent or guardian to sign a consent form. Make sure that you properly research the legal requirements for your area related to this, and do it well in advance of the playtest.

Finding a Location, Arranging a Time, and Deciding a Playtest Coordinator

Find a location for your playtest that is appropriate for your team's circumstances. If you are a professional team, perhaps you can use a meeting room or a communal area at your workspace. If you are a student team, you should be able to find a classroom or common room to use. If you are a member of a game-making club or collective, maybe your shared space is available. Coworking spaces offer meeting rooms for rent. To playtest most types of digital game, you will need a location that has tables or desks and chairs. Make sure you have enough chairs for both the playtesters and the people running the playtest, and check that the location has access to drinking water and restrooms.

Block out enough time at the location; how much time you need will be dependent on the length of your game, the amount of time you want to test it for, the number of stations you will have available (see "Preparing the Location" below), and the number of playtesters you'll have. The goal for a formal playtest is to get at least seven and preferably ten playtesters to play through the game, and to give them enough time that they can play the whole game (or nearly all of it).

Decide who is going to supervise the playtest, to make sure that it runs properly and to talk to the playtesters. We'll call this person the playtest coordinator. It's best if the coordinator can be someone other than a development team member. Otherwise, a member of the team can take on this role. For large playtests, several coordinators may be needed to share the duties of managing the location and facilities, talking to the playtesters, making observations about the test, and intervening when necessary.

Most formal playtests take place in seven stages:

1. Preparing the location
2. The arrival of the playtesters

3. Immediately before the playtest starts

4. The play session

5. The debrief session

6. Clearing up after the playtest

7. Analyzing the playtest results

Preparing the Location

Having arranged a time, place, and playtesters, make sure you arrive at the location early to get the playtest set up. Use the checklist under "Preparing for the Day of the Formal Playtest" at the end of chapter 24 and take everything that you prepared.

Each individual piece of hardware running a software copy of the game that will be tested is known as a station (sometimes also known as a seat). You might have just one station or many, depending on your situation and resources. For example, if your game is a single-player game or an online multiplayer game, and you have five stations, you can test with five playtesters at the same time. If your game is a two-player local multiplayer game, you will need ten playtesters for five stations.

If you are testing the same game on many stations at the same time, set up dividers between the stations so that playtesters cannot see the screens of their neighbors. You can create dividers cheaply and easily from cardboard boxes or sheets of foamcore board.

Set up your playtest station or stations and check all your preparations. This will take some time, so start setting up well before the playtesters are due to arrive.

- Install the stable, healthy version of the game that you plan to test. If late changes were made, also install the safety build that was previously checked for major issues.
- Check that the screen and speakers are working well.
- Check that any special hardware (for example, a game controller or virtual reality headset) is working correctly.
- Check to see that the game is running with no problems and use the safety build or take other appropriate steps if issues are discovered.
- In chapter 26, we'll talk about the metrics data that the game will gather about the player's actions in the game. If you are using a game metrics system, check to see that it is working correctly.
- If you're using station dividers, check that neighboring screens cannot be seen from each station.
- Check the method that you'll use to listen in on the playtest as you watch.
- Make sure that your note-taking method is handy and working (that your digital device is charged and turned on, or that your paper notebook has some blank pages and your pen hasn't run out of ink!).
- Make sure that any audio and video recording equipment or software is charged and working correctly.

- Check that the survey is ready to be given out, along with pens or pencils if you're using paper surveys.
- Check that the exit interview questions are at hand.
- Place the controls cheat sheet (see chapter 12) on the table in front of where each playtester will sit.
- If you're planning to use a written hint or helper because of a known issue in the game (see chapter 12), put it somewhere out of sight if each playtester should only see it at a certain time. Otherwise, put it on the table in front of where each playtester will sit.
- Check that your timepiece is showing the right time and is easy to see throughout the playtest.

The Arrival of the Playtesters

As the playtesters arrive, a coordinator should use the pretest script to greet them and thank them for coming. Give them a comfortable place to wait with access to drinking water and restrooms. If you are going to use a pretest survey, this is a good time to give it to the playtesters to fill out.

Use the pretest script to give your playtesters any information that is important to the success of the playtest (content warnings, health warnings, instructions about consenting to video recording, and so on). Minimize your interaction with the playtesters beyond what the script dictates, per our playtest guidelines, but be polite, and if you need to go off-script, think for a moment before you speak to avoid giving out information that will introduce bias.

Immediately before the Playtest Starts

The coordinator should guide each playtester to the station they'll be playing at and get them settled in. Still following the script, give them any help they need to get ready to play. Show each playtester the controls cheat sheet, if you are using one. Ask them to think out loud, if appropriate. Don't tell the playtester anything at all about the game they are going to play that isn't in the script.

Try to avoid having any of the playtesters wait at their station for longer than the others. We want each playtester to gain the same impression of our game, including how long they spend looking at the title screen. As soon as both the playtesters and the coordinator are ready, the coordinator asks the playtesters to start playing, and the playtest begins.

The Play Session

The first part of the formal playtest is known as the play session. This is the part where playtesters play the game. The coordinator—and anyone else observing the playtest—should make a note of the time that the play session begins.

For the duration of the play session, each playtester should be left to their own devices and allowed to play the game in their own way. According to our playtest guidelines, the coordinator and any other observers should observe (a) what each playtester does in the game, and (b) anything they say about what they're thinking and feeling. Even if the playtest is being recorded with audio and video, the observers should still capture as much information as they can by taking notes.

If I'm using a paper notebook, I draw stars and circles in the margins to create "action items" and to annotate issues for further discussion. If I'm typing into a spreadsheet or document, I'll use bold and italics to do the same. Playtest-recording software suites usually allow developers to tag sections of video with notes, creating a log of issues very quickly and easily. During a formal playtest, I become almost robotic in noting everything I see. I'm trying to make it so that when I review my notes later the problems that our game has will immediately jump out at me.

The coordinator should not help the playtester at all, even if the playtester asks for help. If the playtester does ask for help, the coordinator should apologize, and, following the script, remind them that they are not allowed to give any help. If appropriate, follow the script to use the written hint or helper you prepared.

The coordinator should keep an eye on the time. There must be enough time left at the end for the second part of the playtest, the debrief session, using the survey and the exit interview questions. This might mean ending the play session before the playtester has seen everything in the game, and it's the responsibility of the coordinator to do this if necessary.

Sometimes difficulties arise during the play session. The hardware might malfunction, or a playtester might behave in a disruptive way. The better you prepare for the playtest, the more smoothly things will run, but don't get stressed out if things go wrong. The spirit required for a formal playtest is a lot like that needed for a theater production: when things go wrong you just have to roll with it and do your best to rescue the situation. You can always make the best of a bad lot, one way or another, and in fact this is a good attitude to keep for the whole process of game development.

The Debrief Session

After the playtest session, it's time for the debrief session, when each playtester fills out the survey and takes part in the exit interview.

Still following the script, give each playtester the survey the moment the play session ends and have them fill it out right away. Don't talk to the playtester before they complete the survey, beyond politely asking them to complete it. The goal is to capture the playtester's immediate, raw impressions of the game. We want them to use the same mindset to complete the survey that they were using to play the game, with direct access to their thoughts and feelings about it.

If you're focus testing your game title, key art, logo design, or anything else during the playtest, do it immediately after the playtester completes the survey but before the exit interview. You may need to talk to the playtester to successfully complete the focus test, but again, minimize your conversation with them: you are trying to get *their* opinions, and don't want to bias them by introducing your own, even accidentally.

Then it's time to conduct the exit interview. Whether the exit interview is conducted one-on-one, as is preferable, or in a group, which is sometimes more practical, will be dependent on your team's circumstances and resources. Sometimes a playtester or group of playtesters will be taken to a different location for the exit interview, where it is quiet and recording equipment has been set up.

Ask your playtesters the open-ended questions you've prepared, listen to what they have to say, and write down their answers or record them. If you have sequences of questions designed to funnel your players toward the topics you're interested in, use them. If playtesters begin to talk about something interesting but unexpected, ask them follow-up questions to further guide the conversation. If your playtesters are not forthcoming, try to draw them out with different phrasings of the same question or move on to the next question. Not everyone finds it easy to participate in an exit interview, so don't push a playtester who doesn't have much to say.

Eventually, the exit interview will be completed or you will run out of time at the location. The latter is more common—the interesting conversations we have about our games can run on indefinitely! It's time to thank each playtester and tell them how helpful they have been in helping us improve the design of our game. Give them any gifts you've decided to give or pay them if that was part of the agreement. If they are being paid, there may be some paperwork to fill out before you send them back out into the world.

Clearing Up after the Playtest

After the playtesters have left, there will be some work to do to tidy up the playtest location. Be sure to collect up the surveys and put them in a safe place. Everyone who took notes should make sure their notes are somewhere safe, and you should secure any other important documents, like completed parental consent forms. If you are using a game metrics system (see chapter 26), make sure the metrics data is gathered together and backed up immediately after the playtest. Playtests are expensive in terms of time, money, and effort, so don't lose the results.

If the development team was present for the playtest, it's good to take a few minutes to decompress while clearing up, by sharing thoughts and feelings about the test. The mood in the room immediately after a playtest is often a little giddy, just like backstage after the curtain falls at a show. The team might be exhausted, relieved that it's over but happy in their accomplishment. Some might be elated if things went well. Some might be feeling down if they received any particularly difficult feedback. By talking with one another, even for just a few minutes, we can start to come back down to earth. It's a chance to remind each other that it's okay to feel bad, but that we shouldn't be discouraged—receiving difficult feedback is how we learn what we need to know to make our game better.

Analyzing the Playtest Results

A formal playtest gives us a wealth of data to analyze—so much so that it can be hard to know where to start. We now have:

- Completed surveys
- Play session observation notes (and possibly videos)
- Exit interview notes
- Focus test results
- Metrics data, if we collected any

Analyzing the Results of a Formal Playtest Survey

The very first thing that I do after a formal playtest, when beginning to evaluate its results, is to look at the data I've received from the surveys. The answers that our play-testers have given represent a *lot* of information about the thoughts and feelings they have about our game. How can we parse that data in a quick and effective way, to rapidly build up a picture of how our game is landing with people? It's actually very easy, if we use a spreadsheet.

I begin with the template in figure 25.1, which you can find on this book's website, playfulproductionprocess.com. This template has space for the survey data from ten playtesters and shows the same sample questions we used in chapter 24. You'll see that this template has a column for age—you could add columns for any demographic or psychographic information that you gathered from your playtesters.

Whether the survey was filled out on paper or with an online form, it's a quick and easy data entry job to transfer the information from the completed surveys to this spreadsheet, plugging in the numbers that the playtesters selected in the cell corresponding to the row for each playtester and the column for each question. Even going slowly and carefully, this usually only takes ten minutes or so. Of course, tools can be written to automate this process, and you can find paid survey tools online that will save you some time.

You can see a formal playtest data spreadsheet with some example data plugged in in figure 25.2.

The formulae in the rows labeled GROUP AVERAGE and GROUP MEDIAN calculate the average (mean) and median values for each question, derived from the answers of all the playtesters in the test. The average value or mean value is simply the total of all the players' answers, divided by the number of players. The median value is the number that separates the higher half of all the player's answers from the lower half: it sometimes gives us a better sense of what the "middle" answer is than the average does. When all the data has been entered into the spreadsheet, we can get a good sense of what the playtesters thought of our game as a group, just by looking at the GROUP AVERAGE and GROUP MEDIAN rows. Of course, for most of the questions, the higher the number, the more the players liked that aspect of the game.

<Game Name> Playtest
<Date of the playtest>

Playtester #	Name	Age	Q1 — I liked the QUALITY of the GRAPHICS in this game.	Q2 — I found the GAME PLAY in this game to be very ENJOYABLE.	Q3 — Overall I felt the CONTROLS were EASY to use.	Q4 — Please rate the OVERALL level of DIFFICULTY of the game.	Q5 — Overall I ENJOYED playing at the level of DIFFICULTY I rated above.	Q6 — I thought that the CONTROLS of the game were EASY TO LEARN.	Q7 — The CAMERA always worked in a way that best supported game play.	Q8 — Overall I ENJOYED the MAGIC SYSTEM in the game.	Q9 — Overall I ENJOYED the STORY of the game.	Q10 — Overall I think that the PSYCHIC KITTEN CONTROLS were EASY TO USE.
1	Person 1											
2	Person 2											
3	Person 3											
4	Person 4											
5	Person 5											
6	Person 6											
7	Person 7											
8	Person 8											
9	Person 9											
10	Person 10											
GROUP AVERAGE			=AVERAGE(D6:D15)	=AVERAGE(E6:E15)	=AVERAGE(F6:F15)	=AVERAGE(G6:G15)	=AVERAGE(H6:H15)	=AVERAGE(I6:I15)	=AVERAGE(J6:J15)	=AVERAGE(K6:K15)	=AVERAGE(L6:L15)	=AVERAGE(M6:M15)
GROUP MEDIAN			=MEDIAN(D6:D15)	=MEDIAN(E6:E15)	=MEDIAN(F6:F15)	=MEDIAN(G6:G15)	=MEDIAN(H6:H15)	=MEDIAN(I6:I15)	=MEDIAN(J6:J15)	=MEDIAN(K6:K15)	=MEDIAN(L6:L15)	=MEDIAN(M6:M15)
AVERAGE FROM LAST TEST												
MEDIAN FROM LAST TEST												
AVERAGE DELTA FROM LAST TEST			=D16-D18	=E16-E18	=F16-F18	=G16-G18	=H16-H18	=I16-I18	=J16-J18	=K16-K18	=L16-L18	=M16-M18
MEDIAN DELTA FROM LAST TEST			=D17-D19	=E17-E19	=F17-F19	=G17-G19	=H17-H19	=I17-I19	=J17-J19	=K17-K19	=L17-L19	=M17-M19

Answers Key
1 = Strongly disagree
2 = Disagree
3 = Neither Agree nor Disagree
4 = Agree
5 = Strongly agree

Except for...
4. Please rate the OVERALL level of DIFFICULTY of the game
1 = Too easy
2 = Easy
3 = Average
4 = Hard
5 = Too hard

Figure 25.1

<Game Name> Playtest
<Date of the playtest>

Playtester #	Name	Age	Q1 — I liked the QUALITY of the GRAPHICS in this game.	Q2 — I found the GAME PLAY in this game to be very ENJOYABLE.	Q3 — Overall I felt the CONTROLS were EASY to use.	Q4 — Please rate the OVERALL level of DIFFICULTY of the game.	Q5 — Overall I ENJOYED playing at the level of DIFFICULTY I rated above.	Q6 — I thought that the CONTROLS of the game were EASY TO LEARN.	Q7 — The CAMERA always worked in a way that best supported game play.	Q8 — Overall I ENJOYED the MAGIC SYSTEM in the game.	Q9 — Overall I ENJOYED the STORY of the game.	Q10 — Overall I think that the PSYCHIC KITTEN CONTROLS were EASY TO USE.
1	Scott	21	3	3	2	4	2	3	3	4	3	4
2	Ethel	24	4	5	4	3	3	5	5	4	5	3
3	Dusty	23	4	5	5	4	3	5	5	5	5	3
4	Rosy	31	5	4	5	3	4	4	5	4	5	3
5	Mabelle	54	5	4	3	4	2	4	5	5	4	3
6	Wilber	42	4	4	4	3	4	5	5	3	4	5
7	Margaret	17	4	5	4	3	2	4	4	4	4	3
8	Clyde	rather not say	2	1	1	4	1	2	1	5	3	1
9	Quentin	27	5	3	4	5	3	4	5	4	3	3
10	Leona	33	3	5	1	5	1	5	5	4	4	3
	GROUP AVERAGE		3.90	3.90	3.30	3.80	2.50	4.10	4.30	4.20	4.00	3.20
	GROUP MEDIAN		4.00	4.00	4.00	4.00	2.50	4.00	5.00	4.00	4.00	3.00
	AVERAGE FROM LAST TEST		4.25	3.5	3.5	3.42	2.83	4.33	4.67	3.25	3.75	2.92
	MEDIAN FROM LAST TEST		4	3	3	3	2.5	4	5	3.5	4	3
	AVERAGE DELTA FROM LAST TEST		-0.35	0.40	-0.20	0.38	-0.33	-0.23	-0.37	0.95	0.25	0.28
	MEDIAN DELTA FROM LAST TEST		0.00	1.00	1.00	1.00	0.00	0.00	0.00	0.50	0.00	0.00

Answers Key
1 = Strongly disagree
2 = Disagree
3 = Neither Agree nor Disagree
4 = Agree
5 = Strongly agree

Except for...
4. Please rate the OVERALL level of DIFFICULTY of the game
1 = Too easy
2 = Easy
3 = Average
4 = Hard
5 = Too hard

Figure 25.2

Games that have been carefully designed using ongoing playtesting and concentric development usually score somewhere in the range of three to five for each question at the first playtest. If they don't, major problems may have gone unnoticed or unaddressed in the course of development up until that point. If a game scores low on a particular question, then the designers have to ask themselves: Do we have a real problem here? Was this an anomaly? Was this by design?

I can imagine a game (probably an art game or a "serious" game) that has deliberately been designed to elicit a negative reaction from playtesters. If a low score is aligned with the designers' intent, then we can safely ignore—or even welcome—the low score. What we're looking for is surprises: both good surprises—we didn't think they'd like our strange main mechanic, or understand our story, but they did!—and bad surprises—we thought our art or sound design was brilliant, but our playtesters think it's only average.

Formal playtests work best when they happen as a series of tests taking place across weeks or months, and in the data spreadsheet there are rows labeled AVERAGE FROM LAST TEST and MEDIAN FROM LAST TEST where you can copy over the results that you got for GROUP AVERAGE and GROUP MEDIAN in your previous playtest. In the rows labeled AVERAGE DELTA FROM LAST TEST and MEDIAN DELTA FROM LAST TEST, there are formulae that subtract your previous scores from your current scores. You can apply conditional formatting in the spreadsheet and use color to highlight when your numbers for a particular question have gone up, gone down, or stayed the same.

Of course, we usually want our numbers to go up over time. Working on the *Uncharted* games, from playtest to playtest we would see small, gradual changes in the scores we received for things like our gameplay, graphics, and audio design, as we completed and polished the game. Even if the average score we received for our gameplay only went up from 4.3 to 4.4, we could be confident that the recent changes we'd made had contributed positively to the experience of the game, rather than harming it. This kind of ongoing and incremental formal playtesting can be very reassuring, amid the subjective artmaking process that is game design.

Analyzing Play Session Observation Notes and Videos

In chapter 12, I gave you quite a lot of advice about analyzing the feedback that we get from watching a playtest and from an exit interview. All of that advice is still applicable to a formal playtest. In particular, consider whether the feedback from the exit interview can be categorized as (1) must fix, (2) maybe fix, or (3) a new idea, and make lists accordingly. By the time we're running formal playtests we are in less of an exploratory phase and are focused on building out our game, so be wary of chasing too many new ideas. That's not to say that there aren't still discoveries to be made that could transform your game in a good way, but keep your main focus on finding and fixing problems.

I believe that, for many types of game, just watching someone play can tell us nearly everything we need to know about how to improve it. It's often easy to discern complex information about the player's mental state from their actions in the game, their body language, and sometimes their facial expressions. You can tell if a playtester understands what they can do and what they're meant to do from the actions they take in the game. You can see if they are putting together concepts that the game has taught them in new ways that they find interesting. You can often tell if someone is interested, bored, or frustrated, just from the way they sit and the exclamations they make. Our play session observation notes and any other recordings we make contain this information.

In a character-action game like *Uncharted*, it's easy to tell when someone isn't see-ing something or has forgotten their goal. When players repeatedly run right past the object they're meant to be interacting with, it's a pretty sure sign that they can't see it—maybe it looks like it's part of the background. If they go up to a puzzle-solving object from time to time and briefly use it, but then leave it alone for a long time, you know they can see it, but they don't think it's important.

It's important to take the time to review the notes we take during playtests, in addi-tion to reviewing our memories of what we saw. Memory is easily colored by emotion, as we've previously discussed, and minor things might prove to be important. When I review my notes after a playtest, I'll look for patterns where I've written down the same thing over and over again, indicating a major problem that should be addressed: "Player can't find the door leading out of the level" or "Player thinks they've already hit all the right switches." I'll transfer my notes to my lists of (1) must fix, (2) maybe fix, or (3) new ideas, to go over them with the team later.

Play session videos and metrics data are often useful when we're reviewing our notes and can give us greater insight into the issues our playtesters were facing. With video, we can see exactly what a particular playtester did as they tried to play a part of the game, if we made a careful note of *when* something took place (otherwise, it can be hard to find the moment you're interested in, among the hours of video you captured). We can use metrics data to get a sense of the way players played over time, as individu-als and as a group, as we'll see in chapter 26.

Analyzing the Results of the Exit Interviews

Next, I analyze the results of the exit interviews. If I wasn't present for some or all of the exit interviews, I'm keen to find out what people said about our game. Using an online service to transcribe the exit interview audio to text can make it easier to review and use. Because we asked the same basic exit interview questions of every player in our playtests (even if our follow-up questions diverged), we can compare what differ-ent playtesters say to gain a good overview of how our game is landing with a variety of players.

The ultimate open-ended question might be: How did the game make you feel? Do the answers align with your experience goals? Of course, as designers we want to meet our project goals, but don't discount things you didn't expect to hear about, especially if the playtesters found some value in the experience. As filmmaker Spike Lee is quoted as saying, "A lot of times you get credit for stuff in your movie you didn't intend to be there." So it goes for games, maybe even more so, because of the nature of interactivity.

Evaluating exit interview feedback is a subjective process. Not everything that's said in an exit interview can be taken at face value, and you'll be called on to use your powers of interpretation and to make nuanced judgment calls about the things that you hear. Bring other people into the process. It's often easier to understand playtester feedback when you work together with a teammate, a friend, or someone else who knows your game and understands your creative goals.

Analyzing the Results of the Focus Test

If you included a focus test of your title, key art, logo design, or anything else in your survey or exit interview, hopefully it confirmed what you already knew: that you've chosen a good title, given it a great graphic design treatment, and have made some good key art for your game. If you got results other than this, it's time to do some more work on whatever is falling short.

Once you reach the alpha milestone, don't delay in finalizing the title of your game. You'll need to start reaching out to your potential audience soon, and in order to do that you'll need a social media account, which will need a name corresponding to your title. Your game needs a strong identity, one that will partly be understood through its title, key art, and logo, so all three will be important as you present your game to the public. We'll come back to this subject in chapter 30.

Acting on the Feedback Received from a Formal Playtest

For each of the low scores that we get in response to a particular question, from each conclusion that we draw from watching playtesters play, and for each of the pieces of feedback that we get from our exit interviews, there's an invitation to action on our part that we must evaluate in the context of the whole project. Do we want to work to improve our score in a particular survey category in the next formal playtest? Will we work to fix something or add something new based on a play session observation or an exit interview response? How many different issues are we already dealing with? How much time do we have left, when we consider all the things we have left to implement?

For me, proper evaluation of all of the different types of feedback from a formal playtest comes back to a simple method. Just make a list of all the things that have been identified as problems, potential problems, and new ideas. Prioritize them as very important, somewhat important, and less important. Choose more levels of prioritization if necessary—your lists might turn out to be quite long.

Then, in your next working session, decide what you're going to tackle first. Because I work using concentric development, I will usually fix a problem with something that's already in the game before I add something new. Remember: players don't know about all the good things that *could* have been in your game, but they will certainly notice the things in your game that don't work well.

It might help if you categorize your lists further. I find that most of the problems that I identify during a playtest fall into one of these three categories:

- **Bugs**, where the game glitches, crashes, or does something else that it's not meant to.
- **Content problems**—perhaps players can't see an interactable object because of the texture map on it, or they can't see the entrance to a corridor because the lighting is too dark.
- **Design problems**, where the design of the game doesn't support the experience that we're trying to give our players.

Very often, these three types of issues will overlap. A bug or a content problem might create a design problem. As a result, it's a good idea to tackle these problems in the order above. Fix your bugs first. It's almost impossible to evaluate a buggy game, and you should immediately fix every bug that you find when you're using concentric development. Then fix your content problems, especially if they're quick and easy to fix. Changing a texture or the lighting is often easy; creating an elaborate new animation will take longer and might need some planning. When the bugs have been banished and the simple content problems are resolved, you'll be in a much better place to properly evaluate your design problems.

Occasionally a bug will add something good to the player's experience, as honored by the old software developers' joke: "It's not a bug, it's a feature." You'll have to decide what to do about these happy accidents as they arise. If in doubt, refer to your experience goals and your game design macro chart for guidance.

Remember that the changes you make as you try to fix things based on the feedback you've received could—and most likely *will*—have unintended consequences that you're also going to have to deal with. That's why it's good to have multiple rounds of formal playtesting, to put your game through a QA (quality assurance) process, to find and remove the last of your bugs and content problems, and to deal with any outstanding design problems.

Dealing with Difficult Feedback

As with every type of playtesting, and as much as we try to avoid getting defensive, formal playtesting can present us with feedback that is difficult to deal with. In those times, it's good to get some distance. Take the evening off, go get some exercise, have a healthy meal, an early night, or some fun with your friends. Come back to the difficult feedback with a cool head and with confidence: you're a talented and resourceful game designer. You've got this.

Feedback might be difficult because you have identified a serious problem, but you have no idea how to fix it. In a situation like this, start to make lists of pros and cons. If you were to try a certain solution, how might it help, and what would it hurt? Enlist another person to help you make the list. They will see solutions that you can't, or they might frame the pros and cons differently.

Feedback might be difficult because it seems like it doesn't give you anything to work with. Most creative people value constructive criticism, but sometimes what comes out of a formal playtest might only seem destructive. We can't expect our playtesters always to be constructively critical—they're probably not game designers themselves. (Although we can and should expect our playtesters to be courteous. Don't tolerate abusive situations when you encounter them. You should immediately end a playtest if a playtester behaves or speaks in an abusive way.)

When you receive feedback that doesn't seem constructive, it's up to you, as the game's designer, to find the fix. Think creatively, by considering the problem from many angles, and remember that in the complex dynamic system of a game, a small change might have an unexpectedly good result.

Going into the Next Round of Formal Playtesting

Once we have analyzed the feedback, decided what we're going to act on, and made some fixes and changes to our game, it will be time for another formal playtest. In the next test, we'll look to see whether we've improved the game, made it worse, or have had no effect. Maybe we'll have fixed one problem but caused another.

Again, formal playtests work best as part of a series, taking place as frequently as we can run them, starting around alpha, and finishing just before the final "release candidate" milestone. Our first formal playtests will be lively, erratic, and full of surprises. Our final formal playtests will—if things have gone well—provide validation that our game has turned out as we desired.

The process of formal playtesting is exacting, detail-oriented work, but it's also tremendously fun and satisfying. If you find yourself enjoying this type of work, consider learning more about user research and user experience (UX). As Mun Lum describes in her Prototypr.io article "Is UX Design a Separate Practice from Game Design?" game studios are increasingly integrating usability specialists into their teams: "As games get bigger with deeper and more complex mechanics and systems, new roles such as UX designer emerge. A new job title may have been created; most UX designers in the game industry were once game designers or came with a game design background."[1]

So, this is a great career path for people who love to do substantive game design work with objectively measurable results. We'll pick up these themes of measurement and creativity in our next chapter, where we'll capture numerical information about how our players play and use it to improve our games.

---

1. Mun Lum, "Is UX Design a Separate Practice from Game Design?," *Prototypr.io* (blog), August 23, 2019, https://blog.prototypr.io/is-ux-design-a-separate-practice-from-game-design-97ae1a03e61c.

Telemetry is a word that means "measurement at a distance," from the Greek roots *tele* (remote) and *metron* (measure). The word is used in the world of software development to describe the practice of collecting data about something that is happening somewhere else.[1] You're probably aware that much of the software you use captures data about what you do and when you do it, and then "phones home" to send that data to the software's developer or another party. The issues of privacy and consent around such practices are often (and rightly) the subject of heated debate.

Telemetry is sometimes called instrumentation by human-computer interaction professionals but is more commonly known as game metrics or analytics by game developers. The use of game metrics goes far beyond simply collecting data and has evolved into the game design practice of interpreting that data to understand how real players play, in order to improve gameplay. It is also an important part of the business of games.

Of course, digital games make measurements all the time. They record what buttons the player presses and when. They might check their internal clock to see what time it is in the real world. It's easy to set up some code to capture data about events in a game that we can use to analyze the game design. So far, we've looked at various ways to study the responses of playtesters to our games: by observation, using surveys, and with exit interviews. We can also use game metrics to gain very detailed information about what playtesters do in our games, which in turn can give us an enhanced understanding of their experiences.

You'll hear game developers refer to analytics when discussing the game metrics used to shape the way that games make money. Game analytics typically focus on the regularity with which players return to games and how much money they spend on the game, but they may also look in greater detail at what players do inside the game. You can find many books and articles online about business analytics for games. Instead of focusing on the business side of telemetry, this chapter will look at how we can gain game design insight into player behavior, using easy-to-understand and simple-to-implement techniques.

---

1. "Telemetry," Wikipedia, https://en.wikipedia.org/wiki/Telemetry.

Game Metrics at Naughty Dog

By the time I joined Naughty Dog in 2004, the use of game metrics was already a long-standing part of the studio's design culture. Going all the way back to *Crash Bandicoot*, Naughty Dog had been using metrics to make sure that their games were providing the right level of challenge for their players, being neither too difficult nor too easy.

In each of the formal playtests that we conducted for the single-player mode of the *Uncharted* games, we used metrics to record a lot of data about the player's progression through the game. Every time a playtester reached a new checkpoint (an automatic save point) in the game, the time that had elapsed since the last checkpoint would be recorded. We would also record the number of attempts the playtester had made to reach that checkpoint—in effect, how many times they'd died since the last checkpoint.

At the end of the formal playtest, we would export all this data into a spreadsheet (or later, into a special tool we made) and begin to make tables and graphs to look at the data easily. We did this mostly by setting things up so that we could look at all ten playtesters' data at the same time, but we could also inspect the data for individual players.

In particular, we would look at the average (mean), median, minimum, and maximum attempt counts for each checkpoint, derived from the data for all ten playtesters. In figure 26.1, you can see a table of player attempts for the checkpoints that we'd identified as potentially problematic, because they might be too difficult to get past. We used conditional formatting and color coding to show when these numbers exceeded certain thresholds. For example, an average or median of greater than six attempts was a red flag that the gameplay leading up to that checkpoint might be too difficult. We set these thresholds by discussing how difficult of a game we were aiming to make overall, but we would also override them for particular checkpoints, whenever we intentionally wanted the player to fail a lot in a short amount of time to create excitement or to make the difficulty in that part of the game memorable.

Once we'd compiled the metrics data into this type of easily readable format, we would share it with the game designers on the team so they could begin to investigate and address these possible problems. In doing this, we created a lens through which to look at how real people—the same kind of people who might later buy our game—were playing.

The time data we recorded for each checkpoint was also useful. Figure 26.2. shows a graph that summarizes the way that nine playtesters progressed through *Uncharted 3* in an early formal playtest. The horizontal axis shows the names of the successive checkpoints that would be reached as the player progressed through the game. The vertical axis shows the total amount of time each player had spent in the game up until reaching each checkpoint. (We recorded the time *between* checkpoints, remember, but it's easy in a spreadsheet to calculate a running total of the total elapsed time for each checkpoint.)

You can easily see how quickly or slowly each playtester is getting through the game. Where a playtester's line gets steeper they're progressing more slowly, either because the

	Min	Average	Median	Max
colombia-museum-break-in-roof	1	1.9	1	7
colombia-chase-fence	2	2.2	2	3
colombia-rooftops-tiles	2	2.8	3	4
syria-syria-turret1-outside	1	2.3	2	7
syria-syria-rpgesus-trapped	2	5.9	6.5	9
syria-syria-area2-start	1	2.9	2	8
syria-syria-area2-return	1	7.5	8	14
syria-syria-escape-hub-exit-mid	1	3.0	2.5	8
syria-syria-escape-bridge	1	3.1	2	8
yemen-temple-yem-temp-exit-combat-mid	1	2.2	1	8
grave-grave-01-freighter-section-2-exit	1	3.4	3.5	6
grave-grave-01-firstyard-start	1	3.7	3.5	9
grave-grave-01-firstyard-combat-mid-left	0	1.4	0	10
grave-grave-01-firstyard-combat-mid-right	0	5.3	6.5	11
grave-grave-01-firstyard-wreck-hatch	0	3.1	2	9
cruise-ship-cruise-container-fight-mid	2	5.0	4.5	8
cruise-ship-cruise-ballroom-fight-start	1	5.4	6.5	10
cruise-ship-cruise-ballroom-fight-mid	3	7.6	8	11
cruise-ship-cruise-chandelier-climb	1	2.8	2	9
airport-car-field-start	1	2.3	1.5	8
airport-car-field-mid	1	2.3	1.5	7
sandlantis-san-desert-battle-start	1	4.9	6	7
sandlantis-san-cistern-noria-tower-start	0	3.1	2.5	6

Figure 26.1
A table showing potentially problematic numbers of attempts in *Uncharted 3: Drake's Deception*, derived from metrics data gathered from ten players during a formal playtest. Image credit: *UNCHARTED 3: Drake's Deception*™ © 2011 Sony Interactive Entertainment LLC. *UNCHARTED 3: Drake's Deception* is a trademark of Sony Interactive Entertainment LLC. Created and developed by Naughty Dog LLC.

game has become more difficult, because they're searching for the hidden treasures that are scattered through the game, or maybe because they just keep stopping to admire the view. It's possible to figure out more about what might be happening by comparing the progression time data against the attempt count data for each checkpoint.

Notice how one player progresses through the game much more quickly than the others, and that one player falls behind straightaway and later leaves the playtest. The rest of the players progress at about the same rate, especially in the first third of the game, which was designed to be quite easy. As the game moves through its middle third, the progression rates fan out. A couple of the players are nearly neck and neck for second place, and one player gradually falls farther and farther behind. Interestingly, this was a pattern that we would see in nearly every formal playtest we conducted, with many different groups of playtesters. Only one player actually reached the end of the game in this playtest, but in later playtests we made sure that everyone had enough time to finish.

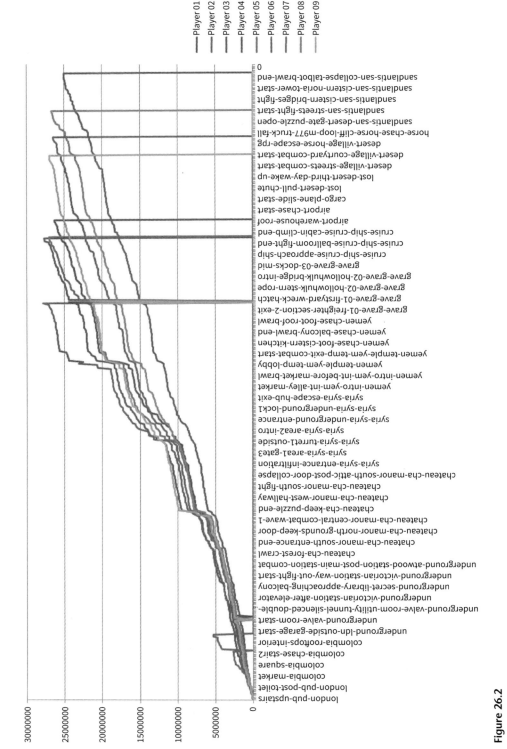

Figure 26.2

A graph showing playtester progression over time in *Uncharted 3: Drake's Deception*, derived from metrics data gathered from nine players during a formal playtest. Image credit: *UNCHARTED 3: Drake's Deception*™/© SIE LLC. Created & developed by Naughty Dog LLC.

We used metrics data to gain insight into many aspects of the *Uncharted* games. How often did players pick up a new gun, hold it for a moment, and then drop it again in favor of their old gun? That was easy to see using metrics data. How often did players attempt to throw back grenades in the throw-back mechanic we'd just implemented? Metrics data helped us fine-tune the interface and controls of this new mechanic.

Metrics data also helped us work on a nasty recurring problem in the *Uncharted* games, one that dated all the way back to the beginning of the series. The game environments in the *Uncharted* series are visually very dense—thanks to the studio's brilliant artists, there is a lot going on in any random *Uncharted* screenshot. As with any videogame, it's easy for things that are important for gameplay to get lost among all that visual information. We found that players would often have a difficult time spotting the "edge grabs" in the environments (the environmental elements that our player-character, Nathan Drake, could jump up to and hang from). This was usually a game design disaster, because it would stop the player from climbing onward to the next part of the game. The problem was compounded by the fact that players would get distracted by things that *looked* like they were climbable but weren't.

The solution to this problem was quite brilliant, and it came from three of my former colleagues at Naughty Dog: Teagan Morrison, Travis McIntosh, and Jaroslav Sinecky. What these clever people did was to set up a system—which we only used during formal playtests—that would record an (x, y, z) coordinate in the three-dimensional space of the game every time a player in the playtest pressed the jump button and didn't end up jumping up to and hanging from a ledge, but instead jumped up and down on the spot.

These coordinates were written to a database on our network, and when the playtest was complete, we could export the aggregate of this data (all the data for all the playtesters) back into the game running on our development systems. When we selected an option in the game's debug menus, a little red sphere was placed where every thwarted jump had taken place for every one of the ten players in the formal playtest. You can see an example in figure 26.3.

We called this our bad jumps system, and we could immediately see the bad jumps clustered beneath objects that looked like edge grabs but that Drake couldn't hang from. The clusters of red spheres told us clearly what we needed to fix. In the days after each playtest, the environment artists and game designers responsible for each level would sit down together and go through their levels with the bad jumps debug spheres turned on. They would discuss the changes that could be made to either artwork or design to improve each situation where our playtesters had mistaken a piece of background art for a grabbable edge.

This not only helped improve our game's design but it eased the collaborative process between artists and designers. Of course, it can sometimes be difficult for artists and designers to reach agreement when the good looks of the game come into conflict with gameplay considerations, especially when all we have to go on are our subjective points

Figure 26.3
The bad jumps system used for *Uncharted 3: Drake's Deception*, showing where players had
attempted to climb upward and had failed. Image credit: *UNCHARTED 3: Drake's Deception*™/©
SIE LLC. Created & developed by Naughty Dog LLC.

of view. The bad jumps system gave us very objective information about whether a particular situation was a major problem or something more minor, and it helped take a lot
of the heat out of this potentially charged collaborative process.

These examples are from the single-player mode of a storytelling action game, but
metrics data can be used to make a positive difference in the design of many types
of games, from eSports games, where we want to investigate the frequency of use of
particular abilities, to interactive narrative games, where we want to see how often
players take a particular story path. I encourage you to think beyond the obvious and
to find ingenious new ways of gathering data that gives you solid knowledge about—
and new insight into—what your players actually do from moment to moment in
your games.

Implementing Metrics in Your Game

Game metrics systems are often simple to implement with a little coding ability,
although this work may require you to learn some new function calls. There are many
off-the-shelf packages you can use, which may not require you to do any coding at all.
At the time of writing, both Unity and Unreal have good in-game analytics plug-ins
that are relatively easy to use.

Start by deciding what kind of metrics data you want to gather. When you haven't
done this before, it's good to begin with just one or two different types of data. You

can add more later. Brainstorm with your teammates about the types of data you could possibly collect and discuss what you could learn from each type.

- A commonly collected type of metrics data records how long the player spends in each part of the game.
- If the player can fail and start over in your game, consider counting the number of attempts they make to complete each section.
- You could record when and where the player uses the mechanics you have given them.
- You might track values associated with resources, such as the experience points the player earns over time, or how much in-game money they currently have.

Think about the granularity of your metrics data: how frequently you make a reading, and therefore how much data you gather overall. Err on the side of too much—you can always filter it later—but be careful: I've seen metrics systems that crashed their games because data was being recorded every frame and the output file became huge. The right granularity of metrics for your game will depend on the type of game you're making and its overall length.

If you wish to create your own metrics data system, you will need to write a script that remains active throughout the course of the game. This script will contain a function that can be called whenever you want to capture some data from the game, which copies one or more variable values into a string, along with some text to make it human-readable, and then adds that string to a text file written out to the computer's hard drive. (The string could also be written to a database somewhere.)

You can either call the function whenever a particular thing occurs in the game or at a regular interval. For example, whenever the player presses the jump button, you could record the current time in the game, and copy it into a string preceded by the text: "player jumped:" Or once every ten seconds you could record the current time in the game and the player-character's health, giving you a relatively fine-grained record of the way the health rises and falls over time.

You can find resources to help you set up metrics data systems for your game on the website for this book, playfulproductionprocess.com.

Metrics Data and Consent

When we design software to capture information about someone else, we should stop and consider whether what we're doing is ethical. The right to privacy is a value held very strongly by many communities in the world, and it is enshrined in the constitution or the law in some places. As game makers, we can ensure that we are behaving ethically by seeking our players' consent before we capture metrics data about them.

This may not be necessary for data about when a player jumps or opens a door, but if it involves personal information about the player (for example, related to their beliefs or to their health), then it is important to get their permission to record that information in your metrics data. You could do this with a screen to opt in or out at the start of the game. If the player doesn't consent, then don't record their data. Err on the side of seeking consent.

Testing Metrics Data Systems

It's important to test metrics data systems regularly to make sure that they're working correctly. In my experience, these can be among the most fragile parts of a game, and, perhaps because they operate silently, it's easy not to notice that they broke. Early in my career, I had an expensive formal playtest fail to give us any metrics data at all, because of a simple problem with our data-gathering mechanisms that we failed to catch in time.

It's easy to test your metrics systems by simply playing the game under the same conditions that your formal playtests will use and looking to make sure that the correct data is being written out successfully. Watch for minor variations between the way that you test the game and the way that the game will be used in the formal playtest. For example, a common way that metrics data problems arise is if the game does not get quit and restarted between successive playtesters, confusing the metrics system.

Visualizing Metrics Data

After a formal playtest, we'll need to visualize our metrics data to make it easier for us to understand. Information design and data visualization are exciting fields worth a lifetime of study for game designers. Edward R. Tufte's *Envisioning Information* and Ellen Lupton's *Design Is Storytelling* contain insightful commentary about techniques that we can use to turn numbers into narratives that people can understand.

Many people learn how to represent data in school by making line graphs, bar graphs, and pie charts, and these are great approaches to visualizing metrics data. Every spreadsheet package includes tools to create graphs from tables of data. They can take a little time to learn but are usually easy to use and powerful. Don't forget to label the axes, to include a legend to clearly describe the data being represented, and to use color and shape to your advantage. Tables that summarize important data work well if they use conditional formatting to color-code important numbers and make them "pop," as in figure 26.1.

Another popular type of data visualization for game metrics data is the heat map, a two- or three-dimensional representation of everywhere in a level that a particular event took place during the course of gameplay. You could use a spreadsheet's graphing tools to create this or code up a special tool inside your game engine to accurately map your data to a view of the environment. Search online for "heat map game" and you'll find many examples from your favorite games.

Remember to think innovatively and to be driven by the design opportunities and challenges that come with your particular type of game. How can game metrics help you become more confident that your game is landing in the ways that you intend?

What would be the "bad jumps" system for your game, where metrics data helps you solve a thorny game design problem in an innovative way?

Game Metrics Implementation Checklist

- ✓ Brainstorm values that can be tracked that will give you some insight into the game's design and the way it is played.
- ✓ Implement a mechanism to record these values as metrics data (simply to a text file or to a database).
- ✓ Seek your players' consent to gather metrics where appropriate.
- ✓ Test that the metrics system is working by playing the game under the same conditions (or as close to them as possible) that your formal playtest will take place.
- ✓ Check that the metrics data is being recorded correctly by looking at the information that was output by the system during the test.
- ✓ Using the test data, start to develop ways to visualize the data, in order to make it easier to read and understand.
- ✓ Test the system again immediately before the formal playtest.
- ✓ Use the metrics system in the formal playtest.
- ✓ Visualize the data you receive during the formal playtest and use what you learn about the behavior of your playtesters to refine the design of your game.

The Opportunities and Limits of Game Metrics

Game metrics are tools, and just like any tool, they can be used for good or for ill. It's good to be rigorous in a technical artform like ours, and user researchers value the scientific method. But I strongly believe that you shouldn't go any further with these techniques than your instincts as a creative designer and artist tell you that you should go.

I use metrics to make sure that my game is giving players the kind of experience I intend them to have. I'm trying to discover the presence of things that might stop my game from landing in the way I want it to land. I resist the temptation to have my metrics data pull me in a design direction that runs counter to my project goals or to my values as a person. You will have to decide for yourself, depending on who you are, what you value, and what kind of context you are making games in—commercial, artistic, or academic—how you are going to use metrics in the design of your games.

I like this quote, often attributed to Albert Einstein but more likely from sociologist William Bruce Cameron: "Not everything that can be counted counts, and not everything that counts can be counted."[2] It's up to you to decide what to count, and what counts.

---

2. "Not Everything That Counts Can Be Counted," Quote Investigator, May 26, 2010, https://quoteinvestigator.com/2010/05/26/everything-counts-einstein/.

In our playful production process, the full production phase has two major milestones: alpha and beta. At alpha, partway through full production, our game will be feature complete and game sequence complete, and we'll be able to play it through, at least in placeholder form. By beta, at the end of full production, the game will also be content complete, which means that everything that's going to be in the game will be present, ready to be polished.

There are two more phases tucked away inside full production: the alpha phase and the beta phase (figure 27.1). In chapter 23, we talked about QA testing, where dedicated quality assurance experts rigorously test a game to find bugs and help solve design problems. An almost universal definition of the alpha phase is that it begins when a software project enters QA testing. The alpha phase ends at the alpha milestone, and then the beta phase begins, which sees us through to the beta milestone. Even if you don't have a dedicated QA department, your project can still have a proper alpha phase, if you just start tracking bugs at some point. We'll look at techniques for bug tracking in a moment.

When a piece of software is in its alpha phase, it is sometimes buggy, unstable, and considerably incomplete. In game development, buggy and unstable software is highly undesirable. We need to keep our game in a highly playable state throughout full production. That way, each time we add a new mechanic or some content, we can run a

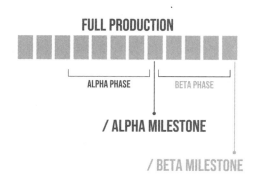

Figure 27.1
The alpha phase and the beta phase tucked away inside full production. Image credit: Gabriela Purri R. Gomes, Mattie Rosen, and Richard Lemarchand.

playtest to evaluate the impact that the new part has on the game as a whole. This is why we use concentric development, as we discussed in chapter 13.

However, as the alpha milestone draws closer, we will probably have to move away from concentric development in order to get all the features and placeholder levels into the game that we need to be there for alpha. This will require us to make another change of gears, keeping the best aspects of concentric development while adopting some new methods that allow us to move forward efficiently. We'll look at this change in approach in chapter 29.

Some game platforms—most game consoles and some mobile and virtual reality platforms—require games to pass a certification process before they can be released. The alpha phase of a project is the right time to begin studying the certification requirements in detail in preparation for the extra work the team will need to do to comply with them. You can read more about this in chapter 34.

A Simple Bug Tracking Method

For every game, large or small, it's important at some point during full production to become methodical about finding, listing, and fixing the bugs that are hiding away inside your game, waiting to mess up the player's experience. Whenever you start doing this during full production you can consider yourself to be in the alpha phase of your project.

Start by developing a test plan. A test plan is usually designed by the head of QA, working with the project's creative leads, producers, and possibly department leads. For a small team, involve as many of the team as is practical. A test plan is a bit like a recipe for a meal or a plan for a weekend away. We have some things we want to accomplish, a sense of the elements and tools we need, and the problems we might face. We draw up lists and give them a hierarchy of importance to tell us what we should tackle first. We might also want to say what the test process *won't* cover, which gives both QA and the development team a chance to set some boundaries around their work.

Test planning is a mature discipline, and you can find a lot of detailed information online about devising a good test plan. Ashley Davis and Adam Single present a lot of detailed and technical advice about creating a test plan for a game in their Gamasutra article, "Testing for Game Development."[1]

Once you have a plan, you are ready to start testing your game. This is usually a question of taking the time to play a build of the game in an orderly way that follows the test plan and keeping a record of the bugs you discover. It is better to test a build, rather than running the game in the editor, as a build may behave differently. Note that QA testers for games usually don't just play the game freely and exploratively as

---

1. Ashley Davis and Adam Single, "Testing for Game Development," Gamasutra, July 26, 2016, https://www.gamasutra.com/blogs/AshDavis/20160726/277825/Testing_for_Game_Development.php.

a regular player would. They carefully check each type of possible interaction as they play, on the lookout for things that are not behaving as they should. If you're on a small team, you'll have to figure how you will test your game. Hiring someone to help you with QA is always a good investment.

Even if your team is so small that you are just testing it yourself as you develop it, you should still make a record of the bugs you find. Professional game developers use dedicated databases, sometimes known as bug trackers, to keep a list of bugs and the information that accompanies each one. Some popular bug tracking tools at the time of writing include Jira, Bugzilla, and Mantis.

For a small project, it's possible to track bugs simply using a spreadsheet. Give the columns these headings (or use the template you can find at playfulproductionprocess .com):

- Bug Number
- Date and Time Submitted
- Date and Time of Build (or Build Number)
- Summary
- Class
- Priority
- Category
- Description
- Location in Game
- Reproducibility
- Steps to Reproduce
- Script Involved
- Assigned To
- Status
- Attachments
- Notes
- Resolution Notes

Let's take a look at each of these headings and the information you'll keep in each column.

Bug Number

Each bug should have a unique number, so that you can refer to the bug quickly and easily.

Date and Time Submitted

When the bug is created, the date and time of creation should be recorded. Many spreadsheets allow you to enter the date and time with a shortcut key combination.

Date and Time of Build (or Build Number)

For every bug that is tracked, you should know the build of the game in which it was originally found. See chapter 5 to read about builds and how to make them.

Summary

This should include a very brief description of the bug and serves as the bug's title.

Class

Bugs come in different classes that describe their degree of severity. The exact definition of each class can vary from studio to studio, but this set of definitions is fairly common:

- Showstopper
  - A bug that must be fixed immediately, because it prevents the game from being played (and therefore tested) beyond a certain point.
- A
  - A severe bug that significantly interferes with the functioning of the game and must be fixed.
- B
  - A bug that significantly interferes with the functionality or experience of the game and that should likely be fixed.
- C
  - A less severe bug that doesn't significantly interfere with the functioning or experience of the game, but that should be fixed if possible.
- Comment
  - This bug class is used by the bug testers to send feedback or ideas to the developers. This can be a valuable channel of communication between QA and the game's developers.

Priority

Within each class of bug, it can be useful to also assign a priority. A "B1" bug needs fixing urgently, although not as urgently as an "A3" bug, while a "B3" bug can probably wait.

Category

If it's possible to say what category the bug falls into, as sorted by the discipline that will be needed to fix the problem, this can make the bug easier to understand, and can make it easier to work out who on the team the bug should be assigned to. Example categories could be:

- Programming
- 2D art
- 3D art

- Game design
- Writing
- Animation
- Audio
- Music
- Visual effects
- Haptics
- UI
- Subtitles
- Other

Description

This is where the bug is described in greater detail than it was in the summary. Writing good descriptions for bugs is an art unto itself. The best description will use clear, concise language to describe **what the bug tester expected to happen** and **what actually happened**. Don't include information about where the bug happens, how often it happens, or how to reproduce it—those things have their own sections.

Location in Game

It can be very useful to the people fixing the bug to know exactly where in the game the bug occurred. This is particularly important for any bug that only happens at one particular place in the game. This is best recorded using 2D or 3D coordinates from the game engine, perhaps supported by a screenshot.

Reproducibility

Some bugs happen reliably every time you try to reproduce them—others only happen sometimes, and some are only ever seen once. You could use these categories:

- Always
- Sometimes
- Rarely
- Seen once

Steps to Reproduce

This is a detailed description of the steps that must be taken in the game to reproduce the bug and can relieve some of the burden from the "Description" section.

Script Involved

If the people testing the game are able to say what script (or other piece of code) caused the problem, it is useful to record it here. Debug messages will often show where in the code an error occurred.

Assigned To

This is where the bug is assigned to a particular team member to be fixed.

Status

Each bug has the status of "New" when it is first created. The status of the bug will change over its lifetime as it gets passed back and forth between QA and other members of the development team, and as the bug gets worked on by each individual in the chain.

- New
  - The status of a bug when it is first created.
- Acknowledged
  - When the bug is received by the developer who is going to work on fixing it, they change the status to this.
- Request information
  - If the person who is going to fix the bug needs more information in order to fix it, they change the status to this, and the bug is passed back to the QA manager or whoever wrote the bug.
- Claim fixed
  - When a developer thinks they've fixed the bug, they mark it "Claim fixed" and it gets passed back to QA for regression, when QA will check to see that the bug has indeed been successfully fixed.
- Unable to reproduce
  - If a developer can't reproduce a bug, they change the status to this, and it gets passed back to QA for regression. The QA department will check to see whether the bug is still happening or not.
- Duplicate
  - The status gets changed to this if the bug is already in the database with a different bug number.
- Fix failed
  - If a "Claim fixed" bug is shown during regression actually not to have been fixed, it gets marked as "Fix failed" and goes back to the developer who had tried to fix it or to their manager.
- Fixed
  - If a "Claim fixed" bug is shown during regression actually to have been fixed, it gets marked as "Fixed" and goes to the great bug graveyard in the sky.
- Closed (can't fix)
  - Sometimes a bug can't be fixed for one reason or another, and then the bug is marked this way. On most teams, only very senior team members can close bugs.

- Closed (won't fix)
  - Sometimes the team members decide that a bug should not be fixed for some reason—maybe it would take too long, it's not a big deal, or someone decides that it's actually a feature, not a bug. Then the bug is marked this way. Again, this decision can usually only be made by very senior team members.
- Reopened
  - Sometimes a bug that has been closed needs to be reopened, and then it's marked this way.

Attachments

It's often useful to attach screenshots or videos that illustrate the bug to the report.

Notes

The notes section for a bug is a good way to pass information back and forth between QA and the development team—for example, when more information is requested about the bug or when a bug is marked as "Fix failed."

Resolution Notes

If there's something special about the way a bug was fixed, or if a bug is closed for any reason, this is the place to record it.

As you can probably tell from these headings, the typical workflow that a bug passes through is:

- The bug is created by someone working in QA or one of the other developers on the team.
- The bug is assigned to a developer to be fixed, who acknowledges they have received it and are going to work on it.
- The developer attempts to fix the bug.
- When they think they've fixed it, the developer marks the bug "Claim fixed."
- The bug then goes back to QA for regression—they check to see if it has been fixed.
- Depending on the findings during regression, the bug is either marked "Fixed" or "Fix failed."
- If a developer needs more information, can't reproduce the bug, or discovers that it's a duplicate, they mark it accordingly and it goes back to QA.
- If a developer can't fix the bug, they take appropriate action, maybe via their manager or a team lead. The bug might then be passed to a different developer who can fix it, or it might get closed.

This simple spreadsheet-based bug tracking method will be useful for small projects and will equip you with the knowledge that you'll need to work with a dedicated bug tracking tool on a larger team. You'll quickly find that tracking bugs in a spreadsheet is unwieldy, though, and I recommend that you find and use a project management tool with a bug tracking feature. Meredith Hall provides a good overview of the bug tracking features of various project management tools in her Gamasutra article, "Choosing a Project Management Tool for Game Development."[2]

⁂   ❀   ⁂

Now that you understand how to track bugs, you're ready to start doing so and to enter the alpha phase of your project. We'll come back to the subject of bug fixing in chapter 32. Equipped with this information about the alpha phase, let's take an in-depth look at the alpha milestone and how we're going to get there.

---

2. Meredith Hall, "Choosing a Project Management Tool for Game Development," Gamasutra, June 29, 2018, https://www.gamasutra.com/blogs/MeredithHall/20180629/321013/Choosing_A _Project_Management_Tool_For_Game_Development.php.

We discussed our project's alpha phase and techniques for bug tracking in the previous chapter. Now let's take a look at the alpha milestone, which marks the end of the alpha phase. At the alpha milestone, the game is "feature complete." This is the meaning of the alpha milestone across most types of software development, from games to business. Every feature that will be in the final game should be present for the game to be considered to have reached the alpha milestone. In our playful production process, we're also going to be "game sequence complete" at alpha—more on that in a while.

Features and Content

Let's take a closer look at this word *feature* and what it means. For the sake of this discussion, we might say that games are made up of two types of stuff: features and content. Generally speaking, features are pieces of functionality. They're the mechanisms that make our game tick. If something in a game is controlled by logic or reacts to the player's input, chances are that it's a feature.

To illustrate this idea, here's a handful of example features:

- The feature in a character-action game that controls the player-character in response to the player's input
- The feature in a social simulation game that controls nonplayer characters (NPCs) as they go about their business in the game environment
- The feature in a city-building sim game that determines what happens to a building over time

Higher-order groups of features, like the ones in my examples above, can usually be broken out into lists of lower-order features:

- A player-character control feature could be made up of separate features that control running and jumping.
- An NPC control feature could be made up of separate features that control walking, taking objects from one place to another, and talking to the player-character.
- The feature that determines what happens to a building over time could be made up of separate features that make the building become dirty, collapse, or catch fire.

We could keep breaking these subfeatures down further until we got to specific functions in code that act on the data structures representing these game entities.

By contrast, content is the data structures and assets that make up the game entities that the features in the game act on: artwork, animation, sound effects, visual effects, music, and dialogue, to name a few, tied together by bundles of data. Of course, you can't have features without content. If you've coded up a system to move NPCs around in your game world but haven't created the artwork, animation, and sounds that represent an NPC, then the feature isn't really in the game. Content often helps features show up in the game world like this, and the blurry line between features and content can sometimes lead game developers into trouble, as we'll see later.

Being Feature Complete

When a game is feature complete, all of its features are present: all of the "moving parts" of the game have been implemented and are working well. This happens more easily if we've been using concentric development, testing the game and fixing bugs as we go along.

When a game is feature complete, every *type* of thing that will be in the game should be in there, whether those are conversations between NPCs and players, logic puzzles, combat mechanics, or AI pathfinding algorithms. If it's a mechanism, and it's going in the game, it should be in there somewhere by the alpha milestone.

However, as the alpha milestone gets closer, game developers are often challenged by the scale of the task as they work to get all of these moving parts into the game. This is where the blurry line between features and content can become relevant and can either be used intelligently to a positive outcome or exploited in a destructive way.

During my time in the game industry, I learned from my colleagues that at alpha you want to make sure you have *one of every type of thing* in the game. If an NPC will have a behavior, that behavior should be used by an NPC somewhere in the game, even if you don't yet have all the NPCs that will use that behavior. Part of the art of hitting alpha well is choosing content to implement that exhibits all of the behavior that all the things in the game could exhibit. These behaviors are the features of the game, and getting all your features in by alpha, when there's still time to refine them, is another key to making an excellent game.

If we have plenty of time for implementing features as the alpha milestone gets close, then we should implement every entity in the game that has a unique combination of features. This is because there could be unforeseen interactions between the features that require us to do more work to get them to play together nicely.

If we have less time as the alpha milestone approaches, then we might consider implementing fewer entities—just as long as, taken all together, these entities exhibit all of the features in the game. This path is much riskier, because even though we will technically have all of our features in the game, as we put those features together in new combinations, we're likely to make radical new discoveries about the way that our game works.

Don't forget to consider every last part of your game's functionality when you're thinking about what to implement for alpha. For example, if the game is going to use an achievements system, either in-game or connected to the achievements system provided by a game publisher or platform holder, then you should set up at least one achievement in your game by alpha.

Part of the point of the alpha milestone is that we are trying to hurry up and make all the major discoveries about the functionality of our game that we're going to make. We want to know how our game works with plenty of time left to fix whatever problems exist, and that means becoming feature complete. The alpha milestone is also a particularly important tool to use in the prevention of feature creep.

I first mentioned feature creep, which is a type of scope creep, in chapter 17. Feature creep happens when developers have exciting ideas for new features during full production, ideas that weren't planned for in the game design macro, but that they decide to add into the game's design anyway, even though the macro was meant to be "set in stone." Sometimes adding a new feature is a good thing to do, especially if the feature will be easy to implement and will add something special to the game. But feature creep can be a destructive, insidious problem.

Trouble is smuggled into the project with each new feature we add, since it's hard to predict the impact that they will have on the project. "Just one more" feature can turn into a steady trickle if the developers aren't disciplined. Each new feature might only take a small amount of time to implement but will probably introduce new design problems and new bugs that could take much, much longer to deal with. As I said in chapter 17, projects that fall prey to scope creep sometimes just don't ever get finished. They can easily become out-of-control messes of bugs and incoherent, competing design directions, with no way of telling when the project will be done.

This is where the danger due to the blurry line between features and content appears. Some game designers seek to get through the alpha milestone by framing new features that they plan to add after alpha as "content groups" of preexisting features. Sometimes this works out okay, but it often goes disastrously wrong, introducing major new bugs to fix and new design problems to solve at a time when the project is meant to have become more stable and better designed.

As a rule of thumb, the more experienced that a developer is—both overall and at working in a particular style or genre of game—the more likely it is that they will be successful when they take risks at the alpha milestone. Developers who are less experienced are exposed to greater risk by not being feature complete in a robust way at the alpha milestone, and new groups of features that they add after the alpha milestone are likely not to work very well when the game is finished, simply because there wasn't enough time left to polish them.

Being Game Sequence Complete

There is another aspect of the alpha milestone that I'm going to invite you to use, and it's tremendously powerful. It's a technique that we developed at Naughty Dog, under the guidance of studio president Evan Wells, and it revolutionized the way that I think about making games. During the creation of *Uncharted 2: Among Thieves* we decided that at the project's alpha milestone we would not only be feature complete, but we would also be "game sequence complete" by having every level in the game in place, at least in rough, placeholder, blockmesh (whitebox/graybox/blockout) form.

Many of the levels of *Uncharted 2* were already very advanced in their development by the alpha milestone. Some of the levels of the game were partway implemented, some were barely begun, and a few hadn't been built out at all. It was those last barely there and not-there levels that we quickly fleshed out, using low-poly blockmesh to create representative levels of approximately correct size and length. We then connected everything together using our level loading system and the game's progression logic, so that we could play through the game continuously from beginning to end.

Being able to play through the game from start to finish at alpha—even if chunks of it were only there in rudimentary form and playing through was more like running through—we were able to get a good and early handle on the overall pacing of the game's play and story. We could see when the game's pace got bogged down or sped along too quickly and were able to make adjustments accordingly. Crucially, we also got an excellent sense of how much work we had left to do. It's one thing to look at a list of tasks that need doing, but it's quite another to run through a largely empty level, visualizing what needs to be built to fill it up with playful events.

As you decide what to cut or change, make sure to update your game design macro chart to keep track of your decisions as you make them. Making a work-in-progress copy of the macro chart and chopping it about to reduce the game's scope and rearrange things so that the game still works is a great way of trying out and then finalizing these important decisions. I've used this game sequence complete at alpha approach on every game I've worked on since *Uncharted 2*, and it works like a charm for helping developers gain an early understanding of whether they should scope their projects further.

Additionally, in order for a game to be considered game sequence complete at alpha, all of the front end, menus, and interface screens should be in place, at least with placeholder art and audio content (including the logo screens, start screen, options screens, pause screens, and save/load screens). All of these elements should be connected together properly so that a playtester can move around the experience of the game from one part to another, just as they could in the finished game. The introductory logos should lead to the title screen, which should lead into the game or the options screen, and so on.

And finally, any animated cutscenes, live action video, or other linear assets that belong in the game should be in place at alpha, at least with placeholder versions or stubs. (We'll talk more about this in the next chapter.) It's easy to become so focused on the gameplay we're creating that we forget about everything else that wraps around the game to make it work. But by thinking about, say, your team's logo screen at alpha, you come to a much greater understanding of the reality of finishing your game than you would otherwise have. Even if you just put in a mouse-scrawled joke logo to stand in for the beautiful animated team logo that you'll eventually have, getting a logo in there will help you get a better handle on your scope.

A Good Onboarding Sequence by Alpha

First impressions count for a lot everywhere in life, and bad first impressions can be hard to shake. The opening moments of a game set a tone for the game and shape our expectations about what it will be like to play.

The beginning of a digital game typically has to teach new players how to play the game. The days of excitedly reading a game's instruction booklet on the journey home from the store are long gone. Today, we download and dive into games, expecting that the beginning of the game will welcome us in and tell us what we need to know.

When you're thinking about how to get a new player into your game—the process known as "onboarding"—it's unwise to rely on what players already know about other videogames and their control schemes. It is important for game designers to know about the control schemes of games similar to theirs, but your players may or may not have played those games, and we want to include people rather than exclude them.

Maybe your players will know about WASD-mouse, for example, but an effective designer will cater to those who don't. The key is to devise a control scheme that suits both seasoned players *and* complete beginners, and that can be learned in an enjoyable way. How can we teach players to control our games and to play them without boring them or confusing them?

At one time, when games had fewer controls than they do today, it was considered enough just to show a "controls screen" at the beginning of the game with callouts showing which buttons do what. Controls screens are good if they're somewhere in a menu for reference; maybe for a player who has spent some time away from a game and needs a memory refresher. But for most people, this isn't a good way to learn, unless the game's control scheme is very simple. Games with even moderately complex control schemes require a better approach for teaching their controls to the player.

A more effective approach to teaching players is to put the player into the game and to introduce the game's controls and mechanics one by one. As each new mechanic is introduced, we prompt the player to use the associated control, and then present them with a situation in the game world that they can get through by using the new mechanic. This way, the player can learn experientially, by doing.

In the 1990s and early 2000s, this kind of player-training was often presented in the form of a tutorial level. But jumping through hoops that a game designer has laid out for you can be tedious. Designers soon realized that players don't want to have to do something that feels like *work* before they can play the game properly—they just want to start *playing*. Today, we still have game tutorials, but the best of them are not recognizable as such. Instead, designers go to great lengths to make their tutorials feel like play, by combining interactivity with something enjoyable, entertaining, funny, or dramatic. A great game tutorial allows players to play freely from the very start of a game, seemingly making interesting discoveries for themselves, all the while learning what the designer wants them to learn.

The setup at the beginning of *Super Mario Bros.* World 1–1, which we discussed in chapter 18, does this very elegantly. The opening train car sequence in *Uncharted 2: Among Thieves* that we talked about in chapter 17 does the same thing, wrapping a tutorial in cinematic action, drama, and surprises, while also setting up the story and building empathy for Nathan Drake, the game's player-character.

Most every game in every style has the opportunity to onboard its players by presenting its game mechanics in such a way that players can learn through curiosity and experimentation. It helps if the game's designers are working to entertain and interest the player at the same time. This is a time when it's good to think about the affordances and signifiers of your game, which we discussed in chapter 12. Does your game give clues about how to interact with it, just by the way it looks and sounds? What could be added to make those clues easier to read?

Not every game needs a smooth onboarding. *Minecraft* was, early in its lifetime, hard to learn without having a friend show you how to play, which didn't prevent it from becoming a huge success. Being difficult to get to grips with might be part of a game's aesthetic or culture. But be careful about neglecting your game's tutorialization. Getting and holding a new player's attention is difficult to do and is crucial for games that seek to be a commercial success.

So, the alpha milestone is the right time to make sure that you have a strong plan for your game's onboarding sequence. It's even better if you can finish building the onboarding and tutorialization sequence of your game by alpha. If you can solve the difficult problems associated with creating a good onboarding sequence by alpha, it will leave you the time and mental bandwidth to focus on everything else that needs to be taken care of between alpha and beta.

The Role of the Alpha Milestone

I like to think of alpha as the first stage of the home stretch. Like the end of ideation and the end of preproduction, the alpha milestone requires us to make some decisions about the scope of our game and provides a defense against both feature creep and scope creep more generally. It also gives us a good moment to check in on the health of our game.

Scoping at Alpha

At the **end of ideation**, we limited the scope of our game in a very general way, by choosing some project goals. Then at the **end of preproduction** we limited our scope in some more specific ways by (a) creating a vertical slice, which showed what a part of our game would be like, and (b) presenting a plan for our game in the form of a game macro.

At the **alpha milestone**, about half or two-thirds of the way through **full production**, we are making even more decisions about the scope of our game, by creating a version of the game that is **feature complete**—that has at least one of every feature, and that is **game sequence complete**. By doing this, we demonstrate both to ourselves and to the world that we now understand in greater detail what our game is like and what it's going to include when it's finished.

When we talk about scope here, we're talking about both features and content. There are really two kinds of scope under consideration: (1) the "possibility space" of the game, the abstract space of all of the different things that might happen when a game is played, and (2) its "content footprint," the amount of content in the game.

Remember that a game's possibility space contains both good and bad things: fun gameplay, wonderful emergent situations, and interesting strategies, along with game design problems, content problems, and bugs. Every time a new feature is added to our game it brings some of the good stuff and some of the bad. By drawing a line in the sand at alpha, beyond which we won't add any more features, we take our next major step toward creating a game that is free of problems.

Alpha also gives us a chance to defend against content creep, another type of scope creep. It might seem like we have some time left after alpha to scope the content of our game, since we don't have to be content complete until the beta milestone. But really, alpha is our best last chance. If we try to reduce the scope of the game after alpha, during the game's beta phase, at the same time as we're building all the content for the beta milestone, then we could well be wasting time building things that we're not sure belong in the game.

So, build out your game with all its features and a complete game sequence at alpha, even if some parts of the game sequence are only stubbed in with blockmesh and other placeholders (as we'll discuss further in the next chapter). Take a good look at the results. Decide what to cut. If it's difficult to decide what to cut, take another look at the project goals that you set all the way back at the end of ideation. They will help to make those difficult last decisions about scope. You might be obsessed with getting some feature or a piece of content in your game, but if it doesn't serve your project goals and you're running out of time, cut it.

Checking In on Our Game's Health

The alpha milestone is an important time to check in on the overall health of our game. How many bugs and outstanding design problems does it have? Alpha is also a good time to take note of any performance issues. Is our frame rate high enough? Are our load times long?

It's important to take note of all these problems, whether design-related, bug-related, or performance-related, because all these issues are going to have to be addressed at some point between alpha and the final "release candidate" milestone. Many of them should be dealt with by beta, which will eat up the time that we have left to implement content. Making a list of our outstanding problems at alpha will help us make smart decisions about whether we need to further reduce our project's scope. The sooner we make decisions to reduce the scope of our game at alpha, the better our game will turn out. The later we leave the decision about scope, the worse our finished game is likely to be.

Choosing a Game Title at Alpha

You may have been running focus tests to get feedback about the title of your game. The alpha milestone is a good time to make a final decision. As soon as you've chosen a title, create a social media account for your game on whatever you think your main social media platform will be. The title on its own might already be taken, but a common convention is to put the words "game" or "the game" after the title of your game to create a unique social media account name.

Based on the audience that you're imaging for your game, you want to find the right social media channel, since different channels have different audiences. Marketing consultant and USC Games professor Jim Huntley recommends that a game team should pick a single channel and make it their social media home. He told me that it's possible to run a social media campaign on multiple channels, but it's going to be exhausting for a small team. (Jim noted that there are free tools that will help you automatically repost content from one channel to another.)

However, even though you've made a social media account for your game, don't post to it yet. Depending on the length of your project, it might be too early to gather your audience around your game. You can only hold an audience's interest for so long before your game is released. For now, make sure you're saving and categorizing everything that you work on in the course of making your game: early concept art that goes unused, GIFs of rough or experimental animations, design ideas that didn't work out. All of these will make for excellent content for your social media presence later on, when you're engaging with your audience.

Summarizing the Alpha Milestone

In summary, at the alpha milestone, our game should be:
- Feature complete
  - All of the functionality of the game should be in place in some form.
  - For a strong alpha, every unique or risky combination of features should be in place.

- Game sequence complete
  - If the game has levels, they should all be in place with at least blockmesh place-holder art and collision geometry that gives us a sense of the size and scope of the overall game.
  - The front end, menus, and interfaces (including the logo screens, start screen, options screens, pause screens, and save/load screens) should be in place, with at least placeholder art and audio content.
  - Placeholder versions or stubs of any animated cutscenes should be in place.
  - Everything should be logically connected together, and we should be able to play or move through every part of the game in a continuous way.

The graphics and audio of a game need not be final at alpha, but we should have created some finished art and audio in every different category of the things we need to make, to show that we can actually make that stuff, and to find out how long each type of thing takes to create. We should try to get placeholders in the game for every major element, giving us a stub to work from and to help us evaluate the game's performance. Don't neglect audio and visual effects as you build out your game during full production! The alpha milestone is a great time to evaluate your audio design and visual effects, and to make sure that you have a realistic picture of how long it takes to make them really good.

In addition, we should ask ourselves:

- How many outstanding game design problems does our game have?
- How buggy is our game?
- How good is our game's performance?

If we do this, we have roughed in our game very effectively. The next stage of our process will see us complete everything that we have roughed in, as we travel through the beta phase to the beta milestone.

For certain types of game developer, the alpha milestone is also a good time to look ahead, beyond the end of your current project. If you plan to roll over into another project after this one, the alpha milestone is a good time to start talking about what you're going to do next.

The Milestone Review That Takes Place at Alpha

The alpha milestone is an excellent time to hold a milestone review with people from inside and outside the team, to get feedback on the state of our project, using the process I described in chapter 20.

The milestone review that takes place at alpha is a lot like the one that occurs at the end of preproduction, except that now there is a lot more game to review. For large productions, you'll have to decide how to present your game in an efficient way. Maybe the milestone review meeting will take place over several days, giving enough time to look at the game and discuss it deeply. For smaller productions, like the short games made for a single-semester class, a review of just twenty or thirty minutes is probably fine.

In their short introductory presentation at the milestone review meeting, the development team leadership should be ready to say:

- Who they consider to be the audience for their game. They have probably refined their positioning statement (see chapter 7) now that they understand more about their game and how playtesters react to it.
- Where their project is at, regarding alpha. For example:
  - They hit alpha strongly and are well on the way to beta, with stub content that is fully representative of the functional parts of their game.
  - They hit alpha right on, and exactly met the alpha requirements, with stub content that is representative of the functional parts of their game.
  - They hit alpha, but have a lot of stub content that isn't fully representative of the functional parts of their game.
  - They're not yet at alpha, and they say what is missing that is keeping them from being at alpha.
- Whether there are any known issues with the project.
- What kind of feedback would be useful to receive from the milestone review group.

At the alpha milestone, we should be careful to give notes that are timely. The review group should—under most circumstances—avoid giving notes that recommend the addition of new features, since the game is now feature complete.

In addition to a milestone review meeting with people from outside the team, the team should also have an internal review at alpha. The internal review should include discipline groups, where the artists look at the art, the engineers consider engineering issues, and so on. It should also include some cross-disciplinary groups. On a large team, the leads of each discipline would come together to discuss the alpha build.

Occasionally it becomes apparent at alpha that the addition or change of a single, simple feature will have a revolutionary and positive impact on the game. You'll have to decide whether the addition of a single feature after alpha represents (a) a safe, sane, positive change for your game, or whether (b) you are falling prey to feature creep, and doing damage to the integrity and quality of your game, and to the health and productivity of your team.

Take full advantage of the alpha milestone review meeting as perhaps the richest source of timely and actionable notes in the whole lifetime of the project. The game is not yet content complete, and we still have a great opportunity to shape it toward excellence, by acting on the design advice that we receive from our playtesters, peers, and mentors.

Some people judge beta as the milestone when you can tell if a game has come together, but I think that alpha gives us a very strong indication of how our game is going to turn out. Committing to hitting alpha well helps us to put in effort in the middle of the project, instead of stacking up the harder work at the end.

So, fly at your alpha milestone keenly and eagerly, and you will find it to be one of the best tools for bringing your game's production under your control, while keeping a playful approach to your work. Remember my "technical rehearsal" analogy for alpha from chapter 22. A theater tech rehearsal can be a lot of fun—it doesn't matter much if the actors miss their cues, if the sound effects are too loud, or if the fog machine completely fills the auditorium with fog. At the tech rehearsal you can sense the potential and the excitement of the artwork that will appear on opening night. Relish your alpha milestone, make it your friend, and celebrate it. Enjoy playing the rough and ready game that appears, and seek out the excellence that it contains.

29 Stubbing Things In

The concept of "stubbing in" features and content can help us reach the alpha milestone in the best possible style and can be useful throughout the whole course of a game's development. When we stub something into a game, we might move away from the principles of concentric development that we've used throughout this book, but we hold on to the functionality and modularity that characterize healthy game design practice.

What Is a Stub?

A stub is a short piece of content or code that stands in for something that will be completed later. For many of us, the first place we encounter a stub is on Wikipedia, where we might see the label, "This article is a stub. You can help Wikipedia by expanding it." It's put in place with just a bare minimum of information, "too short to provide encyclopedic coverage of a subject," but now links can be established leading to it and from it.[1]

Programmers often write functions and methods by creating a stub first, like the one shown in figure 29.1. The stub has the correct name that the finished function will have and can be called by other parts of the code, but it only contains a simple placeholder: perhaps just a comment that describes in "pseudocode" what the function will eventually do, or a print statement that confirms in the debug console that the stub function has been successfully called.

Stubs in Videogames

We can use the concept of stubs when we're building games to make life easier and to work more efficiently. We already discussed a certain type of stub back in chapter 10 when we talked about blockmesh, also known as whitebox, graybox, or blockout level design. Blockmesh is a type of stub: it is a placeholder that gives us the first simple step on the road to the creation of something complex—in this case, our finished level

---

1. "Stub," Wikipedia, https://en.wikipedia.org/wiki/Wikipedia:Stub.

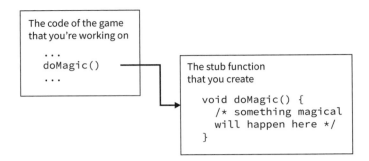

Figure 29.1
A stub function.

designs and level art. Blockmesh gives us low-polygon geometry that we can see and that the entities in our game can collide with, which we will later refine into something more detailed, both functionally and aesthetically.

Just as blockmesh is the beginning of a new level in our game, we can use a stub to begin building any new object or character and to create relationships that involve the new entity. A steel door could start out as a graybox; a tree could be stubbed in as a large green sphere perched on top of a narrow brown cylinder. The characters in a game might begin life as capsule-shaped objects, even though they might eventually end up looking like badgers or basilisks.

Other types of entity in a videogame can be stubbed in too. A text description of an object could start out as a "lorem ipsum" placeholder. At Naughty Dog we had a short video that we'd use as a stub for prerendered cutscenes, hooking it up as a placeholder in the game flow for cutscenes that we hadn't made yet. This allowed us to understand our load times earlier and made it easier to drop the finished cutscenes in later. Interfaces can be stubbed in with placeholder art and simplified interaction to let you select options and access the save menu, but without any of the finesse that the interface will eventually have.

When a game is getting close to its alpha milestone, important entities like the player-character and the key characters, objects, and levels in the game have probably been completed to a good level of polish already. But as alpha approaches, we now have to consider all the *other* entities that will go into the game: switches and doors, tables and chairs, gold coins and secret letters. We don't have to have *all* of these different entities in a finished state by alpha—that will come later, for the beta milestone, when the game is content complete. What we do have to have in the game for alpha is all of the game's features—we have to be feature complete—and stubs can help us achieve that.

An Example Stub Object Process

Let's take the example of a door. Doors give us a great lens for looking at many aspects of game development. They seem simple, but they're actually very complex in game design terms. Liz England is a game designer known for her work on games like *Sunset Overdrive* and *Scribblenauts*. In her insightful and hilarious essay "The Door Problem," Liz uses the game design complexities of doors to illustrate the kinds of issues that game designers have to deal with. She asks:

- Can doors be locked and unlocked?
- What tells a player a door is locked and will open, as opposed to a door that they will never open?
- Does a player know how to unlock a door? Do they need a key? To hack a console? To solve a puzzle? To wait until a story moment passes?
- Are there doors that can open but the player can never enter them?
- Where do enemies come from? Do they run in from doors? Do those doors lock afterwards?[2]

I strongly recommend that you read "The Door Problem." There are a lot of questions to be answered about doors for every member of the development team. We can start to answer those questions by building a stub for the door.

Hopefully we've built at least one finished-looking door by alpha that has final art, animation, audio, and haptics (controller vibration). But let's say that we need a special type of door for a special doorway in our game—maybe a portcullis in a castle or a spaceship door that opens in a cool, complicated way. We should get that door in the game by the alpha milestone if it's complex enough that it warrants being counted as a unique feature. But what if our artists are too busy making other important assets for the alpha milestone? This is a good time to make a stub.

The first consideration when making a stub is: what volume does this object occupy? The more definition that a stub can give to an object's size and shape, the better. If we are making a door that fills a doorway of a certain size and shape, and if the doorway's size and shape are known, then make the door fit the doorway exactly, with exactly the right height and width. Choose the door's thickness carefully too—is it thin and fragile or thick and strong?

The next consideration for your stub door is how it will animate. Does it open inward or outward? Does it slide up into the ceiling or sideways into the wall? Is it a single door or a double door? (See figure 29.2.) Is it a mechanical iris door?

As you think about your door's animation, you should plan to avoid your door crashing on the visible geometry around it. This term, *crashing*, comes from the world of computer graphics (CG) animation. CG objects are said to crash when they visibly interpenetrate each other, overlapping their volumes in a way that would be physically impossible in the real world (figure 29.3). One of the quickest ways to destroy the illusion of reality that we get from CG is to show objects that are meant to be solid going

---

2. Liz England, "The Door Problem," April 21, 2014, http://www.lizengland.com/blog/2014/04/the-door-problem/.

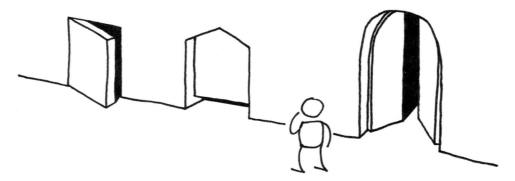

Figure 29.2
Doors in videogames come in many different shapes, sizes, and behaviors.

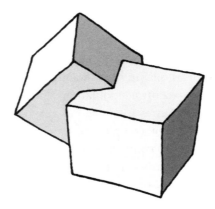

Figure 29.3
Solid-looking objects "crashing" (interpenetrating) and quickly breaking the illusion of the solidity and reality of the objects. Image credit: Mattie Rosen and Richard Lemarchand.

inside one another. People are very sensitive to this, and an audience's eye often goes straight to the part of a CG character's hand that is even slightly inside the CG object that it's picking up.

To prevent your stub door (and the finished door it will turn into) from crashing on the artwork around it, think carefully about how it's going to animate. If you have even a little bit of skill with a 3D modeling tool, you can probably learn to make a simple animation. Choose the point that your door rotates around by thinking about where hinges are on doors in real life, and make the door rotate around a point that won't leave it inside the geometry around it. You can see an example in figure 29.4. If you make this design decision as soon as you stub the door into the game, you will be helping whoever creates the finished art and animation.

Thoughtful stub creation can be something of an art form. Each stub is like the seedling of a finished game object and contains an opportunity to communicate important design decisions. As you work, consider adding a short "readme" file to the object to

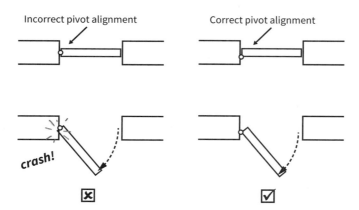

Figure 29.4
Choose the pivot point that a stubbed-in door rotates around carefully to avoid problems with crashing.

say which of the design decisions you made are important and should be preserved in the finished object. The earlier that we can make each key design decision, the more smoothly and efficiently everything runs in the creation of our game, and it's also good for your teammates to know when they have creative flexibility and freedom.

When you're choosing names for your stub objects, remember that, like a Wikipedia stub or a stub function, each stub is not a stand-in: *it's the object itself.* The references to the object will be preserved into the finished game, and you will not replace the whole object later, just the contents of the object. Don't ever name an object that you stub into your game something like "tempBigDoor." Just name it "bigDoor."

Stubs and Functionality

There's always a question around how much functionality a stub should have. A decent answer to this question is: as much as you can manage, but no more than you can create quickly. If stubs are like sketches of objects, then they can have some sketched-in functionality as well.

Level designers often use color conventions when building blockmesh. Adopting color conventions for stub objects can help to convey their form and function, even if the stub object doesn't yet do much. An unbreakable steel door might be light gray, while a smashable stone door might be dark gray. Low bushes that will rustle as the player-character walks through them might be represented by clusters of green spheres and simply have no collision for now. A control panel that will eventually have a detailed model and flashing lights might just be a red box in its stub version.

Simple coding can allow you to approximate an interaction. A smashable stone door that will eventually break apart into detailed chunks of physics-simulating rubble can be coded just to disappear when it's attacked for now.

If you can do some simple animation, even two-frame animations for the open/closed or on/off states of objects, that will give you something to hook up in code. Stubs can aid in the early establishment of the logical relationships between switches, doors, and the other objects in the game. Try to design your content and code in a modular way, so that you can easily make additions and changes as you continue work on the objects and their functionality.

Stubbing in Content versus Concentric Development

As I mentioned earlier, stubbing in entities to make our game feature complete at alpha marks a move away from concentric development. We're no longer polishing each part of the game until it shines before moving on to the next thing. Now we're putting objects into the game quickly, using placeholders. What risks and benefits does this bring?

Concentric development is most helpful in the early stages of a project. Remember, we use concentric development to help us lay the foundations of the game. Concentric development allows us to gain a clear understanding of the most basic, essential, and unique parts of our game. However, at some point in the creation of every game, we now know most everything we need to know to build out the rest of the game, and we can be more confident about the work that remains.

So it's natural that as we progress through full production we gradually shift away from concentric development for a time, as the number of unknowns in our project decreases and as we work to hit the alpha milestone. We'll move back toward concentric development as we work toward the beta milestone, when the game will be complete. Holding a contradiction, like the tension between concentric development and stubbing in the game, is a part of every artmaking practice, and game development is certainly an art form. As you experiment with stubbing in the objects that your game needs, and learn more about what makes an excellent stub, you'll gain confidence and competence in this aspect of our craft.

The alpha milestone is a great time to check in on the work we've been doing that will lead us eventually to connect with the audience for our game. We began this work in ideation, when we considered the possible audience for our game. I encouraged you to continue thinking about your audience by running focus tests for the title of your game, key art, and logo design (during preproduction in chapter 14, and as you began your formal playtesting process in chapter 24). In chapter 28, we talked about finalizing the title of our game and securing social media accounts with names that match our title.

Around the alpha milestone, we should take some more steps to see if we can actually find an audience and speak with them, in the hope that they will want to play our game. Historically, the game industry has done this using marketing, taking out commercials for games in magazines, on TV, and on the Internet. Today, social media gives us new opportunities to reach an audience.

We need to make a concrete plan for how we're going to create and nurture a community for the audience of our game, and then set that plan into action. Early in the development of our plan we will consider how we're going to announce our game. It is typical to go public with our game sometime between the alpha and beta milestones, making an announcement alongside the release of a video trailer for the game, although there are no hard and fast rules about this, as we'll see in a moment. By beta, we will have a good amount of original gameplay and content to show, a title for our game that we're confident we want to use, a logo treatment for the title, and some key art that represents the game in a single image.

There is a lot of debate about how long the gap should be between when the game is announced and when it will be available to play, either in demo form or in its final version. Historically, games could sustain a marketing campaign of up to a year long or sometimes even more. Today, people are often impatient to get their hands on a game as soon as possible after they've heard about it. As marketing consultant and USC Games professor Jim Huntley advises: "You can only sustain consumer interest for so long."

So, if we're not ready to announce our game at beta, we can hold off until we are ready. A marketing campaign can unfold very quickly: Respawn Entertainment's *Apex*

Legends was developed in secrecy and was only announced on the day of its release. It went on to become an enormous commercial and critical success.

You'll have to decide what the right length of marketing campaign is for your game: when to announce it, and how to engage with your audience on the road to release. The right answers will depend on the specifics of your game and the audience that you've imagined for it, but I have a few brief guidelines for you to help you connect with the people who are going to be excited about your game.

Make a Marketing Plan

To run an effective marketing campaign, you need a marketing plan. In their book *Video Game Marketing: A Student Textbook*, Peter Zackariasson and Mikolaj Dymek recommend starting by considering the "marketing mix" for your game—your game as a product, the price you plan to sell it for, the places you plan to sell it, and the promotion you'll use: the "advertising, sales promotion and public relations that are planned."[1] By asking "what, why, when, how, how much, and who?" for each element in the marketing mix, you can set the basis of what Peter and Mikolaj call "the World's Shortest Marketing Plan."[2]

Think about the personality and tone of your game, which may affect who your game appeals to and will inform how you will market it. Is your game serious or silly? Is it playful or intense? Refer once again to the experience goal you set in chapter 7, which you may have refined over time. In *A Practical Guide to Indie Game Marketing*, Joel Dreskin recommends that you ask, "How will my game stand out?" "By thinking about possible unique and compelling characteristics for your game from the very beginning, you can make the process of marketing the game considerably easier. Identify possible hooks, such as a fun new approach to gameplay that's never been done before, a break-through mechanic that showcases a new hardware device or features, highly stylized visuals that will grab players, interesting central characters, storylines and setting."[3]

There's much more to devising a good marketing plan; refer to the books I just mentioned and search online to find detailed advice that will help you make a marketing plan that is appropriate for your game.

Make a Website and Press Kit for Your Game, and Contact the Press

Your game will benefit from having a permanent home on the Internet where people can go to find out more about it. The main page of your website should prominently feature a video trailer of your game so visitors can immediately see the game in action.

---

1. Zackariasson and Dymek, *Video Game Marketing*, 35.
2. Zackariasson and Dymek, *Video Game Marketing*, 37.
3. Dreskin, *A Practical Guide to Indie Game Marketing*, 37.

It should highlight your game's title, development team, platform(s), and where to buy or download it. The key art and logo design that you've been working on will come in handy as you build your website. Add other important information about the game, such as the release date and links to your social media presences, but don't overwhelm your visitors with too much information. Break things out into different subsections of the site, as appropriate.

Professional teams should also create a press kit for their game, which is a website presenting the materials that journalists will use to create compelling stories about you and your game. This will include information about both your game and your team, including your location, history, and business contact details. It will contain still images and videos of your game, your key art, logo designs, and press-quality photographs of the team. "presskit()" is a free tool, created by game developer Rami Ismail and a group of collaborators, designed to help game teams create press kit websites.[4]

When you've made a website and a press kit, you're ready to start reaching out to the press to spread the word about your game. Working with the press falls under the banner of PR (public relations). Build and grow a press list of contacts in a spreadsheet, where you can also keep track of who you've contacted and who wrote back to you. Craft a concise, friendly message that will be received well by your contacts. As Emily Morganti says in her guest chapter about PR in Joel Dreskin's *A Practical Guide to Indie Game Marketing*, "Keep your communications focused and to the point, but also talk like you're talking to another human being. Trying to be formal with your language, using a lot of buzzwords or being too cute in an attempt to grab someone's attention is a great way to be ignored."[5] (Emily's chapter is loaded with excellent advice about working with the press to get coverage for your game.)

Reach out to your contacts with introductions, review pitches, big announcements, or preview copies, and follow up. PR takes persistence, and relationships with the press have to be developed over time. Work to show respect to your press contacts and earn their trust, and the good word about your game will spread.

Running a Social Media Campaign for Your Game

It's not enough to just start hollering about your game on social media: you have to have something to say. You're going to tell a story with your social media presence, and it's that story that will draw the interest of the people who will make up the playing (and possibly paying) audience of your game.

When I asked Jim Huntley for his advice about running a social media campaign, and marketing campaigns more generally, he told me: "Content is king—the more you've got that's relevant to your product or brand, the better. It's easy when you've

---

4. Rami Ismail, Presskit(), accessed December 10, 2020, https://dopresskit.com/.
5. Dreskin, *A Practical Guide to Indie Game Marketing*, 75.

got the content, but it's hard when you haven't, so save and categorize your design materials." In particular, save images, movies, documents, music, and sound. These will become assets in your social media campaign.

A story needs characters. For the story *in* the game, those are the fictional characters in the game. For the story of *the making of* the game, we have a choice: it could be the developers, the community managers, the actors who play roles in the game, or anyone who has something interesting to say about the game, how it's played, and what it took to make it.

Jim Huntley told me that audiences of younger children will respond well to being told the story of the game. He said that older audiences will be interested in that too, but will also be interested in engaging descriptions of the gameplay and in the story of the making of the game. He mentioned that it's important to put the content of the game before any "making of" content. Jim thinks the Marvel Cinematic Universe films do a good job of this in their marketing—they give you a glimpse of the creator's thought processes right *after* they've shown you some new content.

Best practices around social media use evolve very quickly and vary around the world, and you can find some more advice about engaging on social media on the website for this book, playfulproductionprocess.com.

As Jim Huntley told me, "Don't start too early, unless you're sure that you can sustain the dialogue. I've seen people start late, but that's a sin that can be overcome. Engage with your audience—especially those that engage early. Give them stuff to share, or exclusive stuff. Engage with your fans like a friend. As long as you're honest with them, and show them stuff that gets them excited, that's a good place to be. Never, ever take them for granted."

Working with Social Media Influencers

Social media influencers—also called content creators, streamers, or YouTubers—can play an important role as you work to find the audience for your game. Influencers who stream their gameplay sessions can help a game find its audience in a way that is perhaps more effective than any other in the world today.

If you can reach an influencer or their manager to see if they're interested in your game, they might end up showing it to their audience and may say good things about it. Because influencers often have huge audiences—ranging in size from thousands to millions of people—reaching them can be a hit-or-miss business. Maybe your email or direct message will make its way onto their radar—or maybe you'll get lost in the deluge of communication they receive. Use your PR skills to improve your chances of getting a reply to your messages.

Maintain an entertaining and informative social media presence, stay respectful, professional, and friendly in your communications, and you'll be setting up the initial conditions for an influencer to want to pay some attention to your game when they become aware of it.

Integrating Game Development with Professional Marketing

If you have the opportunity to work with professional marketers, whether they're the marketing team at your publisher or a creative marketing company that you hire to help you, *talk to each other early and often*. If you can, start the discussion as soon as you have your project goals, and then stay in touch throughout development. Show them the game and tell them where you think it's headed. Invite them into your creative process by seeking their input. They will have great ideas, and one small idea might revolutionize the opportunities for success that your game has.

As Jim Huntley told me, "I like when a developer asks my opinion before the 'cement has dried,' when they bring me into the process to get my opinion and see what I think. As a marketer, I like being a part of the creative process and feeling that my opinion is valued." Remember, in everything you do, if you show respect to your collaborators and build trust with them, good things will follow.

This chapter has given you just a very brief overview of a huge and important topic. You can learn more in *Video Game Marketing: A Student Textbook* by Peter Zackariasson and Mikolaj Dymek and *A Practical Guide to Indie Game Marketing* by Joel Dreskin. Seek out assistance from marketing and PR professionals, to whatever extent your resources make possible. We'll return to these subjects again in chapter 35.

I realized early that it is essential that game developers and game marketing professionals find ways to work well together. We are all part of the same creative industry, seeking to make great games and get them into the hands of players who will enjoy them. Amy Hennig once pointed out to me that a game director's responsibility for crafting the player's experience of their game should begin the moment that person first becomes aware of the game. That is usually when the player sees an image, reads some text, or sees a video as part of a promotional campaign or press event. That makes it even more important that a game team and their partners in marketing and sales are collaborating closely and effectively.

However you work to reach the potential audience for your game, stay focused on the idea that you have an opportunity to bring genuine value and authentic connection to people's lives. Be clear and engaging in the messages that you send, show respect as you communicate, and work to earn people's trust. Whatever type of game you're making, be it a commercial game, an artistic game, a serious game, or an academic project, the chances are that there are millions of people out there in the world who will enjoy it and appreciate it. Think creatively about how to reach them, and then do the legwork that it takes to follow up.

In our playful production process, the beta milestone marks the end of both the beta phase and the overall full production phase of a game project (figure 31.1).

Beta is often a challenging milestone to hit. In the run-up to beta, we have to make a final round of potentially tough decisions about the scope of our game: what to include and what to cut. Reaching the beta milestone is a very satisfying accomplishment, though, because we can finally see our game in its completed state, albeit with some rough edges.

What's Needed for the Beta Milestone

At alpha, we made our game feature complete and game sequence complete. In order to reach the beta milestone, we must now also make our game content complete. This makes beta a much easier milestone to describe than alpha because at beta the game should essentially be finished, complete in both features and content. We'll have a chance to polish, balance, and bug fix before our final release candidate milestone, but if something is going in the game, it should be in there at beta.

So, at beta, all of the features and content that will be in the game should be in place to at least a first-pass level of polish, including all of the art, animation, audio effects, music, visual effects, and haptic effects (controller vibration). Everything is finished

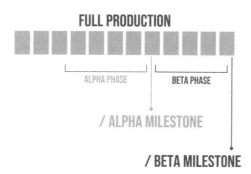

Figure 31.1
The beta milestone ends both the beta phase and full production. Image credit: Gabriela Purri R. Gomes, Mattie Rosen, and Richard Lemarchand.

enough that you *could* ship with it if you had to, even though you'd like some time to make it better. This concept could be important, because at the beta milestone we're often putting things into the game as quickly and efficiently as we can in order to hit the milestone. Bear in mind that unless we have a long postproduction period, it's typically the case that the rougher things are at beta, the rougher the final game will be. It's generally better to cut what you can *before* beta and leave yourself more time to polish everything that makes it into the game.

At beta, the level layout and final art representing the levels and interface screens should all be done, and we should be able to play through the game without any major problems. Our game's onboarding sequence, which teaches new players to play, should be complete. The end of the game (if the game has an end) should be in place and doing whatever it's meant to do. If the game is open-ended, like a sim or a sandbox game, we should be able to play it indefinitely, again without any major problems.

At beta, the icons used by the game's executable or app should be created, in as many sizes as are needed, and the text accompanying the icon should be finalized. If the game will use a pre-game launcher dialogue window when it runs, the text and settings of the launcher should be finalized at beta, and any splash screen images needed for the launcher should be created. If the game will be distributed via an online store, any images required for the game's online store presence are usually created by beta. If the game is going to use an achievements system, either in-game or connected to the achievements system provided by a game publisher or platform holder, then the systems and content for the achievements system must be completed by beta.

If you are going to put any Easter eggs (hidden surprises for the player) in your game, they must be present by beta, and the team's leadership and QA department should be notified of their presence. Surprises and secrets are great for players, but don't hide things in your game without getting everyone responsible on board, in order to avoid bad situations related to everything from copyright problems to defamation liability.

If the game will have to pass a certification process in order to be released on a game console made by a platform holder like Sony, Microsoft, or Nintendo, or on a mobile platform in the Apple ecosystem, the developers should meet as many of the certification requirements as possible by the beta milestone. You can read more about this in chapter 34.

That's a huge amount of stuff to get finished, right? You might be surprised by how early some of these things have to be completed, and now you can see why hitting beta can be such a challenge. The rest of this chapter will give you some advice about reaching this important milestone.

Completeness and the Beta Milestone

In *Game Design Workshop: A Playcentric Approach to Creating Innovative Games*, Tracy Fullerton talks about using playtesting to make sure that a game is functional, complete, and balanced.[1] Tracy discusses checking to see if a game is "internally complete" in its rules and possibility space, and talks about finding and fixing loopholes and dead ends. This is something we should do throughout the whole course of development, of course, but it's a particularly good lens to apply as the beta milestone approaches.

Loopholes, sometimes known as "exploits," occur when the design of the game allows the player to achieve something more easily than they should. For example, if there's a random place in a boss fight level where you can stand and—because of some quirk of the layout or mechanics—the boss can't deal you any damage but you can damage it, defeating it without any effort or risk: that's an exploit.

On occasion, an exploit can add something good to a game, and exploits are less harmful to a design when they take significant skill to use. Glitches in collision that allow the player to take shortcuts through a level are beloved by videogame speedrunners. An unexpected possibility in an eSports game that at first seems like an exploit might be embraced by the player community as a legitimate feature of the game. Perhaps you're making an experimental art game, or a game that comments on loopholes in games, and the exploits in your game are intentional. However, for most types of game, especially those involving competition against the system of the game or against other players, exploits are something to be sought out and eliminated from the game's design. Making judgment calls around issues like this is part of your creative role as a game designer.

A dead end is a situation that arises in a game where the player cannot proceed, possibly because of something they did. Let's say there is a game with a key that the player can pick up and drop anywhere, a locked door that the key unlocks, and a well that is too deep or too narrow to climb down into. The player needs to unlock the door to proceed to the next part of the game, and the key can be found somewhere nearby. But what if the player picks up the key and drops it down the well? Then they're stuck. They can't open the door, they can't get to the key, and they can't proceed in the game. They need to somehow reset the game world so that the key is back in its initial position.

Maybe dying and restarting will do that, but what if objects keep their position across checkpoints? Maybe reloading the game from a previous save will get the key back to its original position (using the technique known as "save scumming"), but what if the game only has one save slot and the game autosaved right after the key went down the well? Then the player is truly stuck, though they might not even realize it. They might keep looking for another key, becoming increasingly bored and frustrated. If they realize what has happened and they want to keep playing, then they will have to start the whole game over again. More likely, they will quit and move on to a different game.

---

1. Fullerton, *Game Design Workshop*, 4th ed., 311.

This situation might sound outlandish, but many games have shipped with this kind of problem lying in wait for unlucky players. Dead ends present a particular problem for games that have a lot of systemic, emergent, and procedurally generated gameplay, though there are usually ways to design them out of existence.

Dead ends can also be embraced as a valid part of gameplay, especially if it's clear to the player that they've wound up in a dead end. Vast new horizons of creative possibility have opened up in this area, with the arrival of games like *Spelunky*, *The Binding of Isaac*, and *FTL: Faster Than Light*, which hybridize the roguelike genre with other styles.[2]

Don't worry if you can't catch all your exploits and dead ends by beta: these are problems that often hide in plain sight, and sometimes they're really good at hiding. The fact that we'll have to seek out some thorny, hidden problems is a part of why we have a postproduction period.

The Beta Phase, Concentric Development, and Game Health

Having spent time stubbing things in for alpha, the beta phase is a good time to return our focus to the concentric development I described in chapter 13, but it can also be a difficult time to practice concentric development. It's an unfortunate game development tradition that we are often putting content into the game as quickly as we can as the beta milestone approaches, not necessarily taking care of the details in the way that concentric development recommends. The structure and discipline of concentric development will create the freedom to be playfully creative when it really matters. We won't be struggling to fight fires at the end, and we'll have more time and mental bandwidth for finesse. If we slap content in too quickly, we might end up with a beta build that has poor game feel, that is much too difficult or too easy, or that is buggy or broken. I try to live by the old adage, "Less haste, more speed."[3]

At the beta milestone, we must check in on the health of our game again, just like we did at alpha. It's now crucial that we attend closely to the technical performance of our game. If our frame rate is poor, if our load times are long, if our lighting is glitchy, this is the time that we *must* start acting to fix these problems. Similarly, if we have any severe design problems or particularly nasty bugs, then we must start fixing them right away. You don't have to deal with all your game's health issues by the time the beta milestone arrives, but you must at least have a good plan for addressing them and must start doing so straight after you reach the milestone. A game that ships with bad bugs or a low frame rate is not cued up for success.

---

2. "Roguelike (or rogue-like) is a subgenre of role-playing video games characterized by a dungeon crawl through procedurally generated levels, turn-based gameplay, tile-based graphics, and permanent death of the player character." "Roguelike," Wikipedia, https://en.wikipedia.org/wiki/Roguelike.

3. "Festina Lente," Wikipedia, https://en.wikipedia.org/wiki/Festina_lente.

Credits and Attribution

If you followed the advice that I gave you in chapter 5, you've been keeping a running record of (a) the attributions for any found and third-party assets that you've used in your game, and (b) the people who worked on your game and what they did. When it comes time to create the in-game credits and the in-game attribution, you should have a fairly quick and easy job on your hands. If you didn't keep a running list, you might have some painful work to do as beta approaches, as you pick through your game's content, building a list of who needs to be credited. Some purchasable asset packs don't require crediting, so carefully check the licensing information that comes with your purchases.

There's an open question when attributing third-party assets of how granular you need to be, and whether you should list every individual asset that you used or just list the names of the individual creators whose work you used. If the license of each asset specifies how it should be credited, you must follow the license closely.

You should always include everyone who contributed to the creation of your game in the game's credits, so think carefully about who worked on the game, especially in the early stages of development. Game developers' résumés and portfolios are very important to their livelihoods, so an omission in the credits of a game can cause them problems.

The Challenge of Reaching the Beta Milestone

Game designers usually have to make some difficult calls in order to reach the beta milestone. As we make our final decisions about the scope of our game and its content, it can become particularly hard to see the forest for the trees. Receiving some external guidance to help us set priorities is often very valuable, and we'll talk about the milestone review that takes place at beta in a few moments.

I have to be honest with you: even though the beta milestone is so easy to define—the game is complete!—beta, like alpha, is sometimes a fuzzy milestone. Just like the dodges that game developers might pull at alpha (exploiting the blurry line between features and content that we discussed in chapter 28), there are dirty tricks we might try at beta to scuttle in under the milestone, as we attempt to make the game content complete in a way that will satisfy our team's leadership. The best-known dodge is to write up a missing piece of content as an "A" class bug in our bug database.

I'd be a liar if I said that I haven't used this trick—I have, although only ever with the explicit permission of my team's most senior leadership, and at least then the missing content is in the bug database, on our radar, and being tracked. Sometimes this kind of dodge is necessary when we're doing triage to hit a beta milestone that *must* be hit, and not all post-beta content additions are equal. Most are risky, but some are safer than others. If you end up with more than a few "A" class bugs that are actually missing pieces of content, then your project could be headed for trouble in postproduction. Fix the bugs—by adding the content—immediately after beta.

After the beta milestone, game developers will sometimes make changes to their content that are so major they might as well be adding new content. This is risky too: the risk comes from adding something to the game late in the day that creates more problems than it solves. As with features, every time we add new content, we risk introducing bugs, content problems, and game design problems. The longer that your postproduction phase is, the less risky major content changes will be, especially if they're made early in postproduction.

It is riskier to add or change content relating to systemic or interactive parts of a game than it is to add or change static assets like title screen backgrounds or linear assets like prerendered cutscene video files. Switching out a placeholder cutscene video for the final, finished version isn't risk-free—the new video file is probably larger and might expose a bug related to memory, for example. But it's much less risky to replace one piece of static or linear content for another than it is to mess around with the systemic and interactive parts of your game, where major problems are much more likely to arise.

Summarizing the Beta Milestone

In summary, at the beta milestone, all these things should be present:

- All features and content of the game should be present in at least first-pass shippable form.
- All front end, menus, and interface elements should be present in at least first-pass shippable form, possibly including but not limited to:
  - A logo image or movie for the development team and/or game studio.
  - A logo image or movie for the publisher or school.
  - A title screen (the interface element that acts as a central hub for decision-making, before the core game experience begins).
  - A credits screen or sequence.
  - Attribution for any found or third-party assets.
  - A "game over" screen, that announces the end of a round of play (if applicable).
  - An options screen or screens, allowing players to configure the experience (if applicable).
- An icon image at all required resolutions for the app or executable and proper titling for the icon.
- A splash screen image for a game that uses a pre-game launcher.
- Any images and text required for the game's online store presence.
- System and content for any achievements, either in-game or connected to a publisher service (if applicable).
- Any Easter eggs (hidden surprises for the player) that you plan to put in the game.
- If the game will have to pass a certification process to be released, the developers should meet as many of the certification requirements (described in chapter 34) as they can.

In addition, at the beta milestone we must make and start to implement an actionable plan to address:

- Any outstanding design problems
- Any performance issues
- The outstanding bugs

The Milestone Review That Takes Place at Beta

When a game achieves its beta milestone and is now feature complete *and* content complete, this presents a great opportunity—and for short projects, perhaps the last big chance—to hold a milestone review meeting and get some feedback from people inside and outside the team to guide us through the postproduction phase.

Like the review at alpha, the beta milestone review for a big professional game will probably take some time, while shorter games can be reviewed more quickly. Make sure that you use your team's time effectively, but don't miss the chance to get one last round of candid, high-quality feedback from your trusted peers and mentors and to dive really deeply into your game. At beta, there are usually a large number of small issues to identify and discuss, and it can be hard for the game team to decide which of the issues are important. As I mentioned earlier, external input is a very effective remedy when we can't see the big picture because we're overwhelmed by detail.

In their short introductory presentation at the milestone review meeting, the development team leadership should be ready to say:

- Who they consider to be the audience for their game. The team's positioning statement (see chapter 7) should now be very refined.
- Where their project is at regarding beta. For example:
  - They hit beta strongly and are entirely content complete, with a game that is free of bugs and well-balanced in gameplay. (We'll talk about game balance in chapter 32.)
  - They hit beta right on and exactly met the beta requirements, being content complete. There is some content polishing to be done, there are bugs to fix, and gameplay needs balancing.
  - They hit beta, and are content complete, but a lot of their content needs polishing, there are many bugs to fix, and the gameplay needs a lot of balancing.
  - They're not yet at beta, and they say what is missing that is keeping them from being at beta.
- Whether there are any known issues with the project.
- What kind of feedback it would be useful to receive from the milestone review group.

At the beta milestone, the review group members should now be very careful to give notes that are timely, as we discussed under "Constructive and Timely Criticism" in chapter 20. The game is now complete, so solutions to problems must come (in most circumstances) from making minor changes to the game. While some might see this—fixing problems without making major changes—as an impossible task, effective designers understand that there is *always* room to maneuver within even the strictest constraints, and will relish the challenge of looking for clever, efficient, and low-risk resolutions to the issues at hand.

The team should also have an internal review at beta, with disciplinary and interdisciplinary groups coming together to talk about the beta build and about what needs to be done during postproduction. (You can read more about internal reviews in chapter 20.) These internal review groups should also be careful to keep their notes timely and should have a discussion about the risks entailed by the action plans they develop.

The quality and health of a beta build can tell us a lot about how the finished game is likely to turn out, especially if the postproduction phase is short. If the game hasn't come together particularly well at beta, it can be a difficult time for the team. They might need some emotional support from their community, their leadership, and each other.

But even if things are rough at the beta milestone, you still have lots of opportunity in postproduction to reach the final release candidate milestone in good style. Lock in the content of your game at beta and move into postproduction, giving yourself time to fine-tune your game until it really sings.

Phase Four: Postproduction—Fixing and Polishing

There's a lot still to do on a modern videogame, once the game is content complete at the beta milestone, and before it can be considered finished at the final release candidate milestone. Postproduction is the time to do everything that needs doing.

The name of this phase is a nod to the postproduction process of film and television production, but be aware that game postproduction is very different from movie or TV postproduction. In film and television, postproduction refers to everything that happens after the film or video is shot. Movies and TV are effectively made in postproduction, sculpted from the raw clay of captured video through a process of editing, sound design, visual effects creation, and color grading.[1]

But a game has already been made and completed in the full production phase of the project. Postproduction for a game is like the very end of movie and TV postproduction, when "picture lock" has been achieved and all the sound design and visual effects work has been done.[2] Then the final audio mix will be made, and any other elements that need work will be fine-tuned. Games need audio mixing and color grading during their postproduction phase, along with other things specific to games.

The need for a formal postproduction game project phase came home to us while we were finishing work on *Uncharted 2: Among Thieves*, a project that was a big success for Naughty Dog, but that had brought a lot of challenges with it. One of those challenges was that we hadn't left enough time between beta and our release candidate milestone to do everything that we needed to do. That work included balancing and equalizing the audio levels of our interactive music and sound, fine-tuning the lighting of the levels, and finessing our color grading and the other postprocessing image effects. All of that work piled up on top of the game balancing and bug fixing that we also had to do at the end of the project.

---

1. "Color grading is the process of improving the appearance of an image. . . . Various attributes of an image such as contrast, color, saturation, detail, black level, and white point may be enhanced." "Color Grading," Wikipedia, https://en.wikipedia.org/wiki/Color_grading.
2. "Picture lock is . . . when all changes to the film or television program cut have been done and approved. It is then sent to subsequent stages in the process, such as online editing and audio mixing." "Picture Lock," Wikipedia, https://en.wikipedia.org/wiki/Picture_lock.

We just about got everything done on *Uncharted 2*, but we only really scraped by in terms of the high standards we set for ourselves, and it meant a lot of stressful last-minute work for the team. So, on *Uncharted 3: Drake's Deception*, we made sure that we gave ourselves a real postproduction phase at the end, where the game's content was locked down properly with an earlier beta, giving us more time to polish it well.

How Long Should Postproduction Take?

There's no one answer to this question that fits every project, but we can seek out the wisdom of our peers. Tale of Tales is a videogame development studio founded by contemporary artists Auriea Harvey and Michaël Samyn in 2003. In their excellent and inspirational 2013 essay, "The Beautiful Art Program," Auriea and Michaël advise: "After the project is finished, we should spend the same amount of time on making it better."[3]

I think that this advice, which might seem paradoxical at first, is excellent. Games benefit hugely from the time we spend improving them once they are complete. I've never been able to spend the same amount of time polishing a game as I spent on building it, but the longer you can devote to postproduction, the better. I recommend spending at least 20 percent of your total project time in postproduction.

Many projects in both industry and academia are strictly time-limited, with a firm and fixed date for the final release candidate milestone planned out a long time in advance. We have to work backward from this completion date to plan the date of our beta milestone, in order to give ourselves enough time for postproduction. For projects that are open-ended in time, we might be able to give ourselves as much postproduction time as we want or need. This could be helpful, but be wary. You'll have to find your own balance between finishing your game properly and continuing to tinker with it indefinitely.

Some projects might have their final release candidate milestone moved further out to give more time to a project that has a lot to do in postproduction. This might be okay as long as we guard against the problem of moving goalposts that we discussed in chapter 15. For many projects, the final deadline *can't* be moved once we're in postproduction, simply because it's too close, and all of the mechanisms that support the launch of a commercial game have already been set into motion. Then we must figure out how best to spend the postproduction time that we have available to us.

Let's take a look at exactly what we do on a videogame during postproduction. Three postproduction activities are common to most types of project: bug fixing, polishing, and balancing the game.

---

3. Auriea Harvey and Michaël Samyn, "The Beautiful Art Program," *Tale of Tales*, August 20, 2013, http://tale-of-tales.com/tales/BAP.html.

Bug Fixing

In chapter 23, we talked about the process of finding bugs and then tracking how they get fixed. By the time a game reaches beta, we usually have a long list of bugs that need fixing, even if we have been dealing with major bugs as soon as they arise. It's normal for new bugs to appear every time we add something to our game, and in the flurry of activity that accompanies the beta milestone, our list of bugs usually grows at a rapid rate. After the beta milestone, the majority of the team's effort may well be focused on bug fixing. This is a time when QA becomes more central to the development process than ever before, since the contents of the bug database represent a major part of the work standing between the team and a finished game.

Individual bugs will be inspected and debated, sometimes energetically or even heatedly, but hopefully always in an atmosphere of respect and trust. This is a time when it is crucial for every team member to keep in mind that we are all working together to achieve greatness in the game. We might be brought into conflict because we value different things in different disciplines or departments. A bug that seems minor to one team member might be a big deal to someone else. We should look past our short-term goals and always think about what will benefit the game and our audience of players the most. Working together, we can figure out how best to handle each issue with the time we have left.

When we're working on a fix for a particular bug, the work that we do can easily introduce other problems into the game. Some fixes are riskier than others: any bug fix that introduces a global change into the way the game works is riskier, while a fix that could only possibly affect one small part of the game is usually safer. Of course, testing should reveal any new problems that get introduced, but the closer we get to shipping, the more likely it is that new problems will go undetected.

In the age of digital distribution, we can issue updates to fix any problems that ship with our game, but we should still be very careful during postproduction. Undetected issues that creep in because of changes we make could still cause us *big* problems. What if there's a nasty bug in the build of the game that we send to an influencer or reviewer or in our shipping build? If people get a negative impression of our game, or can't play it at all, we might miss out on a career-making opportunity. Videos of spectacularly bad bugs that go viral can easily kill audience excitement about a game.

I'm not advocating for total paranoia during postproduction bug fixing—experienced game designers learn to tell how risky any given bug fix is. But we should tread carefully, especially toward the end of postproduction. The closer the final release candidate milestone gets, the safer our fixes have to be—we are running out of the time we'd need to find and fix any new problems that get introduced. So approach your bug fixing during postproduction with an attitude of triage in a medical emergency. Raise the priority of the bigger, riskier fixes you need to make and tackle them first.

Polishing

Once a game is complete at the beta milestone, you may be able to polish some of the content by making small changes to improve how things look, sound, and feel. In the previous chapter, we discussed implementing content to a first-pass level of polish, where we *could* ship with that content if we had to, even though we'd like some time to make it better. Hopefully our first-pass work has a pretty high level of polish—as with any kind of artisanship, the more experienced we become, the more finely crafted our first passes will be.

The more time we have overall in postproduction, and the fewer bugs we have, the more time we can devote to polishing our content. Conversely, if we don't have much postproduction time, and there are a lot of bugs to fix, there won't be much time for content polishing. Bugs typically take precedence over content polish: no one wants to ship a game that doesn't look and sound great, but a buggy game is even less likely to succeed.

Like bug fixing, any work that we do to polish the game during postproduction is risky, since it might introduce new bugs and design problems into the game. As with bug fixing, the bigger the change that the polish requires, the bigger the risk. Major pieces of polish—especially any polish that changes the game globally—should happen as early as possible during postproduction. All polish should be finished by halfway through postproduction, giving us time to spot and fix any problems that do get introduced.

Balancing

In their book *Challenges for Game Designers: Non-Digital Exercises for Video Game Designers*, Brenda Romero and Ian Schreiber give the following definition of game balance:

> Balance: A term used to describe the state of a game's systems as either "balanced" or "unbalanced." When the play is unbalanced, it is too easy, too difficult, or optimal for only certain groups of players. When play is balanced, it provides a consistent challenge for its target audience. For competitive multiplayer games, it also includes the idea that no single strategy should be inherently better than any other, and that no exploits exist that let a player bypass the challenge of the game. We also sometimes call individual game elements "balanced" with each other, meaning that the cost of obtaining it is proportional to its effect, as with cards in a CCG or weapons in an FPS or RPG.[4]

Most game designers strive to balance their game's design all the way throughout preproduction and full production, setting up mechanisms and choosing numbers to create an interesting, enjoyable experience, and attempting to create a game that is neither too easy nor too hard. However, it can be difficult to get a game's balance exactly

---

4. Brathwaite and Schreiber, *Challenges for Game Designers*, 35.

right by the beta milestone. The postproduction phase of a project gives us one last chance to fine-tune our game's balance.

On his blog, *Game Balance Concepts*, Ian Schreiber says:

> While perhaps an oversimplification, we can say that game balance is mostly about figuring out what numbers to use in a game.
>
> This immediately brings up the question: what if a game doesn't have any numbers or math involved? The playground game of Tag has no numbers, for example. Does that mean that the concept of "game balance" is meaningless when applied to Tag?
>
> The answer is that Tag does in fact have numbers: how fast and how long each player can run, how close the players are to each other, the dimensions of the play area, how long someone is "it." We don't really track any of these stats because Tag isn't a professional sport . . . but if it was a professional sport, you'd better believe there would be trading cards and websites with all kinds of numbers on them!
>
> So, every game does in fact have numbers (even if they are hidden or implicit), and the purpose of those numbers is to describe the game state.[5]

Once we reach alpha, all the mechanisms of our game are in place: we're feature complete. By beta, when we move into postproduction, the opportunity for us to balance our game by adding or changing mechanisms is long gone. All the numbers in our game are in place, and hopefully have values that already make the game pretty well balanced. Any balance that we do during postproduction will be done by tweaking the values of those numbers, working slowly and carefully.

Of course, there are some values that we can't change toward the end of the game. As we discussed in chapter 13, if you decrease the height of a player-character's jump by even a tiny amount, it's possible that the character won't be able to reach the ledges that they have to jump to in the game, and the entire game could break.

But some values can be changed in a way that benefits the game. For example, small changes to the numbers governing the movement and combat interactions of characters in an action game could improve the difficulty of the game by making it ever so slightly easier or harder. Tiny changes to the rate at which resources accumulate could have a radical impact on the pacing of a strategy game. Small alterations to the speed at which the text appears in a narrative game might help the player navigate through the story and could help punctuate the unfolding events of the drama. Again, hopefully you've been dialing in these numbers all the way through development. If you must make major changes, make them early in postproduction, giving yourself time to spot any undesirable consequences.

When game balancing, it's essential that you should *only make one change at a time*, and then thoroughly test the game. If you tweak two values, and then see a change that you don't like, you won't know for sure which tweak the change came from. This is good game design practice generally, to make just one change and then test the game.

---

5. Ian Schreiber, "Level 1: Intro to Game Balance," *Game Balance Concepts*, July 7, 2010, https://gamebalanceconcepts.wordpress.com/2010/07/07/level-1-intro-to-game-balance/.

It's not always possible to do this consistently when building out our game during full production, but the further we get through postproduction, the more important it becomes to make just one change, and then test it.

It's easy to get lost in the details during game balancing and end up going around in circles, making tiny changes and then undoing them. Get some outside input to help you stay on track if you find yourself with this problem. You might never find the perfect balance for your game, but if you leave yourself some time for balance during postproduction, you will increase your chances of getting close to perfection. If you want to read more about this subject, Jesse Schell offers lots of excellent advice about game balance in *The Art of Game Design: A Book of Lenses*.[6]

The Character of Postproduction

As we enter postproduction, we're getting close to the end of a marathon. We might be exhausted, limping toward the finish line, and keen to get it over with. But if we've adopted healthy working practices, have scoped our projects well, and have paced ourselves throughout development, we might be tired but still have some energy remaining. It's important that we do everything we can to end up with some charge left in our batteries, because we need to be able to make good decisions in the closing stages of the project, if our game is going to turn out well.

The work we do during postproduction is crucially important. I like to think of postproduction as a time when, having built a house of cards, we are now carefully putting the last two cards on the very top. One small mistake could bring everything crashing down. If we make a design change that appears small but has a major negative impact on the experience of the game—and if we don't notice the negative impact before we ship the game—we could be in big trouble.

Even people who are usually careful and methodical can make mistakes when they're exhausted. That's why it's so important to take care of ourselves throughout the whole course of a game project, by getting enough sleep, exercise, and social time, by eating healthily, and by doing whatever else we need to do to thrive. In this way, maintaining a healthy lifestyle throughout a project is itself a part of the work of game design, because it creates the conditions for us to be able to make great games in an efficient way.

Mobility of Viewpoint

Mobility of viewpoint is a concept used by literary theorists and philosophers, which I find helpful as a game designer.[7] The concept can be applied in many ways but is

---

6. Schell, *The Art of Game Design*, 211.
7. "Cedric Watts characterises Conrad's most complex novel, *Nostromo*, in terms of an enormous 'mobility of viewpoint', with regard to time, space, focalisation and other aspects." Childs, *Modernism*, 85.

essentially to do with being able to switch between different points of view, as an audience member or artist, player or designer. Different points of view come with different modes, priorities, values, and ways of thinking.

When I think about mobility of viewpoint as a game designer, I think about:

- The player's view of the game
- The designer's macroscopic view of the whole game, or a part of the game
- The designer's microscopic view of some detail of the game
- The player-character's view of the fictional world in which the game takes place (or the player-characters' views, if there are multiple player-characters)
- The view of the game world held by the other characters in the game
- The view of the game held by a particular discipline of the development team; for example, the way that a programmer or artist sees the game
- The view of the game held by other professionals that will work on it; for example, the marketing people and community managers who will work on the game

We could keep extending this list for a long time, studying the ways that many different people in the world see the game, and the ways that the fictional characters inside the game see their world, themselves, their goals, their values, and their actions. It's my experience that game developers who have good mobility of viewpoint—who are able to switch quickly between different perspectives on the game—are often able to contribute creatively, problem-solve, and collaborate at a very high level. Mobility of viewpoint is very important for the kind of cross-disciplinary collaboration essential for any complex, creative, technical art form.

Mobility of viewpoint is particularly important for game directors, who must constantly zoom in and out from a macroscopic to a microscopic view of the game. They must see the game from the point of view of many different professional specializations, must see the game world as the fictional characters see it, and must always be advocating for the experience of the player. If the career path of game director is among your goals, take steps to develop your mobility of viewpoint through practice and discussion.

Open-mindedness is in some ways synonymous with mobility of viewpoint, so try to cultivate a mindset that is open to different, and even contradictory, points of view. I find that the more tired I become, the less receptive I am to new ideas, sometimes for emotional reasons. *I'm exhausted, and I just want to get my work done! Why are you asking me to consider a different way of doing things?* is a reaction of mine that I've often had to cool down from. This gives us yet another reason to work healthily throughout the whole course of a project and to avoid ever working to exhaustion.

Postproduction is a time when we often have to switch very quickly between different views of the game. We might have to see the game from a dozen different points of view when we're fixing and regressing a single bug: the player, the person who wrote the bug, the person who passed it to us, the person we need help from to fix it, the person who needs our help with a different bug that they think is more important, the lead producer, the game director, the product manager, the marketing team, and so on. The same goes for the work we do to polish and balance the game.

Your mobility of viewpoint will help you find the best solutions to problems, facilitate good collaboration between team members, and promote the success of your game in the world.

Postproduction Waves

An interesting aspect of postproduction is the way that we *stop* working on the game. On a large team, different disciplines will finish work on the project at different times, gradually completing the game in stages or waves. Of course, if everyone on the team is touching the game up until the very end, there is a high probability that someone will introduce a problem that goes undetected before we ship. We have to move people off the project in waves, gradually handing off work to a smaller and smaller group of people.

In my experience of working on large teams, the process worked like this. First, a milestone is set at the "beginning of the end" of postproduction. At this time, all of the bugs related to content must be fixed. At that milestone, nearly all the artists, animators, audio designers, and visual effects artists have to fix or close all their bugs and stop working on the game. The last few gnarly bugs will be passed to the leads in these disciplines, who will fix them as quickly as they can.

Soon after that, a milestone is set for the game designers, who must finish fixing their bugs related to event scripting, invisible "trigger volumes," camera splines, or whatever is relevant to the style of game being made. Again, the game designers must fix or close their bugs by this next milestone and stop working on the game, with any tough last fixes falling to the lead game designers to resolve.

QA will keep working throughout this time, regressing the bugs that have been claim-fixed, and watching out for the arrival of new bugs. The final milestone is left to the programmers, as they fix or close the last of their bugs. Eventually, the lead programmers will gingerly complete the house of cards that is our game, by fixing the last bug they need to fix. Now the game has become a release candidate and is ready for a final round of extensive testing before it can ship.

There is often an emotional struggle lying in wait for the people who come off the project at the end of each of these waves of work: we're in limbo, waiting for the other shoe to drop, eager for the game to be completed but now not able to contribute directly to its completion. Think of a time in your life when you've waited for news of an outcome that you're deeply invested in, like a test result or a birth. There's a strong feeling of "finished but not yet finished," which for many feels agitated and unresolved.

Perhaps there is not much to do about this unnerving feeling but to tolerate it, and to remember that we did our best, however the game turns out. This is a good time to redouble our focus on health and well-being by eating right, exercising, and doing other kinds of self-care. It's also a good time to turn toward our friends and family.

It's important to try and stay in good spirits throughout the whole game development project, and it's particularly important during postproduction, doubly so for people in leadership positions. Postproduction can be difficult and stressful for the whole team, but there's complex work left to do that will be made even more difficult by bad moods or arguments.

That doesn't mean we have to adopt a fake fixed grin when we're feeling anxious or annoyed. It *does* mean we have to stay aware of the effect our moods have on others. We should find the right time and place to let out any difficult emotions that we're working through—perhaps by talking to a friend or family member outside our game team. Even though postproduction can be very hard, as we struggle to finish the game and make it as excellent as we want it to be, if we all try to keep a positivistic outlook, the work will be a little easier.

In the next few chapters we'll talk about the final milestone—the release candidate milestone—and we'll discuss what happens to a release candidate in the process known as "cert." We'll look at some other things that might need our attention during postproduction, and we'll see what might happen to us and to our game when we've finally finished working on it.

33 The Release Candidate Milestone

The release candidate milestone comes when we finally make a build of the game that we believe could be ready for release. We've fixed all the bugs that we think we need to fix, we've completed all the polish that we had time to do, and we've balanced the game as best we can. We've tested the game thoroughly, and there aren't any major problems that we're aware of. We're now ready to give the game one last round of testing, in order to give it our seal of approval as being ready for distribution. Achieving the release candidate milestone is sometimes known as "going silver"—silver being the stage before gold.

Throughout this book, I've been telling you that the release candidate milestone is the final milestone of a digital game project. But that's not quite true. Releasing software is a complex process, and just like the postproduction phase took place in stages, the end of the project has another milestone hidden at the very end. Once we have tested the release candidate thoroughly, it is alchemically transmuted from silver to gold; it becomes the gold master build, and we have achieved the gold master milestone (sometimes known as the stable release or the release to manufacturing build).

The gold master build gets its name from the recordable CD-ROM discs used in the early '90s, some of which were golden in color because of the organic dyes or actual gold metal used to make them writable.[1] A physical gold master disc would be created at the game studio or publisher and sent to a manufacturing plant to be duplicated onto the cartridges, floppy discs, or CD-ROMs sold in game stores. Today, we can send this information over the Internet with a few mouse clicks and can distribute it online.

In other words, at the release candidate milestone, the programmers, directors, and producers on the project are willing to step away and say, "Okay, we think the game is done now. Test it some more, and let's make sure that's the case. Then we'll have our gold master, ready for release."

What Is Needed for a Release Candidate?

In practical terms for the artisans on a game team, the release candidate is a version of our digital game that:

---

1. "CD-R," Wikipedia, https://en.wikipedia.org/wiki/CD-R.

- Is complete in terms of features and content
- Has had some polish time for both features and content
- Has had some time for game balancing
- Has been in test long enough that we are reasonably confident we have discovered all of the significant bugs
- Has had all of the bugs that the game couldn't ship with fixed and regressed (to check that they are indeed fixed)
- Has had the bugs closed that we've decided not to fix

This last point will probably sound weird or even ghastly to many readers. How can we ship a game with bugs that we know exist? I rebelled against this idea for a long time myself. As a game designer who cares about the high quality of the things I make, the thought of shipping a game with known bugs was anathema to me.

But eventually I had to accept this as a reality of software development. The kind of bugs we're talking about here are not bugs that will definitely cause problems in the player's experience—bugs like that should be fixed. We should only close bugs whose presence or absence is more of a judgment call about the subjective experience of the game. If a bug doesn't affect gameplay, and if many players will not notice it, then we can consider closing it, especially if we're running out of time to fix bugs and there are worse bugs left to fix.

There are other things that we need to do to prepare a release candidate build. Note these things may be required early during postproduction and maybe to meet the beta milestone:

- The debug menus and any shortcut key combinations that we've created should be removed from the build. For example, developers often build in menus and shortcuts to give the ability to teleport around the game, make the player-character invulnerable, or give unlimited resources, as well as to analyze the technical systems of the game.
- Any persistent on-screen debug readouts (showing the frame rate, for example) should be removed from the build.
- Any content and features that will be required by the certification process for the game must be created, if they haven't been already, and must now be finalized. We'll discuss this in greater detail in chapter 34.

Once we've prepared our release candidate, we're ready to test it some more.

From Release Candidate to Gold Master

The process of testing a release candidate to take a game project to gold master is a rigorous one. It requires a complex and comprehensive test plan, a legion of skilled quality assurance people, and some engineers, producers, and other members of a team's leadership. Sometimes artists, animators, audio designers, and game designers are needed as well.

Like detectives on a difficult case, the QA team must comb the build with an eagle eye, looking for bugs. They're after nasty, hidden bugs that happen only rarely or that only occur when the player does something unusual and unexpected in the game. Of course, all this is part of regular QA practice, but it becomes even more important here in the final phase of QA testing.

QA will perform "soak tests," leaving the game running but idle for days on end, looking to make sure it doesn't crash. They'll check over every part of the possibility space of the game one last time to make sure that everything is present and correct. They'll make sure that the game is going to meet the certification requirements issued by the publisher or platform holder, which we'll discuss in the next chapter.

If any problems are discovered, the team's leadership will meet to discuss them and to see whether the problems are severe enough to risk making changes to the release candidate. As we've discussed throughout the previous chapters, every time we make a change to the game, we run the risk of inadvertently introducing new problems. Some QA departments will set the release candidate testing clock back to zero every time a single change is made to the code, starting the whole process over again.

In this way, we make our painstaking progress toward a gold master build. Of course, small teams with limited resources can find this stage of a project very challenging. There are game QA studios that can help teams outsource the burden, but teams without a budget will have to do their own testing.

Professional teams should go through the process of taking their game from release candidate to gold master in a way that's appropriate for the team's resources and funding. There's an open question about whether game projects in academic settings should be taken all the way to gold master or can be considered finished at the release candidate stage. In my opinion, shorter academic game projects of up to a semester in length can be considered finished at the release candidate milestone, but yearlong projects used as thesis projects or capstone projects should be taken to gold master, since the learning that comes from the very last stage of the process is valuable and professionalizing. Of course, any student teams that publish their work on a commercial platform as part of their coursework will take their projects to gold master and may have to go through a certification process too.

Releasing the Game

Once we have given the release candidate a clean bill of health, we can consider ourselves to have reached the gold master milestone, and we can move toward the next stage of releasing our game. If we're releasing our game on our own website or by some other method that is entirely under our own control, then we can just go ahead and release it by making it available for download.

If we are releasing our game on a service like Steam or the Google Play store, there will be a short process of application and approval to go through, and maybe a fee to be paid. The platform holders will check over our game and will either approve it for distribution or deny our application to be hosted on their service.

Even if we're not putting our game out on console, releasing a game is not as simple as just putting it up online. We need to promote our game if we want people to discover it. We'll talk about this some more in chapter 35.

If we are creating a game for a game console made by a platform holder like Sony, Microsoft, or Nintendo, or that is to be released on a mobile platform in the Apple ecosystem, we will need to pass a certification process before we can release our game on that platform. This is also known as a submission process, compliance testing, or passing cert.

In chapter 7, we talked about becoming a developer for this type of hardware platform. When we have been approved by a platform holder as a developer for their platform, we will receive a list of requirements that our game has to meet before it can be released on the platform. These include:

- Technical requirements, how the platform's hardware and software libraries are used by the game, including considerations of screen resolution and refresh rate, disc or drive access speed, and how the processors are addressed.
- Quality control, the degree to which the game must be bug-free and have good interface usability.
- Security in terms of the mechanisms that prevent a game from being copied and that preserve user's privacy.
- Content, whether certain imagery, sounds, and subject matter are permitted, how the game handles multiple languages.
- The implementation of gameplay systems like achievements, which must meet certain standards and conventions.
- Branding, how the logos of the company and game system may be used and modified, including imagery related to the game controller.
- Assets needed to sell the game in the platform holder's online store: text, images, movies, and icons.
- Content ratings, which we'll discuss toward the end of this chapter.
- Localization requirements, depending on where in the world the game will be released.
- Pricing: how much the game will cost when it's sold.

The certification requirements document usually includes several hundred detailed requirements which must be met before the game can be released. Every company has a different set of certification requirements and a different name for them. At Sony PlayStation, they are called TRCs, for "technical requirements checklist." For the Microsoft Xbox they are called TCRs, for "technical certification requirements." Nintendo's certification system is known as the LotCheck process. These are all similar in general terms but have major differences in detail—for example, in terms of how they handle things like player data, multiplayer, and achievements. If you're developing for multiple platforms at once you must study the certification requirements in detail and architect your game to account for the differences.

Be aware that, for most companies, there are actually two parallel processes here: a technical process focused on game development, and a publishing process focused on bringing your game to market. As Tracy Fullerton reminded me: "They are very different beasts and happen on two different timelines, with the publishing/marketing starting earlier and the technical coming in at the end. Then at the very end, publishing comes back and takes over for the pre-launch press effort and then actual shipping." So keep in mind that you will probably need to engage with two different divisions of the platform holder's company, one for development and one for publishing.

The Certification Process Timeline

The game studio receives the list of certification requirements when they are approved as a developer. In order to pass cert first time—or indeed, at all—they must study the requirements throughout their game's development. The earlier they get started on this, the better. The developer should have a good general understanding of the certification requirements from the beginning of the project, starting in the preproduction phase. The full production phase is a good time to begin studying the certification requirements in detail, and they should be clearly understood by alpha.

When a developer is confident that their release candidate build has been thoroughly tested and is free of problems that would prevent it from passing the certification process, they fill out some paperwork and submit it to the platform holder. The platform holder then puts the game into the testing and evaluation process, to make sure that it complies with the certification requirements.

Around the same time that the game is being submitted to the technical certification process, the developer will be working with the publishing division of the platform holder to get their game set up on its digital distribution storefront. The timing of this must be carefully planned and figured into the release plan for the game, which in turn affects the timeline along which the potential audience for the game is engaged using marketing and social media. For example, only after a game has passed cert can promo codes be generated for press and reviewers to help create buzz about the game.

Passing and Failing Cert

The best outcome of the certification process is that the platform holder doesn't find any problems that prevent the game from passing cert. The game is then judged to be compliant with the certification requirements and has truly "gone gold." It can be handed over to the process that will lead to its release.

If the platform holder finds just one major problem (or a handful of small problems), then usually the game has failed cert. The platform holder will stop testing the game and kick it out of the cert process, sending it back to the developer with a description of the problem. If the game developer wants to continue attempting to publish on the platform, they will have to fix the problem, possibly pay a (potentially very large) fee to have their game put through the certification process again, and resubmit. If a game contains several major problems and gets kicked out of cert when the first problem is discovered, the game might be in trouble if the developer doesn't find the other problems before they resubmit.

Developers should do everything that they can to avoid failing cert. Cert takes time: usually at least a week for the rigorous process of testing and evaluation. That means that if we have to go through cert two or three times, we could easily miss our projected release date by a month, which is an eternity in the landscape of modern media consumption and audience attention.

Updating Games after Passing Cert

Game developers often need to "patch" their games. A patch is the replacement and updating of either some part of the build of the game or the whole game. Games are patched to fix problems and sometimes to make an update that adds content and features. Live operations games—games that operate as an ongoing service rather than as a one-time-sale product—must constantly be patched and updated.

For most platform holders, not every successive patch needs to pass cert separately. There is usually a process separate from (but similar to) the first and main certification process that, once passed, will allow a developer to patch their game with a certain degree of freedom.

Content Ratings

Depending on the region of the world where a game is being released, it might be required to receive a content rating before it can be published. The content rating indicates that the game is appropriate for certain age groups and is issued by the ratings board for each region. If you own physical copies of digital games, you're used to seeing content ratings on the box: they're issued by the ESRB in Canada, Mexico, and the United States, by PEGI in Europe, and by many other organizations around the

EXAMPLE VIDEOGAME CERTIFICATION REQUIREMENTS
by Jesse Vigil, USC Games

1.1 Playable on Consumer Hardware

REQUIREMENT: Game can be installed and run on any device that meets the developer's stated minimum specification and target OS.

EXPLANATION:

Games that only run on the developer's personal hardware are not acceptable. Packaged executables, web builds, or mobile packages must install on test/deployment devices indicated by the publisher (instructors) prior to submission. Must comply with 1.2.

1.2 Third-Party Plugins and Drivers

REQUIREMENT: Third-party plugins must be integrated in to the executable or declared to the publisher prior to the beta milestone.

EXPLANATION:

The use of third-party plugins (for controller support, networking shortcuts, etc.) is permitted so long as no special installer or additional permissions are required for installation and playing the game on consumer hardware. Plugins that require the end user to have install permissions (including special hardware drivers) must be declared and approved by the publisher (instructors) no later than the beta milestone.

1.3 Minimum Front-End Requirements

REQUIREMENT: All games must contain the minimum front-end features and content.

EXPLANATION:

Minimum front-end features and content:

- Splash screen/logo display for your publisher or game program
- If a collaboration with another company, institution, or division is involved, appropriate splash screen/logo display
- Title screen/menu screen
- In-game credits

(a)

Figure 34.1

world.[1] However, most of the console platform holders are now moving toward use of the International Age Rating Coalition in order to reduce cost and complexity.[2]

The process of receiving a content rating is separate from the cert process but is somewhat similar to it. The game is submitted to the ratings board for the region of

---

1. "Video Game Content Rating System," Wikipedia, https://en.wikipedia.org/wiki/Video_game_content_rating_system.
2. "International Age Rating Coalition," Wikipedia, https://en.wikipedia.org/wiki/International_Age_Rating_Coalition.

1.4 No Broken User Interface Loops

REQUIREMENT: Users can appropriately navigate between screens/modes without need for reset.

EXPLANATION:

If a menu navigation option leads to a credit screen/instruction screen/supplemental screen, the user must be able to return to the main menu screen via in-game navigation. If gameplay ends, the game must return players to the main menu screen. Accessing or re-accessing any screen in the game should not require closing and re-opening the application.

1.5 Gameplay Input Also Operates Menus

REQUIREMENT: Input method used for gameplay is also functional for menu navigation.

EXPLANATION:

If a gamepad is/can be used in gameplay, the gamepad must also be capable of navigating the menus

1.6 All Debug Functions Removed at Final Cert

REQUIREMENT: Any cheat keys, shortcuts, or other debug functions and tools are disabled/removed/not accessible from the front end by final submission.

EXPLANATION:

No onscreen debug text is visible to the end user. Developer shortcut keys are not findable and cannot be triggered accidentally by end users.

2.1 Standardized Gamepad Requirement

REQUIREMENT: A gamepad-enabled game is compatible with a standard Windows gamepad

EXPLANATION:

Other gamepads can be supported, but gamepad-enabled games MUST support the standard Windows gamepad (an Xbox controller). This device's drivers are part of the standard device drivers inside Windows and do not require administrator permissions to install, therefore making 1.1 easier to comply with.

(b)

Figure 34.1
(continued)

release, sometimes alongside a fee. (Ratings boards are typically affiliated with the government and the digital games trade association for the region.) The game is then reviewed, and a rating is assigned. The rating might include both an age category and some content descriptors that say what kind of content the game contains. If the developer and/or publisher doesn't receive the content rating they wanted, changes can be made to the game and it can be resubmitted, or the rating decision can be appealed.

In many regions of the world, content ratings are optional, and not every game released online needs to receive an official content rating. However, most games released on a game console will be required to receive a content rating by the platform holder's certification requirements and must do so before they are put into the certification process. It can be difficult to deal with the issues arising from the many different content ratings systems and certification processes that a game might go through on its journey to release, and this is one of the areas where game publishers can offer great assistance to game developers.

Some Example Certification Requirements

Jesse Vigil is a writer, game designer, filmmaker, entrepreneur, and educator who teaches in the USC Games program. He developed a set of example certification requirements modeled after those used in the game industry. Our students comply with these requirements when making games in our classes, in order to introduce them to the rigors of "going gold" in a professional setting.

Jesse's cert requirements are a valuable tool for every game developer when learning how to finish a game, and I reproduce them in figure 34.1 with his permission. Since some of them relate to the beta milestone, they should be given to the development teams by alpha at the latest. Jesse and I hope that you find them useful.

⁂

Because passing cert is such a detail-oriented business, the game developers handling it need to be sharp and on point, able to communicate with crystal clarity about every aspect of the process. Some development teams and publishers employ certification experts who know the requirements well and have helped shepherd many games through the cert process, and there are also companies that provide the same service. Passing cert is a rite of passage for every game developer, and while it can be challenging, it brings with it many opportunities for learning. Good luck!

Even when we've passed cert, we're not quite done. There is usually some extra work lying in wait for game designers at the very end of a project. We'll look at that in the next chapter.

35   Unexpected Game Design

The creative journey of a game designer is full of surprises, some of them happy, like unexpected synergies between elements of our gameplay, and some not so great, like hard-to-fix bugs. We continue to make discoveries about our game, our players, our processes, and our tasks throughout the whole course of a project, including at the very end. There's usually some unanticipated work for game designers to do both during postproduction and after the release candidate milestone: work that comes out of the blue and lands in your lap, demanding to be done. This chapter is intended to help you avoid being caught unawares by the unexpected end-of-project duties of a game designer.

The tasks that creep up on us as we get our game ready to meet the world will vary wildly depending on what kind of game we are making, the context in which we are making it (commercial, artistic, academic, or some other), the way our game will be released, the size and nature of our potential audience, and so on. I'll point you toward some general categories of work you might need to do, but you will have to stay alert to the world around you. The cultural, commercial, and media landscape around games is constantly changing—and changes very quickly. Don't be caught snoozing, for your own sake and for the sake of your game.

Types of Unexpected Game Design

Much of the work that takes game designers by surprise relates to the release and promotion of our game. We want people to download, buy, or otherwise experience our game, and making that happen is going to take some effort on our part and on the part of our collaborators.

We already discussed this in chapter 30, and hopefully you've got a plan in place for finding and communicating with the people who might want to play what you've made. However, if you're new to releasing and promoting games, some of the work you'll have to get involved in as a game designer and developer might catch you on the hop. This could include:

- **Helping to make trailers for your game.** You may need to provide raw footage of gameplay and story-based content, and key art assets. You might even have to make the trailer yourself. Creating a good game trailer takes time.

- **Helping to submit the game to receive a content rating.** Even when this process is handled by a third party, there is usually work for the game developers to do to prepare the game for submission.

- **Building and testing demos for your game.** Shipping a demo is challenging and time-consuming in many of the same ways that shipping a full game is challenging. If your game is required to pass a cert and content-rating process, the demo might have to as well.

- **Make a website for the game.** As with a trailer, you may have to provide assets and information for the website, or you might have to make your game's website yourself.

- **Publicity project management.** Running the process of communicating and coordinating with the press and the wider world about your game can be very time-consuming. Professional publicists can take on this work, but if you don't have the budget to pay someone to do it, you may have to publicize your game yourself by reaching out to the press and influencers and by organizing public events.

- **Managing social media accounts.** Creating top-quality content for your game's social media channels can be surprisingly time-consuming. You should also factor in the time it takes to develop both short- and long-term plans for your social media engagement with your audience.

- **Interviews with the games press.** If you're able to attract attention from the press, the interviews you give about your game can do a great job of growing your audience. These interviews might be conducted through email or private messaging, or they might be recorded with audio or on camera. In every case, they take time to do well.

- **Preparing presentations for the press.** In addition to the time it takes to write or record an interview, it will take time to prepare your talking points so that you have something good to say. You will also need to prepare screenshots, videos, and key art to be published alongside your interview.

- **Helping to create the strategy guide.** Many games—especially commercial games—create strategy guides to help players figure out how to play and to act as supplementary content. These might be sold in print or e-book form or made available for free on the web. They take time to create and usually require a *lot* of input from the game's designers and developers. If you will be collaborating with the author of a strategy guide, make sure to build time into your schedule for the communication and attention to detail it will take.

- **Creating "making of" documentaries for short films and in-game bonus materials.** Games have included in-game unlockable "making of" bonus materials for more than a decade now, and short-form documentaries about the making of games have risen in popularity. It takes time to prepare for and record the developer interviews that go into these documentaries, and even more time to plan, shoot, edit, and polish the films themselves.

- **Showing at expos and doing press tours.** Public game expos are an important venue for game promotion for both indie developers and large companies. Preparing for, traveling to, and showing your game at an expo is expensive, time-consuming, and tiring, so plan well ahead. If you are a developer working on a game with a large marketing budget, you may get sent out on a press tour where you talk to journalists and appear in the media, spreading the message about your game as you go.

- **Submitting your game to festivals.** There are many great game festivals, catering to a wide diversity of games. Aside from the fun and the honor of having your game featured in a game festival, they can help a game connect with its potential audience, and the laurels that we see on a game's website can help attract attention to a game. Depending on when the submission deadlines are for the festivals you want to submit to, you might find yourself scrambling to put together the large volume of content that most festival submissions require at the same time as you are trying to "final" your game.

- **Submitting papers and talks about your game to conferences.** Conference talks and submitted papers, whether in industry or academia, are a place to share the knowledge you gained in the process of creating your game, rather than being places to promote your game. However, as with festivals, depending on when the conference submissions are due, you might find yourself with unexpected work on your hands just when you thought you were done.

You might think that much of what I'm describing here isn't game design, it's marketing or PR. That may be true, strictly speaking, but as you can tell from my description of this work, very often, your collaborators in PR and marketing will need input from the development team to carry out these important promotional tasks. On a small development team with a limited budget, the team themselves may well have to do the work.

In chapter 30, I mentioned Amy Hennig's belief (which I share) that the player's experience of the game begins the moment that player first becomes aware of the game. Their experience is shaped by the information and emotion that they get from the promotional materials or press. So this kind of work is actually an aspect of game design—as much a part of the designed experience as the game itself. As such, it benefits from the touch of the passionate developers who are creating the game, working in close collaboration with their expert colleagues in marketing and PR.

There might be other kinds of unexpected game design work lying in wait for you at the end of your project. Maybe you'll get an opportunity to work with nonprofits and have a positive impact on society. Perhaps you'll be called on to address a government assembly about your game. In the worlds of entertainment, art, and business, anything is possible. If you cultivate your game design practice, your character as a person, and your values, you will be able to steer a good course through whatever comes your way.

⚜ ❦ ⚜

In chapter 2, I talked about "the power of the list." Game designers who keep lists and keep them up to date have a kind of superpower, and when unexpected game design comes along, that superpower gets activated. Instead of having to do dozens of hours of work to compile some information that's unexpectedly been requested, you might just be able to produce your list and hand it over.

Now that we have a release candidate, have passed through the certification process, and have dealt with some unexpected game design, we are very nearly finished in our playful production process. The next chapter will talk about what comes after the end, as we release our game and support it, and move on to future projects.

Sometimes when a game is finished, the game's developers can relax, at least for a while. Most of the time when a game is finished and released, it then immediately demands more work from its creators. In either case, another project might also begin. This chapter will look at what we do after we've finished.

Releasing a Game

For the first few decades of professional game design, it was likely that everyone on the team could rest when the game shipped. If the developers had crunched to complete the game—as many did, historically—then families would see their spouses and parents at the dinner table again, and vacation time could be used. For those who crunched, a rest might be more like an exhausted collapse.

Of course, a game that gets released to the public needs a lot of business support. This is true whether it's released as a boxed product, a digital download, or a live service. At big companies, the work associated with releasing the game usually won't fall at the feet of a game's developers (chapter 35's "unexpected game design" excepted). Instead, their colleagues in marketing, sales, operations, and publishing will handle the work. At a smaller company, the game developers themselves might handle their own release.

With the arrival of downloadable content (DLC) as an important way to extend a game's lifetime in the marketplace, and with the growing importance of "live operations" games-as-service, a game's creators will now often find themselves continuing to work on their game after it has shipped. You can imagine how bad this is for anyone who has crunched in the process of shipping their game. If you stumble across the finish line, exhausted and depleted, but then have to keep on running—well, that's a recipe for severe physical and mental health problems. This emphasizes the crucial importance of maintaining healthy working habits throughout the whole life cycle of a game, avoiding crunch so that we will still be healthy and can carry on working on our game once it has shipped.

The Post-Project Review

One of the most important things to do when a project is finished is to hold a post-project review. This usually takes place in a meeting or, more likely, a series of meetings, where the developers discuss the project, looking for lessons that they can learn from it. On a small team, it's natural that everyone will take part in the post-project review process. On a larger team, multiple meetings will ensure that everyone from every discipline will have a voice. Extensive notes are taken to be combined later into a written report. Someone is appointed to gather up all the information and perspectives that surface and to write them up for later presentation to the team, studio, and stakeholders.

This practice is common in the world of games and tech and is often known as a postmortem. The postmortem is a popular genre of Game Developers Conference talk, so seek out and watch the postmortems of your favorite games to learn more about how they were made.

Post-project reviews usually focus on two things: what went well on the project, and what didn't. These lenses can be applied to every aspect of the game: mechanics and narrative, development processes and tools, production and project management methods, communication, collaboration, conflict resolution, and team leadership . . . there's no limit to what we can discuss in a post-project review, as long as we keep it respectful, compassionate, and constructive.

In particular, the developers are looking for ways to improve in the future. It might be useful to apply a SWOT analysis, looking for strengths, weaknesses, opportunities, and threats in the game or the way that it was made.[1] This could feed into the conversation the developers have about what they're good at and how they could stretch themselves in the future (see "Repertoire and Growth" in chapter 7). On my professional teams and in my classes we always make sure to end every project with a post-project review, and the learning that comes from reflecting on process is one of the best ways to improve as a game designer and developer.

Resting at the End of a Project

If you're able to do it, it's valuable to get some downtime between projects. Some studios grant their employees a bonus period of time off at the end of a big project, or individual employees may have saved up their paid time off. Whether you like to travel, hang out with family and friends, read, watch films, play games, make music, a period of "fallow time" between projects can help you recharge and reset whatever it is that makes you feel creative and motivated.

Some studios or teams may be scrambling at the end of a project to bring their next project online or to support their live game, leaving them little time to catch their breath.

---

1. "SWOT Analysis," Wikipedia, https://en.wikipedia.org/wiki/SWOT_analysis.

They may have to keep working to support themselves and their families. If you find yourself in a position to support others in getting some rest at the end of a project, please do so. Downtime is as much a part of the creative process as periods of fierce productivity.

The ideas that come to us when we're daydreaming and directionless are valuable. They might just amuse us and reinvigorate our excitement for what we do. They might bring reflection and growth in ways that we need. They might be the source of a history-making game. So get to know yourself as you gain experience as a game developer and figure out what you need to do to recharge at the end of a big project.

Post-Project Blues

Sometimes, resting at the end of a project isn't so simple. As vacation time begins, some people find a feeling of restlessness and anxiety settling over them, or even emptiness and depression. Suddenly, the exciting, creative, attention-demanding, emotionally rewarding work that filled our days is just—gone. After the end of big projects, I've sometimes felt like Wile E. Coyote from the *Road Runner* cartoons, standing in midair having just run over a cliff edge, looking through the screen at the audience, and then looking down at the abyss below.

Post-project blues can vary in severity. They can be mild or might constitute a serious life problem. Dealing with them is a challenge that can arise for anyone, but it's particularly associated with crunch. When one's life has been entirely consumed by work, and when all of the meaning and emotional connection in one's life comes from work, problems can arise when a project ends and that meaning and connection disappears. Addiction problems can have a bad interaction with both crunch and the post-project blues, as people struggle to fill the void created by unmet emotional needs in unhealthy ways.

I am not a mental health professional, and if you are facing mental health challenges, I hope that you can seek out help, preferably from a professional source. I have had many wonderful experiences of psychotherapy and counseling, and I am always left feeling glad that I sought help. I want to acknowledge that access to psychotherapy is often connected to privilege and wealth, and that psychotherapy may not be available where you live. Group therapy and support groups can provide a relatively low-cost form of psychotherapy. I was a member of a therapy group for more than ten years, which had a hugely positive impact on my life and well-being.

If you have the post-project blues, tell a friend. We often feel shame when we struggle with mental health. But problems that we tuck away in the dark only fester and grow. Problems that are brought out into the light of friendship and compassion can begin to be addressed.

My hope is that if we maintain a healthy process throughout the whole course of a project, in the way that our playful production process aspires to make possible, then we'll still be relatively fresh at the end and will be less prone to the post-project blues. Take note of how you feel at the end of a project and do whatever healthy things you need to do to practice self-care.

The Next Project

Once we've had some rest, and if we're in a good position to be able to make another game, then it may be time to begin our next project. One way to go about that is just to turn to the first page of this book and begin our playful production process again in the ideation phase, with blue sky thinking, research, and prototyping.

On many teams, especially large ones, a dynamic comes into play as we begin work on our next project that we'll need to manage. The different disciplines on our team will move off the project in stages. This means that some people—potentially, very many people—will be ready to start work on the next project before the team's leadership is. This lull between projects can create a problem, since those who are ready to continue will, quite reasonably and naturally, want some direction for the next project before the directors, producers, leads, and designers are back from their vacation and ready to give it. When a team is left without leadership, problems can arise, unless we adopt a strategy to turn a potentially bad situation into a good one.

R&D

During my time at Naughty Dog, the between-project lull was handled constructively by giving time over to research and development (R&D). Team members were asked to spend some time in self-guided work that would help them prepare for the next project in a general way.

Perhaps they would evaluate a new commercially available tool that they thought might be helpful on the next project. Perhaps they would create a tool themselves or do some work to improve the tools pipeline. (A tools pipeline is a mixture of the tools and processes used to create parts of the game, transfer them between tools for further work, and integrate everything into a playable build.)

During R&D, team members might build a prototype of a feature or some content to investigate a wild, creative, experimental idea. Some might attend a training program to improve their skills in a particular area or spend time doing research by reading and watching videos. They could investigate anything from new game technologies to new approaches to art, animation, and audio. They might learn about cutting-edge theory and practice in game design, or best practices related to project management and the development of team culture.

Every studio should be thinking about R&D as a matter of course, to avoid stagnation and to keep them current, and the lull between projects is a natural time to pursue it. An R&D effort may need some guidance from the team's leadership, but R&D can proceed quite well when it's driven by the team members themselves, working independently. After all, the artisans on a team know their tools and processes better than anyone and will have great ideas for areas of improvement.

Starting with Some Direction

The game director (or directors) for the next project will play an important role in set-ting its direction, working across the team to determine what the next game will be like. Most game directors have an ongoing list of project ideas; things that they want to do or try, that they think will be viable from an artistic or business perspective, and that they think their team will like too.

It's good for the director of the next project to set some direction as early as they can, but that direction doesn't have to be very defined. It could be like a very early draft of the project goals that we discussed in chapter 7—maybe just a few sentences about a type of experience, or the practical constraints that the project will embrace (the game's genre or hardware platform, say).

Having no direction at all can cause people to feel lost and demotivated. Given even a little direction, team members feel motivated to contribute to the project, because they know roughly what direction they're headed in. At the *very* beginning of a project, less is sometimes more in terms of direction, since it can allow people greater freedom to explore. Team morale stays strong, because giving people direction helps to show them that you care about them and value their work. While they're giving early direction, game directors should also make it clear that they want to hear everyone else's ideas too. It's important to get input from everyone on the team during the ideation phase of a project.

It's a game director's job to be a strategic thinker and plan ahead—so don't neglect this issue on your team. Start to think about your next project at the alpha milestone of your previous project at the latest, and get ready to give the direction that your new project needs to get it off to a good start.

When to Leave a Team

Making good games is incredibly hard and is dependent on team culture: the work-ing practices, shared knowledge, and shared values of a team. Team culture is a deli-cate thing that often only thrives and lasts when it's nurtured slowly and deliberately over time. Sudden departures and arrivals of individual team members can lead to big changes in team culture, which in turn has an impact on the game that the team is making.

In particular, if someone leaves a project before the game is finished, it can make things almost impossibly difficult. If someone wants to leave a team, I believe that the right time to do it is at the end of a project, when the game has been completed, and not before. Life being what it is, it isn't always possible to make planned transitions like this, but do what you can to see out the projects you've committed to. The game indus-try is a surprisingly small place, and it's good to get a reputation as a finisher, someone who places value on seeing projects through to completion.

That said, you should not tolerate a working environment that is abusive, toxic, or unhealthy. As much as I hold being a finisher as a professional value, I value an individual's right to remove themselves from a bad situation even more highly. I understand that it's a privilege to be able to leave a job, and each individual should navigate a toxic work situation in the way that's right for them. Everyone should strive to create working environments free of toxicity and abuse, and those in positions of power have a particular obligation to do so.

Back to the Beginning

Like the mythical ouroboros that swallows its own tail, the ends and beginnings of game projects are intimately connected. I once heard the game designer Eric Zimmerman say that along with the individual games we make, there's also a greater game design project, one that we work on the whole of our game-making lives. It's the game project that is our entire game design practice, that begins when we make our very first game, and that only ends with the last player of the very last game that we make.

I consider myself incredibly fortunate to have become a game designer. Game design is a deeply rewarding practice and flows like the river of life itself. Every experience and relationship that we have, everything that we learn, and everything that we enjoy can become a part of the design of our games. Go back to the beginning refreshed and excited. Focus on respect, trust, and consent. Follow your interests, refine your craft, and over time you'll figure out how to make superb games in a healthy, efficient, playful style that is all your own.

Epilogue

Game design and development are enormously fun—my friend and colleague Peter Brinson, an artist and game designer, draws parallels between making games and playing games. He points out in his USC Games classes that as we build games we have to learn new skills and use them to solve problems, just like we do in a game. As we proceed, the problems get harder, and we have to acquire even more skills. We end up in the "flow channel," where the rising difficulty of the task at hand is met by our rising skill, and we arrive in a flow state, fully engaged, with all of the good feelings, intense focus, and time dilation effects that Csikszentmihalyi describes.[1]

But that means that making games is also hard work. Countless decisions must be made, with far-reaching impact. And because we're in a flow state, we're rather addicted to what we're doing. We have a tendency to lose track of time and wander off into the weeds, in danger of hypnotically pouring effort into irrelevant things. If we keep working like this, and do it in an uncontrolled way, it's inevitable that we'll eventually burn out. The game that we make will probably suffer in terms of quality, its time of delivery, and in other respects too. We won't be in good shape to make another game when we've finished, and our game-making practice will have become the dictionary definition of *unsustainable*.

Even though creativity is unpredictable, making our work hard to plan, we can begin to bring our work under control by adopting a structured process like the one described in this book—or whatever variation of it works for you. The process must help us manage the limited time and resources we have available to us, without being too rigid and bureaucratic. Then we can bring the scope of our project under our control, while remaining flexible enough to adapt to the discoveries we make as we go along.

It's good to nurture an Agile attitude and to treat change as an opportunity rather than a crisis.[2] The game will reveal itself to you as you make it. It's up to you to set your ego aside, to listen to the project, to understand where it wants to go, and to ride

---

1. Csikszentmihalyi, *Flow*, 4.
2. "Agile Software Development," Wikipedia, https://en.wikipedia.org/wiki/Agile_software_devel opment.

along with it. That's the beauty of creativity, and it's what makes every development experience a unique journey where we can learn new things about the design process.

We have incredible flexibility to continue to shape and finesse the design of our games, right through full production and even in postproduction. In a 2013 interview, the film director Ava Duvernay said, "In the editing room I can remake a whole story. The script is really a guide, and through it I collect all those scenes and words, and once I've done that I can make it into anything I want."[3] Ava can shape a film's story and meaning all the way through to the end of the creative process. Because of the plasticity of digital media, and the explorative nature of our craft, the same is true for games, perhaps to an even greater degree.

But we also have to learn when to commit. I used to struggle with procrastination. I'm a thinker, which means that in my past I was often an overthinker, second-guessing myself as I tried to see things not just from both sides but from every side. Thoughtfulness is valuable, but it can hold us back too, preventing us from making the decisions we need to make so that we can just *build* something.

Eventually I learned to recognize when I had thought about something enough and it was now time to act. This isn't an easy lesson to learn: some are thinkers and some are doers, but most of us are somewhere in the middle, struggling with the question of whether we've thought things through enough, whether it's time to make a move. Eventually, you will get better at knowing when it's time to commit to your decisions.

If you like the sound of what you've read in this book, then consider becoming a game producer. Some books to find out more about game production, listed from newest to oldest, are:

- Clinton Keith, *Agile Game Development: Build, Play, Repeat*, 2nd ed. (Hoboken, NJ: Pearson Education, 2020).
- Clinton Keith and Grant Shonkwiler, *Creative Agility Tools: 100+ Tools for Creative Innovation and Teamwork* (Clinton Keith, 2018).
- Heather Maxwell Chandler, *The Game Production Toolbox* (Boca Raton, FL: CRC Press, 2020).
- John Hight and Jeannie Novak, *Game Development Essentials: Game Project Management* (Clifton Park, NY: Thomson Delmar Learning, 2008).
- Dan Irish, *The Game Producer's Handbook* (Boston: Thomson Course Technology, 2005).

The game industry will always benefit from people who understand the creative process, like to help organize things, are responsible with time and money, and can

---

3. Emma Carmichael, "'I Have Stories I Want to Tell': A Conversation with Filmmaker Ava DuVernay," *The Hairpin*, July 2, 2013, https://www.thehairpin.com/2013/07/i-have-stories-i-want-to-tell-a-conversation-with-filmmaker-ava-duvernay/.

communicate well with a wide range of people. Robin Hunicke once told me that she sees the role of a producer as helping other people on the team to do their jobs as well as they possibly can. We're too often tempted to think of producers as bosses, rather than as facilitators and collaborators. Producers have to be smart and knowledgeable: they need to understand what's happening on the team and with the game, in terms of both the big picture and the small details. They also need to have emotional intelligence and sound values in order to communicate well and to deal with difficult situations as they arise.

A producer always has to look toward the future and plan for it but must also find ways to work with people so that everyone on the team can both hear and be heard. They have to remain optimistic and positive, to help hold a team together when times are tough. Crucially, a great producer will create space for their peers and colleagues on the team to grow, and will constantly be improving the team's culture and processes, in the ultimate service of helping the team make ever-better games as time goes by.

In the past few years, designers and artists of all kinds have been waking up to the opportunities and obligations of their work. The application of design principles to effect social change is called *social design* and is of great importance to game designers working on impact games, educational games, and games for health.[4]

However, I believe that social design is relevant for every game team. As we've discussed elsewhere in this book, even though we've made great improvements over the last few years, the game industry is still struggling with the problem of crunch. The design of the process of game design *is itself a meta-level game design process*, and it deserves as much thought from us as the mechanics and stories of our games. We should take a long, hard look at the social design of game development to make sure that we are supporting, not harming, the people on our teams, as well as the people who play our games.

It's important that we improve our game-making processes so that they welcome and support all kinds of people from every walk of life. In her book *Design as an Attitude*, *New York Times* design critic Alice Rawsthorn talks about the historical problems around lack of diversity in graphic design, typography, and architecture. She says, "If you believe that design plays an important part in organizing our lives and in defining the objects, imagery, technologies, and spaces that fill them, it stands to reason that we need designers of the highest caliber. But we will not get them unless they come from every area of society."[5]

I'm heartened by the fact that many in the game-making community around the world now believe that diversity in games—which can only truly come from diversity in game-making communities—strengthens games as a whole by bringing new game

4. "Social Design," Wikipedia, https://en.wikipedia.org/wiki/Social_design.

5. Rawsthorn, *Design as an Attitude*, 68.

design ideas, attitudes, and audiences into play. It's also ethical that we should make the communities of our games and teams accessible and welcoming to everyone.

Ultimately, respect, trust, and consent are the keys to good game development practice. These three elements form the basis of all good communication, collaboration, leadership, and conflict resolution. Of course, we need skill in game design and development. But without respect, trust, and consent, between designer and player, and between the members of our team, all of our game design ability will likely come to naught. This extends to creating team cultures that are just and equitable, where everyone is treated with respect and given opportunity, whatever their identity or background. If we do that, then we set up the conditions for a more skilled, more innovative, and fundamentally better game development community.

We are on the forefront of culture with the vibrant new art form that is videogames. We have an incredible opportunity to show every type of artist and designer who struggles with complexity and uncontrolled overwork that it is possible to make art more sustainably, using an intentional, compassionate, playful production process.

There is no one right way to make a game. There are just processes and tools, some of which are right for us and our game. The best way to learn how to make games is to make them, and keep making them, and eventually get better. This book has given you a starting point for a better type of game production, one that I've seen working well across game education and industry for projects of all kinds. Please take it and run with it, wherever it may lead you—and then speak about *your* process.

Appendix A: The Four Phases, Milestones, and Deliverables of the Playful Production Process

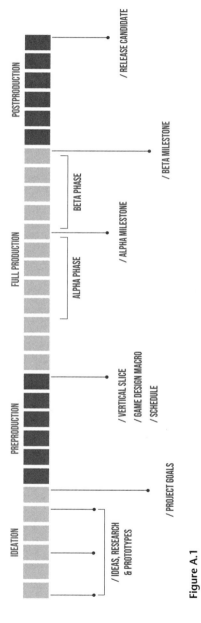

Figure A.1

Image credit: Gabriela Purri R. Gomes, Mattie Rosen, and Richard Lemarchand.

Appendix B: Transcription of Figure 7.1

What Is Uncharted: Drake's Fortune?

1. It's action packed and fast paced.

   We never slow the action down too much to delve into overly complicated puzzles or cumbersome gameplay mechanics . . . we always keep it fast and fun.

2. Uncharted doesn't take itself too seriously.

   We combine elements of suspense, mystery and drama, but keep in mind the fun "pulp action" tone. An occasional wise crack or funny predicament to break the tension is a big part of what makes Uncharted unique.

3. Drake is a fallible everyman.

   Drake is not James Bond. He is never in complete control, always scrambling to get the upper hand by improvising or using whatever means are at his disposal. He doesn't get "souped up" or become a superman, but instead is always operating at the very edge of his abilities.

4. We discover lost and mysterious places.

   We want most of the adventure to be spent exploring "uncharted" places, off the beaten path and forgotten by time. Drake is [a] detective of sorts, trying to put the pieces together.

5. Our world has believable supernatural elements.

   There will be mysterious and seemingly supernatural elements, but it must always be possible for Drake to be skeptical. Uncharted is more like an "X-Files/28 Days Later" supernatural as opposed to a "The Mummy/Ghostbusters" supernatural.

6. Unfamiliar things in a familiar setting.

   From the story to the environments, everything should have some sense of real life historical and visual believability. Once that foundation of believability has been strongly built, a layered element of the "fantastical" has all that much more impact.

Appendix C: Game Design Macro for *Uncharted 2: Among Thieves* (detail) from Figure 18.2

UNCHARTED 2 Macro Design

LEVELS	LOOK DESCRIPTION	TIME OF DAY/ MOOD	ALLY-NPC	ENEMY MODELS	MACRO GAMEPLAY	MACRO FLOW	PLAYER MECHANICS — Free Climb/Dyno	Wall Jump	Free Ropes	Pendulum	Monkey Bars	Monkey Swing	Balance Beams	Carry Objects Heavy	Carry Objects Light	Traversal Gunplay v.1	Forced Melee	Puzzle	Stealth	Swim	Moving Objects	Push Objects	Binoculars
Train Wreck																							
Train-wreck-1	Train Wreckage, Dangling cars	Snowy, Transitioning to White out	Bloodied Warm-weather Drake		Stay alive - injured	Highly scripted moments of Injured Drake traversing injured through wreckage.	X																
Museum																							
Museum-1	Istanbul, Turkey Museum	Night	Drake-1 Flynn-1 Chloe-1 (cut Only)	Museum Guards	Infiltrate - Stealth - Co-op	Co-op w/Flynn to infiltrate the museum. Helping him steal/decipher an artifact there				X	X	X	X			X	X		X		X		
Museum-2	Roman Sewers Below the Museum	Night	Flynn-1	Museum Guards	Escape	Flynn dicks you over, Run from the authorities through an ancient sewer network. Flynn prevents you from escaping - BUSTED!	X									X	X		X		X		
Dig																							
Dig-1	Lush, Wet Jungle/Swamp Lazaravic's dig & campsite structures	Dawn - misty (rainy)	Chloe-2 Sully	Laz Diggers Laz Army HOT Lazaravic Flynn-2	Sabotage - Infiltrate - Fight	Enter Laz dig sight w/Chloe & Sully on radio. Start causing trouble for guards & workers	X			X	X	X	X		X	X	X		X	X			X
Dig-2	Lush, Wet Jungle/Swamp Lazaravic's dig & campsite structures	Dawn - misty (rainy)	Chloe-2 Sully	Laz Diggers Laz Army HOT Lazaravic Flynn-2	Sabotage - Infiltrate - Fight	Explosions - Chaos distracts pulls Laz away from "treasure". Gives Drake clue to find Dagger	X			X	X	X	X	X	X	X	X		X	X	X		
Dig-3	Follow a stream up a mountainside.	Dawn - misty (rainy)	Chloe-2 Sully	Laz Diggers Laz Army HOT Lazaravic-1 Flynn-2 MP's Dead Crew	Sabotage - Infiltrate - Fight	Get to higher ground after scoping Laz's tent - towards mountain in wide world. Stumble onto a temple										X	X		X		X		

(a)

Figure C.1 — Uncharted 2: Among Thieves level progression chart

GAMEPLAY THEME (FOCUS)	Trang-gun	Pistol-semi-a	Assault-Rifle-a	Grenades	Museum Guards	Light	NON-PLAYABLE VEHICLES	CINEMATIC GAMEPLAY SEQUENCES	Vistas
Highly scripted - traversal / L1 + R1 Lock sequence								Exploding Tanker - Washing machine sequence	X
Train Traversal / L1 + R1 Tranquilizer guns / Intro Stealth Attacks / Cover as Stealth	X				X				X
	X				X				
Train Traversal / Train Shooting / Introduce Stealth Attacks / Cover as Stealth / Forced Melee	X	X	X	X		X			X
Forced Melee / Basic Gunplay / Intro Traversal Gunplay / Grenades	X		X	X		X			
	X					X			

(Additional WEAPONS columns present but unmarked: Pistol-semi-b, Pistol-full-a, Pistol-revolver-a, Pistol-revolver-b, SMG-a, SMG-b, Assault-Rifle-b, Shotgun 1, Shotgun 2, Sniper-Rifle, Crossbow, RPG, Rocket Launcher, Turret 1, Pillbox Turret, Mobile Turret. Additional ENEMIES columns present but unmarked: Medium, Armored, Shotgunner, Sniper, Shield, RPG, Heavy, SLA Easy, SLA Hard.)

(b)

Figure C.1

Acknowledgments

With immeasurable love and heartfelt thanks to my parents, Wyn and Derek, and to my brother Jeremy. Love and affection to Nova Jiang, who has always inspired and supported me. Much love to Liz, Shiran, and Mia, to Sarah and her family, to Ros, Peter, Phil, Helen, Paul, and their kids, to Aunt Sheila, Duncan, Teresa, Michael, and Emma, and to Uncle David.

I want to give particular thanks to pioneering game designer and educator Tracy Fullerton, whose inspirational work transformed the world and my life. Tracy, your generous and detailed help with this book was indispensable, and you have my deepest gratitude. Your friendship is elevating.

Sincere thanks to the incomparable Mark Cerny, whose close reading and constructive critique was crucial in bringing this project to completion, as with many others. Mark, thank you for affirming the values in this book and for taking the time to give me your help. You have always been a guiding light.

Many thanks to Evan Wells for his help with the book and for giving me so many great opportunities. Fantastical thanks and love to Amy Hennig, who took me along on an escapade in game design and storytelling, where the treasure at the end was the dearest of friendships.

Thanks with profound admiration for Mary McCoy, whose erudition inspires and uplifts me, and whose authorial advice sustains me. Special thanks to Dan Tarshish for the walks and talk that gave shape to this book. Great gratitude to my expert, ideal readers: Alan Dang, Egan Hirvela, Jeff Watson, Owen Harris, and Timothy Lee. Superlative thanks to Mattie Rosen, whose unexpected offer of help turned into a key part of this book's completion. Many thanks to everyone whose input and encouragement helped in the creation of this book: Adam Sulzdorf-Liszkiewicz, Dennis Wixon, Elizabeth Blythe, Gordon Calleja, Jack Epps, and Jeremy Gibson Bond. Thanks to Loren Chodosh for legal assistance, and to Max and Nick Folkman, whose *Script Lock* podcast sparked ideas. I'm very grateful to MIT Press senior acquisitions editor Doug Sery for his guidance and the trust that he placed in me, to MIT Press editor Noah J. Springer, whose expert advice kept me on track, and to my anonymous reviewers for their valuable input. Special thanks to my production editor, Helen Wheeler, and to my superb copy editor, Lunaea Weatherstone, for their hard work and wise counsel.

Many thanks to everyone who gave me creative inspiration and practical help as I worked on this book: Aniko Imre, Anna Anthropy, Auriea Harvey, Bo Ruberg, Cara Ellison, Chad Toprak, Colleen Macklin, Eric Zimmerman, Frank Lantz, Geoffrey Long, Grant Shonkwiler, Irving Belateche, Jesper Juul, John Sharp, Kris Ligman, Mary Flanagan, Mary Sweeney, Michael John, Miguel Sicart, Naomi Clark, Nathalie Pozzi, Raph Koster, Sam Gosling, Samantha Kalman, Sharon Greene, Steve Gaynor, Tara McPherson, Tobias Kopka, William Huber, and everyone (too many to name) who gave me advice and cheered me on as I wrote. Thanks to everyone not mentioned elsewhere who made contributions to the text and figures: Gabriela Purri R. Gomes, George Kokoris, Jesse Vigil, Jim Huntley, and Marc Wilhelm. Thanks to those who gave me permission to use images related to their work: Aaron Cheney, Chao Chen, Christoph Rosenthal, George Li, Jenny Jiao Hsia, Julian Ceipek, and Michael Barclay. Special thanks in this regard to Arne Meyer, Bryan Pardilla, and Sony Interactive Entertainment.

I am very indebted to everyone I worked with at MicroProse, Crystal Dynamics, Naughty Dog, and in the USC Game Innovation Lab. I learned so much from you all, and we've had such fun making games together. I lack space to thank you all individually, but our collaborations brought great happiness into my life and helped make the ideas in this book clear to me. I would particularly like to thank Robin Hunicke, Hirokazu Yasuhara, Celia Pearce, Sam Roberts, Heather Kelly, Connie Booth, Andy Gavin, Grady Hunt, Sam Thompson, Andrew Bennett, Rosaura Sandoval, Paul Reiche III, John Spinale, Stuart Whyte, Andy Hieke, and Pete Moreland for the mentorship and friendship that you gave me along the way.

Great thanks to all my colleagues in the USC Games program, past and present, from whom I've learned so much, and whose support I have benefited from enormously. Particular thanks go to Peter Brinson, who showed me how to teach; Danny Bilson, whose passion and generosity inspire me; Martzi Campos, who rebooted my creative practice; Jeremy Gibson Bond and Margaret Moser, who taught me to code, and much else besides; Andy Nealen, for opening my mind to minimalism and system dynamics; Jane Pinckard, whose example makes me strive always to do better; and Andreas Kratky, Gordon Bellamy, Kiki Benzon, Laird Malamed, and Marientina Gotsis for their wisdom and friendship. Many thanks to Dean Elizabeth M. Daley, Akira Mizuta Lippit, Michael Renov, and all my colleagues in the USC School of Cinematic Arts, for welcoming me so warmly. A very special thanks to all my students, in the USC Games program and beyond, for all your hard work, creativity, and good humor. A particular shout-out to the alumni of CTIN-532 and CTIN-484/489, for whom chapters of this book were originally written, and who gave me great notes. Teaching you was and is a pleasure—thank you for all that you've taught me.

Great respect and sincere thanks to Sammi Xia Lin, vice president of the Interactive Entertainment Group at Tencent and dean of the Tencent Game Institute, and to Eric Ma, president of human resources for Tencent Games. Our collaborations have led to great friendships and helped to solidify the ideas in this book. Thanks to Li Min, Li Shen, Neo Liu, Cathy Wang, Elaine Wang, Yin Wu, and everyone we've worked with during the Tencent USC Games workshops.

I want to extend deep gratitude to the communities of the conferences, festivals, and summits that I've been fortunate to be a part of, particularly those of the Game Developers Conference and IndieCade. Many thanks to my friends in HEVGA, at Glasgow Caledonian University, and in the wide, wonderful world of games academia. Gratitude to all my teachers, past and present, who've made sure that my world keeps expanding. Deep and dear love to all the friends I've made through the worlds of games, art, and teaching, and to my oldest friends from Newent and Oxford. You cared for me in the hard times, celebrated with me at the high points, and bring me great joy. With deep gratitude and respect for the work of Octavia E. Butler.

In memory of Mrs. Kate Clarke, who taught me how to think; Mike Brunton, who gave me my start; my grandparents, lifelong gamers Doreen and Holden (bridge and chess, respectively), and my grandmother Joyce, who gave me my heart; and my friend and colleague Dr. Jeff Watson, who inspired everyone around him to think deeply, and always to be kind. Jeff's feedback and support were invaluable in the completion of this book.

References

Adams, Ernest. *Fundamentals of Game Design*. 3rd ed. Voices That Matter. Berkeley: New Riders, 2013.

Allgeier, Brian. *Directing Video Games: 101 Tips for Creative Leaders*. Los Angeles: Illusion Road, 2017.

Anthropy, Anna. *Rise of the Videogame Zinesters: How Freaks, Normals, Amateurs, Artists, Dreamers, Dropouts, Queers, Housewives, and People like You Are Taking Back an Art Form*. New York: Seven Stories, 2012.

Anthropy, Anna, and Naomi Clark. *A Game Design Vocabulary: Exploring the Foundational Principles behind Good Game Design*. Upper Saddle River, NJ: Addison-Wesley, 2014.

Aristotle. *Poetics*. Translated by Anthony Kenny. Oxford World's Classics. Oxford: Oxford University Press, 2013.

Block, Bruce. *The Visual Story: Creating the Visual Structure of Film, TV and Digital Media*. 3rd ed. London: Routledge, 2020.

Bogost, Ian. *Play Anything: The Pleasure of Limits, the Uses of Boredom, and the Secret of Games*. New York: Basic Books, 2016.

Bond, Jeremy Gibson. *Introduction to Game Design, Prototyping, and Development: From Concept to Playable Game with Unity and C#*. 2nd ed. Addison-Wesley Game Design and Development Series. Upper Saddle River, NJ: Addison-Wesley, 2018.

Brathwaite, Brenda, and Ian Schreiber. *Challenges for Game Designers*. Boston: Course Technology/Cengage Learning, 2009.

Brotchie, Alastair, and Mel Gooding, eds. *A Book of Surrealist Games: Including the Little Surrealist Dictionary*. Boston: Shambhala Redstone, 1995.

Campbell, Joseph. *The Hero with a Thousand Faces*. Bollingen Series. Novato, CA: New World Library, 2008.

Carse, James P. *Finite and Infinite Games*. New York: Free Press, 2013.

Catmull, Edwin E., and Amy Wallace. *Creativity, Inc: Overcoming the Unseen Forces That Stand in the Way of True Inspiration*. New York: Random House, 2014.

Chandler, Heather Maxwell. *The Game Production Toolbox*. Boca Raton, FL: CRC Press, 2020.

Childs, Peter. *Modernism*. 2nd ed. London: Routledge, 2008.

Csikszentmihalyi, Mihaly. *Flow: The Psychology of Optimal Experience*. New York: Harper Perennial Modern Classics, 2008.

Culyba, Sabrina. *The Transformational Framework: A Process Tool for the Development of Transformational Games*. Pittsburgh: ETC Press: Signature, 2018.

Dreskin, Joel. *A Practical Guide to Indie Game Marketing*. Boca Raton, FL: Routledge, 2017.

Epps, Jack, Jr. *Screenwriting Is Rewriting: The Art and Craft of Professional Revision*. New York: Bloomsbury, 2016.

Frederick, Matthew. *101 Things I Learned in Architecture School*. Cambridge, MA: MIT Press, 2007.

Freytag, Gustav. *Freytag's Technique of the Drama: An Exposition of Dramatic Composition and Art—Scholar's Choice Edition*. Sacramento, CA: Creative Media Partners, 2015.

Fuller, R. Buckminster, and E. J. Applewhite. *Synergetics: Explorations in the Geometry of Thinking*. New York: Macmillan, 1975.

Fullerton, Tracy. *Game Design Workshop: A Playcentric Approach to Creating Innovative Games*. 2nd ed. Boston: Elsevier Morgan Kaufmann, 2008.

Fullerton, Tracy. *Game Design Workshop: A Playcentric Approach to Creating Innovative Games*. 4th ed. Boca Raton, FL: Taylor & Francis, CRC Press, 2018.

Gibson, James J. *The Ecological Approach to Visual Perception*. New York: Psychology Press, 2015.

Gulino, Paul Joseph. *Screenwriting: The Sequence Approach*. New York: Continuum, 2004.

Hight, John, and Jeannie Novak. *Game Development Essentials: Game Project Management*. Clifton Park, NY: Thomson Delmar Learning, 2008.

Huizinga, Johan. *Homo Ludens: A Study of the Play Element in Culture*. Brooklyn, NY: Angelico, 2016.

Hunicke, Robin, Marc LeBlanc, and Robert Zubek. "MDA: A Formal Approach to Game Design and Game Research." *AAAI Workshop—Technical Report* 1 (January 1, 2004).

IDEO Product Development, ed. *IDEO Method Cards: 51 Ways to Inspire Design: Learn, Look, Ask, Try*. San Francisco: William Stout, 2003.

Irish, Dan. *The Game Producer's Handbook*. Boston: Thomson Course Technology, 2005.

Juul, Jesper. *The Art of Failure: An Essay on the Pain of Playing Video Games*. Cambridge, MA: MIT Press, 2016.

Keith, Clinton. *Agile Game Development: Build, Play, Repeat*. 2nd ed. Hoboken, NJ: Pearson Education, 2020.

Keith, Clinton, and Grant Shonkwiler. *Creative Agility Tools: 100+ Tools for Creative Innovation and Teamwork*. Clinton Keith, 2018.

Le Guin, Ursula K. *Steering the Craft: A Twenty-First Century Guide to Sailing the Sea of Story*. Boston: Mariner Books, 2015.

Luhn, Matthew. *The Best Story Wins: How to Leverage Hollywood Storytelling in Business and Beyond*. New York: Morgan James, 2018.

Lupton, Ellen. *Design Is Storytelling*. New York: Cooper Hewitt, Smithsonian Design Museum, 2017.

Meadows, Donella H., and Diana Wright. *Thinking in Systems: A Primer*. White River Junction, VT: Chelsea Green, 2008.

Norman, Donald A. *The Design of Everyday Things*. Rev. ed. New York: Basic Books, 2013.

Phillips, Melanie Anne, and Chris Huntley. *Dramatica: A New Theory of Story*. Glendale, CA: Screenplay Systems, 2004.

Rawsthorn, Alice. *Design as an Attitude*. Documents—Documents Series 28. Zürich: Ringier, 2018.

Rogers, Scott. *Level Up! The Guide to Great Video Game Design*. 2nd ed. Chichester, UK: Wiley, 2014.

Scannell, Mary. *The Big Book of Conflict Resolution Games: Quick, Effective Activities to Improve Communication, Trust, and Collaboration*. New York: McGraw-Hill, 2010.

Schell, Jesse. *The Art of Game Design: A Book of Lenses*. 3rd ed. Boca Raton, FL: Taylor & Francis/CRC Press, 2019.

Sellers, Michael. *Advanced Game Design: A Systems Approach*. Boston: Addison-Wesley, 2017.

Snyder, Blake. *Save the Cat! The Last Book on Screenwriting You'll Ever Need*. Studio City, CA: Michael Wiese Productions, 2005.

Swink, Steve. *Game Feel: A Game Designer's Guide to Virtual Sensation*. Burlington, MA: Morgan Kaufmann/Elsevier, 2008.

Tolkien, J. R. R., Humphrey Carpenter, and Christopher Tolkien. *The Letters of J. R. R. Tolkien: A Selection*. Boston: Mariner, 2000.

Totten, Christopher W. *An Architectural Approach to Level Design*. 2nd ed. Boca Raton, FL: Taylor & Francis, CRC Press, 2019.

Tufte, Edward R. *Envisioning Information*. Cheshire, CT: Graphics Press, 2013.

Vogler, Christopher. *The Writer's Journey: Mythic Structure for Writers*. 3rd ed. Studio City, CA: Michael Wiese Productions, 2007.

Wohl, Michael. *Editing Techniques with Final Cut Pro*. Berkeley, CA: Peachpit Press, 2002.

Yorke, John. *Into the Woods: A Five-Act Journey into Story*. New York: Abrams, 2015.

Zackariasson, Peter, and Mikolaj Dymek. *Video Game Marketing: A Student Textbook*. London: Routledge, 2016.

Games Cited

Apex Legends. Respawn Entertainment. Electronic Arts, 2019.

Bastion. Supergiant Games. Warner Bros. Interactive Entertainment, 2011.

The Binding of Isaac: Rebirth. Edmund McMillen and Nicalis. Nicalis, 2014.

Cities: Skylines. Colossal Order. Paradox Interactive, 2015.

Cloud. USC Game Innovation Lab. 2005.

Control. Remedy Entertainment. 505 Games, 2019.

Crash Bandicoot. Naughty Dog. Sony Interactive Entertainment, 1996.

Crash Bandicoot 2: Cortex Strikes Back. Naughty Dog. Sony Interactive Entertainment, 1997.

Dance Dance Revolution. Konami, 1998.

Dear Esther. The Chinese Room and Robert Briscoe. 2012.

Earth: A Primer. Chaim Gingold, Cliff Caruthers, Michelle M. Lee, Laura Kaltman, and Pete Demoreuille. 2015.

Flow. thatgamecompany. Sony Interactive Entertainment, 2006.

Flower. thatgamecompany. Sony Interactive Entertainment, 2009.

FTL: Faster Than Light. Subset Games, 2012.

Gex. Crystal Dynamics. BMG Interactive, 1995.

God of War. SIE Santa Monica Studio. Sony Interactive Entertainment, 2018.

Halo: Combat Evolved. Bungie. Microsoft Game Studios, 2001.

Jak 3. Naughty Dog. Sony Interactive Entertainment, 2004.

Jak and Daxter. Naughty Dog. Sony Interactive Entertainment, 2001.

Jak X: Combat Racing. Naughty Dog. Sony Interactive Entertainment, 2005.

Journey. thatgamecompany. Sony Interactive Entertainment, 2012.

Keef the Thief: A Boy and His Lockpick. Naughty Dog. Electronic Arts, 1989.

The Last of Us. Naughty Dog. Sony Interactive Entertainment, 2013.

Legacy of Kain: Soul Reaver. Crystal Dynamics. Eidos Interactive, 1999.

The Legend of Zelda: A Link to the Past. Nintendo, 1991.

Marble Madness. Mark Cerny and Atari Games. Atari Games, 1984.

Minecraft. Mojang Studios, 2009.

The Night Journey. Bill Viola, Tracy Fullerton, Todd Furmanski, Kurosh ValaNejad, and USC Game Innovation Lab. USC Games, 2018.

Painstation. Tilman Reiff and Volker Morawe, 2001.

Pandemonium! Toys for Bob. Crystal Dynamics, 1996.

Pong. Allan Alcorn. Atari, 1972.

Proteus. Twisted Tree Games and David Kanaga. 2013.

Ratchet & Clank Future: A Crack in Time. Insomniac Games. Sony Interactive Entertainment, 2009.

Rings of Power. Naughty Dog. Electronic Arts, 1991.

Scribblenauts. 5th Cell. Warner Bros. Interactive Entertainment, 2009.

The Secret of Monkey Island. Lucasfilm Games, 1990.

SimCity. Maxis, 1989.

The Sims. Maxis. Electronic Arts, 2000.

Sonic the Hedgehog 2. Sega Technical Institute. Sega, 1992.

Spelunky. Mossmouth, LLC, 2012.

Spider-Man. Insomniac Games. Sony Interactive Entertainment, 2018.

Spore. Maxis. Electronic Arts, 2008.

StarCraft. Blizzard Entertainment, 1998.

Sunset Overdrive. Insomniac Games. Xbox Game Studios, 2014.

Super Mario Bros. Nintendo EAD. Nintendo, 1985.

Tetris. Alexey Pajitnov and Vadim Gerasimov. Electronika 60, 1984.

Tharsis. Choice Provisions, 2016.

Tinhead. MicroProse UK. Ballistic, 1993.

Uncharted: Drake's Fortune. Naughty Dog. Sony Interactive Entertainment, 2007.

Uncharted 2: Among Thieves. Naughty Dog. Sony Interactive Entertainment, 2009.

Uncharted 3: Drake's Deception. Naughty Dog. Sony Interactive Entertainment, 2011.

Walden, a game. Tracy Fullerton and USC Game Innovation Lab. USC Games, 2017.

The Witcher 3: Wild Hunt. CD Projekt Red. CD Projekt, 2015.

Index